D1563939

PUSHBACK

PUSHBACK

The Political Fallout of Unpopular
Supreme Court Decisions

Dave Bridge

UNIVERSITY OF MISSOURI PRESS
COLUMBIA

Publication of this volume made possible with the generous support of the Kinder Institute on Constitutional Democracy

Library of Congress Cataloging-in-Publication Data

Names: Bridge, Dave (College teacher), author.
Title: Pushback : the political fallout of unpopular Supreme Court
  decisions / Dave Bridge.
Description: Columbia : University of Missouri Press, 2024. | Series:
  Studies in constitutional democracy | Includes bibliographical
  references and index.
Identifiers: LCCN 2023039004 (print) | LCCN 2023039005 (ebook) | ISBN
  9780826223036 (hardcover) | ISBN 9780826274984 (ebook)
Subjects: LCSH: United States. Supreme Court. | Judicial process--United
  States. | Judicial opinions--United States. | Political questions and
  judicial power--United States. | LCGFT: Court decisions and opinions
Classification: LCC KF8748 .B75 2024 (print) | LCC KF8748 (ebook) | DDC
  320.60973--dc23/eng/20231002
LC record available at https://lccn.loc.gov/2023039004
LC ebook record available at https://lccn.loc.gov/2023039005

♾™ This paper meets the requirements of the
American National Standard for Permanence of Paper
for Printed Library Materials, Z39.48, 1984.

Typeface: Minion Pro and Ten Oldstyle

STUDIES IN CONSTITUTIONAL DEMOCRACY

Jeffrey L. Pasley and Jay K. Dow, Series Editors

In partnership with the Kinder Institute on Constitutional Democracy, this series explores the history and development of American constitutional ideas and democratic practices both in the United States and as they have reverberated throughout the world. The volumes in this series showcase interdisciplinary scholarship that helps readers gain insight into both new and traditional themes in American politics, law, society, and culture, with an eye to both practical and theoretical applications.

Titles in Studies in Constitutional Democracy

Contesting the Constitution: Congress Debates the Missouri Crisis, 1819–1821
Edited by William S. Belko

Pushback: The Political Fallout of Unpopular Supreme Court Decisions
Dave Bridge

The Panic of 1819: The First Great Depression
Andrew H. Browning

The Pursuit of Happiness in the Founding Era: An Intellectual History
Carli N. Conklin

Liberal Education and Citizenship in a Free Society
Edited by Justin Buckley Dyer and Constantine Christos Vassiliou

Lloyd Gaines and the Fight to End Segregation
James W. Endersby and William T. Horner

Disestablishment and Religious Dissent:
Church-State Relations in the New American States, 1776–1833
Edited by Carl H. Esbeck and Jonathan J. Den Hartog

Aristocracy in America: From the Sketch-Book of a German Nobleman
Francis J. Grund
Edited and with an Introduction by Armin Mattes

The Federalist Frontier: Settler Politics in the Old Northwest, 1783–1840
Kristopher Maulden

From Oligarchy to Republicanism: The Great Task of Reconstruction
Forrest A. Nabors

A Fire Bell in the Past: The Missouri Crisis at 200, Volume I
Western Slavery, National Impasse
Edited by Jeffrey L. Pasley and John Craig Hammond

A Fire Bell in the Past: The Missouri Crisis at 200, Volume II
"The Missouri Question" and Its Answers
Edited by Jeffrey L. Pasley and John Craig Hammond

(continued on next page)

(continued from previous page)

Bureaucracy in America:
The Administrative State's Challenge to Constitutional Government
Joseph Postell

The Myth of Coequal Branches: Restoring the Constitution's Separation of Functions
David J. Siemers

Reforming Legislatures: American Voters and State Ballot Measures, 1792–2020
Peverill Squire

To Curt,

Your encouragement and friendship made this book possible

Contents

Tables and Figures

Preface

FOR THE REPUBLICAN PARTY, *Roe v. Wade* was the gift that kept on giving. While liberals had successfully defended the precedent, that triumph continually allowed Republicans to win elections on the pledge that one day *Roe* would fall. Promise, compete, repeat—the winning formula worked for nearly half a century. On June 24, 2022, that cycle came to a halt. *Dobbs v. Jackson Women's Health Organization* had overturned *Roe*.

Though we often hear that abortion splits the American public in half, on the eve of *Dobbs*, about two-thirds of those surveyed supported *Roe*. Nevertheless, a significant portion of that majority still voted Republican. With abortion rights secure under the landmark precedent, they could vote based on other preferences (e.g., tax cuts, deregulation, conservative foreign policy). Perhaps this pro-*Roe* Republican-voting faction saw abortion as a symbol for New Right voters. It was a helpful political tool, not a serious policy reform effort.

But the pro-life campaigners proved correct: with enough electoral victories (especially in the White House and Senate), *Roe v. Wade* fell, making *Dobbs* a rare instance of a clearly countermajoritarian decision on an issue that many Americans deemed important. Liberal activists have pushed back. But GOP political operatives probably worry more about the electoral impact, for the Republican Party can no longer campaign on overturning *Roe*; and the Democratic Party can win on anti-*Dobbs* positions. In obtaining what they had always promised, it seems Republicans might have laid the foundation for losing so much more.

This book is about the ways in which majorities can "push back" against unpopular Supreme Court rulings, such as *Roe* and *Dobbs*. It offers four contributions:

Methodological. In searching for countermajoritarian cases, we can do better than Potter Stewart's famous "know it when I see it" standard. I discuss how to identify these cases.

Historical. I look at how grassroots, congressional, and electoral majorities pushed back against unpopular decisions in the 1950s to 1970s. Local communities ignored rulings. Congress maneuvered around them. The GOP used these cases to expand their coalition. In time, those efforts paid off when southern Democrats and northern conservative Democrats (many of whom were Catholic) started voting Republican in 1980.

Analytical. I leverage the variation in pushback in the 1950s–1970s to hypothesize about the conditions under which the Supreme Court can inadvertently hurt the electoral chances of the very faction that desired the original ruling(s). The overall causal web that influences elections is complex, but I conclude with a midlevel theory: that unpopular Supreme Court decisions can be one site (among many) of party-building opportunities.[1]

Generalizable. I apply hypotheses to modern cases, most of which do not meet the criteria to cause an electoral shift. *Dobbs*, though, is different. We stand at a rare moment in political development, when conditions appear ripe for one political party to use an unpopular Supreme Court decision to expand its electoral coalition.

In writing an interdisciplinary book within an interdisciplinary series, I cross methodological boundaries. Sometimes, the inquiry allows for more procedural data collection with measurable observations (e.g., polls, number of congressional proposals, roll call tallies, breakdown of factional affiliations). Other times, I rely on historical narrative to describe complex stories that can only be told by attending to sequence, actors, institutions, and norms. My goal is to help others think about the ways in which our constitutional democracy can push back against rare countermajoritarian Supreme Court decisions.

Acknowledgments

I STARTED THIS BOOK a long time ago and recent Supreme Court developments required addendums. Throughout that process, I worked with the best editorial team imaginable. Editor in Chief Andrew Davidson rarely let a day—let alone an hour—go by without responding to questions, suggestions, or requests for extensions. I do not know if the final chapters would have been finished without his support. Jay Dow and Jeff Pasley oversee the Kinder Institute's Studies in Constitutional Democracy series, and I am grateful for their patience with me and loyalty to the project. I am honored to be a part of the series because I consider this book, above everything else, to be about how democracy works under the US Constitution. My thanks to Kinder for establishing the series, organizing the annual Shawnee Trail Conference, and developing a network of scholars who care about the subject and support each other. Others at Missouri deserve praise: Mary Conley for helping with technical questions; Irina du Quenoy for making the final product so much more polished; Drew Griffith for overseeing the postproduction process; Justin Dyer—a previous series editor who is now at the Civitas Institute at the University of Texas—for first seeing merit in the manuscript; and Aric Gooch—now a colleague of mine at Baylor—for organizing the 2023 Shawnee Trail Conference, where I presented parts of the manuscript. Two anonymous reviewers provided generous, extensive, fair-minded, and constructive critiques of an earlier draft. The final product is so much better because of their efforts and grace.

Many others have helped along the way. Baylor University provided a semester sabbatical, which was essential for writing portions of the book. At other points, Deans Lee Nordt and Kim Kellison allowed teaching arrangements that freed up writing time. My chair, David

Clinton, was instrumental in making sure I continued my research after tenure. Many of my Baylor colleagues have read one part or another of this manuscript: Tim Burns and David Nichols helped me consider the foundations of constitutionalism; Pat Flavin answered research design and methodological questions; and Rebecca Flavin and Ben Kleinerman were my go-to sources for constitutional law and politics. Jenice Langston and Melanie Pirelo provide outstanding staff support—thank you. I enjoyed coming to campus to work, in no large part because of good colleagues (past and present): Linda Adams, Dwight Allman, Steve Block, Matt Brogdon, Joe Brown, Peter Campbell, Jim Curry, David Corey, Elizabeth Corey, Ivy Hamerly, Andy Hogue, Richard Jordan, Sergiy Kudelia, Sarah Lee, Tom Myers, Mary Nichols, Brad Thayer, Ann Ward, and Lee Ward.

I am amazed by the excellence of so many Baylor students who have helped along the way. Adam Carrington was there from the beginning. Ben Betner, Kelli Betner, Chelsea Bryant, Katie Clewett, Alex Eklund, Rocky Katch, Krish Kothari, Blakely Lowe, Jaziah Masters, Caroline Pullella, Ryan Resch, and Peter Wostenberg all provided expert research assistantship. Two former students deserve extra praise. Jordan Cash went from student to co-author to colleague to co-instructor. At some point, the student became the teacher. Haley Stiles contributed thoughts, wisdom, and optimism. She is nothing short of exceptional.

Dan DiSalvo, Ken Kersch, and Keith Whittington read the preface and each of them pushed me to tell my story, and not someone else's. I have been blessed with mentors: Victor Asal, Jeb Barnes, David Clinton, Rich Conley, Richard Duran, Howard Gillman, Mark Kann, and Karen Orren.

I have so many caring friends. My pals from graduate school are still exactly that: Nick Buccola, Juve Cortes, Parker Hevron, Jillian Medeiros and Mike Perez, Jesse Mills, and Dan Walters. Though thousands of miles away, Simon Radford and Nicolas de Zamaroczy are still best friends. My thanks to those in Waco: Scott Spinks and Alex Thiltges, always ready at a moment's notice for a quick get-together; Dave and Maura Jortner, both of whom I try to emulate in faith, scholarship, teaching, and family life. Work/life balance would be impossible without Yoga8's Kim Damm, Maggie Moore, Angela Rankin, and Dollyn Tusa.

My family has heard more about the Supreme Court than they care to admit. Most of all, I thank my wife, Theresa Kennedy, for her love and encouragement. My parents: Melissa and Robert, still encourage my curiosity. My siblings are my longest running friends: Ellen, Dan, Elizabeth, and Lauren are amazing, brave, supportive, and loving. Special thanks to Lauren, a social scientist who uses those skills to help elementary school students learn to read. She read portions of the manuscript and kept me focused on the "so what?" I am lucky to have wonderful in-laws: Dawn and Kurt Crytzer, Victor Mendoza, and Wes Varney.

Finally, Curt Nichols, to whom this book is dedicated, helped generate the original idea. More important than trading theories or reading chapters, he lent his confidence to me. He would not let me give up on the project. Curt is a father, scholar, mentor, veteran, cancer survivor, and a faithful friend. I am proud to know him.

PUSHBACK

Introduction

SENATOR ROBERT KERR (D-OK) must have felt trapped. His colleagues were voting on a bill to curb the Supreme Court's power to hear cases involving communists' rights, everyone knew it would be close, and Kerr's unknown vote might make the difference. His liberal party leaders wanted him to vote "nay" while his conservative constituents wanted to him to vote "yea." But that dilemma was not the reason Kerr felt trapped. Rather, the senator must have felt literally trapped because he could not get out of the side cloakroom and cast his vote. He was not locked in. He was not banned from the Senate floor. He was ready to vote. What kept him from doing so?

It was the politically intimidating and physically imposing Senate Majority Leader Lyndon Johnson (D-TX), who had led backroom efforts to defeat the bill. Johnson had more than one motivation to stop the proposal. He wanted the Senate to move on to other business, specifically the debt limit and defense spending. He harbored presidential aspirations and believed that to promote his national reputation, he needed to appear as more open-minded than other southern Democrats. Perhaps he thought the proposal struck too much at judicial independence.[1] Primarily, though, Johnson opposed the bill because it split the Democratic Party and gave Republicans a chance to forge cross-partisan alliances.[2]

LBJ thought he had the votes to win, but he unexpectedly lost a tabling motion, 39–46. With the bill's supporters shouting "Vote! Vote!" on the Senate floor, Johnson was uncharacteristically paralyzed by the "pandemonium" in the chamber.[3] Noting the late hour (11:30 p.m.), Johnson desperately adjourned for the day and spent a sleepless night whipping votes.[4] He promised favors. He called in others. He lobbied lobbyists to exact pressure on wavering senators.

3

He told northern colleagues that an anticommunism bill would lead to other judicial attacks, such as segregationist proposals. He told southern colleagues that it would lead to liberals pushing for explicit endorsement of desegregation. He disingenuously "paired" one absent senator's anti–Supreme Court vote with another absentee who was likely to vote the same way.[5] When he could not convince Joseph Frear (D-DE) to change his court-curbing vote, he convinced Frear to hide in the Marble Room (a lounge outside the chamber), where the bill's manager (Strom Thurmond, D-SC) could not find and pressure him.

With enough votes to win the roll call, LBJ sought to turn the tables. He no longer just wanted to defeat the bill (although that was still the main objective). He now wanted the vote to result in a tie to put Vice President Richard Nixon in the unenviable position of casting the deciding ballot. Most Eisenhower administration officials, Nixon included, understood the implications of the attack on judicial independence—it was not an issue to be taken lightly, especially on topics that most expected the Supreme Court to defend (e.g., free speech, freedom of association, due process).[6] Yet, it would not have been popular for a Republican vice president (and presumed 1960 Republican nominee) to cast the deciding vote on protecting the rights of communists. Still, Nixon was likely to follow the administration's lead in upholding the court's jurisdiction. And it was that exact vise in which LBJ sought to ensnare Nixon. In twenty-four hours, the "Master of the Senate" had gone from embarrassingly losing the tabling vote to taking the offensive.[7] He was going to put the vice president in a no-win situation.

And that is why LBJ voted against the bill, then immediately "grabbed" and "propelled" his friend Kerr into the Senate cloakroom.[8] Through a combination of congenial banter, the "Johnson Treatment," and, perhaps, sheer physical restraint, LBJ kept the Oklahoma senator in the cloakroom until voting concluded.

The bill failed by a single vote, 40–41. Two items stand out. First, after a 40–40 tie was announced, the clerk noticed that Senator Wallace Bennett (R-UT) had entered the chamber (he, too, had been hiding in the wings during the roll call). With the roll call still open,

Nixon allowed Bennett to vote, which broke the tie.[9] Second, Kerr never voted. Had he done so, he would have been able to make it a tie. In fact, with the result so close to a tie, LBJ allowed Kerr to return to his seat, knowing that the bill's conservative supporters would (and did) call for a revote. Although Nixon had allowed the Senate to run its own business leading up to this point, the vice president immediately seized his president of the Senate role and declared, "The motion is not debatable."[10] The Senate proceeded to the next item on the agenda: a message from the House saying that the lower chamber had passed a bill authorizing a program for the conservation and management of the rare Hawaiian Nene goose. Nixon likely breathed a sigh of relief. Yet, though the bill might not have passed, its supporters had hardly failed in curbing the Supreme Court.

Case Closed?

Even though the jurisdiction restricting bill did not pass, it still accomplished its intended effect: reversing the string of liberal Supreme Court decisions on communists' rights. Shortly after the Senate vote, Justice Felix Frankfurter insisted that the court postpone its next slate of communism cases on the 1958 docket. A year later, Frankfurter and Justice John Marshall Harlan II switched from their 1956–1957 position of protecting communists' rights. Their retreat led to the court scaling back a pair of earlier decisions: *Uphaus v. Wyman* (1959) limited *Sweezy v. New Hampshire* (1957) and reestablished that "subversive persons" included those remotely or unconsciously connected to subversion; and *Barenblatt v. United States* (1959) seemingly overruled *Watkins v. United States* (1957) by upholding the House on Un-American Activities Committee's behavior.[11] Chief Justice Earl Warren criticized his colleague: "*Sweezy* was exactly the same thing as *Barenblatt* . . . Felix changed on communist cases because he couldn't take criticism."[12]

Frankfurter had taken note of the emerging conservative majority, and rather than risk another possible legislative attack on judicial independence (which could bleed into other issues, such as desegregation), he backed off from protecting communists' rights. In the end, Republicans and southern Democrats received the outcome they sought: an effective judicial about-face on communism. Liberal Democrats might have been disappointed with that outcome, but they had avoided congressionally sanctioned court-curbing.[13] Ironically, in backing down from a congressional challenge, the court might have benefited the Democratic Party, which could avoid having to address a major fissure in the coalition. Liberals could suffer the judicial retreat on communism knowing that litigation was still a viable strategy (i.e., a route that avoided contentious intraparty congressional debates) for procuring liberal racial and social policies, such as enforcing desegregation and protecting abortion.

But what would have happened had Frankfurter and Harlan not switched their votes? What would the political fallout have looked like if the court had insisted on a pro-communist jurisprudence? Republican leaders had planned to explore further court-curbing legislation.[14] Southern Democrats would have supported those efforts; liberal Democrats would have opposed them. Could this liberal-southern fault line have threatened to rip the Democratic majority apart?

In short: probably not, because southern Democrats and Republicans opposed communism based on different premises. Republicans opposed communists' rights on national security grounds. Southerners worried about security, too, but they also opposed the Supreme Court's subversion rulings because of their alleged connection to integration.[15] There might have been a policy coalition, but there was not an electoral coalition.

Stemming from their long-standing paranoia about Black insurrection, many white southerners saw supposed ideological and organizational links between communists and desegregationists. For example, Senator James Eastland (D-MS) matter-of-factly told Congress, "It is evident that the decision of the Supreme Court in the school segregation cases was based upon the writings and teachings of pro-Communist agitators."[16] Southern states set up "little HUACs" in efforts to expose a Black communist conspiracy. Under the pretext of subversion, the NAACP was either banned or severely restricted in many southern states. In some parts of the South, supposed anti-communist measures (e.g., voting registration laws) really targeted

Blacks. Take Louisiana, which enacted police-enforced segregation, because, as one state legislator put it, "white control has receded all over the world while communism has advanced."[17]

Republicans refrained from these making these links. Republican Party leaders might have accepted a temporary anticommunism alliance with southern Democrats; but they were unwilling to use opposition to *Brown* as a party building device.[18] Thus, the court's rulings on communism—at least in isolation—were unlikely to create a change in electoral politics.

But what if Republicans *had been* willing to reach out to white southerners with a segregationist platform? What if the court repeatedly transgressed a cross-partisan majority in the electorate, and the minority party sought to publicize those issues to build a new majority coalition? Could the Supreme Court, then, have played a role in the downfall of its elected allies? Put differently, could the liberal court have brought down the Democratic majority? Previous scholarship on congressional court-curbing has designated attacks against the court as successful (e.g., the Sixteenth Amendment overturning *Pollock v. Farmer's Loan and Trust Co.* in allowing a federal income tax) or unsuccessful (e.g., proposed amendments that define life as beginning at conception).[19] But what about ostensibly unsuccessful attacks that do not directly curb the court? Is direct court-curbing the only measure of "success?" In what other ways can anti–Supreme Court majorities express themselves? How can those majorities hold the court accountable for a countermajoritarian decision? *How do they push back?*

This book explores instances in which the Supreme Court transgresses cross-partisan majorities and the pushback that follows in the wake of such decisions.[20] Using case studies from the mature New Deal era, I conclude that by repeatedly ruling on fault-line issues, the liberal Supreme Court of the New Deal coalition likely played a role in the downfall of the Democratic majority.[21] Put differently, by doing what coalitional leaders hoped the court would do, the court brought about the demise of that very coalition. And it is possible we stand on the threshold of another such moment after *Dobbs v. Jackson Women's Health Organization.*

Roadmap

This is the first book to develop a framework for identifying counter-majoritarian Supreme Court decisions and using the different types of pushback to hypothesize about when these rulings have potential to affect elections. Chapter 1 situates the book within the existing literature. It addresses the "countermajoritarian difficulty" thesis, as well as its new wave "regime politics" critics. I flesh out regime politics' baseline assumptions, which derive from scholarship on political parties. I describe how the regime politics paradigm perceives the American polity, including its resulting coalitional politics. After adding assumptions from the political parties literature, Chapter 2 explains why we should not be surprised to see the court occasionally undermining its own coalition in American political development. I generate observable expectations to determine whether a court decision merits the label "countermajoritarian." When listing the expectations, I circle back to the communism cases as an example for how to use the expectations when examining politics.

Chapters 3 through 6 study school prayer, criminal rights, busing, and abortion. Using the observable expectations laid out in Chapter 2, I show that court rulings on these issues ran counter to a national majority. That majority was cross-partisan in nature, and I posit that attacks against the court were part of a larger Republican effort to create a GOP majority by highlighting fault lines in the Democratic Party.

Chapter 7 concludes the New Deal coalition case studies and details lessons for each branch of government. When the lead faction of the majority coalition turns to the court to handle issues that the faction itself cannot guide through Congress, it opens the possibility that secondary factions of the majority party will ally with the minority party. When this happens at the grassroots, implementation of court rulings becomes difficult. When it happens at the legislative level, Congress can curb the court—or at the very least, scale back its rulings. When this happens at the electoral level, we might expect shifts in party advertising and voting behavior. In each instance—grassroots, legislative, and electoral—the cross-partisan majority pushes back. I discuss the normative implications of a judiciary tasked with protecting minority rights but also operating within a larger system that seeks public accountability.

Chapters 8 and 9 apply the analytical framework to recent Supreme Court cases to gauge their potential to change the electoral calculus. I conclude that decisions on "good governance" (campaign finance, voting laws, and apportionment), same-sex marriage, and affirmative action are unlikely to change partisan politics. Health care could affect elections, but the issue's constitutionality appears settled and is therefore unlikely to cause any change. Religious liberty cases have been—and continue to look to be—decided in a direction that would allow both parties to remain content. Abortion, however, remains the "elephant in the room," with the ability to dramatically alter coalitional politics. The book closes by considering this possibility and how the Democratic Party could profit from the reversal of *Roe v. Wade*.

Chapter 1

The Countermajoritarian Difficulty and Regime Politics

THIS CHAPTER DESCRIBES A theory of how the Supreme Court can incite pushback and help bring about the downfall of its own affiliated coalition in the elected branches. In short, by ruling on issues that split the majority party, the court brings to light latent fault lines within the coalition and offers the minority party a chance to appeal to dissatisfied factions of the majority. While there are ways to relieve the pressure on secondary factions in the majority party, repeated violations and/or objectionable rulings on salient issues can lead to grassroots noncompliance, legislative reactions, and electoral consequences.

I begin by reviewing the relevant literature, starting with the "countermajoritarian difficulty" and its successive lineage in both politics and scholarship. Then I describe a newer paradigm, regime politics, and its critique of the countermajoritarian difficulty. I unpack the paradigm's underlying assumptions to propose a theory of how and why an affiliated judiciary can harm its own coalition.

The Countermajoritarian Difficulty and Accountability Problem

Many scholars, judges, and politicians have criticized courts for striking down laws passed by elected officials. This section traces the development of such arguments. I start with the scholarly/legal argument and build toward Alexander Bickel's denunciations of the "countermajoritarian difficulty" and the "accountability problem." Next, I look at how political and judicial actors have used Bickel's reasoning and rhetoric throughout American political history. At the end of this section, I pick up the post-Bickel lineage tale, describing the line of thinkers who come from the judicial restraint family tree, as it were.

The Scholarly/Legal Lineage of Judicial Restraint

While Bickel coined the term "countermajoritarian difficulty" and explicated the accountability problem, he was hardly the first to present these critiques. Philosophical critiques of the American judiciary arose as early as the eighteenth century, when Anti-Federalists, and then Jeffersonians, were skeptical of judicial review. As late nineteenth – and early twentieth-century groups called for judicial reform, many judicial scholars (e.g., Herbert Wechsler) and scholarly judges (e.g., Learned Hand) argued for judicial restraint.[1] Here, though, I focus solely on the direct lineage flowing to and from Alexander Bickel. The roots of the family tree go back to James Bradley Thayer's 1893 *Harvard Law Review* article titled "The Origin and Scope of the American Doctrine of Constitutional Law." In it, Thayer said that judges should grant a "wide margin of consideration . . . to the practical judgment of a legislative body. Within that margin . . . constitutional lawmakers must be allowed a free foot."[2] It is a separation of powers argument, and Thayer argues that courts should be mostly called upon to resolve legal disputes. Courts do have the ability to weigh in on constitutional violations—namely, when the elected branches make a "clear mistake" that no rational person could constitutionally justify—but as Thayer put it later in his career, judicial review "dwarf[s] the political capacity of the people."[3]

Two future Supreme Court Justices had connections to Thayer.[4] Oliver Wendell Holmes studied under Thayer and then practiced law with him. Louis Brandeis, too, studied under Thayer at Harvard. Holmes believed that because legislatures held "paramount" power, courts should give them the benefit of the doubt rather than force legislatures to show the burden of proof. "The decision of the legislature must be accepted," Holmes wrote, "unless we can say that it is very wide of any reasonable mark."[5] His dissent in *Lochner v. New York* bears all the marks of his judicial philosophy. He hints that the New York law limiting the number of hours bakers may work is "injudicious or if you like . . . tyrannical." Yet, he proclaims that the legislators who passed the law were reasonable. Moreover, he emphatically asserts "the right of a majority to embody their opinions in law."[6]

Brandeis's strand of judicial restraint emanates from different sources than Holmes's philosophy. Both believed there was a reasonableness standard. But their methods for reaching that point were different. Brandeis would, on his own, gather the available factual evidence to determine if a legislature's actions appeared reasonable. In other words, Brandeis acted as if he were a legislator—turning to nonlegal facts to determine whether a certain law could be considered reasonable. Often, Brandeis concluded, it was reasonable. (Holmes, on the other hand, "d[id] not need research."[7]) Additionally, Brandeis—a Kentuckian, which many forget—held a strong commitment to the right of state legislatures to experiment with public policy. For instance, in one case, Ernest and Paul Liebmann faced prosecution for bootlegging ice without an Oklahoma state license to sell. The court struck down the Sooner State's regulatory law. Despite evidence that Brandeis strongly agreed with the substance of the majority opinion, he nevertheless dissented. After investigating the causes of the Depression, the impact of overproduction, average monthly temperatures in Oklahoma, and the lack of refrigerators in the state, Brandeis concluded, "Denial of the right to experiment may be fraught with serious consequences to the nation."[8]

A common friend to Holmes and Brandeis, Felix Frankfurter proudly assumed the judicial deference mantle during the New Deal era. In 1963 Frankfurter wrote, "Both Holmes and Brandeis influenced me in my constitutional outlook, but both of them derived theirs from the same sources from which I derived mine, namely, James Bradley Thayer."[9] It is no wonder that Frankfurter wrote to Brandeis soon after the latter released his *New State Ice Co.* (1932) dissent: "Your *Ice* opinion is truly monumental, a most impressive guide for decades to come, one of those dissents that render history."[10] Once, while on the Supreme Court, Frankfurter confronted his colleague, John Marshall Harlan II. Not known for his tact, Frankfurter "put a copy of J. B. Thayer's essay . . . into his hands, with the remark, 'Please read it, then reread it, and then read it again and then think about it.'"[11]

Frankfurter passionately defended the rights of legislatures in *West Virginia State Board of Education v. Barnette* (1943), a case that overturned the short-lived precedent in *Minersville School District v. Gobitis* (1940), which had held that public schools could require students to recite the Pledge of Allegiance. In *Barnette*, Frankfurter dissented: "The judiciary, today, in dealing with the acts of their co-ordinate legislators, owe to the country no greater or clearer duty than that of keeping their hands off these acts wherever it is possible to do it."[12]

Desegregation was trickier. In 1953 Justice Frankfurter believed law, precedent, and legislatures had made segregation constitutionally permissible. Nevertheless, he wanted the racist practice invalidated and searched for an excuse to exercise the activist practices he normally abhorred. He tasked one of his clerks, Alexander Bickel, with studying the legislative history of the Fourteenth Amendment. Like Frankfurter, Bickel believed in judicial restraint *and* in the need to strike down segregation. The young law clerk reported that the Thirty-Ninth Congress of the 1860s might not have intended for segregation to be abolished; but it was also impossible to say that they would have prohibited such an act. Young Bickel deduced that it was "inconclusive."[13] Practically, Bickel gave Frankfurter what the justice probably wanted all along: some kind of constitutional cover for voting with the majority in *Brown v. Board*.[14]

Brown shaped Bickel. We associate the former Yale Law professor with his memorable catchphrases, such as "the least dangerous branch" and the "countermajoritarian difficulty." Those ideas (along with the "accountability problem") are certainly major parts of his scholarly legacy. However, as we do when analyzing political development, it is important to situate Bickel within the context in which he wrote. In large part, Bickel's philosophy was a response to the rising political influence of the Supreme Court in the 1950s, and namely, its ruling in *Brown*.[15] Like Frankfurter, Bickel believed that the court reached the only substantive conclusion that it could have reached: segregation was practically impermissible. The most important fact was that segregation was morally abhorrent. It had to be struck down, and the Supreme Court was an appropriate institution to order its termination. Yet, *Brown* left Bickel uncomfortable. He worried that others could interpret it as the court possessing a broad institutional capacity to be used as frequently and whimsically whenever five justices agreed. He worried that *Brown* might usher in a trend whereby the court would regularly strike down legislative acts as unconstitutional.

Addressing these concerns, in 1962, Bickel published *The Least Dangerous Branch*, arguing that judicial review is countermajoritarian (i.e., opposed to the political will or preferences of the majority). Bickel wrote, "When the Supreme Court declares unconstitutional a legislative act or the action of an elected executive, it thwarts the will of representatives of the actual people of the here and now; it exercises control, not on behalf of the prevailing majority, but against it."[16] Thus, judicial review presents a "countermajoritarian difficulty."

Bickel also argued that there is an "accountability problem"—that the justices employing judicial review are not directly accountable to the electorate. If members of Congress pass a law that the majority finds objectionable, people have a built-in recall mechanism: elections. Entrenched on the bench for life terms, beyond impeachment (which is so rare that it is virtually nonexistent), Supreme Court justices face no such accountability, a fact that Bickel found problematic for a democratic republic.[17]

Bickel argued the court should not exercise judicial review often. Rather, the court should demonstrate "passive virtues" by using justiciability doctrines to dodge controversial cases that portended judicial review.[18] When faced with particularly heated issues, the justices should seek to avoid deciding altogether. Judges certainly had the tools available to credibly dismiss cases. Standing, ripeness, political questions doctrine, jurisdictional restrictions—all of these allowed the Supreme Court to avoid deciding cases that might upset the elected branches and/or the American public.

Yet, unlike Thayer, Bickel's philosophy was not wholly driven by procedure. Bickel did not intend for the court to stay out of policy-making or to clear as high a threshold as "clear mistake." Instead, the passive virtues were a means, not an end. By refraining from stirring controversy, the court could build the kind of capital needed to act when it really mattered (e.g., in *Brown*).[19] Bickel called this a "Lincolnian tension" between principle and pragmatism.[20] As with any court, the US Supreme Court was bound to principle—to judicial practices that upheld the rule of the law.[21] Sometimes, however, the court needed to set aside principle—to be activist, to strike down a law, to get the outcome correct regardless of other concerns.[22] *Brown* was one of those instances.

As is often the case in politics or pop culture, the image of someone or something can be more powerful than the nuanced factual details. The legal profession has treated Bickel's complicated Lincolnian tension fairly, with many acknowledging the passive virtues and Bickel's advocacy for very limited but very important uses of judicial review (e.g., as in *Brown*).[23] Nevertheless, Bickel's main contribution is not his complexity, but his parsimony. Put differently, the catchphrases endure. The "countermajoritarian difficulty" has spawned an entire paradigm in history and political science that seeks to debunk the theory (discussed below). The accountability problem remains and has become the darling of many contemporary conservative jurisprudentialists.[24] The point here is not to debate Bickel's legacy but rather to point out that tenets of his overall philosophy (whether situated in, or ripped from, context) remain. If anything, those arguments were around (if not so cleverly articulated) long before *Brown* or *The Least Dangerous Branch*.

Countermajoritarian and Accountability Criticisms in American History

The Marshall Court was an early target of countermajoritarian and accountability complaints.[25] Granted, though serving alongside an elected Jeffersonian regime, Federalist-leaning John Marshall was especially adept at adhering to public opinion.[26] Even *Marbury v. Madison* (1803) was sensitive to Jeffersonian preferences. Indeed, much of the Jeffersonian critiques against the Federalist court came not against its opinions, but against the Judiciary Act of 1801 and Samuel Chase's partisan behavior.[27] Nevertheless, countermajoritarian rhetoric and accountability rhetoric still emerged. For instance, in trying to repeal the "midnight appointments" scheme of 1801, Jeffersonian members of Congress raised such objections. Representative John Randolph (DR-VA) asked whether constitutional questions should "be confided to men immediately responsible to the people, or to those who are irresponsible?" Worried that judicial review would give judges "absolute direction of the government," Senator John Breckinridge (DR-KY) asked, "To whom are they responsible?"[28] These types of critiques occasionally arose for the next hundred years whenever one side lost an important court case (e.g., *Dred Scott v. Sandford*).

Lochner v. New York (1905) ushered in an unprecedented volume of countermajoritarian demonstrations. They arose from the court itself, with Holmes's dissent commenting on the decision's countermajoritarian nature. Justice John Marshall Harlan quoted his previous opinion in *Atkins v. Kansas* (1903): "Legislative enactments should be recognized and enforced by the courts as embodying the will of the people." Although newspapers (e.g., the *New York Times*) and politicians (e.g., Theodore Roosevelt) denounced decisions as countermajoritarian, the legal community raised the loudest protests. Learned Hand and Roscoe Pound warned of the dangers of judges imposing their will over that of the people/legislature.[29]

In the 1930s a new vision of an activist national government coupled with a growing pragmatist belief in the Constitution as a "living" document led to critiques of the judiciary.[30] New Dealers pegged the justices as outdated relics of a bygone era.[31] Countermajoritarian rhetoric, too, emerged. Robert Jackson, then assistant attorney general, commented, "Either democracy must surrender to the judges or the judges must yield to democracy."[32] Thus, FDR introduced court-packing, which was not just a shot across the bow but a real effort, sanctioned by the Constitution, to reshape the high court.[33] The bill to add justices did not pass, of course, but the court soon began issuing decisions that were more acceptable to the elected branches.[34]

In recent times, Bickel's critiques have been picked up by a new generation of scholars, judges, and politicians. As Erwin Chemerinsky notes,

Modern constitutional theory began with Alexander Bickel's *The Least Dangerous Branch* and its declaration that judicial review is a "deviant institution" in American democracy and that there is a "counter-majoritarian difficulty" in having an unelected judiciary with the power to invalidate the acts of popularly elected officials.[35]

Others have used Bickel as a launching point in developing their own spinoff theories about judicial review. For example, in 1980, John Hart Ely, a Yale Law School colleague of Bickel's, published *Democracy and Distrust*, which refers to Bickel as "probably the most creative constitutional theorist of the past 20 years."[36] Ely calls for limited use of judicial review, saying that the Supreme Court should only strike down a law when doing so either helps majoritarian principles or expands democratic procedures. Cass Sunstein has described "minimalist" rulings that do not go far beyond the facts of the case at hand, which recalls Bickel's passive virtues. Sunstein argues that in some contexts, these virtues are highly preferable.[37] There is even a robust literature review literature. Some scholars focus on Bickel's entire corpus of work.[38] Others focus on his influence and legacy.[39] Still others have published on critiques of Bickel (and his followers).[40] The most famous invocations (or reformulations) of Bickel's philosophy, though, have come from law professors who ascended to the federal judiciary.

Robert Bork claimed that Bickel taught him about the Constitution "more than anyone else."[41] While Bork would later be known as a rejected Supreme Court nominee, he made his name by articulating a minimalist judicial philosophy rooted in originalism. Arguing that judges should base their decisions in the original framers' intent, Bork contended that judicial review is to be—with a few exceptions— avoided. Bork's *The Tempting of America* clearly echoes Bickel: "When the Court, without warrant in the Constitution, strikes down a democratically produced statute, that act substitutes the will of a majority of nine lawyers for the will of the people."[42]

Continuing the judicial restraint line, Bork personally influenced a generation of conservative legal thinkers and actors. He helped start the Federalist Society—a conservative legal organization that lobbies for originalist interpretations. Other members of the Federalist Society have included Antonin Scalia, Clarence Thomas, John Roberts, Samuel Alito, Neil Gorsuch, Brett Kavanaugh, and Amy

Coney Barrett.[43] Scalia, in particular, had a direct tie to Bork, probably because the two served together on the District of Columbia Court of Appeals. Scalia borrowed heavily from Bork's version of originalism. Moreover, Scalia's *A Matter of Interpretation* details his "textualist" philosophy of judicial review and explicitly points to areas of agreement with Frankfurter and Holmes.[44]

In sum, the countermajoritarian difficulty and accountability problem have no shortage of contemporary supporters. From academics (e.g., Steven Calabresi, Randy Barnett) to judges (e.g., J. Harvie Wilkinson, Richard Posner), various arguments against judicial review all seem to incorporate some element of countermajoritarianism and/or accountability. In politics today, countermajoritarian and accountability critiques come from both sides of the political aisle— conveniently enough, whenever that side has lost in court.[45] Scholars still raise complaints about the surface-level countermajoritarian nature of judicial review and the inability to hold justices electorally accountable.[46] Both liberal and conservative political commentators have been quick to label the Supreme Court as countermajoritarian and unaccountable.[47] And while these criticisms still carry a parsimonious message about majoritarian democracy, they underestimate the complexity of American politics, an oversight noted by political scientists, historians, and law professors.

The Regime Politics Paradigm and Its Assumptions

A new paradigm for studying law and courts, the regime politics approach, has largely (but not entirely) debunked the countermajoritarian difficulty as a myth. Scholars in law, history, and political science unite in arguing that because the Supreme Court is part of the national governing regime, it often uses judicial review in regime-friendly (i.e., majoritarian) ways. In the words of one of the leading scholars in the field, Keith Whittington, the court "interposes its friendly hand," striking down laws because the majority coalition wants the court to do so.[48] I provide background of the regime politics paradigm, starting with the four cornerstone assumptions of the paradigm. Then I discuss the various ways in which the court can contribute to the policy and political goals of the national governing regime.[49]

Assumption #1: Presence of a Dominant National Coalition
The regime politics paradigm assumes that the federal government
is—for finite periods of time—managed by an identifiable majority
coalition, or governing regime.[50] Regimes are complex and multi-
faceted coalitions. They carry founding impetuses, critical starting
points, and ideological commitments.[51] Most pertinent to my investigation, though, are the electoral base and congressional delegation
of a coalition. Here, V. O. Key's classic formulation of the party-in-
electorate and party-in-government are helpful.[52]

A dominant coalition has an electoral base with multiple factions,
be they geographic (e.g., northeastern Republicans) or ideological
(e.g., liberal Democrats). The party-in-electorate is responsible for
electing presidents and congressional majorities. The congressional
delegation, then, is a key element of the party-in-government. It
works on behalf of the party in the electorate to deliver promises
on policy. There certainly is a leadership cohort within the coalition.
It includes presidents, members of Congress (e.g., speaker of the
House, Senate majority leader), and other party leaders (e.g., vice
presidents, cabinet members).[53] Beyond the leadership, though, the
rank-and-file members of Congress make up the coalition's majority
in Congress. As with the electoral base, these legislators can come
from different regions and/or ideological wings of the party.

Assumption #2: The Court as Part of the Dominant
National Coalition (Robert Dahl)
The launching point for the regime politics paradigm is that a majority coalition manages the federal government. Using this baseline,
a trio of scholars—Robert Dahl, Robert McCloskey, and Martin
Shapiro—have added other assumptions important for the study of
the Supreme Court. Let us start with Dahl, whose "Decision-Making
in a Democracy: The Supreme Court as a National Policy-Maker" was
his only publication to focus exclusively on the judiciary. Published
sixty-five years ago, the article has remarkable staying power.[54] As
Gerald Rosenberg comments, "The points that Dahl makes can be
seen as precursors of, or contributors to, a plethora of research tra-
jectories. In many ways, he suggested the research road to be taken

by future generations of judicial scholars."[55] For regime politics, Dahl established one of the paradigm's operating assumptions: "The Supreme Court is inevitably part of the dominant national alliance. As an element in the political leadership of the dominant alliance, the Court of course supports the major policies of the alliance."[56]

Dahl examined how often, and under what conditions, the Supreme Court exercises judicial review. First, Dahl investigated how much time had passed between the passage of a law and the court's striking down of that law. He set a four-year limit, reasoning that this is about the time that we can expect lawmaking majorities to stay intact. He found that more than half of all exercises of judicial review (through 1957) occurred more than four years after Congress passed a law. If the pre-1937 New Deal court is excluded, only about one-third of all instances of judicial review took place within four years of a bill's passage.

Dahl then examined the nature of policies struck down within the four-year window. He separated instances of judicial review into times when the court struck down major and minor policies. About 40 percent of cases involved minor policies. Of the other 60 percent, Congress ended up overriding or reversing three-quarters of them. In sum, of all the times the court had exercised judicial review, only 6 percent of those cases were on: (1) major policies; (2) enacted within the last four years of their striking down; and (3) not overturned by Congress. Most of those, too, occurred after a durable majority party had suddenly lost power—"short-lived transitional periods when the old alliance is disintegrating and the new one is struggling to take control of political institutions."[57] Therefore, Dahl reasoned, rather than protecting insular minorities, the main task of the court is to grant legitimacy to the fundamental policies of the dominant coalition.

Two critiques have been raised against Dahl. The first involves methodological questions. What constitutes a major and minor policy? What happens to policies that were struck down and were more than four years old? Does Congress tend to overturn those decisions, too? What about statutory interpretation? Even though the court does not strike down a law in these cases, it still can dramatically affect it in a way that lawmaking majorities did not intend. And what about review of state laws? For instance, under Dahl's scheme, *McCulloch v. Maryland* (1819) is excluded from analysis.[58]

The other critique centers on the mechanism of the alliance between the regime and the Supreme Court. Dahl said that because presidents appoint an average of one justice every two years, there is enough turnover to ensure that the court reflects the preferences of national majorities. Of course, on occasion, presidents fail to appoint a justice who closely mirrors the appointer's preferences. Dwight Eisenhower's nominations of Earl Warren and William Brennan, for example, stand out in this respect. In addition, when Dahl's thesis is contextualized among other institutions, the reason the court rarely strikes down the policies of a "live" majority is not solely because presidents make appointments. It is also because it is very difficult for the court to be a policymaking lone ranger in a system of multiple branches with overlapping powers.[59]

Regardless of these critiques, Dahl's operating assumption—that the Supreme Court is aligned with the dominant alliance and one cannot understand judicial outcomes without considering the political goals and policy preferences of the affiliated coalition—still stands. Dahl lists two important functions of the court: striking down policies preferred by the deposed coalition and legitimizing policies preferred by the sitting, affiliated dominant coalition. And while these seem like relatively passive functions, Dahl also believes the court can play an active role in policymaking. Indeed, scholars in the regime paradigm do not believe that the court merely serves at the pleasure of the coalition. So fundamental to future scholarship (including this book) and so eloquently written, Dahl commented,

> The Supreme Court is not, however, simply an agent of the alliance. It is an essential part of the political leadership . . . [but] it can succeed only if its action conforms to and reinforces a widespread set of explicit or implicit norms held by the political leadership.[60]

In sum, the court is part of the dominant national alliance; it serves with, for, and sometimes in the lead of, the alliance. When the court does make policy, it must count on its political affiliates to back its rulings in order to see a policy stand. Otherwise, we might expect attacks on the court—both on the court's policy prescriptions and on the institution itself.

Assumption #3: "Constellations of Power and Interest"
(Robert McCloskey)

Robert McCloskey contributed to regime politics in two ways. First, he provided the historical evidence showing that Dahl was largely correct: that the Supreme Court is part of the dominant national alliance. Second, McCloskey built on Dahl's assumption. Whereas Dahl believed that the court's behavior had to conform to the norms held by the leadership of the dominant coalition, McCloskey argued that the role and behavior of the court "reflect[s] constellations of power and interest within changing historical contexts."[61] And where Dahl saw the court as needing to satisfy party leaders of the dominant alliance, McCloskey saw the court as answering to a larger, possibly cross-partisan, majority within the government or in the electorate.

Unlike Dahl, McCloskey wrote extensively on the judiciary. Even among an impressive litany of books and articles, *The American Supreme Court* was his magnus opus. In a single short volume, it gives a thorough history of the political and legal development of the court. It describes the early struggles of the court to establish itself as an independent judiciary, as well as the origins of judicial review and its subsequent use by future generations of jurists. Although McCloskey admitted that "a brief book . . . cannot of course . . . cover the story of judicial review comprehensively," it comes very close (published first in 1960, it has been updated by Sanford Levinson).[62] It also offers insightful commentary. McCloskey describes a dynamic institution, capable of adapting to changing political and institutional circumstances. "The interests and values," McCloskey writes, "and hence the role of the Court have shifted fundamentally and often in the presence of shifting national conditions."[63] In other words, depending on the ideological makeup of the court—as well as the makeup of the dominant coalition—the court has taken on different roles (e.g., rubber stamper, bold civil rights leader).[64]

This is McCloskey's major contribution to regime politics: the assumption that politics is not bound by partisan labels and that cross-partisan coalitions can affect how the polity responds to judicial decisions. Rulings will not be supported and/or implemented simply because the justices hail from the dominant national alliance. Their decisions will be accepted or rejected based on whether they can muster the necessary support to carry them out. McCloskey says support comes from "a preponderance of friends over enemies."[65] In the next chapter, I discuss the nature of these friends and enemies. But for now, I point out that regime politics has largely validated McCloskey's conclusion that "it is hard to find a single instance when the Court has stood firm for very long against a really clear wave of public demand."[66]

Like Dahl, McCloskey offers an assumption that seems to limit the power and independence of the Supreme Court. Also like Dahl, though, McCloskey grants agency to the court—an important facet of regime politics. To quote the author:

> This is not to suggest that the historical Court has slavishly counted the public pulse, assessed the power relationships that confronted it, and shaped its decisions accordingly. The process in question is a good deal more subtle than that. We might come closer to the truth if we said that the judges have often agreed with the main current of public sentiment because they were themselves part of that current, and not because they feared to disagree with it.[67]

Assumption #4: Two-Way Relationship (Martin Shapiro)

Martin Shapiro's theory of "political jurisprudence" describes courts as institutions within a larger political system.[68] Similar to Dahl and McCloskey, Shapiro believes that, fundamentally, courts are hybrid institutions with both political and legal missions. One author accurately summarizes this aspect of Shapiro's contribution as: "Courts are courts, but courts are also political institutions."[69] Indeed, Shapiro's two-word catchphrase, "political jurisprudence," captures both aspects. This has dual relevance for the study at hand.

First, as with Dahl and McCloskey, studying courts requires taking stock of other relevant institutions. Second, and more innovatively, political jurisprudence places emphasis not only on how the dominant national alliance (partisan or cross-partisan) affects the Supreme Court. It also looks at the ways in which the Supreme Court affects the dominant coalition. In other words, Shapiro considers not only the effects of politics on the court but also the court's effect on politics. In a seminal "State of the Discipline" essay, Shapiro criticized the public law field for abandoning many of the traditions that allowed law and courts scholars to speak to other Americanists. He lamented the turn to vote counting and constitutional interpretation, and he pleaded for scholars to "bring the courts back in"—to place courts back into the discussion of "the normal nitty gritty politics of pluralist bargaining and compromise that American politics people stud[y]."[70] While Dahl and McCloskey might have granted the court agency within the coalition and the polity, respectively, Shapiro takes the argument a step further—that the court, like the other branches, can transform not only policy and the law, but also politics.

To conclude, each of these scholars helped build a paradigm by contributing an assumption about how the Supreme Court operates in American politics. Dahl saw the court as part of the dominant coalition. McCloskey clarified the possibility of cross-partisan alliances. And Shapiro clarified the ways in which the court could affect other political actors (including cross-partisan alliances). Regime politics scholars have used these assumptions to introduce important theories about the Supreme Court.

New Wave Regime Politics

A generation of scholarship has followed in the wake of Dahl, McCloskey, and Shapiro. Starting with the assumption that the Supreme Court is part of, and rarely deviates from, the dominant majority coalition, the regime politics paradigm clarifies how judicial review can benefit the coalition in complex ways. Table 1.1 summarizes the different ways in which the court can help pursue the policy and political goals of the coalition. To orient one to the nuances of the paradigm, I discuss two of these functions.

TABLE 1.1 Regime Politics Concepts

Concept	Explanation	Example
Legislative deferral	Facing a coalition-splitting issue, coalitional leaders invite the Supreme Court to resolve the issue.	The court tried to resolve slavery in the 1850s with *Dred Scott*.[a]
Deliberate statutory ambiguity	Congress passes a law with purposely ambiguous sections hoping that the court can resolve what Congress could not.	The National Labor Relations Act contained purposely ambiguous labor laws, which were later interpreted in *NLRB v. Jones & Laughlin Steel Corp.*[b]
Judicial entrenchment	Expansion of appointments and/or jurisdiction provides insurance when dominant coalitions suffer electoral defeats.	Republicans in the late nineteenth century packed the courts.[c]
Regional outliers	The court reins in a small number of states or localities that deviate from broad national norms.	Four northeastern states prohibited contraceptives until the court issued *Griswold v. CT*.[d]
Policy-making partners	An ideologically affiliated court issues rulings that the dominant coalition finds preferable.	The Rehnquist Court's federalism jurisprudence aligned with dominant Republican ideology.[e]
Legitimation	The court adds legitimacy to regime policy by confirming its constitutionality.	*West Coast Hotel Company v. Parrish* (1937) upheld minimum wage law.[f]
Overcome entrenched interests	Coalition leaders turn to the court because of institutional roadblocks in the legislature.	Because southerners held gatekeeping chairmanships in Congress, FDR and the NAACP pursued civil rights via the judiciary.[g]
Overcoming fractious coalitions	Coalition members agree to stipulations they normally would not compromise on because they predict the court will strike down those stipulations while upholding the rest of the compromise, which is largely preferable.	In lowering tariffs, Grover Cleveland had to agree to instituting an income tax, which he otherwise found objectionable. When the court struck down the income tax in *Pollock*, Cleveland still maintained the preferred free trade aspect of the bill.[h]

a. Mark A. Graber, "The Nonmajoritarian Difficulty: Legislative Deference to the Judiciary"; Graber, *Dred Scott and the Problem of Constitutional Evil*.

Legislative Deferrals

Mark Graber describes the conditions under which we would expect the dominant regime to pass the buck on coalition-splitting issues.[71] Moderate party leaders can chart a middling course, change the subject, broker compromises, or avoid the issue altogether. Sometimes, though, a highly salient issue requires resolution. If Congress cannot come to an agreement, "legislative deference" is an attractive option. Here, Congress invites the Supreme Court to resolve an issue. Leaders in the majority coalition push legislative deference because it allows them to maintain the partisan cleavages that brought about their majority in the first place. Ideologues—from both sides of the spectrum—support legislative deference because they could win the judicial battle. Even if defeated, politicians can blame an activist court and use position-taking tools to score political points with their constituents.

The court, meanwhile, appears perfectly suited for the role. The court is preexisting and ostensibly nonpartisan—it was not created with the specific purpose to resolve an issue and/or resolve it in a

---

b. George Lovell, Legislative Deferrals: Statutory Ambiguity, Judicial Power, and American Democracy; Scott E. Lemieux and George Lovell, "Legislative Defaults: Interbranch Power Sharing and Abortion Politics."

c. Howard Gillman, "How Political Parties Can Use the Courts to Advance Their Agendas: Federal Courts in the United States, 1875–1891"; Gillman, "Party Politics and Constitutional Change: The Political Origins of Liberal Judicial Activism"; Gerald N. Rosenberg, "The Triumph of Politics: The Republican Party's Takeover of the US Supreme Court."

d. Michael Klarman, "Rethinking the Civil Rights and Civil Liberties Revolutions"; Lucas A. Powe Jr., The Warren Court and American Politics.

e. J. Mitchell Pickerill and Cornell W. Clayton, "The Politics of Criminal Justice: How the New Right Regime Shaped the Rehnquist Court's Criminal Justice Jurisprudence"; Cornell W. Clayton, "The Bush Presidency and the New Right Constitutional Regime"; Cornell W. Clayton and J. Mitchell Pickerill, "The Rehnquist Court and the Political Dynamics of Federalism"; Gerald N. Rosenberg, "The Importance of Being Political: How to Understand the US Supreme Court's Approach to Affirmative Action in Education."

f. Dahl, "Decision-Making in a Democracy"; Graber, "Federalist or Friends of Adams."

g. Kevin J. McMahon, Reconsidering Roosevelt on Race: How the Presidency Paved the Road to Brown; Paul Frymer, "Acting When Elected Officials Won't: Federal Courts and Civil Rights Enforcement in US Labor Unions, 1935–1985"; Terri Peretti, Partisan Supremacy: How the GOP Enlisted Courts to Rig America's Election Rules.

h. Whittington, "'Interpose Your Friendly Hand.'"

particular way. The court is constitutionally authorized to hear cases. Justices are appointed for life; and unlike members of Congress, they need not worry about the electoral implications of the decision they make. Institutionally, justices might be wary of striking down landmark laws or ruling on a salient issue. However, they might be more willing to exercise judicial review or step into a political cauldron after legislators publicly call on the court to take up the issue.

For instance, in the 1850s, after decades of avoiding a showdown on slavery, northern and southern Democrats could no longer legislatively resolve the issue. In Compromise of 1850 legislation and in the Kansas–Nebraska Act, Congress included language that fast tracked judicial appeals and invited judicial participation.[72] Additionally, during debate, Democratic leaders went out their way to invite the court to take on slavery cases.[73] Of course, soon thereafter, the court decided *Dred Scott*. Although it exacerbated the national crisis, that was not the intent; the intent was to solve the slavery issue once and for all.[74]

Regional Outliers

When the Supreme Court strikes down a state law, we might think that it is defying the will of local majorities—that the unelected federal judiciary is imposing its will upon the states. Although it might be easy to label this behavior as countermajoritarian, regime politics scholars have demonstrated that striking down some laws can be entirely in line with national majorities. In these cases, the state policies themselves are the products of countermajoritarianism, and the court's exercise of judicial review is an attempt to bring those states within the mainstream of dominant national preferences. Michael Klarman has referred to this phenomenon as the court reining in "regional outliers"—the last holdouts against policies that are preferred by not just a slim margin but an overwhelming majority. He points to a series of cases that illustrate the court imposing a national consensus on such outliers.[75]

Griswold v. Connecticut and *Lawrence v. Texas* are two of the more familiar examples of the court reining in regional outliers. In the former, the court struck down anticontraceptive laws that applied in only four states.[76] The Supreme Court's striking down of the law may very well have been counter to the majority in Connecticut that passed the law in 1879. However, by 1965, a majority in the United States—and probably even in Connecticut—disagreed with the law. In *Lawrence*, the court overturned *Bowers v. Hardwick* and struck down laws in thirteen states that criminalized sodomy. Though a quarter of the states might seem beyond the bounds of "regional," in reality, nearly all of them did not enforce the law. When *Lawrence* was decided in 2003, a large majority of Americans agreed on sexual privacy in the bedroom.[77]

In both cases, the Supreme Court used judicial review to bring anomalous local policies in line with dominant national preferences. In addition, while Congress could rein in regional outliers, legislative responses are unlikely when problems are relatively isolated and do not attract national attention. By contrast, a politically constructed national courts system is particularly well-suited to accomplish the task.[78]

Conclusion

The regime politics paradigm shows how judicial review can be used in ways to benefit the dominant majority. As such, scholars have all but rejected the countermajoritarian difficulty as the lens through which we should study judicial power. Instead, a "new paradigm for thinking about judicial power . . . Its mantra 'judicial review is politically constructed,' is replacing previous chants that 'judicial review is a deviant institution.'"[79] That said, new wave regime politics has focused so intently on debunking Bickel's thesis that is has overlooked rare, but important, cases of countermajoritarianism. There are some studies, but even they refrain from framing cases as countermajoritarian.[80] This omission is problematic because such decisions can have important negative consequences for the court and its affiliated elected coalition.

Put simply: judicial review is sometimes countermajoritarian, and sometimes that has important effects on the court and the dominant coalition. Nearly all work within regime politics seeks to uncover a variety of coalition-friendly, majoritarian uses of judicial review. This book extends the paradigm in a different way—by accounting for times when the court defies majorities. These are the exceptions that prove the rule, and I suggest that in certain cases, this type of judicial review can cause problems for both the Supreme Court and the dominant coalition. It can lead to the emergence of cross-partisan majorities, which in the short term can push back against the court's effectiveness and independence. In the long term, it can lead to negative consequences for the court's elected affiliates. To understand how and when this occurs, I turn to the political party literature.

Chapter 2

Theory

THIS CHAPTER DISCUSSES REGIME politics' integration of assumptions from the political parties literature.[1] I detail those assumptions to generate observable expectations of a countermajoritarian Supreme Court. I then introduce three effects—the pushback—of those decisions. Throughout the discussion, I use the communism cases of the 1950s from chapter 1 as an example for how to study expectations and effects. Toward the end of the chapter, I address methodological questions.

Assumption #1: Factional Majority Coalitions

Party politics is not a simple one-dimensional clash between two parties. There are fights, also, within the parties, especially within the majority party. Regime politics adopts the political party literature's supposition of "factions" within the dominant national coalition. Parties scholars have long described American political parties as coalitions of different—and sometimes competing—factions. Early work described how: (1) the institutional structures of the Constitution (e.g., first-past-the-post, Electoral College) and (2) the United States' size and diversity (regional, socioeconomic, and ideological) naturally produce, respectively (1) a two-party system in which (2) neither party can accurately represent all the views of the members who associate with that party.[2] Consider the contemporary parties. The Democratic Party houses (among others) cosmopolitans, libertarians who prioritize social issues, Black Americans, Latinos, and LGBT individuals. The Republican Party houses (among others) neoconservatives, libertarians who prioritize economic and/or gun rights, the New Right, and Donald Trump supporters. There are factions, in both parties, who do not see eye-to-eye with copartisans. Put simply: not all Democrats and not all Republicans are exactly alike.[3]

Regime scholars have embraced this supposition, leading to scholarship on intraparty relations that examines how the tension within a party affects the Supreme Court. Accordingly, regime scholars now concern themselves with how judicial power advantages specific institutions or factions within the dominant alliance.

Assumption #2: Leading Factions

The political parties literature explains that within factional majority coalitions, a lead faction directs the party. Schattschneider argues that this lead faction holds the majority party together by uniting others around a shared governing philosophy and constitutional vision.[4] For the party in the government, the leading faction usually includes the president and ideologically affiliated members of Congress.

The regime politics paradigm employs the same assumption. In fact, the phrase often repeated by the regime politics literature is that the Supreme Court advances the preferences of the "presidential wing" of the dominant national coalition.[5]

Assumption #3: Primary Goals versus Secondary Choices

The political parties literature's explanation for how and when a majority coalition ruptures is an important, and overlooked, assumption of regime politics. In the early stages of a regime, factions work together on "primary goals"—overarching and intraparty consensus-building issues.[6] Over time, the regime "matures" and primary goals become either fully realized or impenetrably entrenched (e.g., Social Security). In this phase, majority parties turn to "secondary choices"—issues of lesser importance to the majority party and on which factions within it disagree.[7] Nichols and Myers refer to these late-term coalitions as "enervated political regimes," whereby the lead faction's advancement of secondary choices leads to a decrease in coalitional cohesion and a failure to "keep institutional arrangements functioning effectively under new conditions."[8] Regime politics scholars have properly, if implicitly, used this assumption to generate and investigate some of the most important theoretical claims within the paradigm (e.g., legislative deferrals and regional outliers).

Recap

Before applying the political parties literature's assumptions to the political development of the Supreme Court within a partisan regime, and before offering predictions, let us review. I have rearranged regime politics and political parties assumptions to show their developmental pattern:

There exists a dominant national coalition. (Regime politics assumption #1)

The Supreme Court is part of the dominant national coalition. (Regime politics assumption #2)

The coalition is factional. (Political parties assumption #1)

The coalition is led by a lead faction. (Political parties assumption #2)

The lead faction pursues coalition-uniting goals until those issues are resolved. Afterwards, the lead faction pursues other issues in which factions within the coalition likely disagree. (Political parties assumption #3)

The "constellations of power" between *and within* a coalition affect the Supreme Court. (Regime politics assumption #3)

As the Supreme Court navigates these constellations, its decisions directly affect the coalition. (Regime politics assumption #4)

In sum, the relationship between the court and dominant coalition is dialectical.[9] Because elected members and appointed judges both hail from the same coalition, they will both face similar policy and political challenges. After primary goals are accomplished, the "mature" regime will face a policy challenge: What to work on next? With no coalition-uniting issues left, the lead faction turns to its secondary preferences. This begets a political challenge: How can the coalition manage its internal differences on these secondary issues? When faced with new challenges, the coalition will rearrange its institutional responsibilities.[10] Regime politics scholars have shown how the lead faction has deployed the judiciary as a rearrangement solution. I theorize that this rearrangement can lead to countermajoritarian decisions, which, under certain conditions, can have negative effects for the coalition and the court.

Cross-Partisan Countermajoritarian Decisions

What happens after the Supreme Court hands down an unpopular ruling? This is where I pick up the story. It is foolish to think that judicial decisions under a climate of factional tension will resolve all problems. After all, the court is "politically constructed," meaning affiliated justices might be partisan to the dominant coalition, but they also have preferences on secondary issues that may be at odds with the preferences of other factions in the majority party.[11] When hearing cases on secondary preferences, the justices confront the same coalition-splitting topics that regime managers in the elected branches seek to avoid. Regime politics scholars predict that the court will make a decision that satisfies the lead faction but dissatisfies nonleading factions in the dominant coalition.[12]

I argue that in certain instances, instead of resolving the internal tension in the coalition, the court exacerbates it. That is, factions within the majority party who feel they have suffered injustice will not always blindly accept judicial rulings that go against their secondary preferences. They might push back against the court—both at its rulings and at its institutional independence. Moreover, dissatisfied members of the majority coalition may be joined by opportunistic members of the minority coalition. This cross-partisan combination may even form a majority.

This is key—*when the cross-partisan alliance constitutes a majority, it can effectively push back against judicial decisions.* While the regime politics paradigm has done much to dispel the myth of the countermajoritarian difficulty, *the Supreme Court can still behave in countermajoritarian ways.* The majority, however, might be different from our traditional notions. In other words, in some cases, we must look beyond using partisan labels as a proxy for political preferences. Once again: not all Democrats (or Republicans) are the same. And there are instances in which Democrats and Republicans (legislators and/or voters) might ally with each other to form a cross-partisan majority intent on curtailing the judiciary and the ideas it espouses. I discuss possible consequences in detail below, but in short, cross-partisan majorities might prove successful in delaying or thwarting the implementation of judicial decisions; curbing the court; and/or shifting the electorate so as to bring a new majority coalition into power.

All told, the court is not exempt from reflecting and responding to the developmental challenge of factional in-fighting. When the court upholds the preferences of one faction, the losing factions become understandably upset. And they act on those feelings. Put simply, when the Supreme Court "chooses sides," it does not mend the coalition's fault lines; rather, the court awakens the fault lines. Ultimately, the court's actions can lead, ironically, to the demise of its own institutional authority and its own affiliated coalition.

Expectations

In this section, I use the regime politics assumptions, political party assumptions, and theory to generate predictions regarding cross-partisan countermajoritarian decisions.[13] Here, it is helpful to describe two types of majorities that the Supreme Court could counter. I derive terms from Key.[14] First, the "majority in the government" comprises members of Congress from both parties who are dissatisfied with the court. Second, the "majority in the electorate" comprises dissatisfied voters (again, from both parties).

Now, nearly all judicial decisions on constitutional issues engender some reaction from dissatisfied factions. But the reaction is more likely to have a significant effect—an effective pushback—if a national majority (either in the government or in the electorate) comes together to oppose the court. Granted, it is tough to measure these kinds of majorities with complete precision.[15] Still, were a cross-partisan majority in the government and/or majority in the electorate to emerge, we might expect some observable qualities. I discuss those qualities below and use the introductory chapter's example of the 1950s communism cases as an example to show how the expectations play out in actual political development. Details of the cases are

interesting; but more important than their individual contents was
the collective result.[16] In the first set of cases in 1956–57, the Warren
Court repeatedly ruled in favor of communists' rights. It had declared
that public officials could only prosecute communists based on acts
(or plans to act) and not on political beliefs. Legislatures, administrative bureaucracies, and public service professions had to clear high
bars to, respectively, investigate, fire, and deny employment access
to suspected communists. Thus, the public's (and Congress's) interpretation of the 1956–1957 decisions was that "fourteen communist
leaders had been freed, two suspected communists apparently had
been allowed to practice law . . . and state and congressional investigations had been frustrated."[17]

Expectation #1: Surface-level Indicators

To start, I offer two "surface-level" indicators of a cross-partisan
countermajoritarian Supreme Court decision. While both indicators
are intuitive expectations, I qualify their effectiveness in measuring countermajoritarianism.

First, perhaps the most obvious indicator of a countermajoritarian decision would be public opinion polls showing that a national
majority opposes the ruling. If the court's decision reflects the secondary preferences of the dominant coalition's lead faction, and if a
representative sample of the national majority nevertheless opposes
the decision, then we should suspect a cross-partisan majority.

Public opinion polls from the 1950s show that most Americans
probably would have disagreed with the court's decisions on communism.[18] The National Opinion Research Center (NORC) conducted a
national poll in 1954 entitled "Communism, Conformity, and Civil
Liberties." It found that 75 percent had a "very favorable" or "favorable" view of "committees investigating communism" (e.g., the House
on Un-American Activities Committee). When asked about "some of
the bad things (if any) that you feel these committees have done," 60
percent gave the nonlisted response "not putting enough communists
in jail." Only 2 percent thought the committees created "a general atmosphere of fear and suspicion." Some of the poll's questions asked

about issues that were raised in Supreme Court cases: 94 percent of respondents approved of universities firing communists (*Slochower v. Board of Education*, 1956); 72 percent disapproved of communists making public speeches (*Pennsylvania v. Nelson*, 1956); and 60 percent believed communists should be jailed (*Yates v. United States*, 1957).[19]

The problem with relying solely on public opinion polls is that the court's decision itself may temporarily sway the public. Thus, we might say that the anticommunism majority was not organic; instead, it was a reactionary result of the court's rulings on the issue. This objection is tough to overcome because it is hard to identify *why* respondents believe what they do. That said, the fact that the NORC poll was taken before 1956–57 might give it some independence from the court's decisions.[20]

Second, I look for claims by members of the minority party and the nonleading faction(s) of the dominant party that the court has acted in a countermajoritarian fashion or that the justices are unaccountable. If these members of Congress claim a countermajoritarian difficulty or an accountability problem, perhaps there is one.

After the communism cases, one Republican member of Congress fumed against "the extreme liberal wing of the United States Supreme Court," which had struck down laws favored by the majority.[21] Southern Democrats, too, relayed concerns, such as James Davis's (D-GA) claim that the court was like a king who was "independent of the will of a Nation."[22]

In total, these two surface-level indicators are just that: surface-level. They are inconclusive and have their respective drawbacks. However, they are intuitive checks for a reason. In fact, they are likely the first indicators we would want to see before moving into the two more complicated expectations below. Public opinion polls and congressional rhetoric are not sufficient to identify countermajoritarianism, but when combined with other observable effects, they help triangulate on cross-partisan countermajoritarian Supreme Court decisions. They are informative pieces of the observable effects puzzle. Therefore, I look for public opinion *and* legislators' rhetoric *and* the following expectations.

Expectation #2: Nonleading Faction Response

When the Supreme Court rules in favor of the secondary preferences of the dominant party's lead faction, then we might expect
nonleading factions to try to push back. Going beyond theatrical
rhetoric denouncing the decision as countermajoritarian, members
of Congress have another powerful weapon in their arsenal: court-
curbing proposals. These "attacks" aim to undermine judicial authority and independence. If dissatisfied with the court, nonleading
faction members can introduce attacks that seek to alter the court
and its opinions. The appendix to this book discusses the extension
of a database that registers thousands of court-curbing proposals.[23]
The database provides clues (i.e., home state and partisan affiliation)
about each attacker's factional affiliation.

Note that outside a few high-profile examples (e.g., Sixteenth
Amendment), court-curbing legislation rarely passes or works.
Nevertheless, attacks against the Supreme Court indicate a possibly
countermajoritarian court. Indeed, for the purposes of identifying
such rulings, it does not matter whether a court-curbing bill passes.
Its mere introduction suggests that its sponsor is unhappy with the
judiciary—precisely the type of information I seek to discover.[24]

In fact, members of Congress likely know that attacks are practically futile. They introduce them to send important signals to various
targets. We do not know the full extent of the reasons behind various
attacks, but if combined with other cross-partisan countermajoritarian indicators, then they add another piece to the observable effects puzzle. Obviously, they are a position-taking device that allows
members of Congress to grandstand for constituents.[25] But if linked
to other behavior, then maybe legislators attack to say something to
the court ("back off this issue"), copartisans ("this is an ideological
fault line within the coalition"), or the opposition party ("there is a
cross-partisan alliance opportunity").

Lastly, dissatisfied nonleading faction members of the majority
coalition have a final option available: switching parties. This is an
extreme measure, and we should not expect to see it often. Supreme
Court decisions alone are unlikely to cause such a defection, but they

might trigger, or add to the mounting frustration behind, a political figure deciding to move to the opposition party. One example arises from the communism cases. Ronald Reagan's feelings towards radical leadership within the Screen Actors Guild played a role in him switching to the GOP.[26] By the mid-1950s, Reagan held strong anticommunism stances that aligned with the Republican Party.[27] Though infrequent, even a handful of switches might imply that the court has upset some element(s) of the dominant coalition. If combined with Expectation #3, there is reason to suspect a cross-partisan majority.

Expectation #3: Minority Party Response

Like members of the nonleading faction of the dominant party, we should also expect members of the minority party to alter their behavior. For starters, they too can propose court-curbing bills, such as William Jenner (R-IN) and John Butler's (R-MD) cosponsored bill seeking to strip the court of jurisdiction over cases involving communists' rights.

On a grander scale, the minority party could also move to take advantage of the apparent fault line in the dominant coalition. If conscious of the opportunity, the minority party can attract wavering members of the dominant party. The "issue evolution" strand of the political parties literature explains how minority parties can use newly arising issues to enlarge their coalition.[28] To attract new partisans, minority parties must provide early policy cues—position-taking stances that signal the electorate as to how their party views a new political issue. In addition to providing a clearer sense of the parties' stances, politicians also keep the issue on the agenda, giving it a higher likelihood of being more salient. In time, the consistent blitz of position-taking signals may cause voters from one (or more) faction of the dominant coalition to move to the opposition coalition.

These signals may take many forms: "policy proposals, conventions, speeches, campaign ads, public demonstrations, letters to the editor, talk shows, and so on."[29] Court-curbing attacks certainly qualify as an appropriate, and understudied, issue evolution mechanism, especially since members of Congress are "the most consistently important and recognizable source of partisan cues."[30] I do not mean to say that attacks are the only—or the most important—cue. Indeed, I look to other signaling devices, such as speeches by lawmakers, party platforms, internal party strategy memos, and presidential addresses. In all of these, we would expect to see the minority party changing its *focus, rhetoric, and strategy* on issues raised by the Supreme Court. Put simply, we would expect the minority party to recognize a split in the opposition party, and for the minority party to try to widen that split to win more voters.

Regarding communism, some Republicans doggedly focused on the court's decisions. For example, Craig Hosmer (R-CA) candidly announced that the GOP leadership "instructed [members of Congress] . . . to press vigorously for the enactment of the [court-curbing] legislation before adjournment."[31] Admittedly, this could have been a policy concern rather than a coalition-building effort. In fact, there was not much of an attempt to enlarge the GOP after the communism decisions. Because court-curbing proposals had their intended effect, Republicans had no opportunity to push the communism issue or formally curb the court. Throughout the book, I return to the interplay of court-curbing and judicial responses.

Pushback

If a cross-partisan majority opposes a Supreme Court ruling, then that majority may have recourse. Again, any court decision that involves secondary preferences will lead to some factions being dissatisfied; and those factions, too, have recourse on their own. But when the coalition of objectors encompasses a cross-partisan majority, the options available to that alliance are more likely to have an effect than when a smaller minority faction opposes the court on its own. Even so, a cross-partisan majority alliance will face obstacles. Nonleading factions of the dominant party may not believe that a judicial decision warrants an alliance with the opposition party, or vice versa. Even if the parties are united, it is difficult to overturn a court ruling. Still, if the entire cross-partisan majority is so strongly opposed to the court that members of one party *are* willing to ally with those from another, then we should see some manifestations of that alliance. I present three different types of pushback, depending on the nature of the majority in the government or majority in the electorate.

1. Grassroots pushback. Local citizens and local decision-makers (e.g., sheriffs, school boards) undermine the court's effectiveness. Supreme Court decisions go unenforced, or the extent of those decisions' enforcement are limited by local communities who do not agree with the court's opinion.[32]

2. Congressional pushback. The minority party reaches across the aisle to dissatisfied factions in the majority party to undermine the court's judicial independence. The legislature introduces bills that target the court itself (e.g., restricting jurisdiction) or its rulings (e.g., overriding a judicial opinion). In addition, Congress need not explicitly target the judiciary. Instead, Congress can pass bills that scale back the implementation of a decision.[33]

3. Electoral pushback.[34] The most dramatic and impactful response would be if dissatisfied factional members of the majority party band together with the minority party to form a new alliance that seeks to electorally displace the dominant coalition with which the court is affiliated. In this case, the minority party not only *tries* but *succeeds* to advertise the court ruling(s) in a way to reach out to new voters.[35]

Returning to the communism cases, there were grassroots objections, though they did not consolidate fast enough (i.e., before Congress got involved) to evoke on-the-ground resistance. Still, the American Bar Association expressed disagreement. They first recommended that Congress reverse some of the cases. Then they invited Chief Justice Warren to a conference with the purpose of humiliating him in person with a motion to censure the court.[36] The Conference of State Chief Justices adopted a resolution condemning the decisions and stating they infringed on states' rights.[37] The Governors' Conference passed a resolution praising the FBI, which many saw as a response to judicial oversight of states' antisubversive efforts.[38]

The most apparent majority that formed in response to the communism cases was the one in Congress. Court-curbing sailed through the House with a 249–147 vote. Although a one-vote margin prevented passage in the Senate, we still might say that a congressional majority-in-wait stood ready to strike at the court had the judiciary continued its pro–communists' rights trajectory.

But the court backed off its liberal agenda because—as Earl Warren believed—some justices (namely, Felix Frankfurter and John Marshall Harlan II) were afraid of congressional court-curbing.[39] These justices removed pending communism cases from the docket in 1958. In a pair of 1959 cases, they reversed the ideological trajectory of the earlier decisions.

When analyzing jurisprudential shifts by the Supreme Court from one case (or set of cases) to the next, we must take stock of the justices deciding the cases. Perhaps a liberal-to-conservative flip (or vice versa) was due to replacements on the bench rather than pressure from the grassroots or Congress. With communists' rights, three years had passed between the first case of its kind and the supposed judicial retreat. In that span, three Eisenhower appointees had replaced one justice selected by FDR and two chosen by Truman. It would be easy to conclude that swapping three Democratic-nominated justices for three Republican-nominated others would naturally lead to a rightward shift against communists' rights.[40] But this was not the case.

The justices' voting patterns indicate that appointments were not the deciding factor in the Court reversing its course on communists' rights. Let us take the three new justices one by one.

William Brennan replaced Sherman Minton, first as a recess appointee and then as a confirmed justice. Minton heard three cases before his retirement.[41] He voted against communists' rights in all three. During his recess appointment, Brennan sat in on six of the ten communism cases in 1956–1957. He voted with the liberal majority in all six.[42] He voted with the liberal minority in the post-attack cases.[43] In sum, this seat went from one that voted reliably against communists' rights to reliably pro communists' rights. It did not cause the judicial about-face. If anything, it made liberal entrenchment more likely.

Charles E. Whittaker replaced Stanley Reed, who sat during, and voted conservatively on, the same three communism cases as Minton. Reed heard oral arguments for six other cases but did not vote in them because he retired before the court issued its decisions.[44] Whitaker voted with the conservative majority in the post-attack cases. At base, Whittaker replacing Reed did nothing to the court's final votes. Whittaker voted against communists' rights in 1959, and Reed likely would have done the same. To be fair, Reed had not voted in the pre-attack *Sweezy* or *Watkins*; and Whittaker's vote gave the post-attack *Uphaus* and *Barenblatt* one more vote each.

Potter Stewart replaced Harold H. Burton, who heard all ten 1956–57 cases. Burton joined six liberal decisions, dissented from three of them, and did not vote in one. Stewart sat on the two post-attack cases, in which he voted with the conservative majority. For this seat, we might say that a change in personnel mattered, because Stewart voted with the conservative majority in the post-attack cases. But Burton's votes on specific pre-attack cases cast some doubt. One of the three cases in which Burton dissented was *Sweezy v. New Hampshire*, which was at issue (at least in part) in 1959 in the post-attack case *Uphaus v. Wyman*. In addition, the one case in which Burton did not take part, *Watkins v. US*, was challenged by the post-attack *Barenblatt v. US*. Thus, from *Sweezy* to *Uphaus*, a conservative vote remained conservative. From *Watkins* to *Barenblatt*, a recusal turned into a conservative vote.

Whittaker and Stewart replacing Reed and Burton, respectively, maintained the ideological status quo (see table 2.1). They did ensure that those two seats would cast votes on cases brought to the court. But even if Whittaker and Stewart had been appointed before the first pre-attack cases, the outcomes in all of those cases would have remained the same.[45] The most accurate statement we can make about the impact of appointments on pre- to post-attack communist decisions is that they *added* votes. They did not *flip* any votes from pro communists' rights to against communists' rights. If anything,

exchanging Minton for Brennan flipped one seat in the opposite direction. Nevertheless, Whittaker and Stewart ensured that all nine
justices, rather than seven or eight, would preside over these cases.

TABLE 2.1 Supreme Court Voting on Communism

	Sweezy v. New Hampshire (6–2 liberal decision)	Uphaus v. Wyman (5–4 conservative decision)	Watkins v. US (6–1 liberal decision)	Barenblatt v. US (5–4 conservative decision)
Liberal	1) Warren	1) Warren	1) Warren	1) Warren
	2) Black	2) Black	2) Black	2) Black
	3) Douglas	3) Douglas	3) Douglas	3) Douglas
	4) Brennan	4) Brennan	4) Brennan	4) Brennan
	5) **Frankfurter**		5) **Frankfurter**	
	6) **Harlan**		6) **Harlan**	
Conservative	1) Clark	1) Clark	1) Clark	1) Clark
	2) Burton	2) Stewart		2) Stewart
		3) Whittaker		3) Whittaker
		4) **Frankfurter**		4) **Frankfurter**
		5) **Harlan**		5) **Harlan**
Not voting	1) Reed/Whittaker		1) Burton/Stewart	
			2) Whittaker	

The fourth and fifth anticommunism votes in the post-attack cases
came from two justices, Felix Frankfurter and John Marshall Harlan
II, who had voted for communists' rights in the pre-attack cases.
Some scholars acknowledge the possibility of good-faith judgment
in both sets of cases.[46] Barry Friedman interestingly argues that the
justices felt pressure from the legal community (e.g., the grassroots
pushback from the American Bar Association and state chief justices).[47] The consensus, though, is that appointments did not cause
the shift in jurisprudence. The court—via Frankfurter and Harlan—
backed down because Congress pushed back.[48]

After those decisions, the congressional majority stopped its attack
on the judiciary. With communists' rights off the political agenda,
the Republican Party did not have the opportunity to use the issue
as a party-building device. Granted, the GOP had reservations about
allying with southern Democrats on communism because southerners tried to link the issue to desegregation.[49] Nevertheless, even if

Republicans wanted to exploit the issue, the court's about-face on communism precluded the Republican Party from using the issue as a party building tool. Thus, no electoral majority arose in response to the communism cases.

Data and Methods

The next four chapters look at other cases—on school prayer, criminal rights, busing, and abortion—decided by the Supreme Court during the mature New Deal era. They follow the Expectations and Pushback structure described and exemplified above. Before starting those case studies, I address methodological questions. The appendix describes more details.[50]

Why examine the mature New Deal era? I use this period for two reasons. First, the majority coalition undeniably represents multiple factions, such as southerners, liberals, Catholics, labor, Black Americans, and others. They mostly agreed on economics, but social issues—such as race and religion—exposed different factional preferences.[51] Second, the leading liberal faction is easily identifiable, and by the 1950s, it had captured control of the party's platform writing process, congressional leadership, and presidential nomination.[52] Around that time, the faction also tried to change congressional rules to consolidate its hold on the party.[53] The cases described in following chapters are not exhaustive historical accounts. Rather, they show how majorities can push back against countermajoritarian judicial decisions. The time frame is limited, but the hypotheses under investigation can be applied to other eras. Indeed, chapters 9 and 10 examine recent cases.

Why not start with *Brown v. Board*? For two reasons, I do not start with *Brown*. First, I look at countermajoritarian decisions, and *Brown* was majoritarian.[54] Second, the seminal Warren Court case's story is well-told.[55] Historians and legal scholars have commented on what it did say, did not say, and should have said.[56] Law reviews continue to devote articles, symposiums, and entire issues to the case's legacy.[57] We know the political development narrative. There was massive grassroots pushback (especially, but not exclusively, in the South).[58] Easy to evade, *Brown* did more to create a "hollow

hope" than it supported actual desegregation.[59] Yet, southern violence against *Brown* created northern awareness, which was key for
the push toward civil rights.[60] That, in turn, had long-term effects on
both policy and politics.[61]

Doesn't *Brown* connect to other issues? While I do not start with
Brown, I do loop desegregation into the narrative when it appeared
to connect to other aspects of American politics. For example, in
discussing the communism cases above, I described how southern
Democrats believed that civil rights leaders were in league with
communist agitators. Later chapters discuss how school prayer advocates hinted at *Brown* when discussing the rights of local communities to direct their own school districts. Criminal rights decisions
(e.g., *Miranda*), the crime wave of the 1960s, Nixon's law and order
campaign—these all had racial overtones that recalled the desegregation decision. And, of course, we cannot separate busing from
Brown's failure to integrate with "all deliberate speed." In sum, *Brown*
definitely comes back into play during the 1960s–70s (and beyond).

What are the factions under investigation? I analyze the splits in
the Democratic Party and present three factions: southern Democrats,
liberal Democrats, and northern conservative Democrats.[62]
Democrats held the majority for many of the years under investigation, and one question I seek to answer is how the minority party
can use unpopular court rulings as a site upon which to construct a
new majority electoral coalition. In discussing the communism cases
earlier, I distinguished between northern and southern Democrats,
but the split was more complex.

Economics did not really divide the mature New Deal–era
Democratic Party.[63] Social and racial issues were different, and
northern Democrats split into socially "liberal" and socially "conservative." Liberals were social progressives who supported policies
like immediate integration, the Equal Rights Amendment (ERA), the
right to choose, and the separation of church and state. Northern
conservative Democrats' defining feature was their views on racial and social issues. Many were not outwardly segregationist, but
they opposed some progressive policies on racially charged issues
(e.g., busing). They claimed nonracial bases for doing so (which I

discuss in the chapters that lie ahead). Many northern conservative Democrats were white Catholics with east-central European (e.g., German, Polish) heritage. Their moral and religious beliefs manifested in different ways, such as strong anticommunism stances, support for religion in public institutions, pro-life preferences, and even antibusing positions.

Why the specific focus on Catholics? When tallying roll call votes, I stick with the labels of southern, liberal, and northern conservative Democrats. But when looking at mass public opinion, I operationalize northern conservative Democrat as Catholic and I provide figures for northern Catholic opinion. Moreover, when examining the pushback against countermajoritarian decisions in the 1950s–1970s, I turn to Catholic outlets (e.g., *America*), elite figures (e.g., American bishops), and historical events in known Catholic localities (e.g., violence in Boston).

Why focus on Catholics? Because the GOP specifically did so. Pat Buchanan said "converting the Catholics" was his "constant preoccupation."[64] The story of Republican inroads into the north is not just about Catholics, but that was the group targeted by the party in the 1960s and 1970s.[65] By 1971 an internal White House debate brewed on whether Nixon should go after liberal Democratic or Catholic Democratic votes. A memo titled "The Catholic Vote and 1972" lobbied against the latter, saying that Catholic votes hinged on parochial aid, an issue that alienated Protestant voters.[66] In his response, Buchanan called the memo "remorseless nonsense" and launched into a tirade. He said, "The crucial points are: a) the size of the bloc; and b) the winnability of the bloc . . . the Catholics are where the ducks are."[67] A telling moment came when Michael Novak—a liberal Catholic scholar—published a *Harper's* article (and later a book, *The Rise of the Unmeltable Ethnics*) on the issue. Novak wrote, "On a whole host of issues, my people have been, though largely Democratic, conservative: on censorship, on communism, on abortion, on religious schools."[68] The line hit home with Nixon and structured administration behavior. In looking back, Buchanan claims, "Our Catholic strategy would succeed beyond our wildest expectations."[69] I examine that strategy.

How does one identify the different types of Democrats? I identify three types of Democrats: southern, liberal, and northern conservative. I use former Confederate states as the defining feature for
southern Democrats.[70] I use the social dimension of the Common
Space scores, a member of Congress's religious affiliation, and the
distribution of religious constituents to place northern lawmakers
into the liberal or northern conservative faction. Details are presented in the appendix. The method is not perfect. For our purposes,
though, creating mutually exclusive categories with objective criteria
helpfully shows the clear division in the Democratic ranks (see table 2.2). It also provides a framework for discussing data, as in later
chapters when I use members' of Congress factional assignments to
compare different Democrats' congressional votes. Even if imperfect,
it is still useful.

TABLE 2.2 Democratic Factions in Congress

	House			Senate		
Year	Southern	Liberal	Conservative	Southern	Liberal	Conservative
1961	39.0%	22.0%	39.0%	35.4%	23.1%	41.5%
1965	32.2%	34.3%	33.6%	30.9%	32.4%	36.8%
1969	33.5%	33.9%	32.6%	32.1%	37.5%	30.4%
1973	30.4%	38.8%	30.8%	25.9%	43.1%	31.0%
1977	28.0%	43.3%	28.7%	29.7%	39.1%	31.3%

What are "attacks" on the Supreme Court? Congressional attacks
have commonly been referred to as "court-curbing" attempts. The
terms are interchangeable, and they cover institutional attacks on
the court and issue-based attacks on certain cases. A couple scholars
have laid out useful definitions (see table 2.3).

How are attacks counted? I extend a database that counts all legislative bills and constitutional amendments from 1955–2023 that seek
one of the six tasks laid out by Clark (see table 2.3).[71] I looked for
such proposals in the index in the Congressional Record. Some items

TABLE 2.3 Attacks Definition

Rosenberg[a]	Clark[b]
Legislation introduced in the Congress having as its purpose or effect, either explicit or implicitly, court reversal of a decision or line of decisions, or court abstention from future decision of a given kind, or alteration in the structure or functioning of the court to produce a particular substantive outcome	1) Change the composition of the court[c] 2) Limit or remove the court's jurisdiction[d] 3) Remove or alter judicial review 4) Reverse or remedy particular decisions[e] 5) Dictate internal matters to the court 6) Otherwise target particular decisions

a. Rosenberg, "Judicial Independence."

b. Clark, Limits of Judicial Independence.

c. This includes the size of the court and who sits on the bench. In fact, in 1858 Senator John Hale (FS-NH) claimed that Article 3's claim that "Congress may from time to time ordain and establish" applied to the Supreme Court. "My idea is that the time has come," Hale announced. He sought to disband the entire court and reappoint a new slate of justices. Congressional Globe 1861, 26.

d. Lauren C. Bell, "Monitoring or Meddling? Congressional Oversight of the Judicial Branch"; Dawn M. Chutkow, "Jurisdiction Stripping: Litigation, Ideology, and Congressional Control of the Courts"; Lauren C. Bell and Kevin M. Scott, "Policy Statements or Symbolic Politics: Explaining Congressional Court-Limiting Attempts"; Kenneth Thomas, "Limiting Court Jurisdiction over Federal Constitutional Issues: 'Court-Stripping.'"

e. Barnes, Overruled; Thomas M. Keck, "The Relationship between Courts and Legislatures"; Bethany Blackstone, "An Analysis of Policy-Based Congressional Responses to the US Supreme Court's Constitutional Decisions"; William N. Eskridge Jr., "Overriding Supreme Court Statutory Interpretation Decisions."

required confirmation that the proposal related to court-curbing. I listed the issue involved and the party and regional affiliation (southern or northern) of each attacker. There were 3,649 total attacks, more than a 500 percent increase from the previously most comprehensive list of attacks.[72] Table 2.4 offers a glimpse of the data. Further details on method and results may be found in the appendix.

What other data sources are used? I rely on public opinion polls from respected organizations (e.g., Gallup; ABC). I use data from the American National Election Studies and the General Social Survey to examine subgroups' (e.g., white southerners, Catholics) preferences. Primary documents are invaluable. Speeches from the *Congressional Record*, presidential addresses, platforms, periodicals, GOP strategy memos—these are just some of the primary documents discussed.

TABLE 2.4 Attacks by Decade

Decade	Attacks	Modal attack
1950s	68	Segregation
1960s	865	School prayer
1970s	861	Abortion
1980s	317	Abortion
1990s	268	Abortion
2000s	347	Abortion
2010s	681	Campaign finance
2020s	242	Campaign finance

For insights on pushback, I borrow from the secondary literature that studies the impact of Supreme Court cases, Congress, and elections.

How can the Supreme Court be "liberal" if Republicans made so many appointments? From 1954–80, Republican presidents filled nine of the thirteen Supreme Court vacancies.[73] How can one argue that the court was "liberal"?

Supreme Court appointments are inconsistent. Presidents prioritize different things.[74] The circumstances under which some nominees are confirmed (and others are not) are different.[75] Some justices sit on the bench longer than others.[76] Some have more influence than others.[77] Most importantly, some justices do not vote in a manner consistent with the preferences of their appointers.[78] Eisenhower famously lamented his selections of Warren and Brennan, saying, "I made two mistakes and both of them are sitting on the Supreme Court."[79] He also referred to Warren as his "biggest damn fool mistake."[80] Other "mistakes" abound in Supreme Court history.[81] Appointments are not completely representative of the appointer. They do not equal reliable judicial votes.[82]

Ultimately, it does not matter who did the appointing. It does not even matter what any justice's overall judicial ideology may be (e.g., progressive, originalist, etc.). What matters is the decisions they reach and the opinions they write. And in important social issues cases during the New Deal era, the court repeatedly reached liberal conclusions that advanced the preferences of the liberal faction and highlighted the fault lines within the Democratic Party. Some Democratic appointees (e.g., Arthur Goldberg, Thurgood Marshall) were expectedly liberal. Some Republican appointees (e.g., Warren and Brennan) consistently infuriated conservatives. Other GOP nominees (e.g., Harlan, Stewart, Blackmun, Powell, and even Burger) only occasionally frustrated conservatives. To be fair, though, Segal-Cover scores—which are based on contemporary evaluations of judicial nominees before the Senate—indicate that people at the time probably knew what they were getting with the nominations of Warren, Brennan, Stewart, et al.[83]

What about appointments over time? Don't they matter in how the court rules over time? When I present a change in jurisprudential course, I discuss the slate of justices, as I did above with the post-attack communism cases.[84] I address the hypothesis that personnel changes could account for any particular outcome.

Conclusion

This chapter has detailed the theory behind how the Supreme Court can reach rare countermajoritarian outcomes. It lays out observable expectations and effects of such rulings, using the communism cases as an instructional example. The next four chapters explore other issues from the 1960s–1970s in which the court shook intracoalitional fault lines and cross-partisan majorities pushed back. The story starts with the most congressionally attacked decision in US Supreme Court history: school prayer.

Chapter 3

Prayer

ON JUNE 25, 1962, as the Supreme Court justices took their seats on the bench, the marshal proclaimed, "God save the United States and this Honorable Court!" Minutes later, the court announced that state-sponsored prayer in public schools violated the establishment clause. This chapter examines the response and effects of the court's jurisprudence in the school prayer cases. As will be shown, the decisions were countermajoritarian. The antiprayer rulings did not translate into immediate GOP electoral gains. But they played a part in establishing the narrative of the court as an institution that pursued factional secondary preferences. Prayer did not break the Democratic Party's grip on the majority in the government, but it did split liberal Democrats from southern and northern conservative (namely, Catholic) Democrats. Prayer, then, revealed a new social issues fault line. It might not have paid immediate electoral dividends, but the lessons learned by the GOP in the 1960s would be useful to them after *Roe v. Wade* (1973).

Background

In 1951 the New York Board of Regents adopted the following prayer for New York public schools: "Almighty God, we acknowledge our dependence upon Thee, and we beg Thy blessings upon us, our parents, our teachers, and our country." Composed by a team of ministers, priests, and rabbis, the prayer's broad language and short verse represented its ostensible nondenominational character. The board of regents voted unanimously in favor of the prayer and left local schools to decide whether they would have children recite it. Board chairman John Brosnan saw the prayer as a nonissue: "We didn't have the slightest idea the prayer we wrote would prove so controversial."[1]

Controversy arose immediately. Within months of the board's adoption of the prayer, the New York branch of the American Civil Liberties Union mobilized against it. New York City schools responded by substituting the singing of "My Country 'Tis of Thee." Other districts, however, maintained daily recitation of the board of regents' prayer. On Long Island, the Herricks School Board voted to recite the prayer and left enforcement up to each school's administration. At Herricks High School, the principal passed the decision to teachers, most of whom (either happily or grudgingly) complied. At Herricks Junior High, Principal Wilbur Olmstead enforced recitation, even appointing an assistant principal with the task of ensuring teachers and students prayed. Soon thereafter, a student, Daniel Roth, objected to praying. His father, Lawrence Roth, contacted the ACLU, whose leaders decided to take the case. They asked the Roths to find colitigants. Four more parents signed on: Steven Engel, Monroe Lerner, Daniel Lichtenstein, and Lenore Lyons. When the case came to trial, the plaintiff's names were ordered alphabetically, with "Engel" coming first in *Engel v. Vitale* (1962).

Justice Hugo Black wrote for the 6–1 majority, announcing that state-sponsored prayer was "wholly inconsistent with the Establishment Clause."[2] The opinion of the court cited no precedents. Justice Potter Stewart's dissent became the rallying cry for those who offered a legal justification for school prayer. Stewart argued that the establishment clause only prohibited the government from setting up an official religion. School prayer, Stewart declared, was hardly establishing a state church: "I cannot see how an 'official religion' is established by letting those who want to say a prayer say it." Stewart's dissent asked why God could be called upon in the Supreme Court, House of Representatives, Senate, and at presidential inaugurations, but not in public schools. The majority opinion answered Stewart's question by saying that all religious values and practices need not be extinguished; but schools could not sponsor any of the activities.

Justice William Douglas's concurrence offered a stronger separationist answer. Of all the opinions, Douglas's concurrence received the most attention. In fact, many media outlets reported as if Douglas's concurrence was the majority's holding.[3] Douglas agreed with Stewart that authorizing the prayer was not akin to establishing a religion. However, for Douglas, the establishment clause was meant to create neutrality toward religion, and the regents' prayer violated that provision. Douglas also found the following practices to be unconstitutional: congressional and military chaplains, religious services in prisons, using a Bible when taking an oath, GI bill funds used at denominational schools, "In God We Trust" on the currency, and adding God to the pledge of allegiance.

One year after issuing *Engel v. Vitale*, the court took on two more similar cases. In Pennsylvania, school started with daily readings from the Bible. Outside Philadelphia, the Abington School District coupled scripture readings with recitation of the Lord's Prayer. Ellery Schempp, a high-school student, objected and wrote to the ACLU, asking if they would litigate against Pennsylvania. The ACLU obliged and Schempp won at the district level, where the court held the Bible was a book of worship and being used in this case to promote religion. Pennsylvania then passed a law saying parents could write a note asking for their children to be excused from the practice. After amending its procedures, the Keystone State appealed to the same district court, which again ruled against Bible readings in school. On appeal, the US Supreme Court consolidated *Abington School District v. Schempp* with a similar case out of Maryland with a more controversial litigant.

In Baltimore, teachers read daily passages from the Bible before leading their students in the Lord's Prayer. Madalyn Murray sued on behalf of her fourteen-year-old son. Unlike other litigants, who sought to escape the public limelight, Murray embraced it.[4] Self-described as "the most hated woman in America," Murray publicized her crusades against organized religion, including a lawsuit seeking to bar astronauts from reading the Bible in space. After the USSR rejected her application for Soviet citizenship, she moved to Baltimore. When enrolling her son in the local public school, she saw students praying, whereupon she burst into the counselor's office shouting, "Why are those f******* children praying." The Maryland state attorney general had issued an opinion stating that any student could be excused from class during the recitation. Only three students (including Murray's son, William) out of 170,000 asked to be excused. Eventually, William snuck into class, was exposed to the Lord's Prayer, walked out of class, and sued.[5]

In an 8–1 decision, with Justice Tom Clark writing for the majority, the court ruled that Bible readings violated the establishment clause. To be constitutional, a law needed "a secular legislative purpose and a primary effect that neither advances nor inhibits religion." Bible reading violated both parts of the test. Justices Goldberg and Brennan wrote constitutionally unremarkable concurrences (discussed below). Once again, Justice Stewart was the lone dissenter. He reviewed the same points from his dissent in *Engel v. Vitale*.

All indicators point toward the school prayer/Bible reading cases being countermajoritarian.[6] They also offered the GOP a new type of opportunity when reaching out to cross-partisans. In the end, in part because of the success of grassroots efforts to disobey the decisions, a Republican-southern Democrat-Catholic Democrat coalition never fully formed in the electorate.

Expectation #1: Surface-Level Indicators

Multiple polls from the era show that 70–80 percent of Americans disagreed with the Supreme Court's rulings on school prayer.[7] Relevant to coalitional politics, public opinion polls indicate that southerners and Catholics supported prayer in schools. In 1964, 1966, and 1968, the American National Election Studies (ANES) survey asked respondents when school prayer should be allowed. Collectively, 94 percent of white southerners believed that schools should be allowed to start the day with prayer.[8] The General Social Survey (GSS) found that 70–78 percent of southerners from 1974–78 disapproved of *Abington School District v. Schempp*.[9]

A majority of Catholics also opposed these Warren Court rulings. Notably, Catholic opinion did not hinge on partisanship, either, as Catholics from both parties supported school prayer. For example, in 1969, nearly as many Catholic "Strong Democrats" supported prayer as Catholic "Strong Republicans." This majority held stable throughout the 1960s and 1970s.[10]

Of all the issues discussed in this book, school prayer generated the most complaints from members of Congress about countermajoritarianism. They came from three sources: southern Democrats, northern conservative Democrats, and Republicans. An example of each: Herbert Bonner (D-NC) said, "The Constitution . . . was not designed to permit minorities to deny ruthlessly the rights and needs of others." Robert Giaimo (D-CT) said, "[Prayer] should not be denied because a small minority finds it offensive." Walter McVey Jr. (R-KS) said, "Nearly everyone in America is shocked and sickened."[11]

Expectation #2: Nonleading Faction Response

Members of Congress repeatedly attacked the Supreme Court via court-curbing legislation. If measured by the number of proposals introduced, then *Engel* and *Schempp* are the most attacked decisions in Supreme Court history. In 1962 alone, Democrats launched twenty-eight attacks against the court's anti–school prayer ruling. To contextualize that figure, from 1955 to 1962, all members of Congress (Democratic and Republican) launched twenty-eight attacks against *Brown v. Board*. This is not to say that striking down school prayer generated more passionate opposition than desegregation; for southern Democrats, the opposite is probably true. Rather, I point out that the court's school prayer decisions, quite simply, led to an unprecedented volume of court-curbing proposals.

As expected, southern Democrats attacked. From 1960–80, southern Democrats introduced 169 court-curbing proposals focused specifically on school prayer. When attacking, southern Democrats relied on four rhetorical arguments. First, they contended that taking prayers out of schools was bad policy—that it undermined students' moral education. Second, southern Democrats said the establishment clause did not prohibit prayer in schools. Here, southern lawmakers relied on an originalist understanding whereby the framers of the Constitution did not mean to prohibit religion from public life. Third, even though both cases originated from the north, southern Democrats still claimed the court's rulings violated states' rights.[12]

Fourth, southerners saw links between the court's rulings on various issues. Southerners linked the school prayer rulings to both the desegregation and communism issues. The infamous link to desegregation was that the court had "put the Negroes in the schools and now they've driven God out."[13] Regarding communism, southern Democrats believed that secular policy aligned with communist values. They argued that the removal of prayer and the Bible from public schools was a step toward the kind of atheistic society that communists promoted.[14] John William Davis's (D-GA) accusation captures the long-standing displeasure with the court that many southern Democrats felt: "I have been pointing out and protesting for many years this pattern and plan of the Supreme Court to preserve freedom and individual rights into an instrument to support radicalism, atheism, obscenity, and communism."[15]

One other indicator points toward southern Democratic frustration with the liberal Supreme Court ruling in the school prayer cases: party-switching. In the early 1960s, three Democratic members of Congress switched their party affiliation. However, opposition to *Engel* was likely not a major reason why Albert Watson (SC), Bo Callaway (GA), or Strom Thurmond (SC) switched parties. Watson switched because the DNC stripped him of committee seniority after he supported Barry Goldwater in 1964.[16] Callaway also switched because of his admiration for Goldwater, as well as more hardline views on segregation.[17]

The most highly publicized switch was that of Strom Thurmond, a lifetime Democrat and patriarch of South Carolina politics. After serving in the Palmetto State legislature in the 1930s, he rose to the governorship in 1947–51. In 1948 southern Democrats walked out of the Democratic Convention and nominated Thurmond as the States' Rights Democratic Party (or, Dixiecrats) candidate. Afterwards, Thurmond quietly fell back into the Democratic Party. In 1956 he was elected to the US Senate, where he served for forty-seven years— the third longest term ever, behind Daniel Inouye (D-HI) and Robert Byrd (D-WV).

In 1964 Thurmond switched to the GOP. The Civil Rights Act of 1964 was probably the main reason behind the switch. It had passed only two months before Thurmond officially became a Republican. Nevertheless, when announcing his switch, Thurmond hinted at the court's school prayer decisions as a possible motivation. He said, "The Democratic Party . . . has turned its back on spiritual values . . .

The Democratic Party has encouraged, supported, and protected the Supreme Court in a reign of judicial tyranny."[18]

In addition to southern Democrats, northern conservative Democrats attacked the Supreme Court. The key to understanding these attacks is to recognize the change in pattern from previous lines of assaults in desegregation and communism. From 1955–61, northern Democrats did not introduce a single court-curbing proposal. This clearly changed in the aftermath of the school prayer decisions. In 1962 alone, northern Democrats representing large Catholic constituencies launched nine court-curbing proposals centered on school prayer. From 1962–80, northern Democrats proposed ninety-four attacks on *Engel* and *Schempp*. Of those, twenty-three came from the five states with the highest percentage of Catholics (Connecticut, Massachusetts, New Jersey, New York, and Rhode Island).[19]

When northern conservative Democrats attacked, they made many of the same arguments that their southern colleagues presented. They argued that striking down school prayer was bad policy because it hindered the moral education of students. They protested that the establishment clause did not prohibit prayer in schools. And finally, while northern conservative Democrats did not connect *Engel* and *Schempp* to *Brown* or to states' rights, they did link school prayer to communism.[20] This was a major concern for Catholics who believed American communism was a vehicle for eliminating—or limiting the reach of—the Catholic Church. In other words, communism was antithetical to Catholicism. Catholic publications shared these concerns. *America* and *Commonweal*, for instance, repeatedly worried about the growing "secularism" coming from the court.[21] It came from beyond the United States, too, as the Vatican worried the court had instituted "legal agnosticism."[22] To many Catholics, *Engel* and *Schempp* were not isolated incidents; they were a continuation of a larger judicial problem.

Although southern Democrats proposed more court-curbing bills on school prayer than their northern copartisans, that northern Democrats attacked at all is a marked change from the previous decade. After *Brown* and the communism cases, southerners accounted for 100 percent of Democratic Party attacks. After *Engel* and

Schempp, they accounted for less than two-thirds. These northern Democratic attacks indicate that something changed in 1962. Before this period, the major fault line in the New Deal coalition had always been race. A split on civil rights had existed between the northern and southern wings, with bills (e.g., the Civil Rights Act of 1957) and court rulings (e.g., *Brown v. Board*) occasionally revealing the rift. The decisions on communism accidentally exposed the race fault line (e.g., "Black is red").[23] And according to some southerners, the school prayer rulings were connected to a runaway liberal Supreme Court again imposing itself on the South. But northern Democrats had mostly united on race. After the school prayer rulings, there was not just a rift between northern and southern Democrats; there was also a rift *among* northern Democrats. Specifically, liberals broke from northern conservative Democrats. After *Engel*, the split in the Democratic Party was no longer solely sectional and racial.

Expectation #3: Minority Party Response
Republicans introduced school prayer attacks against the Supreme Court at an unprecedented rate. In fact, *Engel* might also have generated the quickest response to a court case in congressional history. On the very day that *Engel* was decided, Frank Becker (R-NY)—a Catholic who represented the school district from which the case had originated—offered a constitutional amendment "pertaining to the offering of prayers in the public schools and other public places in the United States."[24] Unleashed mere hours after the judiciary announced it holding, the Becker proposal was the first attack, but it was certainly not the last. By the end of 1962, Republicans had proposed thirty-three attacks relating to school prayer. After *Schempp*, it took Republicans only eight days to offer their first court-curbing proposal against the court's decision. Senator Don Short (R-ND) proposed a resolution stating the right to offer prayer, read from sacred scriptures, and refer to belief in or reliance upon God should not be denied or abridged.[25] In 1963 alone, Republicans introduced a staggering seventy-two proposals that sought to curb the court's school prayer rulings. From 1962–80, Republican members of Congress introduced 381 school prayer-focused court-curbing proposals. No

party had ever attacked an issue raised by the Supreme Court with such frequency as the GOP did in response to the 1960s rulings on school prayer.

When Republicans defended their proposals, they argued the same four points that southern and northern conservative Democrats presented. Striking prayer (1) hindered moral education; (2) misread the original intent of the establishment clause; (3) infringed on states' rights; and (4) linked to communism.

Now, Republicans had been leery of the desegregation/communism connection that southern Democrats made in the 1950s. Then, Republican Party leaders had feared that they would be tied to such claims—something the GOP sought to avoid.[26] They did not believe organizational and/or ideological links between communism and integration existed. However, they certainly believed that the elimination of school prayer was tied to the possible spread of communism. "It will fit too closely the Soviet pattern of indoctrination of young people against religion," Representative James Van Zandt (R-PA) commented. "It sounds like something that could have been dreamed up in the Kremlin."[27]

While many Democrats introduced court-curbing proposals related to school prayer, Republicans were always the driving force behind actually trying to pass any bill or amendment. There was a continuous line of Republican leadership on the issue all the way through the 1980s. It includes:

- Frank Becker (R-NY). Representing the district from which *Engel* had originated, Becker was the original leader in the effort to unify Republicans, southern Democrats, and northern conservative Democrats on a constitutional amendment to protect school prayer. No one doubted his sincerity in restoring school prayer—his was not a position-taking motivated effort. Becker said *Engel* was the "most tragic [decision] in the history of the United States" and that June 25, 1962 (the day *Engel* was decided) "will go down as a black day in our history."[28] Born in Brooklyn and a graduate of New York public schools, Becker served as a loyal Republican for decades. A Catholic

himself who represented a large percentage of Catholic constituents, Becker strongly pushed for a vote on his proposed
amendment. He saw it as his mission to save the nation from
the "curse which has befallen all civilizations that forgot and
disobeyed God Almighty."[29]

- Everett Dirksen (R-IL). By 1966 Dirksen had served in
  Congress for thirty-one years (sixteen in the House, then fifteen in the Senate). He had been the Senate minority leader
  for a decade and a stabilizing force in the GOP throughout the
  era. In many ways, Dirksen might have been the most unifying
  leader in the fight for school prayer. A moderate Republican
  who helped secure passage of the Civil Rights Act of 1964,
  he reached out to members of both parties, gaining forty-six
  cosponsors on his 1966 attack. Later, Dirksen's wife referred
  to his efforts to unify the pro-prayer coalition as "his finest
  hour—and his saddest frustration."[30]

- Chalmers Wylie (R-OH). Upon Dirksen's death in 1969, Wylie
  assumed responsibility for organizing the cross-partisan
  pro-prayer coalition. Elected in 1967 primarily on the basis of opposing *Engel*, Wylie understood the latent potential
  that promoting prayer held for the Republican Party.[31] His
  methods differed from those of Becker and Dirksen, both of
  whom mainly lobbied members of Congress one by one. Wylie
  turned to lobbying extracongressional actors and bullying the
  proposal out of committee. Still, for a freshman legislator, he
  proved a remarkably able—if unsuccessful—manager of the
  pro-prayer alliance.

- Jesse Helms (R-NC). In the mid-to-late 1970s, Helms—a former Democrat turned Republican—took control of prayer
  legislation. The original "Jessecrat," Helms embodied southern
  Democrats who over time turned toward the GOP (though, as
  discussed in chapter 6, Helms probably switched parties because of busing rather than religion in schools). He, too, was
  unsuccessful in the school prayer battles—but not for lack of
  effort or ingenuity.

Becker, Dirksen, Wylie, and Helms all failed to curb the Supreme Court. But it is telling that all four came from the minority party—a Republican Party trying to expand the coalition by reaching out to southern and Catholic Democrats on the issue of religion in schools. This strategy was not just confined to the entrepreneurial work of four members of Congress. Top party strategists pursued it, too.

Throughout the 1960s and 1970s, the Republican Party changed its focus, rhetoric, and strategy to attract white southern and socially conservative Catholic Democrats. Although GOP strategists do not specifically mention school prayer as the issue upon which to cleave the Democratic Party, we can intuit that they considered the fallout from the court's decisions on prayer. In detailed fashion, Pat Buchanan admitted:

> The Democratic Party . . . is about twice the size of ours. There is no way we can win a national election, and we had recommended for a long period of time that we move to win to our side certain specific segments of the Democratic Party. And my recommendations are the southern Protestants, if you will, and the northern Catholics . . . This is my long-range analysis of all the possible fissures and faults running through the old Roosevelt coalitions.[32]

While Buchanan does not mention the specific issue of school prayer, he points out two specific religious factions: southern Protestants and northern Catholics. School prayer was exactly the type of issue that would appeal to both groups. Regarding southern Protestants, Buchanan advised President Nixon to appoint a "southern strict constructionist" to the Supreme Court when a vacancy became available. Buchanan believed that such a nominee would force the Democratic Party to "anger either the south . . . or . . . the northern liberals."[33]

Regarding the GOP's courtship of Catholic voters, evidence suggests that, throughout the period in question, Republicans targeted the overarching topic of "religion in schools" as a means to gain this faction's support. For example, Buchanan's "Assault Book" (an internal GOP memo describing ways in which to attack the Democratic Party) highlighted "Catholic/ethnic" issues, including religion in schools. A similar Buchanan memo entitled "Dividing the Democrats" read, "Favoritism toward things Catholic is good politics."[34]

"Things Catholic" included busing and abortion (discussed in later chapters), but also parochial aid, a policy that Catholic leaders and parents requested. Catholic publications advocated that Catholics take their school prayer fight in the direction of federal funding for parochial schools. *America* editorialized, "As the debate over the school prayer question proceeds . . . the case for the independent parochial school gets stronger and stronger."[35] One publication, the *Catholic Register*, in fact lauded the opportunity *Engel* provided: "An adverse decision may not be altogether bad. It should shock many Protestants out of their old complacency and dogged opposition . . . to any aid to the religious school child."[36] Parents, too, explored this route. As they questioned the exclusion of prayer, they began withdrawing their children from public schools and enrolling them in religious schools.[37]

In response, Republicans proactively pushed for federal subsidization of parochial education. The 1968 GOP platform, for instance, called for aid to private schools.[38] In 1970 Nixon met with the National Catholic Education Association. That same day, he directed his staff to announce immediately the creation of the Commission on Non-Public Education. A month later, he told the commission's chairman, "You've got to do this Catholic school job; I want it done well. If you don't do it, I will have to set up a separate commission." When the commission dragged its feet, Buchanan pleaded with Nixon to lean on them: "We are abandoning a political gold mine . . . which splits Catholic Democrats from liberal Democrats right down the line . . .What are Humphrey and Muskie going to say—'I oppose a commission to study the problems of Catholic schools [?]'"[39] True to his word, when the report did not meet Nixon's expectations, he established the Panel on Non-Public Education and appointed the president of Catholic University to chair the group.[40]

In sum, the GOP changed its focus, rhetoric, and strategy after the court struck down school prayer and Bible readings. Statements from national leaders and in national platforms began as early as 1964, when the GOP platform called for a constitutional amendment allowing Americans "to exercise their religion freely in public places."[41] In that year's presidential campaign, the Republican nominee, Barry Goldwater, asked, "Is this the time in our nation's history for our federal government to ban Almighty God from our school rooms?"[42] Of course, Goldwater lost badly. But that part of his strategy would continue as Republicans sought to draw southerners and Catholics toward the Party by taking stances that made the GOP appear amendable to religion in schools. Campaign speeches, platform planks, special commissions, etc. all seem to have been part of the strategy to send socially conservative signals to targeted factions. Altogether, the Republican response to *Engel* and *Schempp* indicates that the GOP viewed—and perhaps *still views*—school prayer as a winning, majoritarian issue.[43]

Grassroots Pushback

The most immediate reaction to the rulings on school prayer was widespread on-the-ground resistance from grassroots majorities. It is difficult to know with certainty the exact percentage of schools that did and did not comply with eliminating prayer and Bible readings. Nevertheless, a synthesis of the impact literature from the 1960s and 1970s shows that while the rulings did have a modest effect throughout the country, there were large pockets in which it seemed like *Engel* and *Schempp* had never happened. Various actors admitted to noncompliance. This included state attorneys general, the chief educational officers of each state, and school district leaders and superintendents.[44] In Tennessee, for instance, seventy school districts required Bible reading, fifty permitted it, and only one banned it. Resistance went beyond the South, too. Take Connecticut, where less than 12 percent of schools stopped reading the Bible. In Indiana, more than half the schools continued to support prayer and Bible-reading.[45] I identify three oppositional tactics: bold opposition, devolution, and alternative measures.

First, some unflinchingly defied the Supreme Court. Senator James Eastland (D-MS) had predicted this in a tone-setting response to *Engel*: "Frankly, I don't believe that the schools of America are going to stop their morning devotions."[46] An anonymous Tennessean school board member put it more candidly: "The Supreme Court decision didn't mean a damn thing."[47] These brash statements came from local leaders from both sections of the country (see table 3.1).

TABLE 3.1 Local Responses to School Prayer Decisions

Governor of Alabama	"I would like for the people of Alabama to be in defiance of such a ruling . . . I want the Supreme Court to know we are not going to conform to any such decision. I want the State Board of Education to tell the whole world we are not going to abide by it."
Governor of Mississippi	"Going to tell every teacher in Mississippi to conduct prayers and Bible reading despite what the Supreme Court says."
Kentucky state superintendent of public instruction	"Continue to read and pray until somebody stops you. I don't want to make anybody stop."
Governor of North Carolina	"We will go on having Bible reading and prayer in the schools of this state just as we always have."
Atlanta superintendent	"We will not pay any attention to the Supreme Court ruling."
Rhode Island state commissioner of education	"Not now or in the future [do I] intend to prostitute the office of the Commissioner of Education of Rhode Island to further the cause of the irreligious, the atheistic, the unreligious, or the agnostic."
Midwest superintendent	"We plan to continue until *forced* to stop" (emphasis in original).[a]

a. Beaney and Beiser, "Prayer and Politics," 486, 487, 487, 488; Lain, "God, Civic Virtue," 513, 513; Dolbeare and Hammond, *School Prayer Decisions*, 42.

Second, many states and communities found that a simple and popular way to avoid the court's decisions was to devolve policy implementation onto decentralized actors, namely, school boards and teachers. In New Hampshire, State Board of Education chairman John C. Driscoll explained that religious practices in public schools were "up to each local school board." In Iowa, Superintendent Paul F. Johnston believed that "custom in th[e] community ought to determine what they should do."[48] Florida, Georgia, Virginia, and Tennessee also used what became known as the "local option." One study from the early-to-mid 1960s surveyed school board members from Tennessee on their religion-in-schools beliefs. Their responses mostly mirrored the same claims made on the floors of Congress (apart from originalist arguments). For example, one board member worried about the moral implications and that removing the Bible put Tennessee on the road to "heathenism." Another believed it raised a "communist atmosphere" in the schools.[49] Some made countermajoritarian claims.[50] In some cases, state level-officials wanted to comply with the court's opinions, but they found it difficult to go against the majority of their communities. For instance, one board member in Tennessee seemed willing to enforce *Schempp* but felt the necessity of "complying with the laws of the state."[51]

Perhaps the most effective way of obstructing the court's school prayer and Bible-reading opinions was to leave enforcement (or, non-enforcement) to the bureaucrats most directly responsible: teachers. For example, in South Carolina, State Superintendent of Education Jesse Anderson said that his state's teachers should continue to do whatever they wanted to do in their classrooms.[52] A survey of 1712 public elementary school teachers across the country found that a majority of schools had no prayer or Bible policy in place, and that both practices were left to the discretion of teachers (see table 3.2).[53]

TABLE 3.2 Survey of Elementary School Teachers

	Prayer	Bible readings
School favors	9.3%	6.8%
School opposes	29.7%	32.1%
No policy, teacher discretion	61.0% (40% of which pray)	61.1% (25% of which read the Bible)

Ohio might be seen as a microcosm of the entire country. When Ohio left the decision to teachers, it resulted in noncompliance. Table 3.3 shows that prayer and Bible reading were both permitted and practiced in a significant portion of the Buckeye State.[54]

It is not much of a surprise that teachers did not enforce the school prayer or Bible-reading decisions because they largely represented

TABLE 3.3 Prayer in Ohio

Bible reading practiced	23%
Bible reading permitted but not practiced	31%
Lord's Prayer required	5%
Lord's Prayer practiced	38%
Lord's Prayer permitted but not practiced	15%
School prayer practiced	33.5%
School prayer permitted but not practiced	46.5%

the American population. One researcher collected elementary teachers' opinions. He found that a majority in every region supported religion in schools.[55]

The third way actors resisted the court's rulings was through creative ways to get around the judicial decrees. These maneuvers took different forms. One common tactic was to claim that neither of the court's decisions affected anyone beyond the schools listed in the names of the cases. Thus, because *Engel* arose from New York and *Schempp* from Pennsylvania, the attorney general of Delaware insisted that his state's statutes on prayer and Bible readings had not been reviewed by the judiciary. In Arkansas, Attorney General BruceBennett said his state law on Bible reading remained intact because, unlike Pennsylvania, Arkansas did not compel children to participate.

Local boards of education and school district administrators found other ways around the rulings. The most common was instituting mandatory moments of silence in which students could voluntarily pray independently. This differed considerably from the New York Board of Regents' policy. Whereas the regents' prayer was spoken, a moment of silence involved just that: silence. The regents' prayer involved an authority figure leading the recitation; a moment of silence put the onus on each individual student to pray on their own. The regents imposed an obviously sacred (even if purportedly nondenominational) prayer; a moment of silence involved no state-sponsored recitation whatsoever. About 22.5 percent of surveyed teachers led moments of silence after *Engel v. Vitale*.[56]

Local policymakers, teachers, and interest groups pursued other means of resistance. On Long Island, where *Engel* had originated, the American Legion printed and distributed one hundred thousand pamphlets containing a short prayer. They encouraged students and teachers to defy the court and recite the prayer every morning in class. In DeKalb, Illinois, one teacher led a (supposedly secular) daily "thankfulness" recitation.[57] In Dade County, Florida, teachers read daily passages from the Bible while not commenting on or teaching about them. In Netcong, New Jersey, the school board passed a policy of reading the section of the *Congressional Record* where the chaplain's prayer was entered. Upon hearing about the practice, Representative Richard Roudebush (R-IN) began reading a different prayer into the *Record* every day, so as to provide teachers with material.

In total, despite the court's rulings, children across the country continued to pray and read the Bible at school. Many local policymakers and bureaucrats turned a blind eye, allowed the practice, or encouraged it. One study offers a brusque but accurate summation of the immediate reaction to *Engel* and *Schempp*: "Whatever was being done before 1962 or 1963 . . . was apparently still being done in 1964."[58] Pro-prayer and pro-Bible majorities on the ground did not merely accept the Court's judgments. They effectively disregarded them in their communities.

Congressional Pushback

Though Congress never passed court-curbing legislation regarding religion in schools, throughout the 1960s and 1970s, there are indications that a legislative majority was always on the verge of coming together. Three months after the decision, the House unanimously voted to inscribe "In God We Trust" directly behind the desk of the speaker of the House. Lest anyone think the inscription was unrelated to *Engel*, William Randall (D-MO) commented, "We have given perhaps not too directly, but in not too subtle a way, our answer to the recent decision of the US Supreme Court banning the Regents' prayer."[59] One southern Democrat tried to include a provision in the budget to provide each Supreme Court justice with a personal Bible.

The pro-prayer coalition was cross-partisan, consisting of Republicans, southern Democrats, and northern conservative Democrats. The constant threat of amending the Constitution to enshrine prayer rights or stripping the court of jurisdiction over the issue loomed large for over two decades. In what follows, I describe the succession of amendments and bills that sought to curb the court, as well as the minoritarian forces that successfully blocked these proposals.

Frank Becker (R-NY) sponsored the first amendment seeking to overturn *Engel*. By 1964, representatives in the House had introduced over 150 constitutional amendments seeking to overturn *Engel* and *Schempp*. But these proposals never got close to a hearing on the House or Senate floor, let alone a public roll call, until Becker organized the pro-prayer lawmakers into an identifiable legislative coalition.

The main obstacle was the House Judiciary Committee, where the chairman, Representative Emanuel Celler (D-NY), was an outspoken opponent of school prayer. Celler fought publicly and behind the scenes against the proposal. For two years, he ignored prayer amendments brought before his committee. Becker then went to the entire House, where he pled with his pro-prayer colleagues to organize their forces and adopt a bill that all of them found suitable. Behind the scenes, Becker began collecting signatures for a discharge petition, a parliamentary maneuver that would overcome the House Judiciary Committee roadblock. It was slow going because of the pending Civil Rights Act of 1964, which southerners delayed in committee. When liberals sought a discharge petition for the act, southerners announced a personal policy of not signing *any* discharge petitions—all in the name of upholding committee jurisdictions. This made it difficult for these same members of Congress to go back on their promise and sign a petition to discharge the Becker Amendment.

Because of the Civil Rights Act, the 1964 discharge petition probably had no chance of working. Still, Becker collected 167 signatures.[60] More importantly, Becker had privately lobbied House Judiciary Committee members, and Celler worried that his own committee would revolt. The chairman had good reason to worry. A quarter of committee members had already sponsored prayer amendments. And it must have concerned Celler when, on February 20, 1964, Representative Michael Feighan (D-OH), the ranking Democrat on the committee after Celler, announced his support for school prayer and that he would chair hearings himself. Sensing a storm brewing, Celler immediately announced he would hold a hearing on the Becker Amendment. Celler delayed the start of the committee meeting until April 22, 1964, not coincidentally, the first day of New York's World Fair—an event that surely would divide the media's attention. In the two months between scheduling and hearing, Celler recruited a host of antiprayer advocates. In total, over two hundred witnesses testified before the committee. Celler allowed for unlimited questioning, leading to the committee hearings dragging out for more than six weeks.[61]

The delay was important, because it gave liberals time to devise a plan. If the Becker Amendment made it out of committee, it would likely garner two-thirds support from the entire House. Already 42 percent of Republicans and 20 percent of Democrats had either introduced a court-curbing proposal or signed the discharge petition. Some lawmakers who personally agreed with the court privately confided that if the Becker Amendment made it to the floor, it would be politically impossible to vote against prayer.[62] Liberals therefore put their resources into stopping it in committee. They artificially increased the amount of antiprayer mail that committee members received. Researchers have put the ratio of pre-hearing pro- to antiprayer letters somewhere between 200:1 to 20:1.[63] From February to June 1964, liberals closed that gap (although antiprayer letters never overtook pro-prayer figures), which relieved the pressure on swing members of the committee to vote for the Becker Amendment. These efforts paid off as the Becker Amendment quietly died in the House Judiciary Committee.

When Becker retired from the House following the 1963–64 session, he levied a pair of threats. First, he pledged to travel to the home district of, and campaign against, every member of Congress who failed to support his amendment. Second, as the congressional session came to an end, Becker's farewell address promised continued support: "I regret this more than I can put in words, and while I will not return to Congress next year, I shall not cease in my efforts to restore a 173-year right to the American people."[64]

In 1966 former Representative Becker returned to Congress to testify on behalf of Senator Everett Dirksen's (R-IL) proposed constitutional amendment seeking to restore school prayer. Like Becker, Dirksen's leadership was religiously motivated. A devout Christian, Dirksen believed that his pending eyesight loss had been avoided by the power of prayer.

Dirksen, as with Becker, faced opposition from a key committee chairman. Senator Birch Bayh (D-IN) chaired the Senate Judiciary Committee and personally obstructed the Dirksen Amendment.[65] As Celler had done, Bayh delayed the hearing of the amendment for as long as possible while liberals organized antiprayer forces. Once again, this gave the liberal coalition time to line up witnesses to testify before the committee. In fact, Bayh scheduled more antiprayer than pro-prayer witnesses: twenty-two to seventeen, a clear misrepresentation of national opinion. At the start of the hearings, Bayh declared that he would not allow discussion of the framers' original intent. Finally, and most importantly, as chairman, Bayh refused to report the bill to the full Senate—despite the fact that by the end of the hearings, Dirksen had recruited forty-six cosponsors for his bill.

To his credit, Bayh realized the difficulties—for himself and fellow Democrats—of opposing school prayer in an election year. As he put it, he did not want to corner his colleagues into having to "vote against God."[66] Although Bayh personally was against school prayer, he strategically offered an alternative to the Dirksen Amendment: a "sense of the Senate" resolution favoring voluntary prayer. Bayh wanted to put the matter to rest by substituting a constitutional amendment with an unenforceable and nonbinding resolution.

Dirksen opposed Bayh's substitute and doggedly sought to bring his own amendment to a vote. Liberals were caught off guard when, on the Senate floor, Dirksen asked for his amendment to substitute the discussion of another bill. Up to this point, hundreds of court-curbing bills and amendments had come before Congress and none of them had come to a roll call vote. Most were introduced and forgotten. Some had garnered floor time, in which Republicans, southern Democrats, and northern conservative Democrats made position-taking speeches while liberal Democrats remained silent, all the while knowing that a one-sided debate without a roll call was useless. Dirksen, though, surprised liberal Democrats with his substitution strategy. Bayh tried to substitute his resolution for Dirksen's amendment, but that move failed.

In 1966, after four years of repeatedly introducing proposals, Republicans finally received a roll call vote on school prayer. A majority, 49–37 (57 percent), supported the amendment; but it still fell short of the constitutionally mandated two-thirds necessary to pass a constitutional amendment. It was hardly a failure for the GOP. The vote not only forced liberals, as Bayh feared, to "vote against God"— it also revealed the coalition-building possibilities available to the Republican Party (see table 3.4).

TABLE 3.4 Congressional Votes on Prayer

	Senate 1966: Dirksen Amendment	House 1971: Wylie Amendment	Senate 1979: Jurisdiction stripping	House 1979: Override bill
Total	49–37	240–163	51–40	255–122
Republicans	90%	84%	68%	90%
So. Democrats	83%	70%	100%	82%
Liberal Democrats	15%	10%	5%	28%
Northern Conservative Democrats	22%	51%	58%	64%

Dirksen reintroduced his amendment in the next session and recruited newly elected Representative Chalmers Wylie (R-OH) to do the same in the lower house. A freshman member of Congress in 1967, Wylie understood the coalition-building opportunities that school prayer afforded to the GOP because he had won office by making the reversal of *Engel v. Vitale* the centerpiece of his campaign.[67] When Dirksen died in 1969, Wylie assumed Republican leadership of the issue.

In 1971 Wylie bullied his way to forcing a vote in the House of Representatives. Bruce Dierenfield gives some of the credit to his association with Louise Ruhlin, an Ohioan homemaker who became concerned when her fourteen-year-old son could not pray at school.[68] With her own savings and loans, Ruhlin established the Prayer Campaign Committee (PCC), a fast-rising lobby group that exerted considerable pressure on Washington. In 1970 Ruhlin was even granted office space in Wylie's district headquarters. That year, she ran a remarkable "coupon" campaign in which newspaper readers could cut out a paid ad that voiced support for the prayer amendment and then sign and mail it. Celler himself directly received half a million coupons.

When Celler still refused to schedule a hearing, Wylie threatened to restart the discharge petition process. Allegedly, Celler put his arm around Wylie's shoulder and condescendingly told the junior congressman, "Well, my boy, that's provided for within the rules of the House."[69] Wylie felt insulted and worked behind the scenes to gather signatures. The PCC coordinated with other interest groups, both religious (e.g., the National Association of Evangelicals) and nonreligious (e.g., the National Conference of Governors). Most notably, they allied with Project Prayer, a group headlined by Pat Boone, John Wayne, and Ronald Reagan.

Altogether, the PCC either acquired the signature of, or met directly with, every representative in the House. It was a 435-pronged campaigned. For instance, Minority Leader Gerald Ford (R-MI) all but dismissed the petition, saying he might sign if he received some constituent mail on the issue. Within days, Ford received five hundred letters and quickly signed thereafter. When Charles Mosher (R-OH) refused to sign, the PCC paid for a billboard in his district that read, "Congressman Mosher did not sign for prayer."

Wylie knew that if the petition gained majority support, some of the signers would withdraw—having only signed because the petition had no practical effect. In fact, some of the signers were liberal leaders in the fight against school prayer, having only signed because, as antiprayer leader James Corman (D-CA) said, it was "an issue that lends itself to pressure."[70] Or, as one staffer put it, "It's just very difficult to explain a vote against prayer."[71] To avoid withdrawal, Wylie built a well of half a dozen Republicans who would sign at the last minute on the floor. Upon gaining the 218th signature, Wylie presented the petition immediately before anyone could withdraw their support. Telling of the cross-partisan nature of the issue, Wylie presented the petition with 111 Republican and 107 Democratic signatures.

Thus, in 1971, Wylie had forced the House to do what Celler had resisted for nearly a decade: vote on a school prayer amendment. As with the Dirksen Amendment, the Wylie Amendment garnered a majority, 240–163 (59.6 percent), but failed to reach the two-thirds needed. The roll calls, though, were indicative of the cross-partisan pro-prayer congressional majority (see table 3.4).

After the amendments failed to receive the required supermajority, school prayer forces turned to the strategy that had worked after the communism cases: jurisdiction stripping, which required only simple majorities from the House and Senate. In 1974 Jesse Helms (R-NC) introduced a jurisdiction bill. The main obstacle to passage came again from the House Judiciary Committee. In fact, school prayer measures probably stood no chance of even making their way to the full committee because Robert Kastenmeier (D-WI), the liberal chairman of the Subcommittee on Courts, Civil Liberties, and the Administration of Justice, presented an immovable roadblock.[72]

Democratic leaders in both chambers, as well as President Jimmy Carter, sought to avoid roll calls, in both chambers, on the Helms bill. But in 1979 the North Carolinian finally secured a vote in the Senate. It passed 51–40, with cross-partisan support. The House, however, passed an override bill rather than a jurisdiction-stripping bill (see table 3.4). Without bicameral support of a single bill, neither court-curbing proposal went into effect. Though the congressional response on prayer did not result in a new constitutional amendment, jurisdiction stripping, or jurisprudential about-face (as with communism), it certainly helped highlight a latent fault line in the Democratic Party.

Electoral Pushback

Scholars have decried *Engel* as countermajoritarian and as one of the most (if not *the* most) unpopular decision in Supreme Court history.[73] Thirty-two state legislatures called for a constitutional convention to amend the Constitution—just two short of the two-thirds required. Even today, a majority of American citizens continue to support the notion and practice of school prayer.[74]

In this section, I argue that even though the prayer and Bible cases did not have large electoral repercussions, they helped expose a hidden fault line in the Democratic Party between liberals and northern conservative Democrats (especially Catholics). One indicator of the latent electoral power was that the liberal justices themselves saw the need to answer the emerging pro-prayer alliance. That is, when deciding *Schempp*, the court took many political steps it normally would not take. For example, the justices knew that Madalyn Murray was "the most hated woman in America," and that it would be a public relations nightmare to make a communist-sympathizing atheist the face of establishment clause jurisprudence. Thus, even though *Murray v. Curlett* had been granted a lower docket number (119) than *Abington v. Schempp* (142), the court listed the later as the styled case.[75] Even the opinion itself is short on details of *Murray*. Where the description of *Schempp* spans seven pages, *Murray* receives only two paragraphs.

Opinion writing was tactical. Justice Tom Clark's reputation as a conservative stemmed primarily from his efforts to fight communism as the former US attorney general. No one could accuse him of aiding communism via secularist rulings. Clark sought to moderate the decision in *Schempp*, namely by distinguishing the *Schempp's* majority opinion from Douglas's concurrence in *Engel*. He made clear that "the place of religion in our society is an exalted one." He lauded military chaplains and the court's cry that "God save this honorable court." And when compared to Black's *Engel* opinion, Clark's *Schempp* opinion was much more accessible to the general public. Moreover, Justices Brennan's and Goldberg's concurrences were designed to add religious diversity to Clark's opinion. In total, a Protestant (Clark), Catholic (Brennan), and Jew (Goldberg) all agreed that reading the Bible was unconstitutional. Brennan's protectiveness of his concurrence is particularly noteworthy. After spending two and a half months on his opinion, Brennan refused to allow anyone to sign on to it. He "wanted to appeal to a Catholic audience as a Catholic," Lain writes, "and for that, he felt the opinion needed to be his and his alone."[76]

The court's efforts worked, to an extent. The media and public response to *Schempp* was gentler than to *Engel*. Whereas the reports on *Engel* were superficial and largely uninformed, those on *Schempp* described the facts of the case and the extent of Clark's opinion. Still, *Schempp* was countermajoritarian and created a conservative frenzy against the Supreme Court. Even if Clark, Goldberg, and Brennan tried to temper the outcry after *Engel*, the fact remains that the court had exposed a rift within the Democratic coalition.

The school prayer and Bible-reading decisions did not directly and immediately translate into the building of a conservative electoral coalition bent on protecting religion in schools. In the long term, though, the issues revealed a new ideological fault line within the Democratic Party. While liberals had always been able to manage the race fault line, the turn to social issues with religious overtones further upset southern Democrats and inspired the realization that conservative Catholic Democrats held different preferences on religion in schools than their liberal copartisans. This divide may not have affected the Democratic Party in 1962. But in the late 1970s, and especially in 1980, many Catholic Democrats began to vote Republican.[77] This is not to say there was an eighteen-year delay before conservatives united to rally against *Engel* and *Schempp*. Rather, I suggest that *Engel* and *Schempp* were part of—or more strikingly, the start of—a slow-motion erosion of the New Deal coalition along the social issues fault line. Over time—decades—the Republican/southern/Catholic alliance did come together, and it composed a unified electoral majority.

Conclusion

It would be easy to think that liberals won on school prayer. In some ways, the school prayer and Bible-reading decisions show the power of the United States Supreme Court. Instead of focusing on noncompliance, congressional pushback, and hard-to-pin electoral responses, perhaps we should focus on the fact that, over time, *Engel* and *Schempp* have largely eliminated state-sponsored prayer and Bible readings from public schools. But to focus solely on the long-term elimination of prayer and the Bible is to ignore the short-term pushback and slow-building medium- to long-term effects. The pushback was vehement; and the effects substantial.

Though it did not translate into immediate gains (i.e., throwing liberals out of Congress), school prayer provided the blueprint for dividing the Democratic coalition in a durable way on nonracial lines. Denunciation from nearly all evangelical denominations and the Vatican, the outcry from Billy Graham and leading cardinals, critical editorials in *Christianity Today* and *America*, the pleas of the National Sunday School Foundation and Knights of Columbus, the congressional testimony of pastors and priests, the flood of mail from evangelical churches and Catholic parishes—surely the GOP did not ignore these developments. Moreover, Republicans could support all the arguments made in favor of school prayer: morality, originalism, states' rights, and anticommunism. When partisans from both sides of the aisle accused the court of countermajoritarianism, Republicans considered ways to unite and exploit that conservative coalition.

Chapter 4

Crime

IN 2000 THE SUPREME Court upheld *Miranda v. Arizona* partly because it had "become embedded in . . . our national culture." Indeed, even Superman was once chastised for forgetting to Mirandize a clearly guilty perpetrator.[1] This public acceptance, though, was not the case in the immediate aftermath of *Miranda*.

This chapter explores the Warren Court's criminal procedure revolution. Though many of the key rulings from the 1960s have fundamentally changed law enforcement practices, in the short and medium term, they had deleterious effects on the Democratic Party. Parts of the story (e.g., uproar from local police, Nixon's law-and-order campaign in 1968) are well established. I highlight that the decisions were countermajoritarian—measurably so—and that they offered Republicans the opportunity to attract disaffected Democrats. Relatively conservative follow-up court rulings, passage of a 1968 anticrime bill, and Nixon's victory did much to relieve the pressure from the issue. But even after the Republican Party claimed credit for addressing the issue, the GOP continued to use it to highlight secondary preferences and cleave the opposition.

Background

The Warren Court decided hundreds of criminal procedure cases, but a small handful of them stand out in constitutional studies, political development, and popular lore. The cases discussed here do not necessarily represent the entirety of Warren Court jurisprudence on the issue.[2] They were, however, of such a high profile as to attract the attention of secondary Democratic factions and Republican coalition builders.[3]

Dollree Mapp lived in a shared residence with a man suspected of a bombing. When Cleveland police demanded entry, Mapp
called her lawyer, who advised her to deny access. Nevertheless,
the police broke down the back door and entered the home. Mapp
demanded to see a warrant, and the police presented her with a
piece of paper (not a warrant), which she promptly snatched and
stuffed in her bra. The police forcibly retrieved it, handcuffed her,
and searched the house, where they found a trunk that contained
pornographic materials. Although Mapp claimed the materials be-
longed to another boarder, she was nonetheless sentenced to prison
for possession of obscene material. Mapp appealed to the Supreme
Court on First Amendment grounds: that Ohio's obscenity law was
unconstitutional. The court stood ready to reverse the conviction
on First Amendment grounds, but a liberal cohort emerged to rule
on procedural grounds. Justice Tom Clark, normally a procedural
conservative, penned the majority opinion in *Mapp v. Ohio* (1961),
which incorporated the exclusionary rule, saying that evidence obtained in violation of the Fourth Amendment was inadmissible in a
state court. Mapp's conviction was reversed.

Massiah v. United States (1964) might not be as remembered as
other cases of the era, but throughout the 1960s, it drew congressional ire. Winston Massiah was caught smuggling 3.5 pounds of
cocaine into New York. Arrested and indicted, he then made bail
and continued his operation. A federal agent co-opted Massiah's
confederate, Colson, to meet Massiah in a parked car to discuss ongoing narcotics business while the agent listened to the conversation over a radio. In the car, Massiah incriminated himself. At issue
before the court was the admissibility of Massiah's comments. The
court ruled against the government, saying the incriminating statements and the federal agent's testimony were inadmissible, because
they had been obtained in violation of the Sixth Amendment's right
to counsel—Massiah did not have counsel while under the interrogative conditions in the parked car. Justice Byron White's dissent
warned of "an overhanging, dangerous threat to . . . innocent people
who will be the victims of crime today and tomorrow." He pointed
out that had Colson not worked with an agent and simply gone

to the police after his parked car conversation, then the evidence would be admissible.

Escobedo v. Illinois (1964) also questioned when right to counsel was necessary. Suspected of murdering his brother-in-law, Danny Escobedo was brought to the police station. Though not indicted, Escobedo was told he was in custody and could not leave. Escobedo asked for his lawyer, who arrived but was repeatedly denied access to Escobedo and told he could not see his client until the police finished their interrogation. Meanwhile, the police told Escobedo that his lawyer "didn't want to see him." While the police separated lawyer and client, an interrogator told Escobedo that another suspect, Benedict DiGerlando, said that Escobedo had fired the fatal shots. Escobedo said DiGerlando was lying. The interrogating officer then brought the two suspects into the same room where Escobedo said, "I didn't shoot Manuel; you did it," thereby admitting some knowledge of the crime. At this point, an assistant state attorney was summoned to take a statement to ensure admissibility of evidence.

The court ruled that Escobedo was denied access to counsel, which was essential to inform him that under Illinois law, admission to "'mere' complicity" in a murder was as legally damaging as firing the fatal shots. Interrogation was the stage where legal aid was most critical to Escobedo—and he was denied it. In the end, the majority ruled that "no statement elicited by the police during the interrogation may be used against him at a criminal trial." Dissents abounded, none more important than Justice White's.[4] "The decision is thus another major step in the direct of the goal which the Court seemingly has in mind," White wrote, "to bar from evidence all admissions obtained from an individual suspected of crime, whether made involuntary or not." In a line that would be much quoted over the next decade, White charged that it was "a rule wholly unworkable and impossible to administer unless police cars are equipped with public defenders."

Similar fears arose the next year with *Miranda v. Arizona* (1966). Ernesto Miranda was arrested and taken to the police station. He was not informed of his rights. After two hours of interrogation, Miranda signed a confession that also acknowledged his legal rights, including that the confession could be used against him. At trial, Miranda was sentenced to forty to sixty years in prison for kidnapping and rape. The court famously ruled that thrusting someone into "menacing police interrogation procedures" without informing them of their rights was unconstitutional. "The Fifth Amendment privilege is available outside of criminal court proceedings," Warren wrote. The chief justice avowed that it did not mean "that each police station must have a 'station house lawyer' present at all times to advise prisoners" and that the ruling "in no way creates a constitutional straitjacket." These reassurances fell on deaf ears within the court as dissenting opinions previewed what would become common arguments (see table 4.1).

TABLE 4.1 *Miranda* Dissents

Justice	Issue	Dissent
Clark	Law	"Such a strict constitutional specific inserted at the nerve center of crime detection may well kill the patient."
Harlan	Unpopularity	". . . the Court's own finespun conception of fairness, which I seriously doubt is shared by many thinking citizens in this country."
	States' rights	"No state in the country has urged this court to impose the newly announced rules, nor has any state chosen to go nearly so far on its own."
	Judicial overreach	"Nothing in the letter or the spirit of the Constitution or in the precedents squares with the heavy-handed and one-sided action that is so precipitously taken by the Court in the name of fulfilling its constitutional responsibilities."
White	Effects	"The Court's rule will return a killer, a rapist, or other criminal to the streets and to the environment which produced him, to repeat his crime whenever it pleases him."

Our final case, *Katz v. United States* (1967), sparked little public resistance, at least when compared to other decisions. Charles Katz used a public pay phone booth in Los Angeles to transmit federally illegal gambling wagers to Boston and Miami. The FBI recorded his conversations with a device placed outside the booth. Katz asked the court to rule on whether physical penetration of a constitutional area was needed to obtain admissible evidence. Justice Stewart's majority opinion said it did not matter, "for the Fourth Amendment

protects people, not places." For the majority, unless a judicially approved warrant allowed for wiretapping, it was unreasonable under
the Fourth Amendment.[5] That the court allowed wiretapping with
a warrant could be interpreted as a win for the police. Indeed, *Katz*
clarified a lot for law enforcement officers who were unclear on
how and/or when to use wires.[6] Nevertheless, shortly after the case,
Congress responded in ways that had political implications. For this
reason, I include it in the discussion of unpopular cases, all the while
noting that it was not in the same realm as, say, *Escobedo* or *Miranda*.

Expectation #1: Surface-Level Indicators

Public opinion polls in the years following the criminal procedure
revolution show that a majority of Americans were not satisfied with
some of the court's rulings in this area. In the 1964 ANES (conducted
after *Mapp* but before the other decisions), respondents had to name
Supreme Court rulings they liked or disliked.[7] Only six said they
liked criminal procedure decisions.[8]

Public opposition to *Mapp* might not have emerged immediately.
But hostility toward *Miranda* was immediate, according to polls. Just
a month after the decision, Gallup showed that 46 percent believed
Miranda was a bad decision. According to a Harris poll, that figure
increased by nineteen points in a matter of months. Polls indicate
opposition to the decision, fear of crime, and dissatisfaction with
criminal courts in general.[9]

In 1970 the ANES asked respondents to place their beliefs on a
1 (protect rights of accused) to 7 (stop crime regardless of rights of
accused) scale. The modal answer was 7.[10] Lest these results be interpreted as outliers, in 1972 the GSS found that 80.3 percent believed
courts did not deal with criminals harshly enough.[11]

In Congress, lawmakers made countermajoritarian complaints.
Some northern Democrats pointed out that *Escobedo* and *Miranda*
were decided with slim 5–4 majorities.[12] To be sure, southern
Democrats highlighted the same narrow split on the court.[13] But
if we can set aside race for a moment (which I discuss later), the
rhetoric coming from southerners regarding the *institutional nature*
of the court was much more direct.[14] When discussing crime, they

referenced the typical countermajoritarian phrases, such as "appointed judges" and "nonelected Supreme Court."[15] Strom Thurmond (D-SC) said it was the "most undemocratic institution in our system of government."[16] Because of "decisions which undermine police powers, favor criminals over their victims, and create favorable conditions for crime," Robert Sikes (D-FL) demanded "to make the Supreme Court more responsible."[17]

Representative John Rarick (D-LA) was especially pointed. On multiple occasions, he attacked not only the substance of the rulings but also the manner in which a "runaway court" overruled federal or state legislative laws. Representing "the vast majority of the nation's population," he called the court "grossly undemocratic" and said the country should not "be subjected to a perpetuation of unpopular Court decisions." He wondered how long the American public would "allow unelected judges to free the guilty and punish the innocent."[18]

Republicans levied similar complaints. Some employed the same arguments and buzzwords used by southern Democrats: 5–4 decisions, "runaway court," "nonelected and accordingly, least representative . . . branch of the national government." "We in the Congress . . ." declared J. Edward Hutchinson (R-MI), "as the people's elected Representatives, rather than the courts, shall write the federal criminal law."[19]

Expectation #2: Nonleading Faction Response

Members of Congress introduced bills and constitutional amendments that attacked the court on its crime decisions. Southern Democrats accounted for half of the twenty-two total attacks; northern Democrats launched six. If measured by the sheer number of attacks of the court, crime figures appear unimpressive—especially when compared to the volume of attacks on school prayer.

It appears as though legislators found another outlet for their frustration, as the years following *Miranda* saw a sharp increase in procedural attacks. For example, 1968 witnessed the fewest substantive (e.g., limit judicial review on crime cases) attacks (eight) of any year

in a two-decade span. Yet, that year also saw the second-most procedural attacks (e.g., limit judicial review altogether) (forty-eight).
From 1962 to 1968, northern Democrats proposed eleven procedural attacks (8.8 percent of all procedural attacks in that span); southern Democrats proposed fifty-eight (46.8 percent). Among those
proposals were requiring supermajorities on the court for exercising
judicial review; term limits; reconfirmation hearings; merit selection procedures; election of justices; retention elections; mandatory
retirement; and allowing Congress to override decisions. Although
the *Congressional Record* does not indicate the substantive motives
behind procedural attacks, the timing coincides with a spike in crime
and rights-of-accused decisions. Perhaps some members of Congress
attacked not just the decisions of the court but its very institutional
structure.

A few years after the decisions, the crime rate increased and riots
spread throughout many American cities. This was very unlikely
due to the court's rulings.[20] But many Democratic lawmakers placed
some of the blame on Supreme Court cases (especially on *Miranda*),
because they had made it difficult for police officers to do their
jobs.[21] Some Democrats—mainly, but not exclusively, southerners—
complained that the court had gone beyond its institutional boundaries and/or that it had violated states' rights.[22]

Democrats split in how they portrayed crime's links to other issues
in 1960s American politics. Part of it was race—that cannot be ignored. Even though southern (or northern conservative) Democrats
did not bring up racial arguments in Congress, we know that the issue
contained well-known "dog whistles" that sent important signals to
racially motivated voters.[23] The rhetoric might have been hidden, but
the connection was still present. "Law and order," "tough on crime,"
and "states' rights"—these are all code words that likely triggered a
reaction from white citizens with blatant, hidden, or subconscious
racist preferences. I do not argue later that by avoiding clearly racist
statements, these politicians successfully removed race from the issue. I argue that, *along with race*, there was an anticommunism argument that the Warren Court rulings paved the way toward anarchy.[24]

In addition, there were arguments made against a further increase in federal spending. Anticommunist and antispending rhetoric might have been spoken in good faith. It might have been used to pander to voters.[25] It might have been a dog whistle itself.[26] In all likelihood, there were multiple, non–mutually exclusive ideologies (racism, anticommunism, anti–Great Society) at play. Given that, opposition to communism and increased federal spending are worth mentioning.[27]

Liberals certainly believed race was the main issue, and they sought to fix it with more Great Society–type legislation. In every branch, liberals tried to explain that criminal procedure problems were inextricably linked to race. In the Supreme Court, when the justices first conferenced on *Miranda*, the majority was ready to decide the case as a vehicle for protecting specifically Black defendants, rather than poor or uneducated ones. They even drafted an initial opinion on these grounds.[28] Under LBJ, two presidentially appointed commissions pointed to racism as the cause of social unrest. The Commission on Law Enforcement and Administration of Justice returned a scathing report on race relations' impact on crime. Meanwhile, the National Advisory Commission on Civil Disorders blamed hopeless police relations with urban Blacks. Accusatorily, it read, "White institutions created it, white institutions maintain it, and white society condones it."[29] Both commissions called for billions in federal funding that targeted at Great Society–type programs rather than tough-on-crime policies.

The reports dismayed LBJ. He knew southerners could interpret them as proof that the Great Society had not produced its intended impact or that race relations could never fully be addressed in the United States.[30] He tried to ignore the commissions' proposals and look for other recommendations. Liberal lawmakers, though, used the findings to push for progressive legislation. In fact, the first law-and-order proposals introduced in Congress were drafted by liberals. They had more to do with social welfare than they did with supporting law enforcement. "Let us not forget that the society which refused to face up to its responsibility to create real equality," Herbert Tenzer (D-NY) stated, "must now bear partial responsibility for the ruins of its urban centers."[31] As explained below, Republicans overtook the legislative process and turned these bills into their own measures.

Survey data shows a split. According to the 1970 ANES, southerners were slightly more ready than northerners to protect the rights of the accused. The same was true in 1972.[32] According to the 1972 GSS, 90.7 percent of New England Catholics felt that courts should be stricter toward criminal defendants. Somewhat stunningly, the three southern regions in the poll returned the highest percentage of those who felt that courts deal with criminals "about right." When separating southern evangelicals (measured as "Baptist" or "Other Protestant"), a slightly below-average 74.4 percent believed that courts were not harsh enough.[33] It is possible that the South was already harsher on criminal defendants, causing southerners to believe that courts were "about right" in their dealings. Even if that were true, though, perception matters in politics. That some northerners— especially Catholic northerners in the electorate—perceived a problem demonstrates the factional fissures that presented the GOP with an opportunity.

Expectation #3: Minority Party Response

Of all the court-curbing efforts under investigation, Republican-led attacks on the criminal procedure decisions represent the smallest tally on any issue by either party. The quantity of attacks was likely small because the Omnibus Crime Control and Safe Streets Act (OCCSSA) of 1968 addressed many complaints. After its passage, there was little need to continue the legislative assault on the court, although the political assault on the Democratic Party continued throughout the 1970s.

Republican opposition to the decisions matched many of the Democrats' reasons. They argued that *Mapp*, *Miranda*, et al. tied the hands of the police and therefore had a direct impact on the crime wave spreading across the United States in the mid-1960s.[34] "I often wonder just whose side the Supreme Court is on," James McClure (R-ID) mused, "since the *Miranda* decision, the safest place for the criminal seems to be in the courtroom."[35] As would become even

more clear in the debate over the OCCSSA, Republicans also lamented the federal intrusion into state matters.[36]

As Republican members of Congress connected the criminal procedure decisions to a host of issues, race was still undeniably present.
Republicans typically shied away from publicly blaming the increase
in crime on Black citizens. Nixon himself would not publicly commit
to the same kind of rhetoric used by, say, George Wallace. Rather
than focus on race, Nixon would admit that racial tension was
present but claim that law and order could be compartmentalized
from it.[37] During a 1968 campaign radio address, he admitted that
America was still "going through an agony of transition" and that
old myths and stereotypes had to give way to new awareness. "But
if progress is to be made, the first essential now is order," he said.
Nixon tried to argue that "law and order is not racism."[38] That said,
Nixon administration officials were fully conscious of the benefits
to be had from southerners making a connection between racism
and Nixon's pronouncements.[39] Lee Atwater, much later, notoriously
admitted that one did not have to say the N-word in order to invoke
it.[40] Yet, for many Republicans, they vehemently opposed "play[ing]
up to the racial minorities."[41] As the debate on how to address crime
moved to legislative policy, congressional Republicans signaled that
federal spending was not the appropriate response to the Warren
Court criminal rights decisions.

Republicans tried to connect crime to communism and spending
in ways that would make the entire issue seem exclusive of race. J.
Edward Hutchinson (R-MI) believed that the causes of crime lay in
the "breakdown of family life," itself produced in part by eliminating
Bible readings from schools.[42] Paul Fino (R-NY) said that federal welfare produced moral degeneration and crime. Like some Democrats,
a handful of Republicans saw communist overtones.[43] During the
1964 campaign, Goldwater proclaimed that a vote for LBJ was a vote
for "the way of mobs in the street."[44] In a piece written for *Reader's
Digest*, Nixon equated crime with "anarchy."[45]

In sum, I am not trying to say that rhetoric on welfare, family
breakdown, law and order, mobs, and anarchy were not callbacks to

race. At most, they were *solely* callbacks to race—which is plausible. At least, they were completely separate from the racial dimension—I believe this is implausible. I speculate the effect was somewhere in between those two extremes: that to many Americans, they knowingly or subconsciously invoked race; and to other Americans, they played on their anticommunist fears and limited government commitments.

Republican opposition to spending manifested in summer 1968, when Congress passed the OCCSSA. Among other things, it empowered states to deal more strictly with crime, allowed federal agents to bypass *Miranda*, and authorized federal wiretapping. Interestingly, what was clearly a conservative response to crime started as a liberal measure,[46] which was drafted because of the presidential commissions under LBJ. In fact, Emanuel Celler (D-NY)—chairman of the Judiciary Committee and the prime obstacle to conservative school prayer attacks—guided the bill through the House. Its object, according to Celler, was to build "better rapport between local officials and local police and minority groups."[47] He moved it from committee to the whole House, where other liberals spoke of the need to legitimize the law "in the ghetto" and to "bear partial responsibility for the ruins of its urban centers" because "police give [Blacks] inadequate protection."[48] The bill was, initially, a liberal measure.

Unsurprisingly, then, House Republicans vehemently opposed the original bill. In particular, Republicans criticized its federal spending implications. As first written, the bill required cities to apply for funds from the federal government, which would then ensure compliance with federal regulations before distributing money. Republicans would have rather allowed states to receive the money and to let them distribute it as they saw fit.[49] They thought federal control would result in another Great Society program.[50] One Republican worried the bill would create a national police force tailored to federal demands.[51] Others believed it was a purposeful attempt to bring local law enforcement agencies under control of the attorney general.[52] Playing his role on the campaign trail, Nixon complained that addressing poverty would not resolve the crime issue.[53]

After the House passed the progressive bill, it moved to the Senate, where Republicans amended it so much that it did not resemble the original proposal. Republicans inserted a block grant system, where the federal government would allow states to distribute money. Responding to *Katz*, Congress eased the pathways for federal agents to employ wiretapping. It all but overrode *Miranda* in federal cases by allowing confessions to be admissible in evidence if they were given voluntarily. As the law read, "The presence or absence of [*Miranda* rights] . . . need not be conclusive of voluntariness." This was as much a policy reversal as an attempt to bring *Miranda* before the court again and have it overruled. With a 5–4 ruling in *Miranda*, some Republicans thought they could tip the scales with a new court and/or the provocations of the 1960s crime wave.[54]

Congressional Quarterly reported, "The bill bore little resemblance to the [original] legislation . . . Taken as a whole, passage of the bill was a major defeat for the Administration and congressional liberals." LBJ strongly opposed the block grants and the attacks on Supreme Court decisions. He called the bill "unwise"; yet, because of mounting public pressure to combat crime, he nevertheless signed it. Afterward, he instructed the Justice Department to follow *Miranda*, stating that despite what Congress passed, they still had to comply with the ruling. His goal was to avoid interrogative situations that might result in a Supreme Court case, where *Miranda* might be overturned.[55]

Republicans also scored smaller victories in anticrime policies. They installed more lights to the White House lawn after a secretary was mugged. They hired more police in Washington, DC, and allowed judges to jail suspects for sixty days before trial. They empowered DC police to enter homes without knocking. Nixon enforced a provision of the 1968 Higher Education Act that made a student convicted of a serious campus violation ineligible for federal scholarships or loans for two years. He tasked the FBI with infiltrating college student groups. The Justice Department took students to federal court on constitutional and criminal procedure issues where the students might have had a winning legal argument but did not have the funds to litigate.[56]

Republican leadership extended beyond policy and into using liberal Supreme Court crime cases as an electoral tool. While we associate the law-and-order response with Nixon's 1968 campaign, Republicans deployed the issue even earlier. In 1964 Barry Goldwater blamed the Supreme Court for allowing criminal defendants to go free, "even though nobody doubts in the slightest he is guilty."[57] During that year's GOP convention, Eisenhower urged delegates to be tough on offenders and to resist "the weakness of many courts to forgive his offense."[58] In his acceptance speech at the convention, Goldwater linked crime and protests, lambasting the Democrats' "failure . . . to keep the streets from bullies and marauders."[59] Two years later, Nixon campaigned nationally for congressional Republicans during the 1966 midterms. As he trekked across the country, the former vice president realized that crowds responded most vigorously when he denounced the court's criminal jurisprudence and the liberal faction's response.[60]

Of course, 1968 was the high-water mark of law-and-order campaigning. Nixon repeatedly highlighted *Escobedo*, *Miranda*, and the cases' supposed effect on increasing crime rates. He particularly emphasized the eventual outcomes of Supreme Court cases: that the court had freed defendants previously convicted of murder, rape, and kidnapping.[61] He attacked the Democratic ticket, proclaiming that presidential candidate Humphrey had "a personal attitude of indulgence and permissiveness toward the lawless" and that his running mate Edmund Muskie gave "aid and comfort to those who are tearing down respect for law across the country."[62] Table 4.2 presents just some of the rhetoric used on one of the most successful issue-dominated campaigns in American history. Nixon knew, too, that it was not simply a policy debate but also a political weapon that Republicans could use against the incumbent Democratic Party. Writing to Eisenhower about focusing on crime, Nixon stated, "I have found great audience response to this theme in all parts of the country . . . [even] where there is virtually no race problem and relatively little crime."[63]

TABLE 4.2 Nixon on Crime

"In the past 45 minutes this is what happened in America. There has been one murder, two rapes, 45 major crimes of violence, countless robberies, and auto thefts."

"Cities plagued by fire; entire neighborhoods destroyed, buildings gutted, thousands hospitalized or homeless, businesses wiped out . . . this destruction is the work of other Americans, transformed into a mob . . . the whole federal effort is handcuffed by red tape."

"Among the contributing factors . . . are the decisions of a majority of one of the United States Supreme Court. The *Miranda and Escobedo* decisions . . ."

"How did it happen that last summer saw the United States blazing in an inferno of urban anarchy?"[a]

---

a. Powe, *Warren Court*, 408; Nixon, "Order & Justice"; Richard Nixon, "Remarks in New York City: Toward Freedom from Fear," May 8, 1968; Nixon, "What Has Happened."

Even after passage of the OCCSSA and victory in 1968, top Republican strategists in the Nixon administration still highlighted crime in the 1972 reelection bid. When compiling information on George McGovern, they indicated that the senator had largely ignored rising crime rates.[64] In the infamous "Assault Book," Pat Buchanan and Ken Khachigian wrote that the campaign should refrain from "pressure to go 'all out' in September" and instead "'hold back some powder' for October" in the form of "horror clippings of 1968, war, riots, coffins, urban violence, crime."[65] A month before going on the full offensive, Buchanan wrote a memo detailing when and how to campaign on crime: "Law and order . . . the issues are ours this time, and if we can get McGovern talking on them, they are winners. No name-calling—just point out here the radical record."[66]

It was not just Nixon, either; across three decades, the entire Republican Party emphasized the Supreme Court, increased crime, and perceptions of anarchy. Table 4.3 compares the platforms of the two parties from 1968 to 1980.

During this period, the GOP repeatedly connected crime to other issues and ideological positions. In the 1968 and 1972 platforms, the Republican Party hinted at the communist threat posed by blaming Democrats for "not prosecuting identified subversives" and for "lawlessness . . . undermining the legal and moral foundations of our society."[67] More consistently, the GOP platforms from 1968 to 1980 always came back to the importance of local rule on fighting crime:

TABLE 4.3 Party Platforms and Crime

Democratic Platform	Republican Platform
1968	
• "In fighting crime, we must not foster injustice."	• "Vigorous and even-handed administration of justice and enforcement of the law"
• "The right of privacy must be safeguarded."	• "federal-state-local crusade against crime"
• "A proper respect for the legitimate means of expressing dissent"	• "determined effort to rebuild and enhance public respect for the Supreme Court"
1972	
• "Free speech and free political expression . . . as guaranteed by the letter and spirit of the Constitution"	• "turning back toward a nightmarish time in which . . . our horrified people watched our cities burn, crime burgeon, campuses dissolve into chaos"
• "epidemic of wiretapping"	• "our unrelenting war on crime is being won . . . more marshals, more judges, more narcotics agents . . . 600 new Special Agents to the FBI"
• "We can protect all people without undermining fundamental liberties by ceasing to use 'law and order' as justification."	
• "Crime and drug use cannot be isolated from the social and economic conditions."	• "Appointed judges whose respect for the rights of the accused is balanced by an appreciation . . . of law enforcement"
1976	
• "jobs, decent housing, and educational opportunities provide a real alternative to crime"	• "A society that excuses crime will eventually fall victim to it."
• "oppose . . . anti-civil libertarian measures in the guise of reform of the criminal code"	• "Emphasis must be on protecting the innocent and punishing the guilty."
1980	
• "enact a criminal code which scrupulously protects civil liberties"	• "real problems that face Americans . . . dangerous streets and violent crime"
• "minorities in some areas have been discriminated against by such police actions"	• "support a vigorous and effective effort on the part of law enforcement agencies"
• "commitment to affirmative action in the hiring of law enforcement personnel"	• "application of strong penalties"[a]

a. Democratic Party Platform, 1968, 1972, 1976, 1980; Republican Party Platform, 1968, 1972, 1976, 1980.

"encouraging communities to solve their own problems"; "vigorous support of local police"; "fighting crime is—and should be—primarily a local responsibility"; "the most effect weapons against crime are state and local agencies."[68] These linkages might have been dog whistles, but regardless of their target, they mapped directly onto arguments made by disaffected Democrats and made the court out to be a repeat offender with multiple disappointing rulings.

In short, the Republican Party continued to highlight crime (and the party's preferred solutions) because they knew the topic fractured the Democratic coalition (for a host of non–mutually exclusive reasons, not the least of which was race). And as opposed to the historical racial fault line, which hinged on region, this issue split the Democrats outside the South, with some northerners breaking from their liberal copartisans. Republican Party leaders knew this and directed their focus, rhetoric, and strategy toward it.

Grassroots Pushback

At the grassroots, there was widespread opposition from many involved in the handling of criminal suspects. In this section, I focus on *Miranda v. Arizona*, primarily because this case seemed to generate the most publicity.[69] Nearly all statements from district attorneys, police officers, and judges expressed vehement opposition. As a young district attorney in Philadelphia, Arlen Specter was brought to testify before a Senate subcommittee on the OCCSSA. He said *Miranda* had caused "very acute problems" for his office and that he maintained a search for a good test case to bring to the Supreme Court to try to overturn it. In the meantime, he advocated that Congress override the holding as much as possible.[70]

Many police officers, especially, were apoplectic. Hundreds of police chiefs were brought to Washington to tell the supposed horror stories caused by recent Supreme Court cases. Table 4.4 samples some of the opposition from police officers across the country.

Similarly, many judges denounced the majority ruling in *Miranda*. Judges were specially positioned to explain cases where defendants exploited technicalities. I discuss some examples later but turn attention here to various judges' concerns with the institutional duty of the Supreme Court. In short, many judges were quick to point out the emerging countermajoritarian nature of *Miranda*. Because *Miranda* soon allowed some confessed defendants to go free—and because these cases made good newspaper copy—judges often had to face questions regarding how the Supreme Court had reached such an outcome. They pointed out the public's reaction to these types of decisions, as indicated by statements I discuss below that were made before the previously mentioned subcommittee (see table 4.5).

TABLE 4.4 Police Chiefs' Responses to *Miranda*

Police chief	Comment
Los Angeles	"[This] will do nothing to enhance the security of America against crime."
Boston	"Criminal trials no longer will be about a search for truth, but search for technical error."
Cincinnati	"These rulings have taken from the police the tools that are essential to do an effective investigative job."
Texas	"It's the damnedest thing I ever heard—we may as well close up shop."[a]

a. Powe, *Warren Court*, 391, 399; CR 1966, 16250; Friedman, "Part Four," 212.

Many newspapers editorialized against the court.[71] More sensationally, their reports of suspects let off the hook were elemental in stoking the public fire. In Buffalo, a teenager had set fire to a Jewish Community Center. Twelve people died in the conflagration. Tape recordings revealed that Miranda rights had not been read. The confession was tossed, and there was a lack of evidence to convict. The *Buffalo Courier-Express* read, "The *Miranda* decision and the results which will continue to flow from it are a travesty on [*sic*] justice."[72] The most circulated story came from Brooklyn, where a woman had stabbed her common-law husband in the leg. He seized the knife and attacked the woman and her five children, stabbing them more than one hundred times and killing all six. He confessed but was not read his Miranda rights, making the confession inadmissible. On reporting the outcome, the *Washington Post* commented that the Supreme Court had sounded "the death knell of effective criminal law enforcement."[73]

As local actors became more disillusioned with *Miranda*, they began to find ways around it. Some of this fell on prosecutors and judges. When confessed defendants seemed prime to win on Miranda grounds, prosecutors would dig deeper into the defendants' criminal

TABLE 4.5 Judges' Responses to *Miranda*

Judge	Court	Comment
Homer L. Kreider	Trial judge, (Harrisburg, PA)	"I have had the painful duty under recent US Supreme Court decisions to take from the jury murder cases . . . the jurors and the public in general were literally dumbfounded."
J. Edward Lumbard	Chief judge of US Second Circuit (NY)	"I believe that to the great majority of the American people, it is unthinkable that law enforcement should remain as impotent as it is today."
Laurence T. Wren	Trial judge, (Flagstaff, AZ)	"The hue and cry of *Miranda* has created an out and out bitterness in Arizona."
Oliver. P. Schulingkamp	US district judge (LA)	"The defendant walks out of the court . . . results in the loss of respect for the judiciary."
Edward S. Piggins	Appeals court (MI)	"One cannot be entirely out of sympathy with an American public that voices a vigorous protest when it watches confessed rapists and murderers go free to repeat their crimes."[a]

a. "Statement of Hon. J Edward Lumbard, Chief Judge of the US Court of Appeals for the Second Circuit, New York City," in *Hearings before the Subcommittee*, 170; "Statement of Hon. Homer L. Kreider, President Judge, Court of Common Pleas, Harrisburg, PA," in *Hearings before the Subcommittee*, 268; "Statement of Laurence T. Wren, Judge, Superior Court, Flagstaff, AZ," in *Hearings before the Subcommittee*, 526; "Statement of Judge Oliver P. Schulingkamp, District Court, New Orleans, LA," in *Hearings before the Subcommittee*, 842; "Statement of Hon. Edwards S. Piggins, Judge of the Circuit Court, Third Judicial Circuit of Michigan," in *Hearings before the Subcommittee*, 887.

history and try to charge them for unprosecuted crimes. Judges, meanwhile, allowed prosecutors the discretion to fight procedural defense claims, which sometimes opened opportunities to elicit the very confession that defense counsel sought to suppress. In fact, in *Miranda*'s retrial, when Miranda took the stand to discuss whether he was read his rights, he ended up confessing to the rape for which he was charged.[74]

The actors with the most agency to work around *Miranda* were detectives. Some detectives followed *Miranda*, while others ignored it.[75] More common, though, was compliance with the letter of *Miranda* mixed with clear violations of its spirit in which detectives exhibited the exact psychological behavior that Chief Justice Warren sought to eliminate from interrogation rooms. This led one group of researchers to conclude that if measured by "tangible effect on the interrogation process," then *Miranda* was "an act of judicial futility."[76]

Two strategies stand out in particular: tricks and threats. First, many interrogators dutifully read rights but still psychologically tricked suspects into confessions. One researcher witnessed a detective congratulating a suspect on a statutory rape, saying, "She's pretty nice. I probably would have done the same thing myself. She probably just let you have your way, and now she's making this charge because she's mad at you. So just tell me how it really happened and I'll see what I can do."[77] One detective admitted to an embedded ethnographer that he liked to impugn the victim's character because it caused the suspect to let down their guard.[78]

Second, and related to psychological tricks, many police officers acted as though they could cut a deal with the suspect. Although plea bargaining formally takes place between a prosecutor and counsel for the defendant, often police officers would appear to negotiate with suspects directly in the interrogation room. They would read suspects their rights, and when met with silence, they would tell suspects that they might be able to recommend a lower charge or the possibility of bail—but only if they received a signed confession after rights were read. In essence, these were threats: if the suspect did not cooperate, worse outcomes were more likely. Some suspects were even told that it would make them look bad if they remained silent.[79] In important ways, this violated the central tenet of *Miranda*: that because silence and representation might matter most before legal proceedings begin, suspects should be made aware of, and allowed to exercise, those rights. Bargaining discouraged silence and counsel at the very moment when the suspect probably needed it most.

The Denver police force employed a clever strategy that fell within the letter, but not the spirit, of *Miranda*. The opinion said that a heavy burden rested on the government to show any waiver of rights was made "knowingly and intelligently." The Denver police created a form that they presented to suspects asking for two signatures. The first was recognition that Miranda rights had been read; the second was the knowing and intelligent waiver of those rights. Because judges deferred so much to these forms, interrogations really centered on

getting suspects to sign both parts of the form. For this outcome to
be achieved, interrogators told suspects that they would be charged
with the most serious crimes if they did not sign the form. The key,
to Denver police, was waiving right to counsel, because "when the
suspect is induced (either consciously or unconsciously) to bargain
away his right to counsel, his Fifth Amendment privilege [against
self-incrimination] becomes impaired and ineffectual."[80] Follow-up
interviews with suspects who signed revealed that 60 percent of them
believed that their consent would have no legal effect.

Miranda v. Arizona might have set off a storm of controversy
among detectives, but in reality, they still held a great deal of agency because they largely controlled the interrogation room and the
manner in which warnings were delivered. They decided whether a
suspect could leave or had to stay. They controlled the flow of information to courts—especially if interrogations were not recorded.[81] In
instances where defendants and interrogators disagreed on the reading or timing of the reading of Miranda rights, judges were much
likelier to defer to law enforcement. Officers could also do minor
things that had large effects. For instance, many officers read the
rights in an overly bureaucratic tone. Or they would read the rights,
start the interrogation with benign questions (e.g., name, age, phone
number), and then move into tricks and threats once the suspect felt
comfortable. Some changed the warning slightly: "Whatever you say
may be used *for* or against you." Some reiterated that suspects did not
have to talk but that it would be best to get everything cleared up as
soon as possible. Eventually, police would comply with Miranda in
the long term. But immediately after the decision, some found ways
to effectively nullify the court's ruling.

Congressional Pushback

Though liberal Democrats were the primary faction of the majority
party in Congress, the cross-partisan coalition of Republicans, southern Democrats, and northern conservative Democrats comprised
a majority that opposed the Supreme Court's criminal procedure
jurisprudence. This cross-partisan majority never institutionally
curbed the court, such as restricting its jurisdiction or requiring

supermajorities for exercising judicial review of state criminal codes. But within the alliance, members of both parties worked to pass the sweeping OCCSSA, which dramatically scaled back the court's rulings and served as notice that Congress could, and would, flex its legislative muscles in the face of unpopular criminal cases.

As mentioned, the original crime bill started off in the House as a liberal-introduced measure. House Republicans and conservative Democrats argued against many of its provisions, but none more than its plan for distributing federal funds through the attorney general's office. The cross-partisan coalition believed this plan gave the federal government too much authority; they preferred block grants that allowed states to distribute the funds. Though the Nixon administration is generally credited with inventing the concept of block grants, the first instance of one was the 1968 OCCSSA, which passed before Nixon took office. The brainchild of a trio of Republican Party leaders—Gerald Ford (MI), Charles Goodell (NY), and Albert Quie (MN)—block grants quickly became a way for Nixon (indeed, all future Republican presidents) to advocate the expenditure of federal funds while also maintaining a conservative respect for states' rights. This respect was inscribed into the preamble of the OCCSSA, which declared itself "an act to assist state and local governments in reducing the incidence of crime." The section on funding clearly laid out Republican beliefs: "Crime is essentially a local problem that must be dealt with by state and local governments." One could easily substitute "crime" for "school prayer," "busing," or "abortion." In other words, passage of the OCCSSA was not just a knee-jerk reactionary measure; it contained elements of a governing philosophy and constitutional vision that would become a cornerstone of the emerging Republican majority.

Moreover, although court-curbing bills related to crime were fewer in number than other issues studied here, the OCCSSA was highly successful. The bill all but overturned *Miranda* for federal officers. Granted, many federal agents still complied with *Miranda* by reading suspects their rights and making sure they were understood. Nevertheless, the OCCSSA made this a luxury, not a necessity, for federal apprehension, arrest, and interrogation.

In addition, the bill widened the possibilities for obtaining a warrant to wiretap. In a series of five amendments, the Senate rejected provisions that would have restricted wiretapping to when a crime had already been committed (as opposed to about to be committed), emergencies, hard-core crime, national security matters, and for only a five-year period (whereupon it expired without renewal).

Voting patterns on the five wiretapping amendments tell the story of the anticrime coalition in the 1960s (see table 4.6). Southern Democrats and Republicans voted quite similarly, with 85 percent of each group voting for wiretapping across the five aggregated roll calls. The more interesting split, though, was among northern Democrats, who voted for wiretapping nearly half the time. As repeatedly shown, this Republican/southern Democratic/northern conservative Democratic bloc comprised a clear majority of members of Congress.

TABLE 4.6 Congressional Votes on Wiretapping

	Republicans	Southern Dems	Liberal Dems	N. Conservative Dems
% of pro-wiretapping votes	85%	85%	41%	54%

Other votes on the OCCSSA demonstrated the same pattern. I highlight the 1968 amendments regarding block grants and overriding *Miranda* (see table 4.7). Southern Democrats and Republicans predictably voted for the devolutionary and tough-on-crime amendments. Once again, though, northern Democrats split, and it was this cross-partisan, bi-regional coalition that represented the congressional majority.

TABLE 4.7 Congressional Votes on Crime

Amendment	Block grants (48–32)	Override *Miranda* (55–29)
Republicans	100%	79%
Southern Democrats	64%	95%
Northern Conservative Democrats	31%	50%
Liberal Democrats	18%	22%

The only votes that liberals won dealt with explicit court-curbing. Two proposals sought to limit the jurisdiction of federal courts. Liberals succeeded in striking those portions from the final bill. The first would have barred federal courts from hearing cases dealing with admitting confessionary evidence if a state supreme court had already decided the case. The second would have stripped federal courts of jurisdiction in appellate cases dealing with admission of eyewitness testimony. Although formal court-curbing never passed, those attacks likely played a role in the court reversing its liberal jurisprudence (discussed in this chapter's conclusion).

Electoral Pushback

The same cross-partisan majority that passed the OCCSSA in Congress started to form in the electorate, too. Part of the mechanism for this electoral coalition was race—that dog whistles on crime conveyed racially motivated signals to voters.[82] I do not dispute this. I raise the point that the Supreme Court gave the GOP a very good opportunity to make those overtures.

Top Republican strategists outlined a tough-on-crime stance as instrumental in building a new GOP majority in the electorate. In the mid-1960s, the Warren Court's criminal procedure decisions were among the most unpopular Supreme Court rulings in American history. The president of the American Bar Association denounced *Mapp*. Observers have since called *Miranda* the "most controversial" and "most reviled" criminal case in history.[83] At the time, it was a symbol of what was wrong—not only in the justice system but also in society at large.[84] And there is nearly unanimous agreement that the decisions were countermajoritarian.[85]

The decisions themselves upset the public, but media reports and unfortunate timing played a role, too. We can imagine a period in which the court protects Fourth, Fifth, and Sixth Amendment rights, the media does not overreport extraordinary instances of guilty criminals going free, and no crime wave coincides. But the media did overreport. And when the crime rate spiked sharply, it all but ensured a hostile retaliation against the court. Ordinary people, newspapers, politicians, law enforcement officials, and even judges asked, "If crime control had been stable, what caused violence, riots, and

disorder to emerge so quickly?" They accused multiple supposed cul-
prits: permissive hippie culture, subversive communist efforts, a de-
emphasis on morality and biblical teachings, and pent-up Black rage.
But no scapegoat received more condemnation than the US Supreme
Court. By 1967 the narrative was that the court had made it easier for
criminals—especially violent criminals—to go free and perpetuate
their terror on law-abiding citizens. Thus, crime increased. In truth,
the court did not cause the crime wave; it was a coincidence.[86]

Yet, the coincidence did not guarantee that the Republican Party
would win votes. It still required purposive GOP efforts to transform
the public outcry into electoral gains. Republican leadership took
these steps, and one of the keys to their success was identifying the
exact factions dissatisfied with the state of politics.

Crime could have reexposed the long-standing racial fault line,
as some southerners surely believed that the increase in crime was
due to race. There is not much evidence of this in the *Congressional
Record*, but it is more likely to manifest in the electorate. Beyond dog
whistles, it appears the GOP was unwilling to explicitly cross that
line; they would not publicly endorse Jim Crow to gain southern
votes. Of course, they did not have to, as racist white southerners
made the jump without having to be told.[87] But the GOP's approach
to crime mirrors the coalition-building during the communism
cases, as Republicans refused to go public with the racial argument.
Nevertheless, the effect was that some southern Democrats in the
electorate voted Republican.

Furthermore, a sizable bloc of northern conservative Democrats
in the electorate considered switching their vote. Two items deserve
comment. First, northern Catholic Democrats might have been especially upset with the uptick in crime and the court's rulings. Already
more conservative than other northerners, Catholics were probably
among the most likely nonsoutherners to be tough on crime. There
are ideological/theological reasons why we might think Catholics
would so staunchly support law enforcement. The church itself is
quite ordered, from the Vatican to any given parish. Given Catholics'
familiarity with institutional hierarchies, they might have been particularly dismayed at the lack of social order. In addition, we cannot

ignore the connection to communism, which again, Catholics saw as a threat to their faith and the church. Certainly not every Catholic voter made the link. Some Catholic Democrats surely saw crime as a race issue. But a plausible hypothesis is that some of them saw an increase in crime as a manifestation of communism.

Second, whether Catholic or not, northern Democrats considered switching because, to them, crime felt more real than, say, desegregation. Whereas *Brown* mainly applied to the South, *Escobedo* and *Miranda* applied everywhere. In addition, while rioting (which was almost always connected to race) did occur in the South (e.g., Birmingham, Atlanta), many of the most publicized outbreaks were in the North (e.g., Watts, Chicago, Harlem, Detroit). Northern conservative Democrats perceived crime in their communities, and it hit home in way that desegregation did not in the 1960s.

Regardless of the GOP's ideological motives, the effect was to align rhetoric perfectly with that of disaffected Democrats from both regions. Republicans, southern Democrats, and northern conservative Democrats all claimed the police could not do their jobs and that the Supreme Court was to blame. Further, the court had overstepped its bounds in legislating from the bench, which, as Republicans reminded, was not the first time the Warren Court had done so. The solution, then, was a break from Great Society federal programs, a return to states' rights, and more local control of criminal enforcement. Republicans and conservative Democrats also believed communist subversion was at the root of the breakdown of law and order.

The rhetoric turned into concrete policy responses, but it also had the political effect of altering elections. Nixon's focus on law and order in 1968 is well known, and more than his Southern Strategy, it was his focus on crime that delivered the White House.[88] The breakdown of the 1968 results typically suffers from a couple of misperceptions. The Electoral College shows a landslide, but Nixon's popular vote margin was less than 0.7 percent. That said, George Wallace's campaign skewed the results, taking away nearly ten million popular and forty-six electoral votes that otherwise would have gone to the two major parties. Had Wallace not run, Nixon's margin likely would have been higher. Nixon estimated that if forced to choose, two-thirds of

Wallace voters would have gone for the GOP.[89] In the short term, the Warren Court's criminal procedure revolution at least affected and, at most, swung the 1968 presidential election.

Conclusion

As with *Engel* and *Schempp*, despite contemporary opposition, the criminal procedure revolution has largely stood the test of time. Future decisions took issue with parts of *Mapp*, but the exclusionary rule is still good law. *Escobedo* still affects interrogation procedures and right to counsel jurisprudence. And, of course, *Miranda* is a constant in criminal law enforcement. Ironically, in *Dickerson v. United States* (2000), Nixon appointee William Rehnquist upheld *Miranda*, declaring that the warnings were too embedded in our national culture to overturn. If Warren Court liberals intended to make criminal procedure more rigorous, they largely succeeded.

While some suspects went free because of procedural violations or missteps, the police soon adapted to judicial opinions. Stories of suspects evading the law became rarer as law enforcement agents found better implementation practices.[90] Passing the OCCSSA provided an effective and highly publicized legislative response to a pressing issue and unpopular court decisions. When federal law changed and the crime rate subsequently dropped (either causally or simultaneously), members of Congress felt less pressure to mount a constant attack on the court. To wit, court-curbing bills on crime all but ceased immediately after the OCCSSA passed.

Post-*Miranda* rulings were a mixed bag. To be sure, a court staffed by Warren, Brennan, Marshall, and Douglas continued to release liberal criminal procedure decisions. For instance, the court extended the right to counsel in posttrial proceedings (*Mempa v. Rhay*, 1967) and during police lineup identifications (*Gilbert v. California*, 1967; *United States v. Wade*, 1967). In other cases, though, the court upheld law enforcement practices. *Hoffa v. United States* (1967) and *McCray v Illinois* (1967) made it easier for police to use and protect informers. Two other cases, in particular, had important effects for law enforcement and coincided with legislative efforts in Washington.

In *Warden v. Hayden* (1967), Joe Hayden had committed armed robbery against the offices of Diamond Cab Company in Baltimore. Two cab drivers followed Hayden to his home and called in a description of Hayden's physical makeup, including the clothes he was wearing. The police arrived at Hayden's home, and his wife allowed them to search the house. One officer found Hayden, a shotgun, and a pistol upstairs. Another officer searched the cellar and found clothes in the washing machine that matched the two cab drivers' description.

Two issues arose at the Supreme Court. First, did the police have a right to enter and search Hayden's home without a warrant? The court answered that speed was essential—that because the police had information that made Hayden a suspect and that placed him at his home, the exigencies of the situation made an immediate search imperative.

Second, were the clothes in the washing machine admissible as evidence? Precedent (*Gouled v. United States*, 1921) dictated the searches could only uncover the instrumentalities or fruits of a crime or contraband. Officers could not seize "mere evidence," items taken for the purpose of proving a crime, such as the clothes in the washing machine. The court overruled *Gouled*, saying that if officers had probable cause, they could seize evidentiary items. In Hayden's case, the two cab drivers' descriptions—plus the fact that the officer in the cellar was purportedly still looking for weapons when he found the clothing—made the seizure valid.

Of the forty-five precedents overturned by the Warren Court, *Warden v. Hayden* was the only one that pointed in a conservative direction.[91] In important ways, the decision loosened the Fourth Amendment. It reinforced the police's right to enter and search in exigent situations, and it made it easier for prosecutors to admit evidence beyond instrumentalities, fruits, and contraband.

Six months after *Hayden*, the court heard *Terry v. Ohio* (1968). Between oral arguments and the release of *Terry*, the anticrime wave had swelled. The Senate had eviscerated the original liberal version of the OCCSSA, and both chambers passed it. Nixon's law-and-order campaign was in full swing. Segments of the population called for

Earl Warren's impeachment. Martin Luther King Jr. and Robert Kennedy had been assassinated, publicly highlighting violent crimes. Faced with this anticrime outpouring, the chief justice penned a pro–law enforcement opinion in the *Terry* case.

Along with two other men, John Terry crossed the same store window twenty-four times. After each pass, two or three of the men would conference. Officer Martin McFadden witnessed this and suspected the three were "casing" the store to rob it. He approached them and patted Terry down on the outside of his clothes. He felt a pistol in Terry's coat, removed the coat, took out the weapon, and searched the outer clothing of the other two, finding another gun in one of their coats. Both were charged with carrying concealed weapons. They claimed the search was not based on probable cause, and therefore unlawful. The court ruled against Terry, saying there are circumstances in which it would be reasonable for a policeman to search for weapons even in the absence of probable cause. In making this judgment, Warren separated search and seizure from probable cause and established (even if he did not label) the "reasonable suspicion" standard. In Officer McFadden's case, there was reasonable suspicion based on the behavior of the three suspects. The evidence, therefore, was admissible.

Were the conservative outcomes in *Warden v. Hayden* and *Terry v. Ohio* due to changes in personnel on the court in the 1960s? It is hard to reach that conclusion. For starters, there were only three changes on the court from *Mapp* to *Terry*. For at least two of them (Arthur Goldberg replacing Felix Frankfurter and Thurgood Marshall replacing Tom Clark), we would expect the seat to have become more liberal. For the other (Abe Fortas replacing Arthur Goldberg), we would have expected it to at least remain about the same, if not trend left.[92]

Voting patterns indicate that some liberal justices switched their votes (see table 4.8). Let us start with *Warden v. Hayden*. Four justices (Clark, White, Harlan, and Stewart) maintained their patterns from previous cases and voted conservatively.[93] Three liberals (Warren, Douglas, and Fortas) maintained their patterns and dissented against the conservative ruling. Two liberals (Brennan and Black) broke from their recent votes. Brennan even wrote the majority opinion in *Warden*.

A similar dynamic appears in *Terry v. Ohio*. Some justices maintained a conservative vote. Douglas authored a solo dissent. Marshall, who had replaced Clark by then, provided a rare conservative vote. Brennan, Black, and Warren joined the majority, too. As with *Warden*, a supposed liberal (Warren) wrote the majority opinion in *Terry*.

TABLE 4.8 Supreme Court Voting on Crime

Justice	*Escobedo* & *Miranda* (5–4)	*Warden* (6–3)	*Terry* (8–1)
Warren	Liberal	Liberal	Conservative
Douglas	Liberal	Liberal	Liberal
Fortas	Liberal	Liberal	Conservative
Brennan	Liberal	Conservative	Conservative
Black	Liberal	Conservative	Conservative
White	Conservative	Conservative	Conservative
Harlan	Conservative	Conservative	Conservative
Stewart	Conservative	Conservative	Conservative
Clark	Conservative	Conservative	Retired

Moreover, *Warden v. Hayden* came six months before the court's ruling in *Katz v. United States*. In fact, the court heard *Katz*'s oral arguments after it issued *Warden v. Hayden*. If new conservative appointments were the cause of the jurisprudential switch in *Warden*, then why the liberal ruling in *Katz*? Simply put, this was still a liberal slate of justices who preferred liberal outcomes. *Katz* delivered that but was relatively minor when compared to, say, *Miranda* or *Terry*.[94] The facts—busting a gambler—were not as headline-grabbing.[95] Nor did *Katz* set free a suspected rapist and murderer. *Warden* and *Terry*, meanwhile, allowed law enforcement to prosecute and foil armed robberies.

This was a clear break from the liberal criminal procedure jurisprudence of *Mapp* through *Miranda*. Indeed, many scholars have questioned how "Terry stops" ideologically fit with the same court that initiated "Miranda rights." William Stuntz comments, "One cannot read the two opinions without sensing that something in the author's thinking changed between 1966 and 1968."[96] One of Warren's clerks admitted that the liberals on the court were unwilling to be perceived as the institution that checked the police in a time of rising violent crime.[97]

Even if not meant to do so, *Terry v. Ohio* had the effect of rear-guard action against the threat of court-curbing from Congress. The OCCSSA had not stripped the court's jurisdiction. But a provision to do so had been added to the bill and was only stricken during roll call. The OCCSSA signaled pushback against the Warren Court's liberal rulings on criminal procedure. A coalition of Republicans, southern Democrats, and northern conservative Democrats stood ready—perhaps eager—to lash out further against a court that released one more criminal rights decision. Did *Terry v. Ohio* mark the court's capitulation to—or at least the court's recognition of—this coalition? One can reconcile *Miranda* with *Terry*. Indeed, they deal, fundamentally, with different parts of the Bill of Rights. Nevertheless, I agree with Powe's reflection: "One cannot help but wonder if *Terry* would have been similarly decided two years earlier."[98]

Cases such as *Warden v. Hayden* and *Terry v. Ohio* made the court's jurisprudence more acceptable to conservatives, who in turn eased their criminal rights assault on the judiciary. Meanwhile, Nixon's election released some of the electoral frustration built up by conservative Democrats. When crime rates fell, the issue decreased in salience, and many of those Democrats probably found their way back to the Democratic Party.[99] Still, Nixon's 1968 election was directly traceable to liberal crime decisions.

Less appreciated than the law-and-order campaign of 1968 is the long-term effect that crime had on the shifting nature of coalitional politics. Even after police adapted, Congress passed the OCCSSA, the court retreated, and Nixon won, the GOP still stressed crime rates to win elections. In 1972 Nixon reelection strategists accentuated the administration's record on crime and the prospective danger in allowing George McGovern to tackle the issue. All Republican platforms of the era spelled out a stark contrast between the two parties on criminal procedure. Long after crime no longer dominated the news, the GOP continued to press the issue because a majority of voters agreed with the party's positions. To some Democratic voters who had already been disappointed with other Supreme Court rulings on communism and prayer, the criminal rights cases were another reminder that the opposition party held preferable positions on some issues.

Thus, the issue drove a deeper wedge into the Democratic Party and sparked legislative and electoral coalitions that bucked the normal state of mature New Deal–era politics. Republicans correctly identified their targets: southern and northern conservative (including Catholic) Democrats. And although the court would scale back its criminal procedure revolution, it took up other issues that soon drove the wedge deeper into the cleavages that threatened to rip its affiliated coalition apart.

Chapter 5

Busing

ON OCTOBER 27, 1969, the most senior justice, Hugo Black, accused his newest colleague, Chief Justice Warren Burger, of disingenuously representing court's unanimous antisegregation ruling in *Alexander v. Holmes County Board of Education* (1969). In voting with the majority, Chief Justice Burger assigned the per curiam to himself; and he produced an opinion that hardly represented the majority's view. Black confronted the chief in conference, saying that the court's ruling should more strongly oppose the Nixon administration's position.[1] In couched terms, Black accused Burger of being too deferential toward his appointer. The charge was accurate. Burger wanted to spare the court from an interbranch showdown on integration via busing. The chief justice's efforts, though, were short-lived.

This chapter looks at busing in the late 1960s and early 1970s. In *Swann v. Charlotte-Mecklenburg Board of Education* (1971), the court issued a ruling that stood in direct contrast to the will of a majority of Americans. Busing divided the Democratic Party, and it did so across more than just the racial fault line. Even some reliable liberals splintered. Republicans consciously used the issue to drive a wedge in the opposition. In some instances, Republicans prevailed, which, along with ideological retreat from the court, relieved enough pressure to stave off immediate rupture of the mature New Deal coalition in 1974. Nevertheless, busing cases once again revealed the court pursuing factional secondary preferences. And while it is easy to cast the issue as simply racial, the ideological/coalitional story is more complex.

Background

Brown v. Board I (1954) declared that "separate but equal" was inherently unequal. A year later, *Brown v. Board II* (1955) ordered local authorities to desegregate their schools "with all deliberate speed." In issuing an oxymoronic phrase, the court tried to remain sensitive to the rate of change that could be expected—especially within the South—in overcoming centuries of discrimination. Segregationists used the phrase as license to delay, and in some cases completely obstruct, desegregation. As a result, until the Civil Rights Act of 1964, integration was at best slow, and at worst practically nullified by determined segregationists.[2]

1950s: Post-*Brown* Inconsistencies and Follow-Through

Two judicial developments encouraged segregationists. First, Fourth Circuit Chief Judge John J. Parker, a failed nominee to the Supreme Court, gave hope to those who believed the *Brown* decisions were limited in scope. Upon remand of one of the original consolidated *Brown* cases, Parker ruled that *Brown* did not say that schools must integrate. "All that it has decided," Parker wrote, "is that . . . the Constitution . . . does not require integration. It merely forbids discrimination."[3]

Parker gave judicial credence to segregationist claims that *Brown* only required eliminating pro-segregation laws. Erasing laws and simultaneously establishing new racist practices and norms kept segregation alive. Several states turned to "pupil-placement" procedures, whereby students were arbitrarily assigned to one school or another. Although race was not officially a factor in determining students' placement, it so happened that districts would place nearly all the white students at one school and all the Black students at another.

The other development that likely encouraged segregationists was the Warren Court's reluctance to follow through—immediately, completely, and consistently—on *Brown*. In particular, the court declined to hear a 1957 Fourth Circuit case, decided by Parker, which upheld pupil-placement procedures (*Carson v. Warlick*, 1956). In 1958 the court considered whether one Black child in a white school constituted desegregation in Alabama. Although the court's one-sentence per curiam in *Shuttlesworth v. Birmingham Board of Education* (1958) did not explicitly support the policy, it also did not strike it down. Segregationists took the justices' silence as consent.

1960s: Leading up to *Swann*

To be fair, the Supreme Court did somewhat chip away at segregation after *Brown*. Four cases preceded the court's pro-busing ruling in *Swann*. They affirmed the range of equitable powers and that the judiciary tired of segregationists' delays.

First, in Prince Edward County, Virginia, local officials reacted to the *Brown* ruling by refusing to levy any school taxes, which led to the closing of all public schools. However, the state and county distributed tuition grants and tax credits for parents to send their children to private schools, all of which accepted only whites. Black students, meanwhile, went unschooled. The court chastised the county and expressed a clear frustration at segregationist foot-dragging. The majority opinion read, "There has been entirely too much deliberation and not enough speed . . . The time for more 'deliberate speed' has run out" (*Griffin v. School Board of Prince Edward County*, 1964).

Second, after the passage of the 1964 Civil Rights Act, which withheld funding from schools that segregated, many southern states replaced pupil-placement with "freedom of choice," which allowed students to attend their school of choice. The policy continued segregated patterns, in part because white southern racists threatened Blacks with violence should they send their children to white schools. Rural New Kent County, Virginia, contained two segregated schools—one for white students and one for Black students. By the time the New Kent County case came before the Supreme Court, in three years under freedom of choice, no white student had ever chosen to attend the Black school. Meanwhile, 85 percent of Blacks attended the Black school. In oral arguments, the Virginia attorney said that *Brown* did not require integration; it had merely "take[n] down the fence." Chief Justice Warren retorted that New Kent had replaced the fence with booby traps. The court announced frustration with the failure to observe "all deliberate speed." The school board was to devise a plan that "promises realistically to work, and promises realistically to work *now*" (emphasis in original). In addition, the burden was placed on school boards, which had "the affirmative duty to take whatever steps might be necessary" to eliminate "dual systems" (i.e., separate white and Black schools). Finally, until desegregation occurred, district courts would retain jurisdiction, assuming the responsibility should school boards fail to integrate (*Green v. County School Board of New Kent County*, 1968).

Third, in *United States v. Montgomery Board of Education* (1969), the Supreme Court upheld a district judge's use of Black-to-white ratios when determining the assignment of Black and white teachers. In doing so, the court signaled that affirmative numerical goals (such as white-to-Black ratios) assigned by judges could become the standard by which federal courts ordered desegregation. This would be a higher standard that segregationists would have to overcome. In addition, the court chastised Alabama for "attempt[ing] in every way possible to continue the dual system of racially segregated schools in defiance of our repeated unanimous holdings." The decision reaffirmed *Green*'s decree to desegregate "now."

Fourth, in the case mentioned in the introduction to this chapter, *Alexander v. Holmes County Board of Education* (1969), the petitioner sought to end the delay of desegregation plans. The US Department of Health, Education, and Welfare (HEW) had backed delay, and Justice Black believed this was Nixon's nod to the South for helping him win election. Although Burger initially hedged by writing a softer opinion, the other justices forced a stronger condemnation of segregationists. As the per curiam in *Alexander* states, "'all deliberate speed' for desegregation is no longer constitutionally permissible . . . every school district is to terminate dual school systems at once." The court remanded the case back to the circuit court, empowering the latter with "the execution of this judgment as far as possible and necessary"—language that indicated that federal courts could intrude further than previously believed.

1970s: *Swann v. Charlotte-Mecklenburg Board of Education* (1971)

Like many other cities, Charlotte, North Carolina, had hardly desegregated its schools in the decade following *Brown*. The district was somewhat unusual in that it encompassed a swath larger than the city limits. In 1959 local voters approved a referendum to merge the city's schools with those of Mecklenburg County. Many white voters did not realize the implications of consolidation: that with a larger district, inner-city Blacks could attend suburban white schools, and vice versa.

Granted, at the time, Charlotte had all but ignored *Brown's* mandate. By 1960 only five Black students had ever integrated into white schools. In a famous photograph, one Black student, Dorothy Counts, entered a white school amid a raucous mob. Picked up by the international press, the photo was published in India and was seen by Counts's friends, Darius and Vera Swann, who were serving as missionaries in the subcontinent. After the Swanns returned to Charlotte in 1965, their son was assigned to an all-Black school. They challenged the placement in court, kicking off a historic legal battle.

When *Swann* began, Charlotte-Mecklenburg's student population stood at 71 percent white and 29 percent Black. Yet only 2 percent (490 out of 20,000) of Charlotte's Black students attended schools with any whites. About 400 of the 490 attended one school that had seven white pupils. In short, the Queen City's schools were highly segregated.

Judge James B. McMillan presided at the district court. A former segregationist, in 1961 McMillan had declared, "May we forever be saved from the folly . . . of requiring that students be transported . . . so that some artificial 'average' of racial balance might be maintained."[4] He only reluctantly agreed to hear the Swanns' case. Yet, when McMillan ruled, the plaintiffs could not have asked for a more favorable decision. He invalidated Charlotte's policies as discriminatory, ordering the district to devise a new plan that aimed for a 71–29 ratio in all schools. Upon submission, McMillan found the plan unsatisfactory. After two more false starts, he appointed an outside consultant to prepare a desegregation proposal. The consultants rezoned Charlotte's junior high and high schools into wedgelike shapes, with inner-city Blacks attending outlying white schools. For elementary education, it paired Black schools with white schools. In grades one through four, Blacks would bus to outlying white areas; in grades five through six, whites would bus to inner-city schools. Charlotte appealed to the Fourth Circuit, which vacated McMillan's ruling on elementary schools. Swann then appealed to the Supreme Court.

The court unanimously upheld McMillan's ruling. The opinion announced that when local authorities fail to desegregate, district court judges hold broad equitable powers. In exercising them, the court said, district judges may use mathematical ratios as a starting point, rezoning, or pairing of schools (even in noncontiguous areas). Most controversially in *Swann*, the court upheld busing: "We find no basis for holding that the local school authorities may not be required to employ bus transportation as one tool of school desegregation."

Expectation #1: Surface-Level Indicators

Public opinion polls from the 1970s indicate that a majority of Americans, consistently between 70 and 80 percent, opposed busing.[5] Both southerners and Catholics opposed the practice. For instance, in 1972, 80 percent of southerners and 77 percent of Catholics registered the most antibusing response in the ANES.[6] Though not representative of the entire nation, a handful of states voted against busing in referenda.[7]

At the time of *Swann*, antibusing politicians were quick to point out that they stood on the side of the majority.[8] Nixon, in fact, cited the abovementioned polls in the 1972 presidential campaign.[9] Nixon's chief political officer, Pat Buchanan, commented that "the president's stand upon . . . busing [is] closer to what the American people want."[10] Members of Congress, too—from both parties, and from the North and South—delivered speeches containing strong denunciations of countermajoritarianism. For example, Herman Talmadge (D-GA) said, "An overwhelming majority of the American people are opposed to having their children bused to school."[11] Similarly, Frank Annunzio (D-IL) declared, "The American people are opposed to busing."[12] And Bill Roth (R-DE) proclaimed, "The will of a vast majority of the American people, both Black and white, has been callously ignored and subordinated to the views of a relative handful who are largely unaccountable."[13]

Expectation #2: Nonleading Faction Response

From 1970 to 1980, Democrats were responsible for 57 percent (121 out of 214) of the court-curbing proposals related to busing. Of those 121, southern Democrats contributed 88 (73 percent of all

Democratic attacks on busing). Echoing the previous chapters' ac-
knowledgment of obvious racial overtones and dog whistles (which
were even more present with busing), southern Democrats repeatedly made two facially nonracial claims. The first was a combination of
arguments. Busing was bad policy (1) because it took students away
from neighborhood schools, which (2) undermined states' rights/lo-
cal rule. Different southern Democratic members of Congress highlighted different aspects of this argument. Some focused on the daily
operations of schools and the educational environment.[14] Others
stated that the best way to ensure students' success was to have them
attend the school closest to their home, where they could appreciate,
and be part of, the local community.[15] And predictably, a number of
southern Democrats contended that the Supreme Court had overstepped its bounds in allowing federal courts to dictate local policy.[16]

Second, in the early 1970s—before busing came to the North—the
most common and passionate argument from southern Democrats
involved complaining about "sectional harassment."[17] This was not a
claim of states' rights, but a charge of hypocrisy. Southern Democrats
claimed that the court was quick to demand integration south of the
Mason-Dixon Line while simultaneously doing nothing to fix similar
problems north of the line. A year before *Swann* came down, Senator
John Stennis (D-LA) caused a stir by introducing an amendment to
the 1970 education funding bill that stated that federal guidelines on
school desegregation—be they de jure or de facto—had to be applied
equally in the North and South. When northern liberals scoffed,
southern Democrats became incensed. As Thomas Abernethy (D-
MS) put it, the government continued "to deplore school segregation
in the South . . . [but] wink at school segregation in the north."[18]

Stennis found an unlikely ally in liberal Abraham Ribicoff (D-CT).
"The north is guilty of monumental hypocrisy," the New Englander
alleged, "northern communities have been as systematic and as consistent as southern communities in denying the Black man and his
children the opportunities that exist for white people."[19] With every
southern Democrat voting in favor, the Senate added the Stennis
amendment. The House Judiciary Committee, chaired by liberal
Emanuel Celler (D-NY), kept the provision out of the House bill.[20]
In conference committee, it was dropped. A year later, Ribicoff

reintroduced the amendment, but the *Swann* decision had changed the political calculus.

A final note on southern Democrats: some prominent politicians switched their party affiliation to the GOP soon after *Swann*. Here, I highlight two important individuals. As a civic-minded white Mississippian, Trent Lott naturally came of age as a Democrat in the one-party South. In 1968 he went to Washington to serve on the staff of Representative William Colmer (D-MS), who, Lott says, "helped make a Republican out of me . . . I watched him day in and day out philosophically identify with the Republicans—not the Democrats."[21] When Colmer stepped down in 1972, Lott switched to the GOP and ran for the seat. Lott claims that he "crossed the Rubicon" after a "Young Burros" meeting in which Democratic National Committee Chairman Lawrence O'Brien gave a speech. By the end of the meeting, Lott concluded, "I don't agree with anything that's being said here, so I guess I'm a Republican."[22] Journalists speculate that political strategy likely played a role in his decision to switch parties.[23] Lott himself admits that "in those days, in the south, it was good to run as one who was not of the Humphrey, Kennedy, and McGovern ilk."[24] To "fight against the ever increasing efforts of the so-called liberals," Lott became a Republican.[25]

As the 1970s progressed, Jesse Helms of North Carolina developed into one of the most ardent foes of busing. When the court released *Swann*, Helms was a Democrat. A year later, he ran for, and won, a Senate seat as a Republican. Like Lott, Helms joined the GOP "in 1972 to try to derail the freight train of liberalism."[26] His memoirs state that his switch was a spur-of-the-moment decision influenced by his eighteen-year-old daughter. But there is reason to believe that the busing issue played major role. The timing certainly fits. And as the 1972 chairman of the North Carolina Republican Party, Frank Rouse, reflected back on the era, "It's race in North Carolina. That is not supposition, that is fact. The Democrats by and large were pro-busing . . . That is why Jesse's campaigns have been so successful."[27] While "Dixiecrat" had always referred to southern Democrats, Rouse's turn-of-phrase "Jessecrat" came to denote southern politicians who had abandoned the New Deal coalition to join the GOP.[28]

Southern Democrats were not alone in their attacks on the Supreme Court in the wake of the busing decisions. Although northern Democratic proposals did not comprise a majority of the party's attacks, it is important, again, to highlight the change in distribution from late 1950s and early 1960s. From 1955 to 1961, northern Democrats accounted for 0 percent of their party's court-curbing proposals related to desegregation. From 1970 to 1980, they launched thirty-three busing attacks—28 percent of their party's total. More than half of these attacks came from lawmakers likely responding to federal court orders in their home state. For instance, Michigan's members of Congress introduced five attacks on the court after a federal district court mandated busing in Detroit. Most of these northern-sponsored measures sought to overturn *Swann* or to strip the court's jurisdiction in school segregation cases.[29]

Some of these districts—not by design, but by chance—contained a significant Catholic population (e.g., those in Boston, Philadelphia, Chicago). While disapproving of liberal school prayer and abortion rulings would seem intuitive for Catholics, a significant number also held strongly antibusing views. Beyond obvious racial explanations, I pause here to explain why they opposed busing.[30]

Catholic opposition to busing was different from southern opposition to busing, which was hard to separate from centuries of historical racism. Instead of simply focusing on racial arguments, I argue that Catholics' opposition was due, in part (1) to their political and economic development in the early New Deal era and (2) more importantly, to their very Catholicism—their theological beliefs and religious traditions.

During the Depression and after World War II, a majority of northern Catholics lived in urban areas, where they represented one of the strongholds of the New Deal coalition. The relationship between party and faction strengthened when the Democrats nominated the first Catholic candidate for president in 1928 (Governor Al Smith of New York). Moreover, Catholic voters appreciated Franklin Roosevelt appointing several Catholics to important positions (e.g., Thomas J. Walsh as attorney general; Frank Murphy as Supreme Court justice). Primarily, though, northern Catholics likely identified with the Democratic Party because key parts of New Deal ideology fit urban Catholic preferences. In particular, Catholics supported a larger federal role in the economy and its regulation.[31] For instance, many benefited from New Deal initiatives that stressed jobs (e.g., Civil Works Administration), regulation of business (e.g., Securities and Exchange Commission), and expanding labor/union rights (e.g., Wagner Act).

And while northern Catholics supported policies that appealed to the working class, they simultaneously held strong beliefs about local rule. As one scholar notes, Catholic political thought called for "decentralization *and* federal action."[32] They backed the New Deal, but their working-class and urban roots historically fostered a strong commitment to one's ethnic enclave. This was especially true in the North. For example, one square-mile section of Chicago encompassed two Polish, two Irish, two German, one Lithuanian, one Italian, one Slovak, one Croatian, and one Bohemian churches. All of these parish communities largely excluded each other.[33] Combined with conservative views on social issues (e.g., school prayer), this parochialism led to a "politics of family and neighborhood," which opposed outsiders' intrusions into "unmeltable ethnic" communities.[34]

Most pertinent to busing, Catholics harbored very strong feelings about local rule. This stemmed from the Catholic church's doctrine of "subsidiarity," which originated from a section in Pope Pius XI's encyclical *Quadragesimo Anno*: "It is an injustice and at the same time a grave evil and disturbance of right order to assign a greater and higher association what lesser and subordinate organizations can do."[35] The papal call for decentralization especially manifested itself in educational issues, where the church historically fought against state intervention into schools. In total, generations of Catholic parents had been led to believe that their rights over children's education superseded the government's ability to intervene.[36]

Such a philosophy would have led most Catholics to oppose busing. But it became magnified with Catholics' general upward socioeconomic development and subsequent migration to the suburbs. According to the ANES, the ratio of suburban to urban northern Catholics in 1960 was slightly less than 1:1. By 1970 the ratio was 3:2.[37] Put simply, in the 1960s millions of working-class Catholics dramatically improved their lot and left the inner city. As they moved to outlying areas, they carried with them a "politics of family and neighborhood."

This philosophy was qualitatively different from historically/racially rooted southern complaints. Certainly, a contingent of Catholics held racist views. However, there is little evidence to suggest that a majority of Catholics were especially prone to such views.[38]

It might be more accurate to describe Catholics' views on race as passive rather than hostile. One researcher's 1970s interviews with local Catholic community leaders reveals an ethnic parochialism. For instance, one leader remarked, "Do-gooding for minority groups. . . There's nothing there for Catholic ethnics . . . The ethnics in the Church have to fend for themselves." Another Italian American Catholic commented, "White Catholic ethnics don't have the guilt feelings about the Blacks that Liberals have."[39] If anything, examination of letters to the editor in leading Catholic periodicals, *America* and *Commonweal*, display a deeper concern with class than with race. This was especially the case with busing (see table 5.1).

TABLE 5.1 Catholics on Busing

Name	Publication	Comment
Thomas C. Farrelly	*America* (1976)	"To Catholic parents struggling to keep their own children's schools open, the proposition [of busing] is infuriating."
Katharine Keeley	*America* (1976)	"The 'limousine' Liberals of the East—they want integration and no standards for the poor."
Michael C. O'Neill	*Commonweal* (1975)	"Maybe the Blacks and whites of Boston will start to realize that their problems do not being and end with a bus ride to school or the color of a person's skin, but are embedded in a society which discrimination against the poor and lower-middle classes . . .is a fundamental element."[a]

a. Thomas C. Farrelly, "Letter to the Editor," *America*, 1976; Katharine Keeley, "Letter to the Editor," *America*, 1976; Michael C. O'Neill, "Letter to the Editor," *Commonweal*, 1975.

For many Catholics, school desegregation was a separate issue from busing. The former involved the elimination of state-sponsored discrimination via "separate but equal." The latter involved governmental meddling in the communal lives of neighbors and children. *Brown* was heroic; *Swann* was intrusive. In fact, a number of northern

Democratic members of Congress who represented large Catholic populations went out of their way to clarify their position on desegregation versus busing.[40]

One researcher found that opposition to busing in 1974 was not correlated with racism, prompting him to conclude, "School busing is not just another in the long series of racial issues."[41] I do not suggest that race can be fully eliminated from the discussion of busing—that would be ridiculous. Yet, many Catholics sincerely opposed *Swann* because it called for the busing in of outsiders and the busing out of insiders.

Furthermore, whereas southerners linked busing to northern racial hypocrisy, many Catholics linked it to communism. Table 5.2 shows a sampling of northern (or, border state) anticommunist concerns.

TABLE 5.2 Catholics on Busing and Communism

Speaker	Quote
Parent (Boston suburb)	"They tell me where my kids have to go to school. This is like living in Russia. Next they'll tell you where to shop."
Parent (Wilmington, DE)	"There is a sort of Communistic conspiracy in the country to lower the standard of education here."
Student (Louisville, KY)	"My dad called it communism."
Parent (Baltimore, MD)	"This isn't Russia and nobody's going to tell my kid where to go to school."
Parent (Boston)	"I can't believe that in the United States of America we are being ordered, as if we lived in a Communist State."[a]

a. Formisano, *Boston against Busing*, 192; Brett Gadsden, *Between North and South: Delaware, Desegregation, and the Myth of American Sectionalism*, 202; Tracy E. K'Meyer, *From Brown to Meredith: The Long Struggle for School Desegregation in Louisville, Kentucky, 1954–2007*, 67; Howell S. Baum, *Brown in Baltimore: School Desegregation and the Limits of Liberalism*, 161; "Letter to Judge Garrity from Mattapan Resident," *Wendel Arthur Garrity Papers on the Boston School Desegregation Case, 1972–1997*.

American Catholics were not the only group to connect busing to communism, but they were especially prone to make the connection.[42] As already indicated, Catholics historically opposed communism, sought local control (especially over schools), and, after *Engel* and *Schempp*, were already primed to believe that secularly motivated federal courts were determined to destroy schools.[43] Catholics worried about a slippery slope: if the federal government could transport students out of their own community, then who knew the limits of Washington's control over the home? The anticommunist angle never took the fore in the busing issue, but for Catholics, it was always lurking in the background.

The main rallying cry for Catholics was the need to respect "neighborhood schools." Granted, for some, this was undoubtedly a veiled racial argument. For example, one Bostonian complained that Blacks had "changed the face" of a neighborhood and made it a "hellhole."[44] For others, though, opposition to busing could have been driven by good-faith support of neighborhood schools. At the very least, the rhetoric was different from much of the overtly racist speech after *Brown* (see table 5.3).

TABLE 5.3 Catholics, Busing, and Neighborhood School

Source	Year	Quote
America letter to ed.	1975	"Community is a positive religious and social value. The neighborhood school develops it demonstrably."
NY Times letter to ed.	1971	"The strength and effectiveness of the neighborhood school may be far more useful tools in child development than are bureaucratic busing schemes."
NY Times letter to ed.	1971	"I applaud those parents who reject the notion that courts or bureaucrats can heedlessly discard the obvious sanctuary of the neighborhood school."
Letter to Boston mayor	1973	"I was born and brought up in South Boston and so was my husband. We went to school in South Boston and we want our children to go to school in South Boston."
Letter to Boston mayor	1973	"Why does it make any difference what school a child goes to as long as it is near their home?"
Letter to Boston mayor	1974	"We support the right of parents to send their children to schools in their own neighborhood."
Letter to Boston mayor	1974	"What is considered a neighborhood? To me a neighborhood consists of my place of worship, a health clinic, my shopping area (Uphams Corner), and our schools. Now the state tells me my neighborhood is Columbia Point and Roxbury. Next will they tell me I must attend church there?"[a]

a. George W. Casey, "Busing in Boston: Weighing the Values," *America*, September 1975; "Letter to the Editor," *New York Times*, 1971; "Letter to the Editor," *New York Times*, 1971; *Garrity Papers*.

On the whole, northern Democratic congressional lawmakers
failed to get ahead of the antibusing movement within their constituencies, especially when compared with Republicans. While they
might have voted for, or took positions on, antibusing measures,
they rarely attempted to lead the antibusing charge, even though it
would cater to a majority in their voting bases. That said, there were
rare instances in which northern Democrats took the lead fighting
Swann. The best example is probably then-freshman senator Joe
Biden (D-DE), a liberal-to-moderate Catholic who had won his
seat by a slim margin (1.4 points) in 1972. Without a safe electoral
majority, Biden probably felt pressure to shore up his base. As such,
he introduced legislation that would limit the courts' ability to order busing.[45]

Biden acknowledged the strange turn of events that led to a liberal senator fighting against busing: "I am sure it comes as a surprise
... that a Senator with a voting record such as mine stands ... [with]
the Senator from North Carolina [Jesse Helms]."[46] Biden attacked
busing's effectiveness, but his main argument was against the federal government meddling with local affairs. "People are beginning
to get fed up and when, in fact, you lose the basic support of that
so-called great unwashed middle class—of which I am a part—you
are not going to get any social policy in this Nation."[47] His most
powerful statement against busing created a vivid image: "Busing
is the atom bomb of discrimination. It may be needed on occasion
but it should not be used unless it is an absolute last resort."[48]

Biden's measure failed, but he hoped it "made it reasonable for
longstanding Liberals to begin to raise the questions I've been the
first to raise in the Liberal community."[49] With his original electoral victory so slim, Biden rightfully worried that he would be
unseated in 1978. But with the social conservative position-taking
on busing, Biden's 1977 reelection campaign focused on outflank-
ing the Republican candidate to the right. Indeed, Biden castigated
his opponent as too liberal and subsequently won reelection by a
convincing seventeen points. Still, it was Republicans who most
skillfully capitalized on the public's antibusing sentiment.

Expectation #3: Minority Party Response

From 1970 to 1980, Republicans in Congress launched ninety-two attacks against busing, twenty-three of which came from representatives from the traditionally Catholic-concentrated northeast, and forty-eight of which came from Members of Congress who identified as Catholic. When debating busing, Republicans brought up many of the points that southern and Catholic Democrats expressed. Like southern Democrats, Republicans said that busing was a bad educational policy that also undermined states' rights/local rule.[50] A few Republicans paid lip service to southern Democratic claims of sectional harassment.[51]

More important to this analysis, Republicans—much more so than Democrats—capitalized on the "neighborhood schools" argument earlier in the busing debate. That is, in the two or three years following *Swann*, Republicans were much more likely than Democrats to make rhetorical overtures not only to the position but also the argument, favored by northern Catholics: that federal courts would rearrange neighborhood schools. For example, Bill Young (R-FL) stated, "The neighborhood school system is . . . the best system of public education in the world. That system is now being destroyed by nine men in black robes."[52] The comment not only hits on political anxieties of conservative Democrats (federal courts' intrusion) but also reflects Catholic (and less so, southern) concerns about the role of neighborhood schools. Thus, Republican attacks aligned with Catholic and southern preferences, and the arguments made in favor of those attacks resonated with conservative voters. Republican lawmakers hammered at "neighborhood schools" as if it were a concerted party effort.[53] Presidents Richard Nixon and Gerald Ford also publicly highlighted the phrase.[54]

A final note on ideological arguments: Republicans connected federal courts' busing decisions to other rulings from the Supreme Court. In this way, the GOP not only targeted busing as an individual issue but also reminded conservative Democrats of the string of liberal decisions that had come out the court. With discussion of "carrying children from safe and pleasant neighborhoods to

high-crime slums," the connection between busing and crime probably had underlying racial tones.[55] Like Catholic voters, Republicans
hinted at a communist conspiracy. Take Senator Sam Ervin (R-NC),
who described busing as "no different from the tramping boots of
the Communist."[56] In probably the most widely cast net, Rep. John
Schmitz (R-CA) introduced a bill that would have stripped federal courts' jurisdiction over busing, obscenity, abortion, prayer and
Bible readings, and challenges to criminal procedure.[57] Whether the
linkages made sense is less important than the fact that busing not
only upset southern and Catholic Democrats in its own right; it piled
on to other rulings (e.g., communists' rights, school prayer, crime)
that had upset these very factions.

As the 1970s progressed, Republicans increasingly asserted legislative leadership over antibusing measures. The turning point was
1971–72, when antibusing policy leadership switched from southern
Democrats to the GOP. The timing aligns perfectly with the court
issuing *Swann v. Charlotte*, after which Republicans offered major
support for antibusing, and/or resistance for pro-busing, measures
each year. This went beyond position-taking proposals for constitutional amendments that had no hope of passing. Rather, Republicans
in the White House and on Capitol Hill forcefully and effectively led
a policy campaign to obstruct busing efforts.

In 1971 President Nixon proposed an educational funding bill that
would grant $500 million in 1972 and $1 billion in 1973 to school
boards. Proposed as a "desegregation measure," the main purpose of
the bill was to improve the quality of urban schools so as to deflect
interest away from wanting to bus Black students to white neighborhoods. Moreover, the bill stipulated that school boards need not
adopt any one method of desegregation (i.e., busing).

Two Republican-sponsored 1971 amendments stand out. First,
John Ashbrook (R-IL) proposed the first version of "defunding"—
that any federal money could not be used to buy or pay for the use
of buses. Second, William Broomfield (R-MI) introduced the first
version of "postponement"—that any federal court order requiring
busing be postponed until all appeals had been exhausted. They
passed the House, but the Senate did not act on the bill.

The next year, Congress reconsidered the bill. In 1972 the main story was the interchamber politics. The House, once again, passed defunding and postponement, as well as a stipulation that the "neighborhood school" was appropriate for determining pupil assignment. The more liberal Senate stymied the antibusing coalition, defeating three Republican-sponsored amendments: Howard Baker's (R-TN) call for a significant postponement of federal court decisions requiring busing and Bob Dole's (R-KS) and Robert Griffin's (R-MI) separate amendments to strip federal courts of jurisdiction in busing cases. The two chambers' bills were clearly at odds.

The conference committee met more than twenty times in 1972, including a final all-night session. Republicans were disappointed with the final version. For instance, upon signing the bill, Nixon quipped, "Not in the course of this administration has there been a more manifest congressional retreat from an urgent call for responsibility." He approved it because it at least added some antibusing measures, but he called the provisions "inadequate, misleading, and entirely unsatisfactory."[58]

A look at the bill, however, reveals the Republicans had much to celebrate. The conference rejected the requirement that students only attend their neighborhood school. But House conferees had mostly followed through on Earl Ruth's (R-NC) resolution (which passed 272–140) that conference members insist on defunding and postponement. The final bill defunded busing when the school had not requested the money, and it prohibited spending whenever students would be bused to inferior schools. Congress also postponed federal court busing orders by two years. In addition, the final bill included a watered-down version of the Stennis/Ribicoff amendment: that the rules of evidence to prove racial discrimination be uniform throughout the country, and not just in areas with a history of segregation (i.e., the South). In sum, the bill significantly thwarted busing.

Nevertheless, Republicans still clamored for stronger attacks against *Swann* and lower federal court rulings. Republicans' expressed disappointment with the conference bill suggests that despite a policy victory, they saw antibusing positions and measures as not yet fully tapped political boons. To wit, on the day Nixon signed the

bill, domestic affairs advisor John Ehrlichman announced that the
president would use the 1972 campaign to build support for a constitutional amendment against busing.

Moreover, Republican Party leaders learned a valuable lesson in
1972: that coalitional opportunities in Congress existed between
Republicans and conservative Democrats from both regions. Two
episodes stand out. First, Senate conservatives from both parties
worked together to prevent assigning the Education Bill to the Labor
and Public Welfare Committee. Packed with liberals, the committee
likely would have killed a bill that contained any substantive attacks
on busing. Working with James Allen (D-AL), John Sparkman (D-
AL), and Harry Byrd (I-VA), Robert Griffin (R-MI) coordinated a
parliamentary maneuver to ensure that the bill would go directly
on the Senate agenda, without committee assignment.[59] Second, the
House Rules Committee uncharacteristically intervened to discharge
an antibusing constitutional amendment (proposed by New York
Republican Norman Lent) from the House Judiciary Committee. A
majority of the votes to discharge came from Democrats—and one-
third of those were from northern Democrats, indicating that the
busing cleavage was not merely a regional split.

Republican leadership of antibusing policy, which included ex-
posing the fault line in the Democratic Party, continued into the
1970s. In 1973 cross-partisans Jesse Helms (R-NC) and John Dingell
(D-MI) introduced identical amendments in the Senate and House,
respectively, to the Energy Conservation Bill. In the midst of an oil
shortage, the North Carolina Republican and Michigan Democrat
argued that fuel should be cut from buses used to transport students
outside their own neighborhoods. That same year, Republicans sponsored a bill to bar the federal Legal Service Corporation from using
money to litigate desegregation cases.[60] In 1974 Nixon threatened to
veto a $25.2 billion education bill if the Senate's more liberal version
came to his desk. In 1976 President Ford called on Congress to create
busing guidelines for federal courts. He also backed a bill that would
place a three-year expiration date on court-ordered busing.[61]

The Republican Party knowingly sought to publicize the issue to
attract conservative Democrats. In fact, with busing, we have the closest thing to a "smoking gun" as possible. That is, we cannot reasonably

expect politicians to admit that they exploit a policy issue area for the primary purpose of enlarging their coalition. Nevertheless, H. R. Haldeman's diary reveals a striking story. I quote it here at length to drive home that Supreme Court rulings can open up coalition-building opportunities:

> A long discussion of school problem,[62] with even [Senator Hugh] Scott [R-PA] agreeing we should go for another Congressional vote against busing, to try to impress the Courts and deflect their present trend toward ordering end to de facto segregation nationwide at any cost. P[resident] made *very* strong statement of his position and his real concern that we may be headed for total chaos unless the courts let up. They all seemed to agree. This has become the major cause of the moment, and may really be very serious. Great advance political possibilities . . . if we don't move out on this, a southern Democrat like Russell will, and might unite the right and left-wing Democrats on a strange basis, both against the Courts, but for opposite reasons. Feels we can preempt the proper position by going first.[63]

The quote deserves analysis. First, though a Republican, Senate Minority Leader Hugh Scott (R-PA) was a busing proponent. That he agreed to allow antibusing stances to be used to enlarge the Republican Party is telling. Second, lest we think that Republican behavior was only political, it appears that Nixon wanted to stop liberal court decisions and that he reasoned that congressional votes would slow the judiciary.[64] Third, not only did Republican leaders see "political possibilities," but they also realized that if they did not "move out on this," then southern Democrats might be able to unite their own party.[65] Instead, Republicans wanted to pick off antibusing Democrats; to do so, they would have to act quickly. In sum, the quote is as honest as we can expect from politicos. A top-level Republican strategist admits to pushing the policy issue against the court in order to attract members of the opposition party. Indeed, Haldeman insisted that Nixon get "clearly on the record again by being against busing."[66] Afterward, "I am against busing" became a Nixonian mantra.[67]

Another top Republican strategist, Kevin Phillips, hinted that Nixon would win votes by refusing to require school districts to bus students.[68] However, the immediate reaction from the Nixon White House was to look halfway complicit with Supreme Court rulings, stall, and use the issue to drive a wedge in the Democratic Party. As one aide put it, the administration's position was a "calculated waffle."[69] In other words, the executive branch would not do enough to ensure forced integration, but it would do just enough to keep busing alive as a threat to those who opposed it.

To keep the issue on the minds of anxious white voters required Nixon to enforce Supreme Court decisions—albeit minimally. In a press conference ten days after the court ruled in *Swann*, Nixon said, "Nobody, including the President of the United States, is above the law as it is finally determined by the Supreme Court." The president then went on to interpret *Swann* as requiring the elimination of de jure segregation without answering the de facto question. He reiterated his opposition to busing as a means for addressing de facto segregation. "Where it is de jure, we comply with the Court," the president said, "where it is de facto, until the Court speaks, that still remains my view."[70]

Even in carrying out court rulings, Nixon made it clear that he did not want executive branch officials going overboard. After *Alexander*, Haldeman advised, "Do only what the law requires . . . do it quietly without bragging about it; hit hard on the administration position against busing at every opportunity."[71] As Nixon put it, "I don't want a young attorney going down [South] being a big hero kicking a school superintendent around . . . I'll not have such a pipsqueak, snot-nosed attitude from the bowels of HEW."[72] Nixon even met with his HEW secretary to order him to do nothing except what was specifically required. They were not to take the initiative; instead, they were to "go straight down the line, and not one step beyond."[73] In another directive: "*Quietly* do our job."[74]

Besides "rolling his eyes," Nixon also tried to ensure the court would go no further than *Swann*.[75] In a phone conversation with Chief Justice Burger, Nixon brazenly asked whether the court would hear any more busing cases. The chief justice responded that it was "way down the road," to which Nixon replied, "That's good. The longer, the better." The president also suggested that impending legislation (e.g., defunding, postponement, jurisdictional court-curbing) might resolve the issue before the court became further embroiled.[76]

In addition, internal strategy memos regarding the 1972 reelection campaign are rife with mentions of how to exploit busing. A Democratic operative believed Nixon was "playing a very cute and deceptive game": barely following judicial decrees and keeping "our conservative southern friends convinced that we are not doing any more than the Court requires."[77] Republicans attacked Democratic challengers hard for their alleged busing connections, with Nixon himself advocating the strategy.[78] The Committee to Re-elect the President targeted presidential hopeful Edmund Muskie by creating signs that read, "Pro-Busing Ed's Kids Go to Private School." Acting under the auspices of a fictitious liberal interest group (the Mothers Backing Muskie Committee), GOP operatives hung posters that advocated the nonexistent group's call to "Help Muskie in Busing More Children Now."[79] Pat Buchanan drafted an internal memo entitled "The Muskie Watch," in which he pushed the Nixon administration to "force Mr. Muskie to take the kind of stand that would either alienate the suburbanites . . . or appear again as an appeaser of the Right in the eyes of the professional liberals."[80] Buchanan's memo "Dividing the Democrats" proclaimed that the sectional "dividing line is essentially that of the race issue . . . which does not sit well with the essential 'suburban conservatism' . . . of Democrats in the south." Buchanan suggested "more than just rhetoric . . . elevation of the issue of compulsory school integration . . . via 'bussing' [sic] . . . This puts northern liberals like Muskie on an untenable hook."[81] Even after George McGovern won the Democratic nomination, Buchanan believed "'forced busing' . . . can be publicly hung around the neck of the Democratic candidate."[82]

Grassroots Pushback

Judicial decrees faced highly publicized grassroots resistance. Perhaps the most common response was stalling via assertions that immediate action was impractical. In Charlotte, for example, where *Swann* had originated, metropolitan school officials complained that immediate desegregation via busing was impossible and that local politicians, city and suburban principals, parents, and school children needed time to adjust to the sweeping changes mandated by federal courts. While this cry might have been true in places, often it was a tactic to delay (and hopefully erase) judges' orders.

When stalling failed and further federal court rulings reinforced busing orders, many localities took to questionable and/or extralegal maneuvers. Table 5.4 shows the wide distribution of noncompliance. North, South, working class, upper class, suburban, city, metropolitan—the demographic makeup of a community did not matter.[83] Where local majorities did not want to bus students in and out of the neighborhood, they were able to thwart, evade, or minimize court orders.

TABLE 5.4 Local Responses to Busing

Location	Response to busing
Louisville	• Closed all-Black schools and required Black students to bus into neighboring counties with white-only schools • Blockades, violence, and vandalism toward buses required National Guardsmen to ride with Black students. • Klan threats to gas stations created fuel shortage for school buses.[a]
Baltimore	• Mayor, school board president, and superintendent all ignored new measures. • Riots[b]
Jackson, MS	• Parents providing fake addresses when enrolling students • Not allowing bused Blacks into the school • Churches forming new private schools overnight[c]
San Francisco	• Ballot initiative directing city to avoid busing • Integrated schools, but not integrated classrooms[d]
Oakland	• Violent school board meetings • Assassination of superintendent[e]
Dayton, OH	• Creation of new organization (Save Our Schools Party) that ran its own candidates • Assassination of university professor appointed to create desegregation plan[f]
Nashville	• Protests shut down US court hearing[g]
Charlotte	• Three-year delay before busing began • Require Blacks to bus into white neighborhood schools[h]

TABLE 5.4 *(continued)*

Location	Response to busing
Richmond	• Transfer of guardianship to move children into neighboring counties • Renting apartments in other districts, filing false addresses • Make transportation financially difficult for working-class Blacks[i]
Norfolk, VA	• Private school enrollment • Make transportation financially difficult for working-class Blacks • Bus drivers would not stop at bus stops to load school children[j]
Columbus, OH	• Violence • Discontiguous school zones, gerrymandered pupil assignment, race-based employment[k]

a. K'Meyer, *From Brown to Meredith.*

b. Baum, *Brown in Baltimore.*

c. Teena F. Horn, Alan Huffman, and John Griffin Jones, *Lines Were Drawn: Remembering Court-Ordered Integration at a Mississippi High School.*

d. "City and County Propositions," San Francisco Public Library, https://sfpl.org/, June 2, 1970.

e. David L. Kirp, "Race, Schooling, and Interest Politics: The Oakland Story."

f. Joseph Watras, *Politics, Race, and Schools: Racial Integration, 1954–1994.*

g. Richard A. Pride and J. David Woodard, *The Burden of Busing: The Politics of Desegregation in Nashville, Tennessee.*

h. Schwartz, *Swann's Way.*

i. Robert A. Pratt, *The Color of Their Skin: Education and Race in Richmond, Virginia.*

j. Jeffrey L. Littlejohn and Charles H. Ford, *Elusive Equality: Desegregation and Resegregation in Norfolk's Public Schools.*

k. Paul R. Dimond, *Beyond Busing: Reflection on Urban Segregation, the Courts, and Equal Opportunity.*

The most infamous cases were Boston and Detroit, where white parents fought (sometimes violently) against federal court orders to desegregate via busing. After a federal judge ordered busing, 22,000 white students left the Boston school system. Many of those who stayed boycotted the schools. For instance, on the first day of busing at one traditionally white school, only 186 of 1,539 students attended; at a traditionally Black school, only 10 of the 525 assigned whites enrolled.

Local officials encouraged grassroots antibusing groups: the mayor came out against busing; the Boston School Committee refused to name a desegregation coordinator even though the court mandated it; and police officers visibly sympathized with protestors by tying ribbons around their handlebars. More concerning were the threatening and violent displays. Messages such as "N****** Go Home" and "This is Klan Country" were spray-painted on inner-city-to-suburb bus routes. At one school, a mob threw rocks and glass bottles at incoming Blacks while chanting, "Die, N******, Die."[84]

Two photographed incidents made the country aware of the civil unrest in Boston. "The Soiling of Old Glory" won a Pulitzer Prize for photography.[85] In the picture, a white man appears to thrust the tip of a flagpole, with the American flag attached, toward a Black man. The Black man was knocked to the ground and suffered a broken nose. The white man was convicted of assault with a deadly weapon and sentenced to two years in prison. The sentence was subsequently suspended.[86]

Another photograph shows blood running down the face of André Yvon Jean-Louis, a Black man driving through a part of Boston where antibusing protestors had assembled. Stopping at a red light, Jean-Louis's car was surrounded by a mob that rocked the vehicle. He locked the doors, whereupon protestors broke the windows and forced open the doors. They dragged Jean-Louis into the street and held him down, while one man punched him in the face. Jean-Louis broke free and ran away but was caught after trying to hop a fence. He was beaten with a hockey stick and kicked in the groin. A responding police officer then fired two shots into the air, which caused the mob to stop long enough for Jean-Louis to board a police cruiser. Guns drawn, the car backed away from the crowd.[87]

In Detroit, US District Judge Stephen Roth ordered cross-district busing, in which children living in a suburban school district were bused into the city, and vice versa. Enraged suburbanites defied the judge's ruling. Roth was hung in effigy, suffered death threats, and required federal marshals to protect his family. Bumper stickers proclaimed "Roth is a four-letter word" and "Judge Roth is a child molester."[88] Largely because of the reaction to his decision, Roth suffered two bypass surgeries and three heart attacks, the last of which he did not survive.[89] While he was in intensive care, the hospital fielded multiple callers who telephoned to say, "I hope the bastard dies."[90]

On-the-ground resistance ran rampant in Detroit. Roth's decree set off the largest and longest non-labor-related protest in the city's history. In one county, the antibusing group Save Our Children recruited ten thousand members who pledged to boycott busing, resulting in twenty thousand students not showing up to school. School board members worked with antibusing groups in drafting a measure to allow local parents to form private schools that could use public school facilities after hours.[91] White students' mothers chained themselves to buses and were subsequently sentenced to fifteen days in jail. A half dozen women gained national exposure in the *New York Times*, and encouragement from House Minority leader Gerald Ford (R-MI), by walking 620 miles from Pontiac, Michigan, to Washington, DC, to protest busing.[92] Most shockingly, the Klan took to bombing empty school buses.

These grassroots efforts affected congressional behavior. Before 1971 every white member of Congress from Michigan voted against spending cuts on busing. Afterward, all but one switched their votes. Even noted liberal Democrats desperately called upon Congress to scale back busing. Rep. James G. O'Hara (D-MI) was an outspoken liberal who eventually proposed a court attack. One historian notes that for O'Hara to win reelection, "he had to forswear his integrity."[93] If anything demonstrates the widespread opposition to busing in Michigan, it was that 51 percent of Democrats—*in a northern state*—voted for George Wallace in the 1972 presidential primary.

Congressional Pushback

Throughout the 1970s and into the 1980s, Congress repeatedly signaled its displeasure with liberal Supreme Court rulings on busing. Many proposals passed, substantively scaling back the effectiveness of *Swann*. Other initiatives stood no chance of passing (e.g., a constitutional amendment), but they still allowed conservative lawmakers to take important antibusing positions.

While conservative congressional majorities significantly curtailed busing, they did not restrict it as much as they would have

liked. Minority liberal factions in two gatekeeping institutions stood
in their way. First, in the immediate aftermath of *Swann*, the House
Judiciary Committee refused to administer proposed constitutional amendments. Chaired by Emanuel Celler (D-NY), who single-
handedly obstructed school prayer proposals, the committee refused
to schedule public hearings on any busing constitutional amendments.[94] This included Norman Lent's (R-NY) proposed amendment
that "no public school student shall, because of his race, creed, or col-
or, be assigned or required to attend a particular school." Realizing
Celler would not schedule a hearing, Lent began gathering signatures
to discharge his amendment from the House Judiciary Committee.
When the total signatures reached a third of the entire House, Celler
scheduled a hearing.[95] After a parade of antibusing sentiments, the
liberal-packed committee refused to discharge any proposal, whereupon the Rules Committee discharged the Lent amendment from
the Judiciary Committee to the full House. It never received a floor
vote, however.[96]

The other gatekeeper was the group of Senate liberals who provided rearguard resistance. Leading up to the 1972 elections, they
filibustered the defunding and postponement amendments that the
House had passed (described earlier). Liberal senators knew the filibuster was unpopular, but a number of them either were not running
in 1972 or had especially safe seats, allowing the faction to effectively
thwart the conservative majority. They also secured appointments to
the 1972 interchamber conference committee, which still produced
conservative results but did not go as far as Republicans wanted.[97]

By 1974, however, antibusing groundswell had become impossible
for Congress to ignore. With more liberal Democrats' seats becoming
less safe than they had been in 1972 (precisely because of busing)—
Congress reached its antibusing nadir in the months leading up to
the 1974 elections. Despite an embattled Republican Party dealing
with the Watergate fallout, the GOP could still count on popular and
legislative support on the busing issue. If anything could help draw
coverage away from Nixon's resignation and toward public sympathy
for the GOP, it was busing. At its extreme, Republican Party leaders
might have even hoped for *more* busing to deflect attention from
Watergate, as well as to provide a winning Republican campaign

issue. Nevertheless, in 1974, the institution responsible for creating the national controversy, the Supreme Court, reversed course just enough to quell congressional hostility.

In *Milliken v. Bradley* (1974), the court ruled that federal judges could not issue metropolitan busing orders. That is, judges could not consolidate multiple school districts and force suburban children in one district to attend an urban school in a separate district. Originating in Detroit, the decision alleviated tension in both the Motor City and between the legislature and judiciary. After *Milliken*, congressional lawmakers did not pursue court-curbing as vigorously. They still proposed jurisdiction stripping and constitutional amendments, and defunding still passed. But the public clamor to repudiate the court quieted.

Did the court back off because of congressional and/or grassroots majorities? Thurgood Marshall's *Milliken* dissent says so: "Today's holding, I fear, is more a reflection of a perceived public mood that we have gone far enough."[98]

Or was *Milliken*'s outcome, in part, an effect of new appointees to the court? After *Swann*, Nixon created a litmus test for Supreme Court appointees—he would only accept candidates if they swore their opposition to busing.[99] Indeed, he extracted promises from William Rehnquist and Lewis Powell that they would vote against the policy.[100] Those two justices replaced Hugo Black and John Marshall Harlan II, respectively, both of whom had voted for busing in *Swann*.

Rehnquist and Powell were in the *Milliken* majority. Both justices had complicated voting records, opinions, and histories on Black civil rights. As a law clerk for Justice Robert Jackson, Rehnquist infamously wrote a memo defending *Plessy v. Ferguson*.[101] Scholars debate whether the memo represented Rehnquist's true preferences or not.[102] Regardless, when taking his seat on the bench in 1972, he was very conservative, especially on positive integration measures.[103] Like the many Catholic citizens who supported desegregation but opposed busing, Rehnquist could have supported *Brown* and opposed busing. Without taking sides on the memo issue, the latter was likely true in the 1970s. In sum, the Rehnquist appointment probably made a difference in that seat's vote in *Milliken*.

Powell, too, was against busing. His law firm represented one of the southern school districts in the consolidated *Brown* case. After *Brown*, as chair of the Richmond school board, he was mostly silent on integration.[104] He also took issue with much of the civil disobedience and rhetoric of Martin Luther King Jr.; though, that seems to be rooted in Powell's strong anticommunist feelings.[105] As with Rehnquist, though, the point is not to determine if Powell opposed *Brown* or Black civil rights in general. The point is that Powell "abhorred busing."[106] He even filed an amicus brief against it in *Swann*.[107] Thus, Powell's appointment mattered to the outcome of *Milliken*—he gave conservatives a vote they might not otherwise have had.[108]

The other three votes came from Warren Burger, Harry Blackmun, and Potter Stewart—all of whom had voted in the unanimous *Swann* majority. What accounts for this trio's switch?

Burger might have felt more comfortable not supporting buses and/or he might have felt pressured by the president. The chief justice was in constant personal contact with the White House, and we know from *Alexander* (1969) that he tried to pacify Nixon, who, after *Swann*, "lit into" Burger.[109] Burger responded by saying that *Swann* was actually trying to put limits on busing and that the media had misrepresented the holding. This did not assuage the president, and Burger soon thereafter exhibited behavior that indicated a *Milliken*-type vote was in the cards. Soon after *Swann*, a stay application regarding busing came to Burger from the circuit that he oversaw (ironically, from North Carolina). Burger refused the application, saying that it had been filed too late and contained insufficient information to overturn the busing order. But, strangely, he wrote a ten-page opinion that chastised lower court judges who believed that *Swann* required racial balance in the schools.[110] Burger wrote, "Judges were not required to use busing."[111] He then mailed copies of the opinion to federal judges across the country.[112] Was this because Burger's true conservatism began to emerge and *Swann* was an outlier vote? Perhaps—the chief justice had shown himself rather difficult in trying to write a more moderate-to-conservative draft of *Swann*.[113] Others have said that Burger felt more comfortable voting conservatively because the government was more receptive to antibusing stances.[114] Nathaniel R. Jones, general counsel for the NAACP at the time (and later a federal judge), noted that *Milliken* should be "viewed in light of the political climate created by the [Nixon] administration."[115] Given Burger's close personal ties to the White House, he likely would have been the justice most influenced by the other political branches.

Blackmun's confirmation was not straightforward. He came to the court after the failed nominations of Clement Haynsworth and G. Harrold Carswell, both of whom were southerners with checkered pasts.[116] At Blackmun's congressional hearings, he attested to his sensitivity toward Black civil rights. When he was confirmed 94–0, both sides read into Blackmun what they wanted to see. Democrats thought he was a moderate. Republicans could see conservative bona fides. Indeed, his Segal–Cover score, derived from contemporary assessments, rated him even more conservative than Rehnquist.[117] Eventually, Blackmun turned leftward. But at the beginning of his service on the Supreme Court, he tended to vote more conservatively. Other scholars (including Linda Greenhouse) confirm as much.[118] Final assessment on Blackmun is murky. Maybe the combination of *Swann* and *Milliken* represents his moderation on race in the 1970s. Maybe he lent his support to fellow "Minnesota Twin" Warren Burger in both cases. Maybe Burger caved to Nixon in *Milliken* and Blackmun followed suit. Still, Blackmun sat during *Swann*. We might attribute his conservative vote in *Milliken* to something other than political pressure. But it was not due to intervening appointments.

Likewise, Potter Stewart had sat on both *Swann* and *Milliken*, voting for busing in the first and against it in the latter. While his seat did not change—and therefore we cannot assign a new appointee as the cause of a directional shift—his concurrence in *Milliken* says much about the Supreme Court's jurisprudence and politics. *Swann* had laid out broad equitable powers to address segregation; Stewart's concurrence put boundaries around those powers. Moreover, Stewart raised the bar for demonstrating that school districts knowingly segregated when making policy.[119] Owen Fiss believes the effect was dramatic: "It constitutionalized the difference between de jure and so-called de facto segregation . . . Stewart refused to treat the demographic pattern of student attendance—Black students in one set of schools, whites in another—as a constitutional wrong."[120] Stewart's concurrence, then, summarizes *Milliken's* effect: it put a halt to a court primarily interested in results-oriented desegregation.[121]

What caused the court to reach this conclusion? It could have been because of the appointment of two antibusing newcomers. It could have been good-faith judging: Rehnquist and Powell had genuinely conservative views on the constitution; Blackmun had not yet made his liberal turn; and Stewart and Burger could reconcile *Swann* and *Milliken*, arguing that *Milliken* set *Swann's* boundary.[122] Nevertheless, the fact remains that the court changed course at the same time it felt intense public and congressional scrutiny. The justices must have noticed how busing went unenforced—in the North and in the South. How could they not look across Washington and see Congress searching for ways to immobilize federal judges' orders? Maybe it is true that appointments account for *Milliken*—after all, four of the five justices in the majority were Nixon appointees. That would not account for the change from *Swann*, though. Maybe, then, *Milliken* was about jurisprudential fine-tuning.

Maybe it is simultaneously true that the court caved after the justices learned how unpopular *Swann* was. Woodward and Armstrong's *The Brethren* reported that Stewart, in particular, thought interdistrict busing was too far outside the mainstream of public opinion and that the court would have been irreparably damaged by ruling differently in a case like *Milliken*.[123] Legal experts have similarly concluded that *Milliken* was a reaction to grassroots and congressional pushback.[124] Indeed, in a televised address, Nixon had specifically denounced interdistrict busing. It is hard not to notice that the court adopted the exact position of the president.[125]

Electoral Pushback

With a congressional majority coming together to fight busing, GOP managers must have questioned whether the combination of Republicans, southern Democrats, and socially northern conservative Democrats could be transposed from the majority in the government to the majority in the electorate. The highest level of Republican strategists (e.g., Pat Buchanan, HR Haldeman, John Ehrlichman,

Kevin Phillips) saw the opportunities available. When the Supreme Court allowed lower federal judges to remedy segregation with busing, it exposed fault lines within the New Deal coalition.

Busing revealed the long-standing rift between southern and northern Democrats on the issue of race. Busing in the 1970s was certainly not the first time southern Democrats broke from party ranks. And given the development of desegregation in the 1940s–1960s, the Democratic Party deserves credit for maintaining coalitional cohesion in the face of divisive episodes. The Dixiecrat Revolt, Truman's desegregation of the military, *Brown*, Little Rock, the 1957 Civil Rights Act, Kennedy's executive order against housing discrimination, the 1964 Civil Rights Act, the assassination of Martin Luther King Jr.—all these could have triggered a durable split in the Democratic coalition. Busing, therefore, was not just a fault line issue; it also built upon the decades of pent-up southern frustration with slowly progressing desegregation. For white southerners, it was the latest in a line of racial issues that chipped away at Democratic coalitional cohesion. For the Republican Party, busing was a major opportunity to use socially conservative stances to realign the South.

It differed from previous segregationist episodes because the Republican Party outwardly claimed that busing was not just about race. While the Republican Party of the 1950s–60s enjoyed the fruits of Democratic divisions on race, the GOP did not necessarily exploit the divisions to their fullest. This changed with busing. Consider the congressional attacks surrounding the Supreme Court's protection of communists' rights in 1957–58. Southern Democrats split from liberals, in part, because southerners believed there were ideological and organizational links between communism and desegregation. Republicans opposed the court's rulings because they valued fighting communists over protecting their rights. And while Republicans welcomed southern Democratic votes on communism court-curbing, the GOP did not look to turn the temporary pact into a lasting alliance, because Republicans were wary of being accused of having a segregationist ideology.

Republicans shed that concern with busing. After *Swann*, the Republican Party was eager to use an issue with clear racial overtones to attract white southerners who historically voted Democratic.

Granted, Republican leaders might not have seen antibusing positions as solely and/or purely as segregationist. That is, they could
have held a good-faith commitment to both desegregation and
neighborhood schools. Even so, these same Republican leaders could
not ignore that most white southerners fought busing primarily on
segregationist grounds.

So why did the GOP try to attract white southerners in the early
1970s when it rejected race-based opportunities such as *Brown* or in
the communism cases? I believe that busing hit "closer to home" and
was therefore more salient to northern Republicans, who might have
opposed the racism of Deep South Jim Crow in part because they did
not see it in their daily lives.[126] Busing, though, transcended region.
And whether the true reasons for opposition between the North and
South were in good faith (neighborhood schools versus segregation,
respectively) or not (both regions were racist), the proposed solution
(fight against busing) and rhetorical defense of that solution (neighborhood schools and local rule) were the same in both regions. In
sum, not only did GOP leaders have incentive to attract southern
Democrats but the public discourse from, and between, the two
groups aligned perfectly.

This supposed alignment of ideologies leads to the second fault
line exposed by busing: that between liberal Democrats and northern
conservative Democrats, in particular, Catholic Democrats. In many
ways, this is the untold story of busing: that it stoked the disagreement between two different kinds of northern Democrats. We can
easily see how Catholics would have been upset at decisions on school
prayer or abortion (or even communism). But their Catholicism
had just as big of an effect on their general disagreement with the
federal courts' use of busing as a desegregation remedy. When we
consider Catholics' social, religious, and political culture, we can begin to understand why 1970s Catholics-in-the-pews opposed busing.
Ardent anticommunism, theological belief in decentralized decision
making, a historic commitment to education, provincial loyalty, and
a deep suspicion of outsiders all contributed to Catholic protests of
busing and promotion of "neighborhood schools."

Republican strategists understood this, and attacks on busing were not merely part of the Southern Strategy. They were grander in scope and meant to attract both white southerners and northern Catholics. They accomplished their ends. Catholics' opposition to busing might not be as straightforward as their support for school prayer or their pro-life preferences. And busing itself probably did not cause enough Catholics to switch their party affiliations to realign the electorate. But in the 1970s the importation of outsiders and the deportation of neighborhood kids angered northern Catholic voters in a significant manner. It probably did cause some Catholics to switch parties. At the very least, as Republicans consciously sought to attract northern Catholics, busing became another chink in the Democratic armor.

Conclusion

Milliken v. Bradley allowed white suburban parents and Congress to ease their assault on the court. Attacks still came, but with the judiciary backing down from its original liberal decisions, the pressure had been somewhat relieved. As the 1970s progressed, the court continued to wade into busing.

In *San Antonio ISD v. Rodriguez* (1973), the same majority coalition decided that public education systems could rely on local property taxes, even if it created haves versus have-nots. In *Keyes v. School District of Denver* (1973), the court ruled that districts maintain the burden of proof to show that their entire jurisdiction is free of segregation. Two years later, the court ruled private schools did not have a right to segregate (*Runyon v. McCrary*, 1976). *Milliken* came back to the court in 1977 asking whether federal courts could issue orders that went beyond the bounds of pupil assignments. The court unanimously answered in the affirmative, adding that federal courts could even require states to help foot the bill, even if states were not party to the suit. Taken together, these outcomes waffled between liberal and conservative, with neither side claiming an overwhelming victory that upset the government or electorate to the extent that *Swann* had.

Still, *Swann* shook coalitional fault lines. For southerners, it unearthed the racial division that Democratic leaders struggled to avoid

since the Jacksonian era. For Catholics, it exposed another, maybe
not entirely racial, fault line. Many Catholic arguments appealed to
southerners and were amenable to established Republican ideology.
Republican party leaders encouraged their politicians to pick up on
these arguments to attract Catholics and southerners. And the GOP
would continue this strategy as the court issued perhaps its most polarizing decision of the twentieth century.

Chapter 6

Abortion

THIS CHAPTER EXAMINES THE political development of abortion politics in the 1970s. *Roe v. Wade* was historic not only for its ruling on the merits but also for its effects on coalitional politics. Once again, Republican Party leaders knowingly exploited the issue to divide the opposition. It took time for the politics of abortion to become clear enough to show a partisan split. But by the late 1970s, the pro-choice and pro-life divide between the Democratic and Republican Parties, respectively, helped transform American political parties. *Roe* was not the first episode to expose differences within the mature New Deal coalition. But *Roe* had two important effects. First, it introduced a topic that attracted single-issue voters. Historically Democratic voters would contemplate voting Republican because they deemed pro-life stances and policies salient enough. Second, it was a tipping point for frequently frustrated conservatives who sought a change on a variety of issues, among them prayer, crime, busing, and abortion.

Background

Roe originated in Texas, where state law on abortion dated back to 1854. Under the statute, it was illegal for anyone to perform an abortion, an act punishable by up to five years in prison. The law made no provision for rape or incest, but it did contain a clause allowing for abortions in cases where it was necessary to save the life of the woman. In 1970 Norma McCorvey became pregnant and sought an abortion. Recruited by a pair of Texas lawyers seeking to repeal the Lone Star State's regulations, McCorvey—under the pseudonym Jane Roe—sued Dallas County district attorney Henry Wade.

Three items raised in district court oral arguments played a role in the Supreme Court's eventual decision.[1] First, the three-judge panel asked whether it made a difference how far along in a pregnancy a woman was. They wondered if different restrictions could apply to different times during a woman's pregnancy. Second, although McCorvey's counsel argued that the Texas statute violated the First, Fourth, Fifth, and Fourteenth Amendments, the heart of their constitutional argument rested on a right to privacy.[2] Third, a district judge asked why McCorvey had sued Wade. Even if the court enjoined Wade, other Texan district attorneys outside of Dallas County could still enforce the antiabortion law. McCorvey's lawyer admitted, "We goofed."[3]

The district court struck down the Texas law on Ninth Amendment/privacy principles. However, because of counsel's "goof," the court did not enjoin Wade to stop the enforcement of the law. Wade announced he would continue to prosecute those who performed abortions, which forced McCorvey to appeal that part of the district court ruling. Normally, such an appeal would go to the Circuit Court. But with a slew of other states handling abortion cases, she bypassed this stage and appealed directly to the Supreme Court. In fact, the key to obtaining a writ of certiorari may very well have been that neither side of the abortion debate could at the time claim widespread victory. Pro-choicers had won the constitutional argument in Texas and Georgia. In Louisiana, though, a federal judge had ruled that life began at conception and that if a woman did not want to become pregnant, then her options were "abstinence, rhythm, contraception, and sterilization" (*Rosen v Louisiana State Board of Medical Examiners*, 1970). Likewise, Ohio ruled that life began at conception and that judges could not ignore "the laws of nature" and "the facts of biology" (*Steinberg v. Brown*, 1970). It was within this context that the Supreme Court accepted *Roe v. Wade* and *Doe v. Bolton*, a companion case from Georgia.[4]

Only seven justices sat during oral arguments, due to Hugo Black's and John Harlan's recent retirement. In conference, a host of opinions emerged: Douglas, Brennan, and Stewart found Texas's law unconstitutional; White believed the state had a compelling interest in protecting potential life; and Marshall and Blackmun suggested that the state's interest changed as the pregnancy progressed. Chief Justice Burger equivocated but the next day declared that he was in the majority.[5] He then suggested the court hear rearguments a year later after two new justices had joined the court. In the meantime, Burger assigned Blackmun to write a rough draft of the majority opinion—even if the text would need editing after reargument.[6] Blackmun subsequently acquired writing space at the Mayo Clinic, where he studied the medical side of abortion.

After reargument, Blackmun was again assigned to write. Constitutionally, he found a right to privacy in the Fourteenth Amendment (through the Ninth Amendment), which allowed for abortion under certain circumstances. His time at Mayo played a prominent role in the opinion arrived at by the court. Blackmun divided pregnancy into trimesters, with states having varying levels of regulatory authority in each trimester. In the first, in consultation with a doctor, women had a right to terminate an unwanted pregnancy; in the second, states could regulate when it related to the health of the mother; in the third, states could prohibit abortion (except when it was necessary to preserve the mother's health).

Justices Burger, Douglas, and Stewart concurred, while Justices Rehnquist and White dissented. Rehnquist granted states more latitude in regulating abortion. He also claimed that an explicit grant of a right to privacy was nowhere to be found in the Constitution. White complained that Blackmun's opinion "disentitled" states from making the exclusively political decision of weighing the development of the fetus versus the impact on the mother.

Blackmun went to lengths to try to explain that the court was not providing "abortion on demand." In fact, he originally drafted a statement that was not part of the opinion that he read on the day *Roe* was issued. It reads, "The Court does not today hold that the Constitution compels abortion on demand. It does not today pronounce that a pregnant woman has an absolute right to an abortion."[7] It made no difference. For pro-lifers, relatively unrestricted first-trimester abortions meant abortion on demand.

Expectation #1: Surface-Level Indicators

Unpacking national opinion on abortion in the early 1970s is complex. There was no pro-life majority, but there was an anti-*Roe* majority. The two categories are different, and the latter existed before

Roe but only revealed itself after the decision. That is, it was not that more than half the nation identified as strictly antiabortion. Rather, more than half opposed the details of *Roe v. Wade*.

The most telling indicator of an anti-*Roe* majority is public opinion polls on the regulatory trimesters taken before Blackmun wrote his opinion with that framework. Five months before *Roe* was decided, a Harris poll found that 46 percent opposed, and 42 percent supported, first-trimester abortions.[8] Mere weeks before *Roe*, Gallup reported that 45 percent opposed, and 46 percent supported, first-trimester abortions.[9]

Other public opinion tallies, before and after the decision, suggest that a majority was likely dissatisfied with the particulars of *Roe v. Wade*. Two months before *Roe*, Gallup found that 58 percent opposed liberalizing abortion policy.[10] Nearly two-thirds (65.5 percent) opposed laws permitting second – and third-trimester abortions.[11] A clear majority (64–67 percent) believed that life began either at conception or at "quickening" (i.e., around the end of the first trimester).[12] Only one-third (33 percent) approved government funding of abortion. And on the whole, a majority of Americans consistently disapproved of elective abortions.[13]

What should we make of these figures? One interpretation is that the issue presented a "nonmajoritarian" difficulty in that neither side could conclusively claim that they represented the dominant position.[14] In fact, precisely because national pro-life *or* pro-choice policy would have resulted in a large contingent becoming upset, members of Congress claimed that abortion was a "judicial issue," to be resolved by appointed federal judges not subject to retention elections. In other words, policymakers willfully passed the buck—this was especially true in the Democratic Party, where abortion preferences were split between liberals and conservatives (e.g., Catholics and southerners).[15] While Democrats wanted the court to decide the issue for coalitional reasons, my research demonstrates that a different majority (made up of southern Democrats, Catholic Democrats, and Republicans) disagreed with the outcome of *Roe*. In other words, southern and Catholic Democrats might have wanted the court to weigh in; they just wanted a different judicial result.

Was there a pro-life majority? Possibly. But, again, I make the more qualified claim that instead of an identifiable and consolidated pro-life majority before *Roe*, there was a reactionary anti-*Roe* majority that emerged after the decision. At the very least, there were pockets of the country where a majority did seem to oppose the court's decision. Fifteen polls from thirteen states showed a district majority opposed to *Roe*, in favor of a constitutional amendment to prohibit abortions, or in favor of letting states decide the matter. For example, in Ohio's Eighth Congressional District, 67.3 percent of respondents opposed *Roe*. In Texas's Seventh Congressional District, 61 percent wanted states to have jurisdiction over abortion policy.[16]

Perhaps it was these district-wide polls that caused some lawmakers to claim that *Roe* was countermajoritarian. More than the other issues discussed, congressional debate on abortion centered on moral arguments and not institutional complaints. Only a few members of Congress directly raised the countermajoritarian or accountability arguments, such as George O'Brien, who said, "A majority of the nation's citizenry oppose the easy abortion practices which the *Roe* decision mandates."[17]

Expectation #2: Nonleading Faction Response

Southern and northern conservative Democrats' responses to abortion was different from those groups' reactions to other issues. Whereas southern Democrats accounted for a majority of court-curbing proposals on prayer and busing, northern conservative Democrats took the lead on abortion. In fact, southern Democratic contributions to the collective assault on the *Roe* court were paltry. From 1973 to 1984, southern Democrats sponsored only nine abortion-related attacks.

More than any other faction, southern Democratic politicians recognized that abortion politics were a landmine. With rare candor, Representative Dale Milford (D-TX) admitted as much, saying, "I cannot possibly cast a vote on the abortion issue without making a large number of people in my district very angry . . . It's a no-win situation."[18] As such, in the initial years after *Roe*, southern Democratic representatives and senators—at least when compared with other conservatives in Congress—were more likely to complain about procedure (e.g., states' rights) than substance (e.g., life begins at conception).

Make no mistake, southerners opposed easier access to abortions. But instead of portraying the dominant southern opinion as "fixedly" pro-life in the 1970s, it would be more accurate to say that it "trended" that way. The sharp traditionalism on abortion that would characterize the New Right base of the South did not come about until the Reagan or George H. W. Bush years.[19] In 1973, when *Roe* came out, this wing of the GOP was far from an identifiable, consolidated, and organized movement (discussed later). Put simply, there was no monolithic hard-line southern position.

While southern Democrats disagreed with each other on the conditions under which the government should and should not restrict abortion, one unifying theme did emerge: that legislatures should implement *some* restrictions. Early congressional votes on abortion skirted the main issue, but they still reveal southern Democratic conservatism on the issue. For example, in 1973 Congress voted on a "right to conscience" provision that prohibited hospitals from compelling their employees to perform abortions; southern Democrats in the Senate voted 19–1 (95 percent) in favor; and those in the House voted 55–3 (95 percent). The same year, the House amended the incorporation of the Legal Services Corporation (LSC, which helped those who could not afford counsel) to provide a right-of-conscience provision for pro-life lawyers. Southern Democrats voted 53–4 (93 percent in favor) on that amendment. Later, the House further banned LSC funds from being used on litigation that sought to procure, or provide facilities for, an abortion. Southern Democrats voted 61–6 (91 percent) in favor of the ban (see table 6.2).

Within the larger abortion issue, these were marginal bills. In truth, southern Democrats were the most flexible members of Congress, and they tried to strike creative compromises between and within parties to avoid destructive fault lines (discussed subsequently). It was not until special interest pro-life leaders merged

Catholics into a coalition with evangelicals that the South became the pro-life bastion we know it as today.

Catholics' antiabortion views are well known. Even before *Roe*, the Catholic Church had committed itself to strict opposition. Pope Paul VI's *Humane Vitae* from 1968 reads, "Abortion[s], even for therapeutic reasons, are to be absolutely excluded as a lawful means of regulating the number of children." Stateside, the National Conference of Catholic Bishops (NCCB) declared, "Reverence for life demands freedom from direct interruption of life once it is conceived. Conception initiates a process whose purpose is the realization of human personality. A human person, nothing more and nothing less, is always at issue once conception has taken place."[20]

The NCCB issued a "Pastoral Plan for Pro-Life Activities," which declared that the court had violated the moral order. They called for the passage of a constitutional amendment and for federal and state law "that will restrict the practice of abortion as much as possible."[21] Meanwhile, the NCCB created the Family Life Bureau, which set out to build a network of information distributors and donors. The bureau then created the National Right to Life Committee (NRLC)—the self-proclaimed "nation's oldest and largest pro-life organization."[22]

With direct support from the NCCB, the NRLC was an instant, if somewhat haphazard, force in abortion politics. It oversaw protests in all fifty states and was most strongly felt, naturally, in those states that had a significant Catholic presence. In Michigan and Connecticut, for example, the church organized successful parish-by-parish efforts to block liberal abortion bills.

The NCCB managed early lobbying efforts in Congress, too. They coordinated pro-life organizations in all 435 congressional districts. They helped write pro-life legislation, encouraged constitutional amendment proposals, and considered judicial paths for overturning *Roe*. At the presidential level, the NCCB held private meetings with both Gerald Ford and Jimmy Carter to encourage both parties to adopt a pro-life plank in their 1976 platforms. The Democratic Party platform disagreed with the NCCB's position, stating, "It is undesirable to attempt to amend the US Constitution to overturn the Supreme Court decision in this area." The GOP assented, and its platform recommended "a constitutional amendment to protect the unborn." This matched the NCCB's belief that "a pro-life constitutional amendment [was] a priority of the highest order."[23] No wonder, then, that Archbishop Joseph Bernardin—the central figure in political negotiations between the parties and the church—threw his support behind Ford. Responding to the Democratic plan, the archbishop expressed "outrage."[24]

Catholic elites were unified in opposition to *Roe*. Archbishop Francis J. Furey called the justices in the majority "fetal muggers."[25] Cardinal John Krol of Philadelphia said it was "bad logic and bad law." The Reverend Monsignor James T. McHugh called it "terrifying" and predicted it would "energize the pro-life movement rather than destroy it." Cardinal Terrence Cooke's condemnation touched nearly every procedural anti-*Roe* argument: "Seven men have made a tragic utilitarian judgment regarding who shall live and who shall die. They have made themselves a 'super legislature.' They have gone against the will of those American people who spoke their minds in favor of life as recently as last November in referendums in Michigan and North Dakota. They have usurped the powers and responsibilities of the legislatures of 50 states to protect human life." In an unprecedented move, American Catholic leaders called for civil disobedience of any proabortion law.[26]

Major Catholic publications expressed disapproval. The *Catholic Lawyer* likened it to *Dred Scott*. The *Wanderer* called for William Brennan's excommunication. *Triumph* urged Catholics to unite with evangelicals. Both *America* and *Commonweal* criticized the decision after its release.[27]

Catholics in-the-pews opposed *Roe*. Table 6.1 shows 1976 ANES data on the proportion of Catholics who, according to party identification, answered questions with pro-life and pro-choice responses. In total, 71.9 percent of Catholics took a pro-life-oriented stance. Partisanship was not the driving force at the time of the survey. In fact, "Strong Democrats" were more likely to be against abortion than any other group.[28]

TABLE 6.1 Catholics Opinions on Abortion

Party ID	Pro-Choice	Pro-life
Strong Democrat	19.1%	80.9%
Weak Democrat	24.3%	75.7%
Independent Democrat	40.3%	59.7%
Independent independent	35.2%	64.8%
Independent Republican	35.6%	64.4%
Weak Republican	29.5%	70.5%
Strong Republican	20.6%	79.4%
TOTAL	28.1%	71.9%

Northern Democratic congressional roll calls on early abortion issues provide one indicator of the unerupted fault line. Table 6.2 breaks down congressional votes on funding bans for LSC legal services in abortion litigation and for abortion services themselves. As expected, Republicans and southern Democrats supported funding bans. But the table also shows that many northern Democrats had misgivings about pro-choice positions.

TABLE 6.2 Congressional Votes on Abortion

Group	Legal Services Corp	Hyde
Republican	94%	91%
Southern Democrat	90%	85%
Northern Conservative Democrat	92%	79%
Liberal Democrat	38%	32%
TOTAL	301–68 (81%)	290–91 (76%)

In time, partisanship became the primary determinant in abortion funding votes. But in the immediate aftermath of *Roe v. Wade*, the DNC had not clearly articulated the party line on abortion. In the absence of mandates from party leaders, many factors influenced politicians' positions. We might think northern conservative Democrats from, say, Massachusetts voted against funding abortion because such positions would win points with their heavily Catholic constituency. Or perhaps they voted pro-life because they themselves were stridently pro-life. Speculations aside, these votes showcase the split in the party: it was not simply regional. Northern conservative Democrats—especially Catholics—did not adhere to nascent pro-choice norms in their coalition. I describe subsequently how the pro-life movement and GOP mobilized these northern conservatives. For now, I simply point out that a sizable faction of northern conservative (likely Catholic) Democrats stood in opposition to liberal copartisans.

Expectation #3: Minority Party Response

The GOP did not immediately assume a monolithic pro-life stance, but the early internal splits on abortion were neither as deep nor as durable as the fault line in the Democratic Party. Republicans were much less likely to struggle with abortion positions—both personally and as a party. Moreover, Republicans led the court-curbing efforts on abortion, both in quantity and in organizing pro-life congressional forces.

As with previous liberal court decisions, *Roe* drew an immediate response from congressional Republicans. The first attack was nine days after *Roe's* release. In 1973 alone, Republican MCs introduced twenty-six abortion-related attacks on the Supreme Court. From 1973 to 1980, they introduced 128 such resolutions.

When debating the court-curbing bills, Republicans pressed arguments that matched the philosophical and religious beliefs put forward by southerners and Catholics. For instance, Republicans echoed the long-standing southern Democrat complaint that the court usurped a legislative power and trampled on states' rights.[29] These arguments were probably not advanced with the same vehemence as those, say, after *Brown*. But as time wore on, and as pro-life positions became more important to Republican politicians, they would become more important.

A small handful of Republican politicians made an additional argument against abortion: they said it was yet another in a line of liberal decisions that undermined conservative values. Just as conservatives had linked desegregation to communism or prayer to busing, they now connected abortion to a general decline in morality. Angelo Roncallo (R-NY) stated, "The abortion culture that has grown in the United States since the Supreme Court decision extends far beyond the abortion issue itself." Obviously alluding to sexuality and homosexuality, John Zwach (R-MN) said *Roe* "would be following in the footsteps of Sodom and Gomorrah." Marjorie Holt (R-MD) asked, "What will be the effect of unrestricted abortions upon the family structure and our value system?"[30] School prayer, Christian education, sexuality, homosexuality, family values, obscenity— Republicans linked abortion to all of these. As will be shown, these efforts later evolved into conscious—and successful—attempts to attract conservative Democrats by uniting seemingly disparate issues.

Outside of verbal assaults and hopeless constitutional amendments, Republicans made other important, if small, forays into abortion politics. President Nixon changed the Department of Defense's policy regarding abortions in military hospitals.[31] Previously, any military hospital could perform a therapeutic abortion, regardless of the law of the state in which the military hospital was located. Nixon changed the policy such that hospitals would have to follow the laws of the home states. In announcing the new policy, the president used emerging pro-life catchphrases, such as maintaining "the sanctity of human life—including the life of the yet unborn." Adviser Pat Buchanan had recommended the reversal because abortion was "a rising issue and a gut issue with Catholics" and would help Nixon steal voters from George McGovern.[32]

The first major fight on abortion—on the 1977 Hyde Amendment that prohibited funding of the procedure—helped the GOP consolidate the party's emerging pro-life position. Both chambers had passed separate health, education, and welfare funding packages, and Senate liberals would not concede to the House's passage of the Hyde Amendment.[33] Senate liberals insisted on a House revote. It failed 164–252 (Republicans voting 29–113). Soon thereafter, the Senate dropped its provision for funding abortions in cases of mental illness, genetic damage to the fetus, and statutory rape. The only exceptions were for rape and incest, which had to be reported promptly to prevent women from falsely claiming rape or incest to secure a subsidized abortion. In cases where the woman's health was negatively (but not mortally) affected, the House included language requiring the consent of two doctors. Moreover, the House changed the Senate's original language from "severe *or* long lasting physical health damage" to "severe *and* long lasting." Thus, abortions could not be funded if damage was minor and/or short-lived. In short, the resulting negotiations resulted in a major conservative victory.

Throughout the Hyde debate, Democrats tried to find a solution that would avoid a national debate. Southern Democrats led the efforts to compromise, likely because they appreciated abortion's ability to shake the social issues fault line with their party.[34] House Republicans repeatedly rebuffed these efforts and held their hard line. Northern Democrats, meanwhile, grew increasingly frustrated and torn. Representative Dave Obey (D-WI) claimed "20 or 30" members of Congress told him that various iterations of the Hyde bill were reasonable compromises but that "they just couldn't vote for it . . . if you compromise at all, you spend half your life explaining why. People just didn't want to have to go through that." For his part, Speaker of the House Tip O'Neill (D-MA) refused to whip House Democrats into voting for compromises. He claimed he "just can't twist the wrists" on the abortion issue.[35]

Both politicians and lobbyists understood that pro-lifers had won the standoff. Pro-choice group National Association to Repeal Abortion Laws called the final bill "inhumane";[36] the Women's Lobby admitted that they had lost sight of how narrow the bill had become. The National Committee for a Human Life Amendment called it a two-thirds victory and presciently concluded, "The most important aspect of this entire thing is that the pro-life movement established itself as a major political force."[37]

This early battle shone light on how the GOP could use abortion to build a national majority, and Republican leaders recognized the coalition-building potential of pro-life politics. The earliest, strongest, and most continuous calls for pursuing a pro-life political agenda came from the Nixon administration.[38] Many focused on winning new Catholic votes. Pat Buchanan suggested the strategy before *Roe* and repeated it throughout his tenure as senior adviser. He pushed Nixon on the conservative military abortion policy, saying the president's stance "should be made public and strong."[39] Buchanan also convinced Nixon to send a letter to Cardinal Cooke expressing gratitude for the Catholic Church's campaign to fight abortion. Behind the scenes, Buchanan encouraged the cardinal to leak the letter, which announced to the public, "this is a matter for state decision" and that "unrestricted abortion policies . . . seem to me impossible to reconcile with . . . our religious traditions."[40] After the letter was made public, those in the administration publicized it further. Henry Cashen, deputy counsel to the president, penned separate memos indicating he worked with Cardinal Patrick O'Boyle, archbishop of Washington, DC, on pro-life campaigns, as well as with the Knights of Columbus to adopt a resolution at their national convention thanking Nixon for his positions on abortion. Other Nixon officials pursued further publicity (on the Knights' commendation and other pro-life episodes) in Catholic journals.[41]

The 1972 election gave the GOP the chance to paint the Democratic Party as liberal on abortion. Buchanan specifically targeted the type of Catholics "who join the K. of C. [Knights of Columbus] . . . who fight against abortion in their legislatures . . . they are where our votes are."[42] High-level strategist Kevin Phillips predicted that "betting on traditional values" would "woo conservative Catholics, senior citizens, and other traditionalists."[43] Even when George McGovern tried to hedge on abortion, GOP leaders were confident that Catholics knew his pro-choice preferences, in part because "Republicans won't let them forget it."[44]

Granted, party strategists understood the trade-off of pro-life stances—that they would *lose* some voters. Phillips mentioned that traditionalist stances would alienate "upper-middle and upper-class GOP liberals." Cashen believed those voters were already not going to vote Republican and that pro-life stances might help turn those "who might be inclined to support the president." Buchanan, in particular, was fine with those "far-left losses." "The women's libbers would moan and groan about this," he wrote, "but, this group we never had, and never will have." In another note, he wrote, "But in terms of those who will vote for or against on the basis of this one issue, it is clearly a political windfall—as it is 'the' issue to tens of thousands of conservative Catholic Democrats." In the early 1970s, Buchanan's bottom-line math—"there is tradeoff but it leaves us with the larger share of the pie"—was likely correct.[45]

Grassroots Pushback

Some state legislatures passed antiabortion laws, many of which were within the bounds of the court's decision (e.g., regulating in the second and third trimesters). Given that so many laws (189 in 1973 alone) were proposed immediately after *Roe*, it is clear that states were reacting against the ruling.[46]

The combined effect of post-*Roe* abortion legislation in the fifty states was substantial.[47] Some states, in fact, passed statutes that outright defied *Roe*. Rhode Island guaranteed Fourteenth Amendment equal protection to unborn children. Montana declared its existing state laws valid until those specific laws were struck down by a court. North Dakota and Arkansas banned abortions—even in the first trimester—with the only exception being to save the life of the woman.

Most bills, though, sought to deter abortion rather than ban it outright.[48] States closed facilities offering abortions, discouraged insurance providers from covering abortions, and restricted medical schools from teaching abortion procedures. Second-trimester abortion availability, coverage, and training became rarer.[49] Table 6.3 highlights some of the other restrictions on abortion after *Roe*.

On the whole, *Roe* might have made first-trimester abortions easier to obtain, but as a 1984 study commented, because of the statutes passed in response to *Roe*, "many women still find it difficult or impossible to obtain abortion services."[50] Pro-life organizations in the 1970s found these restrictive measures to be substantive victories. They still pushed for items such as a constitutional amendment or judges who would overturn *Roe*. But "incrementalist" pro-lifers

TABLE 6.3 Abortion Restrictions

Restriction	Explanation	State
Residency requirement	Must be a resident of the state to perform an abortion	TN
Support for amendment	Resolution dictating state support to amend US Constitution to overrule *Roe*	NE
Define viability	Narrow the window before which the fetus becomes "viable"	MN, KY, PA, UT
Parental consent	Minors must secure parental consent to obtain an abortion	FL, KY, OR, SD, PA, CO, UT, MA
Paternal consent	Women must secure consent from the father to obtain an abortion	PA, MO, WA
Civil liability	Practitioners cannot be held liable for refusing to provide abortions	ME, CA, SD, UT
Right of conscience	Practitioners can refuse to provide abortions if they are morally/religiously opposed	KY, NE, AZ, NY
Reporting requirements	Practitioners must report information on women who procured abortions	PA
State Hyde amendments	States will not provide funding for abortions	Many

turned away from solely opposing all abortions and toward seeking meaningful and possible victories. Indeed, while the quest to appoint Supreme Court justices who would overturn *Roe* garnered half a century of publicity, it was at the margins where pro-lifers experienced the most success.[51] One legal scholar has called these efforts an "evisceration" of privacy rights.[52]

Congressional Pushback

In clear up-or-down votes from 1973 to 1983 on abortion itself (and not on tertiary issues such as the Hyde Amendment), Congress showed close splits. In 1981 Jesse Helms (R-NC) introduced a measure that would have declared that "human life shall be deemed to exist from conception." Practically, the measure sought to prohibit lower federal courts from granting injunctions against states or localities that prohibited, regulated, or defunded abortions. Also in 1981, Orrin Hatch (R-UT) proposed a constitutional amendment to grant concurrent power to Congress and the states to restrict and prohibit abortions. In cases where state law was more restrictive, it would be considered supreme. Moreover, the Hatch Amendment "declare[d] that the Constitution does not secure a right to abortion." Both proposals received extensive and emotional committee hearings. And both were reported out of committee by narrow margins: 3–2 for the Helms Amendment and 10–7 for the Hatch Amendment. The Hatch Amendment was soon buried, but Helms maneuvered his proposal to a key tabling vote. It was close: 47–46 to table. Republicans voted 19–33 in favor. Democrats voted 28–13 in favor, with southern Democrats voting 6–5.

In 1983 a Human Life Amendment seeking to overturn *Roe v. Wade* came to a vote. It registered a 49–50 split in the Senate—clearly below the two-thirds needed to amend the Constitution but again indicative of the narrow division between those on different sides of the abortion issue. Republicans voted 34–19 in favor. Democrats voted 15–31 (8–6 for southern Democrats).

Meanwhile, the House introduced a constitutional amendment in 1983 that would ban all abortions except when the life of the mother would be endangered. When the bill became bogged down in four separate committees, its supporters filed for discharge motions. We do not have official data on how many representatives signed the discharge, but the bill had obtained seventy-eight cosponsors, which included twenty-two Democrats (three from the South and five from the five states with the highest percentages of Catholics) and fifty-six Republicans (forty from the South and six from the five Catholic states).

The aforementioned proposals represent as close to an up-or-down vote as Congress would have on banning abortion outright. Their tallies accurately portray the closeness on abortion with which both chambers struggled. Put simply, what would become a *deep* division in American politics started off as a *narrow* division. The slimmest of majorities in the House and Senate seemed reticent to overturn *Roe* wholesale. Yet, a different majority acted repeatedly to scale back the decision. As mentioned, a coalition of Republicans, southern Democrats, and northern conservative Democrats (e.g., Catholics) consistently nipped at the margins of *Roe v. Wade*. They barred the LSC from representing litigants in abortion cases, passed right-of-conscience laws, withheld federal funding of abortions, and allowed for conscientious objections. In sum, some in Congress might not have been ready to overturn *Roe*, but they were eager to attack it.

Electoral Pushback, Part 1: Building the Pro-Life Coalition
Roe initiated a developmental course that galvanized the pro-life movement, which took some time to consolidate but eventually helped transform abortion politics in a way that had durable electoral repercussions in two ways. First, it turned some reliably conservative Democrats (northern and southern) into single-issue voters who switched to the GOP solely because of their pro-life preferences.[53] Second, it was likely the tipping point for other conservative Democrats (again, in both regions) who had endured a consistent line of liberal Supreme Court decisions (starting with *Brown* or communism, and continuing with school prayer, crime, and busing).[54] Along with other issues in the political system, I put forward that the electoral repercussions of developing abortion politics played a role in paving the way for the Reagan Revolution. In what follows, I discuss the development of the pro-life movement via the Catholic Church and the emerging "New Right." I then discuss the ways in which it affected electoral politics.

Catholic Church Leadership
Prior to *Roe*, the Catholic Church had done much to fight abortion. Pro-life organizations existed well before *Roe v. Wade*, but the general belief was that antiabortion lobbying was primarily a Catholic effort.[55] Cardinal Cooke's letter to Richard Nixon on military abortions helped publicize the earliest salient federal abortion episode. The

church also helped lead the way in publicizing George McGovern's pro-choice tendencies on abortion.[56]

The Catholic Church was instrumental in funding and helping to organize the defeat of two 1972 state referenda in North Dakota and Michigan that would have made abortion legal. The Michigan initiative involved a dramatic turn of events. When first introduced, polls indicated that voters supported the referendum 57–37. Understanding that they might lose at the ballot box, the Michigan Catholic Conference sued to stop the referendum wholesale. After losing in court, they teamed with other pro-life organizations to mobilize opposition to the measure. The tide-turning moment came when pro-lifers publicized that abortions could be obtained up to twenty weeks into a woman's pregnancy. They combined that fact with images of eighteen – and nineteen-week-old fetuses. When the measure failed 61–39, the *Detroit Free Press* called it "one of the most startling and successful campaigns in Michigan political history."[57]

The Catholic Church's initial post-*Roe* activity was at the policy level—lobbying to enact pro-life guidelines, legislation, and court rulings. In 1975, the church entered the electoral fray to try to influence the selection of pro-life politicians. Their first test was the elections of 1976, and although they were not completely successful, they were encouraged by some of the effects. Specifically, as discussed earlier, the NCCB lobbied both parties to adopt a pro-life plank. More broadly, the NCCB politicized abortion in a way such that presidential candidates could no longer sidestep the issue.[58] Put differently, the NCCB was instrumental in forcing possible candidates for president to declare their respective stance on abortion. This itself barred candidates—especially Democrats—from avoiding an issue that might split their base. Table 6.4 indicates many of the candidates who did run or considered running for president in 1976 and their view on abortion.[59]

We might think the campaign to force candidates to declare their positions would have had the most profound effect on Gerald Ford, in part because of his wife Betty Ford's support for *Roe v. Wade*.[60] After all, he won the GOP nomination and clearly leaned more pro-life than the other major party contender (Jimmy Carter). Yet, the

TABLE 6.4 1976 Presidential Candidates on Abortion

Candidate	Party	Stance
Gerald Ford	R	Constitutional amendment for states' rights; abortion for rape and life of the mother
Ronald Reagan	R	Opposed abortion
Sargent Shriver	D	Opposed abortion but not in favor of constitutional amendment
Jimmy Carter	D	Personally against abortion, but not in favor of constitutional amendment
George Wallace	D	Constitutional amendment
Milton Shapp (PA gov)	D	Blacklisted by pro-lifers for vetoing an anti-abortion law
Birch Bay (SJC Chair)	D	Refused to act on constitutional amendment
Henry Jackson	D	Opposed, but not in favor of constitutional amendment
Morris Udall	D	Supported *Roe*; opposed amendment
Fred Harris	D	Supported *Roe*; opposed amendment
Eugene McCarthy	I	Supported *Roe*
Robert Byrd	D	Constitutional amendment against abortion except in cases of rape or to save the mother's life
Ellen McCormack	D	Opposed abortion

NCCB's pressure probably had a greater effect on Ford's primary and general competitors.[61] For starters, despite having signed liberal abortion laws in 1967 as California's governor, Ronald Reagan came out early and strong against abortion in the 1976 campaign.[62] Also, whereas Ford preferred to devolve the issue to the states, Reagan argued more on the merits, arguing that abortion itself was wrong and should be constitutionally banned. Though it might have taken time, these stances, reinforced four years later, would help Reagan win a considerable number of Catholic votes.[63]

Additionally, Jimmy Carter's campaign was damaged by his prevarication on abortion. No one doubted that Jimmy Carter, a born-again evangelical, personally opposed the procedure. But his public stance and political commitment remained cloudy. In the early days of the primary, Iowa voters pressed Carter for his beliefs. He said he morally opposed abortion but did not support a constitutional amendment to ban it. Then, he hinted that he might support an amendment to ban some types of abortions. In one of the presidential debates with Ford, Carter finally offered the clearest articulation of his stance on abortion. Even then, he was accused of waffling.[64] Later, although the Democratic platform opposed an antiabortion constitutional amendment, Carter asked Catholic Democrat Joe Califano—who would later be appointed as HEW secretary and help thwart federal funding of abortions—to reach out to Catholic leaders and tell them of Carter's opposition to abortion and his intention to cut off funding. In the end, Ford and the GOP's pro-life stance might have disaffected pro-choice voters. But as Republican strategists had rightfully noted, those voters were likely to vote Democrat anyway. For Carter, though, there existed a sizable contingent of pro-life Democrats. He did not lose enough of them to overcome a wave of suspicion against the post-Watergate GOP. But key leaders in the Catholic Church (e.g., NCCB) and in politics (e.g., Ronald Reagan) experienced their first taste of abortion's effect in electoral politics.[65]

The Catholic Church led this initial post-*Roe* movement because it was the only nationally organized force.[66] A handful of organizations did represent conservative American Protestants, but the "New Right" (the Christian coalition we know in the twenty-first century) was unnamed, untapped, and unidentifiable. It certainly did not have clout to fight abortion on a national level. Moreover, there existed a schism between fundamentalists and more mainstream evangelicals (e.g., Billy Graham) over how literally to interpret the Bible. Beyond overcoming theological disputes, though, organizational problems presented the main obstacles.[67] They cut two ways. Some groups (such as the National Association of Evangelicals) had the membership, standing, and funds to tackle a pro-life agenda, but they did not focus exclusively (or at least focus enough) on abortion politics. Other groups might have focused on abortion, but they were either too regional (such as the Minnesota Citizens Concerned for Life) or plagued by start-up costs.[68]

The Catholic Church did not merely "fill the void" of leadership because mid-1970s conservative Protestants stood unable to lead the antiabortion charge. Rather, the Catholic Church took positive action. For starters, the church had fought abortion even before *Roe* and was already practiced in nationwide lobbying efforts. Going back to the 1960s, cardinals and bishops had been the earliest spokesmen of the pro-life movement. The church had identified state-level battles and contributed resources to fight against pro-choice measures.[69] *America, Commonweal,* the *National Catholic Reporter,* and the *Wanderer* all opposed abortion before 1973. The NRLC submitted an amicus brief during *Roe.*

Perhaps the most important reason why the Catholic Church led the early pro-life movement was the inherently hierarchal structure of the church. With a top-down organizational model, the church could mobilize more easily than, say, congregationalist churches or municipal organizations. American Catholic cardinals and bishops dictated the church's stance on abortion. The NRLC led the fact-finding, coordination, and communication efforts. And, perhaps most importantly, taking their orders from above, local parishes provided the on-the-ground drumbeating necessary for any grassroots movement to work. Take three examples, two from before *Roe* and one afterward.

In 1970 the Catholic Church in California mobilized against Democrats after the party adopted a pro-choice plank for the state platform. On August 30, 1970, Catholic priests across Orange County organized voting registrars to set up tables outside their respective churches. Parishioners then listened to a homily asking all Democratic members of the congregation to change their party affiliation to protest the abortion plank of their party. The strategy worked. For example, in Santa Ana, 530 parishioners became Republicans.[70]

In 1972 the Catholic Church played a major role in transforming public opinion in Michigan to help defeat the referendum that would have liberalized abortion law (discussed previously). Presbyterian Richard Jaynes sought to unite more than two dozen pro-life groups in Michigan. But the pro-life campaign did not consolidate until the Michigan Catholic Conference stepped in. The conference encouraged priests to devote two preelection Sundays to preaching on abortion. They also appealed to local Catholic churches to raise more than $200,000 for the campaign. Parish leaders received information kits, which included tips on advertising the pro-life agenda, pamphlets for distribution that featured color photographs of fetal development, and a twelve-minute slideshow. It is not a stretch to say that the measure owed its defeat not only to the central leadership of the Michigan Catholic Conference but also to the decentralized response of priests and congregants.[71]

After *Roe*, the NCCB (to whom the NRLC reported) announced their Pastoral Plan for Pro-Life Activities. It included involving every parish in the country organizing prayer drives, providing education on abortion, and actively pursuing pro-life political efforts in all three branches. Each parish was encouraged to set up their own decentralized pro-life committee, which would report to diocese leaders. Above them sat officials who monitored district – and statewide politics. These officials maintained files on every elected official and potential candidate's abortion positions.[72]

New Right Coalition between Catholics and Evangelicals

The modern New Right—the religiously motivated coalition of Christian conservatives within the Republican Party—did not exist during or immediately after *Roe*.[73] In fact, in the mid-1970s, the Catholic Church's stance on abortion was so high profile that many believed that the pro-life movement was synonymous with the church.[74] To wit, the justices themselves viewed opposition to abortion as an exclusively Catholic belief.[75] Catholics fought this perception. Before *Roe*, the New Jersey Catholic Conference asked, "Are Catholics the only ones against abortion?"[76] And even though they provided anecdotal evidence of non-Catholic pro-lifers, the very asking of the question shows the confluence of religious identity and antiabortion activism.

Moreover, most politicos considered Catholic involvement as a single-issue campaign against abortion. In the early 1970s the perception was that the church did not have a broader social conservative message; they fought solely against abortion. Greenhouse and Siegel's documentary collection of abortion material repeatedly refer to the Catholic Church's early-1970s efforts as "single-issue."[77] And while today's American Catholics has come to express liberal (e.g., firearms, death penalty) and conservative opinions (e.g., free exercise, abortion) on a wide variety of issues, in the immediate aftermath of *Roe*, the church's hierarchy was primarily—if not solely—concerned with abortion.

As the 1970s progressed, however, the Catholic Church did not want to be singularly synonymous with pro-life politics. More accurately, the church did not want pro-life politics to be singularly synonymous with Catholicism. Catholic leaders wisely realized that for the pro-life movement to have a wide and lasting political and electoral effect, it had to reach beyond their own congregations.[78] In the late 1970s, pro-life efforts decoupled from the church because of two groups' efforts: (1) Catholics actively courted other socially conservative Christians; (2) other socially conservative Christians came to realize their commonalities with Catholics.

Even before *Roe*, Catholic leaders understood the importance of attracting non-Catholics. As early as 1968, the NCCB grounded abortion not only in Catholic theology but also in ecumenical "Judeo-Christian traditions inspired by love for life."[79] Immediately after *Roe*, the NRLC sought to attract non-Catholics to the pro-life cause. They created an interfaith/intergroup committee, which looked for opportunities to do pro-life workshops at Bible colleges and to work cooperatively with evangelical leaders. Yet, the NRLC resolved not to take up "biblical tracks" and "sectarian issues," which might attract "one or two religions" but would alienate others. They hoped to appeal a broad base of religionists: conservative evangelicals who would be naturally attracted by the pro-life stances and mainstream Protestants who could sign on because the NRLC reined in its anti-contraception message. They even adopted resolutions that expanded their directorate to non-Catholic pro-lifers. Indeed, by 1974, they elected a Mormon as director of the executive committee, which also contained an Episcopalian, a Baptist, and two Presbyterians. The goal was to get the NRLC away from representing a purely Catholic point of view and toward taking the lead in representing all pro-lifers.[80]

Early Catholic efforts to attract other pro-lifers largely failed. Part of the problem was Protestant suspicion of all things Catholic. Pro-choice groups strategically played up these misgivings. The founder of NARAL unleashed harsh anti-Catholic vitriol meant to link the pro-life movement to the church. In 1976 the pro-choice Religious Coalition for Abortion Rights sought to convince evangelicals into thinking they were assuming Catholic dogma.[81] It worked. For instance, the chairman of the Southern Baptist Convention's Christian Life Commission believed that the crusade against abortion was a Catholic conspiracy.[82]

Thus, in the early and mid-1970s, the Catholic Church might have been ready to unite with evangelicals. But evangelicals remained skeptical of allying with Catholic organizations. It was not until 1978–79 that evangelicals took their first steps in creating a con-solidated Christian pro-life movement. A host of abortion-related developments came together around 1978–79 that would push evangelicals—especially southern evangelicals who had historically voted Democrat—toward the GOP.[83] In short, conservative activ-ists assisted with organizational and financial ties between the two Christian sects. The key to the alliance was not just abortion but an overarching conservative ideology that encompassed pro-life posi-tions. More than just an advocate for conservatism, the New Right sought to be an electoral force.[84] The Republican Party transformed it into a partisan bloc by offering a platform that wedded many of their concerns—not the least of which was abortion.

Perhaps no one was more responsible for southern Protestant realignment than a pair of blue-collar Catholics, Paul Weyrich and Richard Viguerie.[85] Weyrich helped found the Heritage Foundation, a conservative think tank that still wields considerable influence in Washington. Viguerie was the originator of direct mail campaign contributions whereby he targeted carefully selected individuals with mass mailings both to advertise conservative positions and raise money in the form of small contributions from thousands of donors.[86] He was one of the first lobbyists to use computer databases, and he later became a leader in the conservative push to use internet funding and organization. Both experienced disillusionment with establishment Republicanism in the 1970s and sought to rebrand the party.[87]

Weyrich coordinated activism and communication between Evangelical leaders of different denominations, while Viguerie raised start-up money for the New Right via various political action committees (PACs). Together, the two helped organize the antiabortion Life Amendment Political Action Committee, which would become an organizational leader in pro-life politics.[88] Viguerie also worked with the National Conservative Political Action Committee, which raised far more money than liberal abortion PACs. By 1978 the pair's efforts had a noticeable effect on congressional elections. But their most lasting effect was showing that a rightward turn on abortion attracted more followers than the NRLC's previously more inclusive efforts. In other words, pro-life forces had more to gain by consolidating conservative voices than by seeking a broad-tent coalition.[89]

After the 1978 midterm elections, Weyrich and Viguerie advertised hard-line stances on abortion, which they connected to other issues of concern to evangelicals. Soon, they had the attention and alliance of major evangelical organizations, such as the Moral Majority, the Religious Roundtable, and Christian Voice. In 1979 they secured a sit-down with Jerry Falwell in Lynchburg, Virginia. There, the trio discussed how to split the Catholic bloc from the Democratic Party.[90] After meeting with Viguerie and Weyrich, Falwell said, "The Roman Catholic Church for many years has stood virtually alone against abortion. I think it's an indictment against the rest of us that we've allowed them to stand alone."[91]

Electoral Pushback, Part 2: Attracting the Pro-Life Coalition

Pro-life momentum helped create the conservative Catholic/evangelical alliance, but pro-life preferences also fit into a larger traditionalist political philosophy that sought to combat 1970s liberalism. This was the true genius in the construction of the New Right: abortion politics went from single-issue to a piece of an encompassing ideology that was broad enough for different people to take away different messages from it. At its core, the New Right advocated for a smaller federal government that would refrain from intruding into traditionalist family life, which had already come under attack from judicial activism, radical feminism, and communism. The Republican Party met these linkages by putting forward a similar overarching ideology.

The New Right's Connective Ideology
Foundational New Right ideologues worked to convince social conservatives (many of whom voted Democratic) that *Roe v. Wade* was not an outlier in an otherwise stable country. Instead, they portrayed the United States as losing its moral compass and producing a host of policies that hurt both the traditional family and the collective American citizenry. What might have started with pro-life positions grew into a broader critique of "secular humanism."[92] New Right activists attacked what they believed were interrelated parts of liberal America, including the gender revolution, a decline in family values, and a trend toward atheism.

Perhaps the most vocal opponents of the gender revolution of the 1970s were a cadre of conservative women activists, who ideologically linked radical feminism to pro-choice stances. Phyllis Schlafly stands out. She said abortion was connected to undermining traditional gender roles, homosexuality, and feminism, both of which were "antifamily goals."[93] Specifically, she tied the passage of the ERA to abortion. During the International Year of the Woman, Schlafly organized a counterconvention that protested the "common goals" of those enemies of the American family: "the ERAers, the abortionists, and the lesbians."[94] Schlafly particularly reached conservative evangelical homemakers by claiming that the ERA would force them into the workplace and the Selective Service. The ERA would not liberate these women; it would only make them more like men. Tapping into a latent antifeminism among conservative women, Schlafly inspired a generation of female evangelicals to take up the conservative mantle.

Consider Beverly LaHaye, who started Concerned Women for America (CWA), which today claims to be "the nation's largest public policy women's organization" that is "on the frontline" of "a cultural battle."[95] Her book, *The Spirit-Controlled Woman*, used Bible verses to advocate a more submissive role for women. Quoting St. Paul's letter to the Colossians, LaHaye explained that "I wasn't just picking up dirty socks for my husband; I was serving the Lord Jesus by doing this."[96] In total, Schlafly, LaHaye, and other anti-ERA women of the 1970s uncovered a value system that cut across issues and religions and allowed the New Right to unite antifeminists—especially female antifeminists—with pro-lifers.

New Right activists also linked abortion to a host of issues that they believed hurt the traditional American family. Abortion was present- ed as more of an effect—rather than a cause—of a decline in moral values. This deterioration led to other problems that liberals sanc- tioned: easier access to divorce, cohabitation of unmarried couples, drug use, increased sexual activity, access to obscenity, graphic sex education in school, a loss of a sense of community via busing, and, of course, abortion on demand. In addition, activists advertised that the nation stood on the verge of adopting radically liberal policies, such as same-sex marriage or allowing gender-neutral bathrooms. Underlying their belief in a decline in moral values was the claim that the country was becoming less rooted in religion. New Right propo- nents charged liberals with promoting atheism in the public schools, a growing separation of church and state, and a subversive commu- nism threatening American households and the nation as a whole.[97] They lambasted the elimination of school prayer. They warned fol- lowers that the government sought to shut down Christian education by taking away religious schools' tax-exempt status.[98]

These other planks of the New Right ideology—antifeminism, family values, and support for religion—connected to each other, and to abortion, in loose ways. This allowed ardent followers of one movement to dovetail into other conservative forays. Pro-lifers be- came antifeminists because they were convinced pro-choicers had allied with feminists. Today, CWA focuses on, among other things, "the family, the sanctity of human life, religious liberty, education, [and] national sovereignty."[99]

At the beginning of the New Right's formation, leaders proposed making abortion the "keystone of their organizing strategy, since this was the issue that could divide the Democratic Party."[100] On the flip side—and perhaps these organizers did not intend this—it fused together different conservative factions. It was an emotional issue that roused conservatives to mobilize where they otherwise might not have done so. Abortion was salient enough to unite Catholics with evangelicals in a durable way. And pro-life arguments struck at the Supreme Court, the punching bag of the New Right's procedural critiques of liberal overreach into American society and family life. True, abortion was not the only issue to cause shifts in voting, as short-term events always play a role.[101] In fact, Weyrich later claimed that abortion "wasn't sufficient" for the New Right's emergence.[102] He was likely correct. Nevertheless, *Roe* might not have been sufficient for the New Right's emergence, but it was probably necessary because it (1) had an independent effect that itself affected so many voters on a singular dimension and (2) brought together different kinds of conservatives (e.g., Catholics and evangelicals), after which they advertised united positions on other, nonabortion, conservative policies, such as:[103]

1. Law and order: anticommunism, tough on crime
2. Family values: prayer in schools, religious education, opposition to the ERA, opposition to sexual revolution, antihomosexuality, concerns about obscenity
3. Procedural judicial critiques: opposition to judicial activism, restoration of originalism
4. Procedural federal critiques: local rule, states' rights, antibusing[104]

Opposition to the federal government writ large, and especially to judicial activism, became a linchpin for the New Right and underlay all their policy concerns. The federal government intruded into matters either of local communities (e.g., school prayer, crime, busing) or of the family (e.g., abortion, relaxing divorce requirements, teaching about sex in schools). According to Weyrich, the New Right was held together by the "long-held conservative view that the government is too powerful and intrusive."[105] To New Right activists, the most egregious violator of limited government and states' rights was the Supreme Court, a collection of unelected and unaccountable judicial activists who sought to undemocratically impose not only their views but also their lifestyles on conservative households.

In part, New Right conservatives opposed judicial activism because court decisions went against their preferences. Thomas Keck has shown that the court can be both activist and conservative—and in those scenarios, conservatives might tolerate judicial decisions.[106] Regardless of procedural objections or substantive grievances, the call against judicial activism was an effective weapon in the New Right's coalition-building arsenal.

The Pro-Life Coalition and the 1970s

It took the GOP some time to assemble a comprehensive constitutional vision that would appeal to New Right conservatives. Nevertheless, we see some congressional Republicans (e.g., Marjorie Holt, John Zwach) immediately linked *Roe v. Wade* to other issues. In 1972—even before the court decided *Roe*—Senate Minority Leader Hugh Scott (R-PA) labeled George McGovern the "triple-A candidate," who stood for abortion, amnesty, and acid. Nixon operatives seized on the moniker and connected abortion to other issues.[107] For instance, in putting out a position flyer on abortion, Buchanan suggested that it also include Nixon and McGovern's stances on parochial schools and obscenity.[108] This fit Kevin Phillips's goal of attacking on "social morality" by linking McGovern to "a culture and morality that is anathema to Middle America."[109] In addition, some early 1970s Republicans also objected to what they saw as unwarranted judicial activism, an intrusion on legislative powers, or the trampling of states' rights. When writing to Cardinal Cooke about abortion, Nixon stated that he believed it was "a matter for state decision outside federal jurisdiction."[110]

These early linkages were a primitive form of what became a party-wide attempt to unite seemingly disparate issues under a common philosophical banner. The differences between the 1972 and 1976 Republican platforms provide the earliest glimpse at a winning philosophy that could tie single issues to notions of limited government and states' rights. In 1972 the party was, simply, "irrevocably opposed to busing." In 1976 it explained why busing was so bad: it turned local school boards into "bookkeepers" who could not navigate federal "red tape restrictive regulations." In 1972 the GOP announced, simply, "Voluntary prayer should be freely permitted." In 1976 prayer was a matter for "local communities," and thus the GOP sought to eliminate "bureaucratic control of the schools by Washington." The implication of these justifications was that not only did Republicans oppose busing and prayer— they also based their opposition on a notion of a federal government with very limited powers and a devolution of power back to states and localities.

The 1976 platform also contained a section labeled "The American Family," which was the GOP's first attempt to define a comprehensive set of social concerns. Under this heading, the party presented its abortion plank. Yet, the same paragraph that announced that the GOP "values human life" also mentioned "neighborhood schools" and "education systems that . . . are responsive to parents' concerns"— buzzwords and arguments used in the school prayer and busing debates. The paragraph also introduced financial concerns and called for "economic and employment policies that stimulate the creation of jobs so that families can plan for their economic security," as well as a "welfare policy to encourage rather than discourage families to stay together."

Although the 1976 platform took the GOP more toward the kind of comprehensive program that would ideologically and electorally unite different types of conservatives, it was still not a conscious partywide effort. The words were right, but the emphasis was off. The best indicator of this was Gerald Ford's 1976 presidential election campaign. At times, Ford seemed to understand the rhetorical linkages needed to be made to fuse together various wings of American conservatism in 1976. For example, in a presidential debate, the candidates were asked which of the proposed constitutional amendments before Congress they would support. Jimmy Carter said, "I honor the right of people to seek the constitutional amendments on school busing, on prayer in the schools, and on abortion, but . . . I won't actively work for the passage of any of them." Ford pointed to the GOP platform's position of an amendment that would outlaw abortions. Strangely, though, he also seemed to rebuke it by stating that he preferred an amendment that would hand the issue to the individual states. He gave a rambling answer about supporting a prayer amendment, too.[111] His response technically matched conservative voters' preferences, but he failed to tap into a larger ideological vision in a conscious, systematic way that mobilized voting behavior.

The Pro-Life Coalition and the Rise of Reagan

The problem in 1976 (aside from the lingering effects of Watergate) might have been that Republican Party leaders did not understand the factional breakdown within the electorate.[112] Conservatives comprised a majority of the electorate (or at least a majority within some salient issues). Yet, the GOP failed to garner enough of their votes to take control of Washington. This was a problem for the Republican Party, and even articulating it took time. Finally, in 1977 Ronald Reagan issued a challenge that would become a turning point in American political development. He said:

> The so-called social issues—law and order, abortion, busing, quota systems—are usually associated with the blue collar, ethnic, and religious groups [that] are traditionally associated with the Democratic Party. The economic issues—inflation, deficit spending, and big government—are usually associated with the Republican Party . . . The time has come to see if it is possible to present a program of action based on political principle that can attract those interested in the so called "social" issues and those interested in the "economic" issues. In short, isn't it possible to combine the two major segments of contemporary American conservatism into one political effective whole?[113]

The speech came from the right person at the right time in the right place. A Republican primary candidate in 1976, Reagan had been the darling of the New Right just a year before the speech. Finding Gerald Ford not conservative enough, New Right activists had turned to alternative candidates for the GOP nomination. Not wanting to hitch their ideological wagons to the race-fueled rhetoric of George Wallace, and after some waffling, they threw their support behind Reagan. When he lost the nomination to Ford, they tried to mount a third-party campaign for Reagan, who rejected the request. Still, New Right leaders saw Reagan as a viable challenger for the 1980 race.[114] In 1977 they asked him to speak at the relatively new Conservative Political Action Conference (CPAC). Only in its second year, CPAC might not have been as well-known as it is today. But important leaders in the New Right movement still attended. Moreover, Reagan's call came only a year after Ford lost to Carter. It gave conservatives (candidates and activists) nearly an entire presidential term to develop a strategy that could win electoral majorities. In sum, the speech was nothing short of prophetic.

Fittingly, then, it would be Reagan who presided over putting together a "program of action based on political principle" that would unite the "the two major segments of American conservatism." Of course, economic conservatives had long been part of the Republican coalition—especially after the New Deal. But Reagan made a special effort to court social conservatives, and in 1980, he presided over the construction of a comprehensive constitutional vision (that of an original intent understanding of limited government and states' rights) that appealed to a new, larger, coalition of conservatives. In fact, more than any substantive policy issue area, this philosophical argument itself might have been the primary goal that fueled Republican ascendancy in the late twentieth and early twenty-first century.[115]

Devolution (i.e., returning power to the states) and originalism abound in Reagan's 1980 campaign. For instance, in a primary debate, Reagan was asked whether pro-life Catholics and fundamentalists should base their vote solely on abortion. Reagan replied that not all pro-lifers were single-issue voters; rather, many of them were broad-based social conservatives who believed that abortion fell under a larger belief system.[116] It was almost as if he rejected the notion of single-issue voters and forcibly lumped their pro-life stance with other conservative positions on a host of issues—as if he told the voters where they stood. Later, he lumped pro-life positions with one's views on scope of government and welfare policy. Abortion created a "welfare burden," which was "too onerous for local governments to bear."[117]

Original intent was the constitutional justification for why Washington should step away from economic and social regulation.

According to this argument, the Founders never intended for Congress to enact large entitlement programs or for the Supreme Court to control neighborhood schools. Only by returning to their vision of a limited federal government and robust federalism could the economic and moral wrongs of the country be righted. The 1980 GOP platform spelled this out. The government, "steeped in Judeo-Christian ethic," was based on "the intent of the Founders . . . that the Central government should perform only those functions which are necessary." Not only did the platform tie the political to the religious, it also gave an historical-legal justification for limited government—the foundation of modern economic conservatism. It continued, "The durability of our system lies in its flexibility and its accommodation to diversity and changing circumstance." Here was the call for states' rights and local rule—the vehicle through which social policy preferences could be enacted.

The 1980 Republican Party platform included sharp language designed to appeal to social conservatives. "For the first time in our history," it warned, "there is real concern that the family may not survive." Wedding economic and social matters, it called for tax, spending, and welfare policies that promoted American families. It promised that the party would appoint "judges at all levels of the judiciary who respect traditional family values and the sanctity of human life."

A single line in the 1980 GOP platform encapsulates the party's overarching philosophy: it was "time to shift the focus of national politics from expanding government's power to that of restoring the strength of smaller communities such as the family, the neighborhood, and the workplace." This one sentence covered everything and everyone that Reagan had originally called for at the 1977 CPAC. Reference to "the workplace" signaled economic conservatives who prioritized economic issues (e.g., balanced budgets, expanding welfare, tax rates). And while these voters had always been in the Republican fold, the exhortations to "family" and "neighborhood" appealed to social conservatives of various stripes. Importantly, the catchphrases were broad enough to attract both single-issue voters (e.g., post-*Roe* pro-lifers) and those interested in a range of culture wars issues (e.g., the Moral Majority, Focus on the Family).[118]

It allowed the GOP to tap into voters concerned with any number of issues: school prayer, busing, abortion, obscenity, crime, divorce, feminism, homosexuality, sex education, parochial schools, drugs, and so forth.

Moreover, the proposed solution (i.e., devolution) was conservative enough for social conservatives. Stating that "the best government is the one closest to the people," the platform called for decentralization. It would be less costly, more accountable, and more responsive. Block grants, revenue sharing, reduction in the size of the executive, and "strict budgetary control of the bureaucracies"—social conservatives could sink their teeth into these proposals.

Reagan's efforts culminated in what has become his most quoted phrase, from his First Inaugural Address: "Government is not the solution to our problems; government is the problem." He stood for the economic conservatism that the GOP had long advocated. But he also advocated a social conservatism based on original intent, limited government, and states' rights. All these constitutional justifications registered with both of the major segments of American conservatism. It was, in a word, accessible, and GOP supporters could see a path to tangible and preferable results. It started, though, with winning majorities in national elections—converting the New Right movement into a partisan voting bloc. And *Roe v. Wade* was integral to these efforts.

Conclusion

Roe v. Wade was a durable force in both American politics and constitutional law. For half a century, it was the starting point for nearly all political and legal discussions of abortion policy. It changed how most states handled abortion restrictions, and as such, it garnered an immediate and vociferous response from pro-lifers. They attacked the court, introducing hundreds of amendments to constitutionalize the right to life and/or to define when life began. They sought ways to combat *Roe*, from the Hyde Amendment to banning partial birth abortions to heavily restricting second-term abortions. And yet, *Roe* still stood for a long time.[119] Part of its durability may be due to later cases—especially those immediately after *Roe*—in which the court allowed for restrictions on abortion. For instance, *Connecticut v. Menillo* (1974) upheld the state's restriction that all abortions be performed by physicians. And, importantly, the court upheld the most powerful tool (short of amendment or judicially overturning *Roe*) in the pro-life arsenal—defunding abortions at the federal (*Harris v. McRae*, 1980) and state (*Williams v. Zbaraz*, 1980) levels. Later, *Planned Parenthood v. Casey* (1992) might have upheld *Roe*, but it also created a new wave of antiabortion restrictions.[120] As communism, crime, and busing show, judicial retreat from a landmark decision can lead to opponents of the court to backing down on institutional reforms (e.g., packing the courts, eliminating judicial review).

But conservative activists did not back down from using *Roe* to win elections. It is difficult to say with precision how many voters switched. In pro-choice pockets of the country, *Roe* probably did not change the electoral calculus whatsoever. However, in pro-life pockets with a nonexclusive combination of a majority of Democrats and a critical mass of pro-lifers (e.g., the South, and districts and states with Catholic pluralities), *Roe* was more likely to change vote tallies. Richard Viguerie's *Conservative Digest* recognized this fact in the early days of the New Right. By 1978 the pro-life movement and the New Right "had become powerful enough to provide the margin of victory."[121] Put simply, *Roe* did not have to turn every Catholic and southerner into a single-issue pro-life Republican voter. But it did turn *some* of them into GOP converts via single-issue and overarching traditionalist concerns. And even if the GOP lost some liberal Republicans because of the party's rightward turn on abortion, the net gain was large enough to help break the New Deal coalition's decades long grip on national politics.

In the end, *Roe* was an anvil upon which to forge a larger, more vocal, influential, and durable New Right bloc. In allying with evangelicals, the early pro-life Catholic-driven lobby forced the issue upon the nation. This consolidated bloc and the GOP then established a symbiotic relationship in which the party stood for pro-life principles and the New Right voted Republican. Single-issue voters, links to other issues, originalist rhetoric, a return to states' rights—all these played a role Republicans gaining more votes. And the court's involvement at most created, and at least accelerated, a vigorous social conservative movement—one that would become a defining feature of twentieth – and twenty-first-century American politics.

Chapter 7

Lessons

THIS CHAPTER RECAPS THE mature New Deal–era narrative and links it back to Alexander Bickel's complaints regarding countermajoritarianism.[1] In doing so, I hypothesize about the extent to which liberal Supreme Court decisions played a role in the shift in the electorate. Next, I talk through some of the political lessons that can be gleaned from this period.

The Court Joins the Party

In some ways, the mature New Deal narrative was predictable. Although we cannot discount the agency of political entrepreneurs (from community organizers and local litigants to national party leaders and Supreme Court justices), the institutional framework of American politics makes court-driven development possible.[2] Here, I revisit the assumptions from chapters 2 and 3 and briefly contextualize them within the 1950s–80s narrative. Altogether, they show how the combination of the political parties and regime politics literatures predict the conditions that lead to the intersection of coalitional and judicial politics.

A dominant national coalition exists. The New Deal regime gained control of Washington in 1932. Even if brief moments of divided government (e.g., 1947–49), "preemptive" presidential administrations (e.g., Eisenhower), or even unified Republican government (i.e., 1953–55) arose, they all passed quickly.[3] Even in those years, the politics were still defined by New Deal commitments. The New Deal regime—with its ideological, political, and policy commitments—was durable.[4]

The court is part of the dominant national coalition. By the 1950s there was a clear liberal majority on the Supreme Court.[5]

Democratic nominations were not the only mechanism that brought the court into the regime. Republicans, ironically, appointed liberals (e.g., Warren, Brennan) and unreliable moderates (e.g., Blackmun, Stevens).[6]

The coalition is factional. The election of 1932 brought together the largest partisan coalition in modern US history. Liberals, labor union members, Blacks, southerners, and Catholics—all these copartisans voted similarly.[7]

The coalition is led by a lead faction. The liberal faction drove the New Deal coalition's agenda, especially by the 1950s. Liberal measures, such as desegregation, did not always receive legislative votes. But maintaining the liberal status quo implemented by the court was easier and less politically dangerous than positively making policy.[8] The Democratic Party was in control, but liberals controlled the Democratic Party.

Coalition-splitting issues replace coalition-uniting issues. In the 1930s the liberal faction could garner, say, southern support for the Tennessee Valley Authority or blue-collar Catholic support for the Wagner Act. In the 1970s the DNC had a harder time selling pro-choice policies to those more conservative Democratic factions. When economic-based primary goals were replaced by secondary preferences on social issues, it split the party.[9] These issues changed over time.

The coalition affects the court. Liberals exploited the Supreme Court as an outlet for pushing more liberal policies than they could hope to achieve through legislation. FDR delegated desegregation to the courts to avoid rupturing the racial fault line.[10] In the 1940s a "liberal-labor" coalition perceived economic rights as inextricably tied to civil rights.[11] LBJ reorganized federal courts to establish a pro–Great Society judiciary.[12]

The court affects the coalition. Just as the coalition influenced the court, so did the court change coalitional politics in the second half of the twentieth century. It expanded communists' rights, struck down school prayer, instituted stricter criminal procedures, implemented busing, and protected abortion rights. These instances were not just jurisprudential opinions; they were policy-setting cases that forever changed the national agenda, as well as the inter – and intra-coalitional alliances.

Canaries in the Coal Mine

In 1962 Alexander Bickel lobbed two complaints against the Supreme Court.[13] First, judicial review is countermajoritarian. Second, justices cannot be held accountable for their actions. Put together, according to Bickel, the "least dangerous branch" of the mid-to-late twentieth century was squarely undemocratic. Presidents, members of Congress, states, local communities, and the American people could do nothing but sit by idly, while the Supreme Court repeatedly imposed its countermajoritarian will with impunity.

These assumptions are misguided. The court was attacked, frequently and on different fronts. If anything, the era demonstrates that majorities can find relief from countermajoritarian decisions. Specifically, the Constitution provides three response mechanisms from different parts of the polity—all are effective in their own sphere. First, because enforcement of court decisions requires local cooperation, grassroots majorities can seriously hinder implementation. Second, the majority in the government can curb the court, tighten the purse strings, and/or execute decisions listlessly. Third, the majority in the electorate can elect a new party intent on reversing the decisions of the countermajoritarian court. Abortion likely had the most lasting electoral effect in this regard. But other issues previewed the schism in the Democratic coalition. They were canaries in the coal mine. Table 7.1 lists the ways in which the court faced these three majorities in the cases discussed.

This is the irony, and the tragedy: liberal Democrats wanted the Supreme Court to hand down liberal decisions on social issues. When those very opinions came to pass, the fallout likely played a role in dethroning the Democratic Party from the seats of government. In getting what they wanted, liberals lost their grip on Washington, and with it, a good deal of opposition to, and trimming/reversal of, the judicial opinions they originally sought. The issues discussed here had different outcomes, but all involved hard-fought battles long after the court delivered its opinions.

TABLE 7.1 Summary of Case Studies

Issue	Grassroots	Congressional	Electoral	Short-term implementation and long-term political effect
Communism	Opposition from Conference of State Chief Justices and Governors' Conference	Nearly successful court-curbing attempt		Short-term implementation: avoidance and reversal Long-term political effect: canary in the coal mine—communism cleaves Democratic Party
Prayer	Superintendents and teachers refuse to stop praying or find easy workarounds	Constitutional amendments supported by Senate majority	Socially conservative cross-partisan majority emerges	Short-term implementation: as if court never ruled Long-term political effect: canary in the coal mine—morality cleaves Democrats and prayer relates to communism and local rule
Crime	Tricks and threats avoid *Miranda*	OCCSSA scales back rulings; hands enforcement to state and local governments	Nixon runs successful law and order campaign	Short-term implementation: *Miranda* not followed, then (along with *Katz*) rendered impotent by Congress; court eases up in *Hayden* and *Terry*; election of Nixon Long-term political effect: canary in the coal mine—crime cleaves Democrats and relates to communism, prayer, and local rule
Busing	Delay, nonimplementation, protests, violence	Defunding and postponement; 1979 discharge petition to amend the Constitution	Liberals ready to turn away from busing in 1974 GOP ready to build coalition on racial issue	Short-term implementation: *Swann* rendered impotent; court eases up in *Milliken* Long-term political effect: canary in the coal mine—busing cleaves Democrats and relates to prayer and local rule; *Swann* is not *Brown*
Abortion	States push back	Hyde Amendment; constitutional amendments	New Right emerges and unites with GOP	Short-term implementation: pro-life lobby has mixed success; court issues pro-life and pro-choice decisionss Long-term political effect: some southern and Catholic Democrats become Republicans

Because southerners saw a supposed ideological link between desegregation and communism, the Republican Party could have tried to fashion a durable coalition. GOP leaders, however, refused to make segregation the foundation of a conservative majority. Moreover, the communism attacks worked: the court backed off.[14] With favorable judicial results, the possible anticommunists' rights coalition lost steam. Nevertheless, the episode was the first "canary." It provided valuable information that, if deployed skillfully, could rupture the Democratic Party and give Republicans a pathway to national majorities. The controversy around the communism cases revealed that anticommunist sentiment lay not only within the GOP and the South but also among Catholic Democrats who feared the atheistic elements of communist ideology.

Striking down school prayer and Bible readings offered a similar opportunity to build a Republican, southern Democrat, and Catholic Democrat coalition. For two reasons, it never came to fruition. First, grassroots efforts made it unnecessary. Put simply, kids still prayed after *Engel*. Second, the issue was not salient enough to drive national electoral politics. Still, it split the Democratic coalition in a new way, along a fault line that raised new moral issues and contained an anticommunist ideology and local rule governing philosophy. The decision on school prayer did not substantially change American electoral politics, but its fallout offered a glimpse into what could occur should a salient enough issue arise.

The criminal procedure narrative is complicated. When combined with a spike in crime, it created a nationally salient issue. In many ways, the response to these decisions was the most severe of any of the topics discussed. In local police stations, detectives easily found effective *Miranda* work-arounds by tricking and threatening suspects during interrogations. Congress subsequently passed a law dictating that *Miranda* did not apply to federal investigations. The court then, in *Hayden* and *Terry*, backed off a uniformly liberal criminal procedure agenda. All these factors relieved the pressure off the issue. Yet, it still was not enough to deflate crime from becoming a foundational issue in the election of 1968. The court's causal effect on the increase in crime in the late 1960s is questionable, if not tenuous. But that does not matter as much as Richard Nixon successfully selling the causal link to the American electorate in the 1968 law-and-order campaign. Whether it was true or not, enough voters (especially southern and Catholic Democrats) *believed it was true*. And it was that election that ultimately resulted in the growing criminal procedure counterrevolution. Even so, it had even longer-term effects by furthering the rifts in the Democratic Party, as crime's causes were linked to anarchic communism, the elimination of Bible readings, and a runaway Supreme Court.

After *Swann v. Charlotte*, school districts avoided compliance for some time. Congress legitimized those actions by defunding and postponing busing. By 1974 all Democrats faced electoral pushback for their association with court-ordered busing. Ironically, their seats might have been saved by *Milliken*, which gave local antibusing leaders enough leeway to effectively and durably sidestep federal courts' intervention. More than congressional action or presidential rhetoric, this court decision mollified white suburban parents.

But busing was another canary in the coal mine because it raised different dimensions of an old fault line. Unlike *Brown*, the antibusing majority in the electorate did not arise purely because of racist zealotry. Granted, one clearly cannot eliminate race from busing. But there are reasons to believe that *Swann* was different from *Brown*, especially in the North. In the 1970s Catholic Democrats worried about an activist Washington government reaching too deeply into matters that were best governed by those who lived within the church parish. This, then, was the busing canary: that the Republican Party's ideological commitment to local governance was not only compatible with the South's historic (and racist) commitment to states' rights but was also congruent with Catholics' theological belief in subsidiarity and neighborhood schools.

Roe v. Wade witnessed considerable pushback. States restricted and banned abortion. Congress federally defunded abortion with the Hyde Amendment. The court protected key pro-life restrictions. But neither the grassroots efforts, congressional majorities, nor the court's post-*Roe* jurisprudence could stop abortion from changing electoral politics. In its simplest terms, conservative organizers and financiers united pro-life Catholics and evangelicals into an identifiable movement: the New Right. It paved the way not only for single-issue abortion voters but also for an overarching constitutional commitment to a smaller federal government that fostered traditionalist family life and challenged judicial activism, radical feminism, and Soviet communism. It was only natural when the New Right fell into the partisan fold after the Republican Party advertised a platform built on originalism, limited government, devolution, and the American family.

Thus, *Roe v. Wade* was an important—perhaps even necessary—component of Ronald Reagan's successful bid to realign American politics. To conservatives, *Roe* was not a stand-alone decision, and its effect cannot be understood without taking communists' rights, school prayer, crime, and busing into account. *Roe* was not a canary in the coal mine. It was a critical juncture both in its own right and because it was the culmination of decades of cross-partisan conservative frustration with liberal Supreme Court rulings.

Political Lessons

Here, I take the viewpoint of political actors to describe some of the political dynamics of countermajoritarian court decisions. Various actors might be described as "political" in the previous chapters' narratives. For instance, teachers leading prayers or mothers chaining themselves to buses were indeed key political players. To simplify, though, I discuss the lessons of the three branches of government, beginning with the executive.

Presidents and the Countermajoritarian Difficulty

Dahl originally posited that presidents hailing from the dominant national alliance could expect to work with a friendly Supreme Court that would strike down the policies of the old guard and uphold those of the new guard.[15] In many ways, Dahl is still correct—the court rarely acts in a countermajoritarian fashion, and presidential appointments to the bench are a key reason why. However, the appointment power assumes that presidents can only affect *who* accedes to the court and not *what* comes after. Of course, presidents cannot order justices to decide cases one way or the other. But this does not mean presidents are impotent in the face of unfavorable decisions—especially those that are countermajoritarian.

Other than nominating justices, presidents hold other powers. These powers are constitutional, derived either from plain meaning or from accepted (if controversial) interpretations of Article II's "Vesting Clause." They are isolated: nearly uncheckable from other institutions, including the other two branches. And they are unilateral: vested solely in the one person in the Oval Office. These powers extend farther than we might think, but I focus on two realms of presidential power: execution of laws and agenda setting.[16]

When presidents take the inaugural oath to faithfully execute the law, they assume considerable prosecutorial discretion in choosing how much or how little they will enforce judicial rulings. Sometimes presidents are meticulous about following through on Supreme Court rulings. Even if enforcement typically is delegated to state and local authorities, control of federal agencies can make a difference. Take, for instance, Eisenhower's decision to send the national guard to Little Rock to enforce desegregation when Governor Orval Faubus refused to do so.[17] Or consider LBJ's insistence that federal agents follow *Miranda*, even after Congress eliminated the need for such protections in federal investigations. These examples demonstrate presidential compliance with court rulings, but we can imagine a hypothetical president George Wallace responding to Little Rock differently.

We need not look far to see how another president would approach *Miranda*. Less than six months after Inauguration Day in 1969, the Nixon administration issued a memorandum to all US attorneys explaining that failure to give *Miranda* warnings would not necessarily result in the exclusion of a resulting confession.[18] The discrepancy between LBJ and Nixon does not indicate that one president was right and the other wrong. It does not mean that one cared more than the other about the rule of law (either from a criminal procedure or law-and-order point of view). Rather, it shows the level of agency granted to presidents in carrying out Supreme Court rulings. Even if Congress had not passed the OCCSSA, LBJ and Nixon still would have the authority to dictate how the FBI, CIA, ATF, and so forth, carried out their duties.

Presidents are constitutionally empowered to set the national agenda. They make legislative recommendations through the constitutionally required State of the Union Address. Following *Swann*, Nixon mentioned "unnecessary busing" in 1972; in 1974, he devoted an entire section of the address to the issue. He, and later Gerald Ford, also rarely missed an opportunity to lay blame on the crime issue.

The executive is the only branch of government with a unitary actor, which makes media attention more concentrated.[19] All presidents from Eisenhower through Reagan used some combination of press conferences, proclamations, primetime Oval Office speeches, and radio addresses to set the agenda on issues decided by the Supreme Court. After the court ruled against his administration's ability to deny passports to suspected communists (*Kent v. Dulles*, 1958), Eisenhower stressed the need to update statutory law to allow the State Department to take such action.[20] In a press conference two days after *Engel v. Vitale*, JFK indicated his broad support for the court while also recognizing the decision was unpopular.[21] As *Roe* percolated through the federal courts, Nixon issued a statement about abortions performed at hospitals on military bases.[22] Declaring that the military hospitals had to follow the laws of the states in which they resided, it was an early signal to Catholic leaders that the GOP was more in line with pro-life stances than the Democratic Party.[23] These incidents demonstrate the executive's immediate and direct line of communication to the people—an important tool in setting the terms of political debate.

Congress and the Countermajoritarian Difficulty

I highlight two broad types of responses available to members of Congress after a countermajoritarian Supreme Court ruling. First, Congress can seriously impair a court opinion (without amending the Constitution) through *substantive responses*—measures passed by Congress that noticeably scale back the effectiveness, breadth, and/or depth of the court's judgment. The case studies here are full of examples. After the communism cases, Congress tried to permit states to enact laws that barred subversive activities. Moreover,

congressional conservatives pushed for those laws to stand even if
they went further than federal antisubversion laws. Congress all but
overturned *Miranda* and *Katz* for federal law enforcement. It postponed the busing decisions and refused to allocate federal dollars
toward that mode of desegregation. And the Hyde Amendment similarly restricted federal funding for abortion.

All these policies were attempts to substantively oppose the court.
While some blatantly overrode the thrust of judicial opinions (e.g.,
the OCCSSA), others simply made enforcement or enactment more
difficult (e.g., Hyde), if not impossible (e.g., postponement of busing).
The lesson from these substantive congressional responses is that,
in an "intercurrent" system of overlapping institutions, Congress is
hardly shut out of the policymaking process after the court rules on
the constitutionality of a policy.[24] Further, when the court strikes
down a practice supported by the majority in the government and/or
the majority in the electorate, then Congress has ample political cover to fight back. Indeed, members of Congress have not only cover
but also incentive to curtail the effects of the court's opinion.

That incentive leads to the second type of reaction available to
members of Congress: *position-taking responses.* These do not seek to
meaningfully trim the effects of countermajoritarian decisions; they
are symbolic and electorally connected.[25] Some have a minimal substantive effect, such as hiring more police in the District of Columbia
after *Miranda*, addressing the oil shortage by not allowing buses to
travel far outside their home school district, or not allowing the LSC
to handle abortion cases. These are not inconsequential; but neither
are they consequential at a nationwide level. Other actions, meanwhile, are trivial—clearly meant as a shot across the bow instead of
a solution to policy problems (countermajoritarian or otherwise).
For instance, installing more lights on the White House lawn was
not a solution to a perceived problem; it was an opportunity for lawmakers to blame the Supreme Court for a Nixon aide being mugged.
Similarly, funding Bibles for Supreme Court justices did not resolve
post-*Schempp* hostility.

Yet, proposals that appear marginal, passive-aggressive, or even
practically meaningless still have value to their introducers. They give

members of Congress position-taking stages upon which legislators can grandstand for constituents. Likely, they are posturing for their constituents and working to enhance their own reelection prospects. But even if unintentionally, this type of behavior has the added benefit of contributing to issue evolution and signaling to cross-partisans the cleavages that exist in the opposition party.[26]

In this sense, claims of countermajoritarian Supreme Court decisions have the same effects. We saw such examples in every case described here. Some of the claims were obviously true: some opinions (e.g., *Engel*, *Swann*) clearly went against national majorities. Abortion was more complicated, but there is evidence that an odd mix of pro-life and pro-choice Americans were opposed to the particulars of *Roe v. Wade*.

Sad though it sounds, the truthfulness of these claims is less important than the sheer fact that they were made. In fact, countermajoritarian complaints might be particularly attractive because they allow members of Congress to dictate which positions are the majority and minority. Those who make these claims might do so in good faith—they might truly believe that countermajoritarianism needs to come to light. But surely these kinds of statements are delivered, also, with the intent to increase the chances of reelection bids. And as with proposals of minimal/trivial impact, these positions have the added bonus of coalition-building. Perhaps these positions are even more important, as they allow secondary members of the dominant coalition to feel like they do not have to settle for the lead faction's preferences. They might empower secondary factions to look across the aisle and see what cross-partisan majoritarian possibilities exist. At the very least, in terms of expanding one's minoritarian coalition, making claims that one's position is majoritarian does no political harm.

Finally, I point to one more method of position-taking unique to this study: court-curbing attacks. The appendix details a database that counts 3,649 attacks on the court from 1955 to 2023. More than two-thirds of those were attempts to amend the US Constitution, none of which succeeded in their constitutional aim. The statutory attempts also failed. The closest Congress came to formally curbing the court in the late twentieth century was when the Senate fell one vote short of restricting jurisdiction on communism cases. Yet, that too did not pass. With an overwhelming rate of failure, why then are these proposals worth consideration?

The mere introduction and sheer volume of attacks on certain issues can play a role in the political evolution of an era. Attacks do not need to formally curb the court to produce their intended direct effect. That is, even if Congress votes a measure through, it can still achieve judicial retreat on the issue in question. Consider the following:

- Communism. After Congress attacked, the Supreme Court delayed hearing communism cases, then reversed two of its previous decisions, thereby allowing a broad definition of "subversive persons" and condoning HUAC's actions. Afterward, it refused to take any more communists' rights cases.
- Criminal procedure. Politicians and voters alike pinned the 1960s crime wave on the Supreme Court. Even before Nixon won his law-and-order campaign, the court retreated from its line of decisions that protected criminal rights. *Warden v. Hayden* (1967) and *Terry v. Ohio* (1968) scaled back the evidence-collection implications of *Mapp v. Ohio* (1961).
- Busing. *Swann v. Charlotte* (1971) produced vociferous pushback that led to local majorities looking to replace their normally liberal members of Congress. Indeed, to save their own seat, liberal Democrats even began voting against busing. Then, seemingly out of step with recent jurisprudence, the court ruled that federal judges could not consolidate multiple school districts. *Milliken v. Bradley* (1974), decided only three years after *Swann*, gave suburban parents, superintendents, and politicians the outlet they needed to avoid busing.
- Abortion. Some cases in the immediate aftermath of *Roe* suggest judicial withdrawal from the historical 1973 decision. They supported some state restrictions (*Connecticut v. Menillo*, 1974; *Planned Parenthood v. Danforth*, 1976) and upheld state and federal Hyde Amendments (*Harris v. McRae*, 1980; *Williams v. Zbaraz*, 1980).

The retreats listed here range from concessions (abortion) to enabling (busing and crime) to full-scale reversal (communism). It is difficult to conclusively point to why the court would behave in this way. Of course, constitutional law is complicated. New appointees would provide a good answer, but as the respective chapters demonstrate, the court's membership did not change enough in any of these cases to warrant a jurisprudential tilt. The same justices sat on the communism cases. If anything, Abe Fortas and Thurgood Marshall made the court more liberal on criminal procedure.[27] Between *Swann* and *Milliken*, Lewis Powell and William Rehnquist likely swung the court farther to the right on busing, but that does not account for going from unanimity to a split court. And only John Paul Stevens was added to the court in the immediate aftermath of *Roe*. In sum, there is not enough evidence to say that new justices led to new rulings.

Perhaps the justices saw nuances in the particulars of the cases before them and issued good-faith rulings on each case's individual merits.[28] From a post hoc historical point of view, they appear contradictory, but placed within political development—as it was developing—perhaps the justices were trying to sort through complicated issues with complicated facts that led to seemingly disparate opinions. For example, instead of thinking of *Swann* and *Milliken* as contradictory, perhaps we should see them as complementary—that busing was permitted, but only so far. Or maybe *Terry* was the natural limit of *Mapp*.

Appointments and jurisprudential complexity have merit, but another explanation that deserves consideration is that the court backed off when Congress expressed displeasure with its rulings. Earl Warren thought this was the case with communists' rights. Even in that instance, the court-curbing measures before Congress had not passed. Not only had they failed, but some lawmakers, as well as President Eisenhower and Vice President Nixon, were relieved to see them off the legislative docket. If a majority in Congress was unwilling to go so far as to formally curb the court, then why would the justices ease off their line of jurisprudence?

The answer is that members of Congress do not need to pass their attack bills to receive the results they want. The legislature can introduce bills that affect the rollout of a decision. Defunding, overriding, overseeing operations—these all can scale back countermajoritarian decisions. They also send important signals to the justices. They indicate that members of the branch of government closest to the people are dissatisfied with judicial pronouncements. Attacks, then, are also important signals. They might be offered as electorally connected and individual position-taking efforts. That is, legislators likely attack because they believe that doing so will help them retain their seat. However, they have the side benefit of relaying to the court that others are not content with its decisions. When the issue at stake involves the court directly—such as stripping jurisdiction, mandating retirements, or amending the Constitution to overturn a decision— then we might think the justices are even more likely to respond by reversing their jurisprudential course or, at the very least, stopping their jurisprudential trajectory and letting interbranch politics naturally scale back the original objectionable ruling. Put differently, maybe Congress does not need to curb the court in order to curb the court.

We might even think that members of Congress, if they were conscious of the court backing down in the face of majoritarian threats, would *not want to* curb the court, even if they propose measures to do so. This is for two reasons. First, institutionally, the court has not seriously been curbed many times in American history. In the Jeffersonian era, Congress shut down the court for a year. During Reconstruction, Congress prohibited the court from hearing certain cases involving former Confederates. The legislature has passed constitutional amendments overturning judicial rulings (e.g., the Sixteenth Amendment) and occasionally changed the size of the court, but nearly every attack dies either in the halls or on the floor of Congress. Even the most famous attempt (FDR's court-packing) ultimately did not pass.[29] Though individual lawmakers might be upset at a particular ruling, on the whole, there is an institutional commitment—coming from Congress—to grant as much judicial independence as possible. Put simply, Congress does not like to curb the court. It is willing to do so, but only in rare circumstances.

Second, politically, congressional lawmakers might not want to curb the court because winning the policy debate would mean shelving a winning electoral issue. Individually, members of Congress might prefer having a majoritarian view on a counterma-joritarian court ruling. This might occur, also, on a coalitional level. That is, taking issues back to constituents is all the better if it unites a lawmaker's own party and splits the opposing party. Indeed, a coun-termajoritarian decision is likely going to unite the minority party with factions of the majority party. Under these conditions, minority party members might want the issue to linger to sow dissent within the opposition, not only for their own reelection chances but also for those of their copartisans in office and those challenging the seats of the incumbent majority party's members. In sum, sometimes it is better to be on the losing side of a court case because it provides an anvil upon which one can hammer against the opposition, and perhaps even forge the outlines of a new majority.

The Supreme Court, the Countermajoritarian Difficulty, and the Accountability Problem

Bickel's simplistic charges carry political weight, and contemporary Democrats and Republicans deploy the trope whenever it is conve-nient.[30] Yet, the regime politics paradigm has largely debunked the countermajoritarian difficulty as a myth.[31] Nearly every time the court decides a case of public interest, it is in line with the majority in the government or with the majority in the electorate (or most likely, it is in line with both). When exercising judicial review, the court may be striking down old guard policies, reining in regional outliers, or resolving nonmajoritarian issues. When upholding or interpreting a law, the court might be legitimating the dominant national alliance's agenda or deciding in a way preferred by the dominant national al-liance. Even if the alliance is split, the court likely helps the coalition overcome fractious coalitions or entrenched interests. At base, the court is rarely countermajoritarian.

Thus, in most instances, Bickel was wrong: the court is almost never countermajoritarian. But in select and extremely important instances, Bickel was right: the court *is* countermajoritarian, and that fact can be problematic for American democracy. These instances are rare, but their rarity make them even more outstanding. Obviously, they are important on their own merits: they change constitutional law in a way that matters for legislators and the American people. But their effects go beyond jurisprudence; they trickle into American politics, too. And this is where Bickel might not have recognized the depth and extent of his claim. That is, countermajoritarian decisions do not just present a theoretical "difficulty" for constitutional ideals. They trigger visible, measurable reactions that attempt to course correct what some see as a runaway court.

In addition to the countermajoritarian difficulty, Bickel also lamented that the court was unaccountable for its actions. Once the court issues a decision, there is little anyone can do, because Supreme Court justices are insulated from elections. This view, though, seems somewhat myopic in that it views one part of the Constitution as directly comparable to another. That is, Bickel wants to compare members of the House of Representatives to Supreme Court justices. When representatives flout the will of the people either repeatedly or on highly salient issues, their likelihood of reelection decreases. When justices deliver unpopular decisions, they remain on the bench.

To be fair to complaints about the accountability problem, short of impeachment, there is no method of holding justices directly accountable. Even then, impeachment is more republican than democratic; it is indirect: justices are not removed by the people but by officials elected by the people. While justices themselves will never be held to simple majoritarianism, their rulings will certainly face trial, as it were. Majorities have outlets, and they can impose significant short – and long-term effects. Table 7.1 lists examples of how grassroots, legislative, and electoral majorities can oppose court decisions. Countermajoritarian decisions can be left floundering at the grassroots, tied up in congressional oversight, or used as a foil to win elections. Majorities do not have to kick justices out. They have plenty of response mechanisms.

In this way, it is more helpful to see the *Supreme Court* as accountable rather than the *justices*. And given the complex nature of the Constitution, this makes sense. The document works holistically. Parsing out a single slice of the Constitution (life tenure for federal judges) and evaluating it against criteria used to judge other slices (e.g., electing representatives) is just not fair. Instead, it would be more appropriate to see how all parts of the document work together to form a functioning government. In looking at the judicial branch, we see that its relationship to the whole polity is not all that different from the legislative and executive branches' relationships. It is embedded in a system of separation of powers and checks and balances in which institutions have overlapping, concurrent, and intercurrent powers. The Supreme Court is subject to majoritarianism; the Supreme Court is held accountable—even if we never see the justices' names on a nationwide ballot.

I would argue this is a normatively good aspect of the US Constitution. It helps pursue dual, and dueling, goals of public accountability and tolerance of minority rights.[32] Some might say that the court primarily protects those with wealth, status, and power.[33] This happens. But I maintain that an unelected high court empowered with judicial review can theoretically provide rearguard action against federal and state laws that subtly—and sometimes blatantly—infringe on the protected civil rights and civil liberties of minorities. Indeed, this happens. Some of these decisions were cornerstones for Black civil rights (e.g., *Brown*, *Loving*, and *Smith v. Allwright*). Many are known by a single word: *Gideon*, *Brandenburg*, and *Frontiero*. Others (e.g., *Engel v. Vitale*, *Texas v. Johnson*, *US v. Virginia*) are contemporaneously controversial. Perhaps we do not want our political conversations about school prayer taking place in elementary school classrooms where teachers interpret court rulings as they see fit. But such is the complicated nature of a large, diverse, and federalist republic. Moreover, it seems appropriate that Congress have a say in policymaking, even if it is responding to judicial policies.[34] At the very least, given popular sovereignty, surely we would want for there to be ways for the people to express their electoral preferences. All these are public accountability mechanisms. Majorities cannot run roughshod over tolerance of minority rights, but minorities cannot always rule, either.

We should see the institutional design of the Supreme Court as working in harmony with the rest of the system, rather than in opposition to it.[35] The court is rarely countermajoritarian. But sometimes it is—and those cases might be the most important ones. And while the Senate and Electoral College can also be countermajoritarian, it is hard to see Congress or the White House going too far out of their way to protect discrete and insular minorities the way that the court sometimes does. Put simply, the judiciary is probably a necessary outlet for minorities to seek protection. Without the court, the Constitution might be *too majoritarian*. Still, minorities cannot always dictate policy; and that is why grassroots, congressional, and electoral majorities can form against consistent and/or salient unpopular rulings.

It would be silly to suggest that before drafting opinions Supreme Court justices should take stock of public opinion polls, foresee likely countermajoritarian rhetoric on the floors of Congress, identify evolving factional and coalitional politics, or predict how national elections will turn on their rulings. This is not the work of judges. Instead of prescribing how the most powerful judges in the history of the world should do their job, I instead offer the following: actions have consequences.

Sometimes, an action must be taken, consequences be damned. For many pro-choice advocates, this describes their feelings toward *Roe*. Despite whatever pushback occurred, *Roe* still set the foundation for access to abortions. It is this balancing act that legal actors (litigants, interest groups, and, most importantly, judges) must consider, for the case studies here demonstrate that there is a limited amount of countermajoritarian capital. A string of decisions along linked ideological lines can push majorities over the edge. A single decision on a highly salient issue can do the same. Tolerating minority rights *must* be prioritized sometimes—especially by the Supreme Court. But other institutions must also simultaneously prioritize public accountability. This is the ultimate lesson for the court and its scholars: it all hangs together.

Chapter 8

Contemporary Issues

PERHAPS THE MOST IMPORTANT takeaway from studying the countermajoritarian decisions of the 1950s–70s is that such opinions have the ability to affect the way parties and people approach electoral choices. Historians, legal scholars, and political scientists all have interest in exploring the extent of this effect. How do legal institutions interact with political ones? Does history repeat itself? What are the limits of the judiciary's institutional independence to rule against the majority's preferences? Is the pattern generalizable across case studies? In what follows, I hypothesize about the conditions under which an unpopular Supreme Court decision can lead to opportunities to shift electoral coalitions. The discussion is meant to be an initial foray rather than the final word on the subject. At the very least, it provides a starting point for scholars to explore how countermajoritarian Supreme Court decisions can affect elections.

Two basic conditions must be met for a political party to have the opportunity to use a Supreme Court ruling to enlarge their coalition:

1. The decision must cleave the national majority along cross-partisan lines[1]
2. The issue must be salient to the cross-partisan majority

The first condition is simple. The decision must be countermajoritarian in way that unites members of both parties. Typically, the court rules in line with the primary faction of the dominant party. Secondary factions, then, will need to have the same preferences as the minority party. This is easily measured, through counting (e.g., court-curbing attacks) and/or archival (e.g., party memos) methods.

The second condition is trickier, and it raises many questions. What makes an issue "salient": the effect of an issue on vote choice? Attention paid to an issue by politicians? Attention from the media? Is it dichotomous—either an issue is salient or not—or is there a sliding scale? A pair of scholars offer a helpful definition: "The extent to which people cognitively and behaviorally engage with a political issue."[2] This allows salience to be identified by the amount of influence an issue has in affecting the way people think and act on an issue. This, though, raises another question: What is the *exact threshold* for determining the extent to which thoughts and actions on a salient issue are significant?

Even if we cannot pinpoint the threshold, is there a fair selection method for determining a salient issue? Many public opinion polls include a question about "the most important problem." Yet, using this measure would assume that the most important is the only important issue and that nonproblematic issues are unimportant.[3] Is a salient issue a problematic one? Is it an important one?

Instead of "most important problem," I use newspaper mentions, a method made popular by Mayhew's "sweeps" in *Divided We Govern*.[4] Clark, Lax, and Rice present a database that identifies all stories mentioning the Supreme Court from the *New York Times*, *Washington Post*, and *Los Angeles Times*.[5] I merge their case numbers with those from the Supreme Court Database.[6] One issue with newspaper coverage is that salience then can be measured retrospectively—that salience is determined in stories after the event rather than being measured as a true product of its time. Clark, Lax, and Rice address this by including a measure of newspaper mentions before the court even decides a case. They find that it roughly matches any retrospective measure of salience. In sum, newspaper mentions might not perfectly correlate with an issue's importance. But they do demonstrate how much attention an issue was given—at least by three leading national newspapers. That would seem a good proxy for salience. The appendix provides details on the cases' measurements. For now, we can say that Clark, Lax, and Rice's measurement of salience puts communists' rights, crime, busing, and abortion in the top 1 percent of 7,181 Supreme Court cases from 1955 to 2008. These issues were salient—they probably had the ability to affect the way citizens voted. School prayer appears relatively nonsalient. None of the recent cases discussed in this chapter are in Clark, Lax, and Rice's dataset. The appendix tries to predict what their method would say if extended past 2010, but without data, all we have is speculation. I conclude that all the issues discussed in this chapter were salient, but on different dimensions.

If the two conditions are met (cross-partisan bonds and salience), it is still far from guaranteed that a new electoral majority will emerge. Instead, elites (primarily those in the minority party) will only have the *opportunity* to use the controversial ruling. In doing so, the lessons of 1950s–1970s point to two suggestions. Leaders in the cross-partisan majority should:

1. Send signals to voters
2. But not be too successful in reversing judicial policies

The first suggestion is straightforward. If the electorate is to be mobilized to form a new national majority, cross-partisan leaders should direct those voters to a new choice. This book explains many of the available signals: court-curbing bills, congressional speeches, presidential addresses, party platforms, and so forth. Even more subtle signals exist: Nixonian eye rolls when discussing busing enforcement, installing more lighting on the White House grounds after *Miranda*, or providing a Bible to Supreme Court justices after *Schempp*. Even if the signals have no practical effect—even if the court attacks fail, constitutional amendments are held up in committee, or the justices never open their Bibles—they still provide position-taking opportunities for the aggrieved cross-partisan majority. It might be enough to highlight the single issue (e.g., abortion after *Roe*). Alternatively, the minority party might find even more success if it can link the issue to a comprehensive ideology (e.g., states' rights, limited government, American family) so that secondary factions of the majority party feel as if they are repeatedly disappointed by their own party and that switching would be more than emotional reactionary behavior.

The second subpart —not succeeding too much—seems counter-intuitive to what one should want from the policymaking process. But the cross-partisan majority—especially those from the minority party—do not want immediate success is reversing countermajoritar-ian Supreme Court decisions. If grassroots opposition or legislative action render a decision impotent, then voters are satisfied enough to maintain the coalitional status quo. Disaffected members of the majority, then, lose incentive to electorally push back. Parties cannot fix the problem if they want to campaign on the problem.

These developmental lessons are not confined to the mature New Deal era. Several twenty-first-century decisions fit the analytical framework here, and this chapter, and the next, describes contempo-rary Supreme Court decisions. What was the setting under which the court heard a case? What did the court rule? What were the conse-quences (e.g., congressional response) of that ruling? What explains those consequences? How do the cases compare to those of previous chapters?

I discuss five issue areas (good governance, Obamacare, same-sex marriage, religious liberty, and, in the following chapter, abortion). It is not an exhaustive list, and we could imagine even more Roberts Court decisions being eligible for scholarly examination. The exam-ples here, though, provide a good window into analyzing modern Supreme Court politics, and they offer appropriate comparisons from historical examples.[7]

Good Governance

I start by lumping a set of cases into a single group: those that resolve the best ways to administer American democracy. I quickly recap three issues before the court: campaign finance, voting rights, and re-districting. Then I give two reasons why these cases have not created countermajoritarian difficulties.

In *Citizens United v. FEC* (2010), the court ruled that the First Amendment prohibits limitations on corporate spending that funds political campaigns not managed directly by candidates themselves.

The decision also upheld disclosure requirements, as well as indicated that the court would draw the line at overt quid pro quo arrangements between financiers and candidates.

In *Shelby County v. Holder* (2013), the court declared that the standards by which states and localities were held to account under the Voting Rights Act of 1965 were outdated. Roberts wrote that Congress, when reauthorizing the act in 2006, had ignored voting rights developments, kept the focus on "decades-old data relevant to decades-old problems," and not tried to resolve current needs. Procedurally, this meant that previously targeted localities (e.g., the south) did not need federal preclearance before changing their electoral policies. Substantively, it allowed these localities to alter voting practices (e.g., early voting times, number of precincts, or absentee rules). In particular, it led to many states instituting strict photo ID requirements.

The final set of disputes involves the many redistricting cases heard by the Roberts Court. The least controversial was *Evenwel v. Abbott* (2016), where a unanimous court ruled that apportionment be based on total population and not on registered voters. Cases out of Alabama (*Alabama Legislative Black Caucus v. Alabama*, 2015) and North Carolina (*Cooper v. Harris*, 2017) challenged supposed Republican efforts to "pack" Black citizens into a single majority-minority district to dilute other districts' likely Democratic voters. In *Arizona State Legislature v. Arizona Independent Redistricting Commission* (2015), the court ruled that independent commissions set up in response to statewide referendums had constitutional authority to redistrict. In cases involving partisan advantage via gerrymandering, the court has avoided the issue by claiming problems with standing (*Gill v. Whitford*, 2018; *Virginia House of Delegates v. Bethune-Hill*, 2019) and by invoking the political questions doctrine (*Rucho v. Common Cause*, 2019; *Lamone v. Benisek*, 2019).

Public opinion on these good governance issues is somewhat hard to discern because the issues involved are complicated. On one hand, we can find evidence that *Citizens United* was countermajoritarian. Table 8.1 indicates the percentage of respondents who believed the following statements.[8]

TABLE 8.1 Public Opinion on Campaign Finance

Question	%
Wealthy Americans have more of a chance to influence the elections process than other Americans	66
Money has too much influence	84
Most of the time, candidates who win public office promote policies that directly help the people and groups who donated money to their campaigns	55
Fundamental changes are needed for funding political campaigns, or we need to completely rebuild the system for funding political campaigns	85
Groups not affiliated with a candidate should have spending limited by law	78

On the other hand, shortly before the court handed down *Citizens United*, Gallup found that a majority believed campaign donations were a form of speech protected by the First Amendment.[9] However, the same poll also found that a majority also felt there should be limits on individuals and groups. In all likelihood, a 2012 Pew poll captures the most important item: average Americans were uninformed on the issue. The modal respondent had not heard about *Citizens United*. When asked about the main effect of increased outside spending, nearly half had no opinion; a quarter said it would have a negative effect, while another quarter said it was a neutral effect. Perhaps the most telling indicator was that Pew found that 46 percent did not know what a Super PAC was. Nearly 15 percent believed it was a hazardous waste cleanup project, a congressional budget committee, or a smartphone game.[10]

Opinions on *Shelby v. Holder* are also difficult to unpack. A majority of Americans consistently believe that voters should be required to show photo IDs on Election Day before they are allowed to vote.[11] Even when phrased as "opponents of voter ID laws argue they can actually prevent people who are eligible to vote," more than two-thirds still support such laws.[12] Yet, about two-thirds also approve of same-day registration, automatic registration, allowing post-punishment felons to vote, and giving all voters the option of a no-excuse absentee ballot.[13] There were differences between Democrat and Republican respondents. But on all four issues listed previously, a majority of

Democrats and a majority of Republicans approved of the voting access measures.[14]

Setting public opinion polls aside, some Democratic members of Congress would have us believe that the court was countermajoritarian in some of these good governance cases. Chuck Schumer (D-NY) claimed that if there was one thing Americans could agree on, it was that there was too much special interest in politics.[15] Senators Richard Blumenthal (D-CT) and Sheldon Whitehouse (D-RI) both called *Citizens United* "judicial activism." Complaining about *Shelby*, Patrick Leahy (D-VT) said, "All Americans strongly believe in fair and equal electoral opportunities." Congresswoman Lucille Roybal-Allard (D-CA) said the court had undermined "bipartisan supermajorities."[16]

At the federal level, these issues (campaign finance, voter ID, and redistricting) have become largely partisan, with both parties advocating positions that conveniently benefit their respective coalitions. Republicans advocate election spending as free speech, which allows wealthy donors to fund conservative campaigns. Both parties have been taken to the Supreme Court for partisan gerrymandering; both deploy it when they are the majority party in a state and abhor it when they are the minority party. And the GOP has been accused of abusing post-*Shelby* election law reforms to drive out likely Democratic voters. There are certainly instances where local politicians have benefited in ways contrary to the general partisan narrative. For instance, we could imagine how some Democratic leaders who are well connected to wealthy financiers might benefit from *Citizens United*, or how voter ID laws in a rural conservative district without many public service offices could end up hurting the Republican slate. Yet, as is increasingly the case in American politics, these issues track less with what people think is good for democracy than with what they perceive of as good for their party. This explains, in part, why the Democratic Party has launched congressional attacks.

Attacks on campaign finance are the modal type in the last decade, with 424 court-curbing measures after the release of *Citizens United*. Democrats account for a staggering 395 (93 percent) of them.[17] They fell into three categories. Many were constitutional amendments, such as Representative Marcy Kaptur's (D-OH) HJ Res 38

(2015), which read, "the First Amendment to the Constitution does not apply to the political speech of any corporation." Second, there were purely symbolic attacks—those with no real effect but which made for good political copy. Take for example, Representative John Yarmuth's (D-KY) resolution (2010) to "express disapproval of the decision issued by the Supreme Court in *Citizens United v. Federal Election Commission*." Third, statutory attacks sought to scale back the court and re-regulate campaign finance. Senator Dick Durbin's (D-IL) S. 2023 (2014) was a giant catch-all bill. Among other items, it sought to fast-track cases to the Supreme Court, streamline disclosures, regulate online contributions, and increase tax revenues for public financing of Senate elections.

Democrats account for all seventy-eight attacks against voter ID laws. Southern Democrats account for a disproportionate share (about 20 percent) of these measures. Many of these voter ID laws came out of the South and therefore directly threatened the reelection odds for southern Democratic members of Congress.

Furthermore, Democrats launched apportionment/redistricting attacks after the Trump administration tried to insert a citizenship question into the Census. The court struck down the question in 2019. Overall, Democrats expressed mild opposition to some redistricting issues. But it was neither broad nor tractable. This might be, in part, because some Democrats benefited from the way districts were drawn. That is, representatives had been elected based on the current map—perhaps they felt safer in their seat with the status quo than by changing the procedure by which districts were drawn (which could lead to their electoral defeat). Moreover, Democratic-controlled states were not beyond drawing lines in a way that helped the Democratic Party. Gerrymandering cut both ways and some Democrats supported partisan gerrymandering because it helped their own party.

For two reasons, the court's rulings on these types of cases are unlikely to alter electoral politics: (1) because, as described, good governance has an ideological/partisan cleavage; and (2) because it is not in the forefront of many voters' minds. Even if these issues are reported on in news coverage (see appendix), most voters simply do not regularly think about them; and if they do, they are already aligned with the party that promotes their ideological preferences. More likely, they are already registered with the party perceived to benefit from the outcomes of those ideological preferences. Although these cases have a far-reaching impact on elections, and therefore on public policy, they have not drawn the electoral ire of the very clear majority that believes in more egalitarian management of elections. At base, they do not have the raw appeal that moral/privacy (e.g., same-sex marriage, abortion) or economic (e.g., health care) issues carry. If anything, the nonsalience of the issues in the minds of most Americans is an even more powerful explanation than partisanship for why these cases have not sparked a political, electoral, and/or congressional pushback. Put differently, public opinion polls and some congressional rhetoric might indicate a countermajoritarian difficulty, but not enough Americans care deeply enough about these cases for them to have caused major electoral upheaval.

In some ways, the "good governance" issues coming out of the judiciary are unique. This is mainly due to rising partisanship and the role these decisions play on elections. The split on these issues is clearly partisan because Democrats believe *Citizens United* and *Shelby* threaten their chances of winning elections (and vice versa for Republicans). At the congressional level, there is no room for cross-partisan coalitions. In other words, they do not meet the first condition (that a decision cleave along cross-partisan lines).

They might meet the second condition (that they are salient to a majority), but only at the congressional level. Here, they share a trait with the school prayer decisions: they are just not salient enough to use to build a new electoral majority. *Engel* and *Schempp* were clearly countermajoritarian whereas public opinion on the three good governance issues is more difficult to unpack. Voter ID laws appear majoritarian. However, some of the more recent attempts to restrict voting (e.g., making absentee voting more difficult, restricting Sunday early voting) have drawn the ire of national political figures and major interest groups.[18] Moreover, it appears that a national majority opposes the disproportionate influence of unlimited campaign spending and partisan gerrymandering. But even if a national majority opposes the court's rulings, they do not inspire that majority to do much about it. Congressional attacks might indicate public pushback (though they likely represent the electoral threat to those launching the attacks), but nothing has come from attacks. Congress has not passed meaningful overrides. The court has not backed off. And politics has continued as normal. In short, though the good governance cases are certainly important, they are not the type of issue that leads the news every night for a month, let alone a week. They are just not salient enough to create major electoral shifts.

Obamacare

In one of the most controversial cases of the contemporary era, the Supreme Court upheld the Affordable Care Act (ACA). Much of the decision turned on Chief Justice Roberts. Roberts agreed with the court's four conservatives that Congress's commerce powers did not extend to providing an individual mandate for health care. (The four liberals dissented, saying they were unconvinced by the chief justice's distinction between "activity" and "inactivity.") However, Roberts joined the court's four liberals to say that the taxing and spending clause allowed Congress to impose a penalty on those who did not show proof of insurance. (The four conservatives dissented, saying that a penalty was not the same thing as a tax). Separating the court's decision from the politics of Obamacare is thorny because the policy itself created new political pathways.[19] Moreover, although certiorari was granted quickly after passage of the ACA, the case was still decided after intervening elections in which Republicans won a substantial number of new seats (six in the Senate; sixty-three in the House). Still, we can trace the contours of the case, its context, and its aftermath.

Gallup polls tracked support and opposition to Obamacare.[20] The break points are as follows:

- 2000–2009. Nationalizing health care was a popular stance. For example, when Barack Obama won in 2008, those who supported a program similar to the ACA outnumbered those who opposed it by a thirty-one-point margin.

- 2010–12. There was a rough fifty-split split.
- 2013–15. Conservatives claimed a slim majority.
- 2016–21. Liberals claimed a slim, then comfortable majority.

The Kaiser Family Foundation (KFF) also started a running poll that asks about respondents' feelings toward the health reform law.[21] It shows many of the same results as Gallup:

- 2010–12. No majority.
- 2013–15. A modest conservative plurality.
- 2016–21. An emerging and widening liberal majority.

Again, interpreting the causal implications of these polls is difficult. Did the two-year stall in legislation occur because of dwindling support for Obamacare? Or did support dwindle because the Democrats dawdled? Did opposition to federal health care increase because of poor rollout (e.g., the website crashing)? Did support increase after the policy normalized and management improved? Perhaps most importantly, did altering the way that millions of Americans received health care change their views—in liberal and conservative directions—on the role of the federal government and health insurance? Also concerning, Gallup found that the wording of the questions played an inordinate role in determining answers. When asked about the "Affordable Care Act," some were more likely to support the policy. When asked about "Obamacare," some were more likely to oppose it (see table 8.2).[22]

Table 8.2 Obamacare versus Affordable Care Act

	Obamacare	Affordable Care Act
Support	38%	54%
Oppose	54%	49%

Some Republican lawmakers hinted that *Sebelius* held counter-majoritarian elements.[23] But *Sebelius* did not cause a shift in cross-partisan voting coalitions. At the congressional level, only two of the forty-nine attacks related to the ACA were introduced by Democrats, and they were directed, specifically, at free exercise claims.[24] These are a stark contrast to Republican bills, many of which were direct assaults on the ACA, such as Marco Rubio's proposal that "Congress shall make no law that imposes a tax on a failure to purchase goods or services."[25]

At the level of the electorate, the original bill might have mobilized some inactive Republican voters in 2010, but the court's ruling did not durably cause a critical mass of voters to stop voting for one party and start voting for the other. That said, we could imagine what would have happened had the court ruled the opposite—if it had overturned the ACA.[26] This alternative decision would have been much more unpopular than Roberts's original opinion. Whether Obama sought to use policy to change politics, the *effect* of Obamacare has been to shift views on the issue in favor of Democratic preferences.[27] A 2023 KFF poll shows a 62 to 36 percent majority that favor the ACA. A 2022 Gallup poll put it at 57 to 40 percent.[28] Both are sizable Democratic margins.

Additionally, more Democrats in the electorate are becoming entrenched in their party's position than Republicans. That is, more Democrats favor Obamacare than Republicans who do not favor it. Put differently, the 85 percent of Democrats and 15 percent of Republicans who favor the ACA is a larger group than the 8 percent of Democrats and 77 percent of Republicans who do not favor the ACA. Were the court to overrule Obamacare, and were Democrats to net only a fractional increase (say, 5 percent of Republicans), it would still represent a significant shift in the contemporary electoral balance of power. Thus, striking down Obamacare represents a dilemma for the Republican Party. They may prefer that policy outcome, but it might come with political costs.[29]

In 2021 the court had a second chance to strike down Obamacare. President Donald Trump orchestrated a complicated political-legal maneuver to bring a new case before the court that could challenge *Sebelius*'s logic. In 2017 Trump pushed Congress to revise the ACA to lower the penalty for not having health care from $695 to $0. Conservative legal activists found a case to bring the court (*California v. Texas*), where they argued that without penalties, there was no real tax, and the ACA had no constitutional justification.[30] They said that the individual mandate was not severable from the rest of the ACA; if the mandate was struck down, the entire bill collapsed.

Many court watchers expected a conservative ruling. Alito and Thomas still sat on the court. Roberts's *Sebelius* logic might be undone and the chief justice could swing. Moreover, Trump had appointed three new justices (discussed further in the next chapter), all of whom had conservative bona fides and who were expected to ally with Justices Alito and Thomas to form an anti-ACA majority, regardless of how Roberts voted. Instead, the case was dismissed for the plaintiff's lack of standing by a 7 to 2 vote.[31] Justice Alito, joined only by Justice Gorsuch, dissented, saying that standing was not an issue and that the no-penalty mandate was not sustainable under the taxing power. Thomas concurred with Alito on taxing but joined the majority in the ruling on standing.

Sebelius shares some similarities with abortion in the 1970s. They were both salient and did not have clear-cut majorities or minorities as landmark cases reached the Supreme Court.[32] Broadly, about half the country was pro-life and pro-choice in 1973; about half the country supported and opposed the ACA in 2012. Immediately after the decisions, support for the conservative positions increased somewhat, likely because a sector of the electorate was energized by those very rulings. Over time, though, both rulings normalized and their popularity increased. For *Roe*, this took decades (see following chapter), and in the intervening time, Republicans flipped many conservative Democrats. For *Sebelius*, this took only a few years, and the decision had no coalition-building impact.[33] By 2016 there was a national majority in favor of the ACA, to the point where united government under Republican leadership could not repeal it. Trump was not mistaken in setting in motion a plan that might retry the case before the court under a different constitutional logic that might lead to judicial review striking down the original act. Surely the appointment of three conservatives—especially one in Justice Ginsburg's vacant seat—increased the chances of conservatives winning *California v. Texas*. Yet, they lost. The 7 to 2 vote was not even close, and two of Trump's appointees (Kavanaugh and Barrett), as well as Thomas and Roberts, voted to punt the case.

Perhaps the main difference between *Roe* and *Sebelius* was popular support for their underlying basis. On a binary pro-life/pro-choice split, the country was roughly half and half in 1973. On the details, though, a majority opposed fundamental aspects of *Roe* (e.g., allowing any abortions after the first trimester). Meanwhile, before Obama took office, a majority supported national health care, and this could explain the longer-term dynamics of public opinion on Obamacare. That is, the conservative midterm reaction in 2010 could have signaled a shift in public opinion on health care; or it could have been a normal, if larger-than-usual, midterm loss by the president's party. Opinion shifted more conservatively in the years after the ACA's passage, but that was a relative blip. But by the time of *California v. Texas*, Democrats had a comfortable and durable pro-Obamacare majority within the electorate. The shift in public opinion might not have caused the court to rule as it did in *California v. Texas*. But the outcome certainly reflected that opinion.

In this way, *California v. Texas* is similar to the 1958 communism decisions, in which the court legitimated majoritarian legislation. Both issues were salient. Congress was narrowly divided on communism, as the Senate barely failed to pass a court-curbing bill. The public, though, clearly stood against communists' rights, as well as, presumably, against the court's 1956 and 1957 pro–communists' rights decisions. When facing the issue for a second time in 1958, the court reversed a pair of earlier decisions, which then made it easier to prosecute communists. When facing Obamacare for a second time in 2021, the court did not reverse its original opinion. But like the do-over with communism, the court ruled in the direction favored by a national majority. As such, congressional Republicans might continue to attack the court on health care. But those will likely be position-taking measures designed to rile up their home constituency. They are as likely to have coalition-expanding effects as pro-communist sentiments would have had in 1958.

Same-Sex Marriage

In 2015 a 5–4 court ruled that states could not ban same-sex couples from marrying. Justice Anthony Kennedy authored a decision rooted in four principles and traditions that overturned some states' legislative or initiative-driven bans. Every justice in the minority wrote an impassioned dissent. The case was highly salient and widely covered. Yet, it did not cause the kind of pushback that other cases described in this book caused. Put simply, *Obergefell v. Hodges* highlighted different ideologies but did nothing to reshape partisan coalitions. Moreover, there is evidence that the decision was some combination of majoritarian and expected (from both parties).

Public opinion polls demonstrate two things. First, opinion trended toward support for same-sex marriage. Table 8.3 tracks three separate polls in the decade leading up to *Obergefell*. There are minor variations, but the overall trajectory in each is clear: over time, more people began to support same-sex marriage than oppose it. Second, by 2015 there was a clear majority in favor of the policy. Moreover, the numbers in the table were collected before the ruling—they were not influenced by the court's striking down of state restrictions. In fact, the ruling seems to have had little impact, as Gallup found no meaningful movement on support or opposition two months after *Obergefell*.

TABLE 8.3 Public Opinion on Same-Sex Marriage

Poll[a]	2005		2010		2015	
	Support	Oppose	Support	Oppose	Support	Oppose
Pew	36	53	42	48	57	39
Gallup	37	59	44	53	60	37
ABC/WP	32	62	47	50	61	35

a. Pew Poll, 2005, 2010, 2015; Gallup Poll, 2005, 2010, 2015; ABC/*Washington Post* Poll, 2005, 2010, 2015.

Members of Congress were aware of the same-sex marriage majority. In their comments on the floor, they were much more likely to denounce the accountability problem than the countermajoritarian difficulty. The closest we get to the latter is when Tim Huelskamp (R-KA) argued that fifty million Americans, who had voted in state referenda to define marriage as exclusively between one man and one woman, had suddenly been silenced. More common, though, were members who cited "unelected judges" and claimed that "it is the Court's job to interpret the law, not to rewrite the law."[34]

Perhaps these lawmakers railed against the process more than the merits because, like the American people, they sensed that—in one fashion or another—same-sex marriage was soon to be the law of the land. Right before the announcement, Pew found that 72 percent believed that legalizing same-sex marriage nationwide was "inevitable." Interestingly, this number did not waver between partisans: 72 percent of Democrats and 72 percent of Republicans saw it as inevitable.[35] This likely included the dissenting justices, in fact. The four dissenters did not fight same-sex marriage as bad policy as much as they lamented the manner in which same-sex marriage was now instituted (i.e., though judicial decree). Like their congressional counterparts, it was not a matter of *what*, but rather *how*, which indicates that in the judicial conference room, the substantive policy not as contentious as the constitutional process for this type of social change.[36]

It is not that same-sex marriage was not salient. It was—for both sides. But they both saw the endgame as unchangeable and had already adapted their expectations and political behavior. Same-sex marriage mattered to many liberals and conservatives, but they were likely already aligned with the political party that better represented their respective viewpoints. Put bluntly, many LGBT folks already voted Democrat; many religious traditionalists already voted Republican.

Thus, although *Obergefell v. Hodges* was salient enough to have created coalitional changes, the coalitions were already in lockstep with the policy preferences. Moreover, there just was no anti-same-sex marriage majority to be found. If anything, the court ruled with the majority in a way that the minority saw coming and for which it had already braced itself.

Many LGBT activists equate marriage to desegregation—they argue that it was the culmination of a long legal effort and would become the cornerstone of future activism. In reality, *Obergefell* had less in common with *Brown* (or certainly with *Swann*) than it did with *Gideon v. Wainwright*, which granted indigent defendants the right to counsel in criminal trials. *Gideon* was a majoritarian decision that only really pertained to three states that did not already provide counsel.[37] *Obergefell* applied to more than three states; it applied to fifteen, all in the Midwest or South.[38] But nationally, the public opinion tide had turned as a majority already supported same-sex marriage. That majority's margin, too, had not yet plateaued. In sum, the Supreme Court was hardly a lone wolf policy entrepreneur standing up to national majorities to protect minority rights in *Obergefell*. The decision was majoritarian, reined in regional outliers, and garnered very little substantive objections. It was, in a word, expected.

Religious Liberty Cases

Obamacare and same-sex marriage led to free exercise litigation before the Supreme Court. These cases centered on how to navigate religious exemptions, exceptions, or objections under new constitutional constructions. In both issue areas, the court did not seem to upset a majority. If anything, they might have provided rearguard action that made their earlier decisions (i.e., *Sebelius* and *Obergefell*) more palatable for their original detractors.

Affordable Care Act, Birth Control, and Religious Liberty

New Right conservatives objected to the women's health amendment to the Affordable Care Act, which required employers to provide preventive contraceptive insurance to women. The law allowed religious institutions to apply for exemptions when their beliefs ran contradictory to the coverage. However, such exemptions did not exist for for-profit companies, such as Hobby Lobby, an arts and crafts chain which operated its business model on Christian principles. In *Burwell v. Hobby Lobby* (2014), Justice Alito wrote for a 5–4 majority that gave Hobby Lobby the right to the same exemption granted to religious institutions. To apply for the exemption, corporations like Hobby Lobby would have to fill out a form that registered their religious objections, which then required insurers to find a way to pay for such coverage beyond charging the objector (e.g., the government might subsidize that part of the coverage).

Wheaton College, a private Christian institution, then sued, arguing that filling out the form made them complicit in actions that led to birth control methods that violated its core religious beliefs.

Decided a few days after *Hobby Lobby*, *Wheaton College v. Burwell* (2014) stated that the school did not have to sign a form that allowed someone else to provide contraceptive coverage. Instead, Wheaton had to file a letter with the federal government stating its objections. From there, it was incumbent on the government to notify third parties (e.g., insurers) to obtain and provide the coverage.

After winning an election in which he promised, but failed, to repeal Obamacare, President Donald Trump took executive action to scale back the health care law. One administrative guideline expanded who could claim an exemption to the contraceptive requirement. Liberals objected. There were procedural arguments, but at base, at issue was whether Trump could administratively stretch the religious exemption.[39] In *Little Sisters of the Poor Saints Peter and Paul Home v. Pennsylvania* (2014), Justice Clarence Thomas wrote for the court's five conservatives, saying that the ACA's language granted broad discretion, and that the administration's interpretation was appropriate.[40] Agreeing on the merits, Justices Kagan and Breyer concurred, but they would have remanded and asked the lower court to decide if the administration's interpretation fit with the standard of reasoned decision-making (*Chevron v. NRDC*, 1984). In sum, all three cases were split 5–4 on ideological lines. But though the majority was narrow, religious conservatives won all three.[41]

At base, public opinion polls on the contraception coverage issue show a nonmajoritarian setting. For instance, a couple years before *Hobby Lobby*, the public split on whether religious institutions should be allowed to apply for a contraception exemption (see table 8.4).

TABLE 8.4 Public Opinion on Contraceptive Exemption

Poll[a]	Support exemption	Oppose exemption
YouGov	46%	41%
Washington Post	46%	49%

a. YouGov Poll, 2014; *Washington Post* Poll, 2014.

The *Washington Post* poll is particularly interesting because it offers some specifics about the social welfare versus religious liberty tension. Respondents were asked two questions. First, "do you think health insurance companies should or should not be required to cover the full cost of birth control for women?" The *Post* found a 61–35 split in favor of coverage. When the survey followed up with the nuanced question of whether the insurance should be provided through an employer affiliated with a religious, support decreased to 49–46.[42]

In 2012 the Public Religion Research Institute (PRRI) found that support fluctuated when the institution in question changed. Table 8.5 indicates that a majority might have opposed *Hobby Lobby*, *Little Sisters*, and *Wheaton* in their request for an exemption; yet a majority also would have supported churches in asking for an exemption. When compared to other polls, this could be a product of the wording of the question. PRRI asked if these institutions "should be required to provide employees with health care plans that cover contraception." They highlight the social welfare aspect of the issue in the trio of court cases. When questions centered on the religious liberty aspect, results were different, as table 8.4 indicates.[43]

TABLE 8.5 Public Opinion on Corporations and Contraceptive Exemption

Institution	Should be required to provide contraception coverage
Publicly held corporations	62%
Religiously affiliated hospitals	57%
Religiously affiliated colleges	54%
Privately owned small businesses	53%
Religiously affiliated social service agencies	52%
Churches and other places of worship	42%

Moreover, the polls cited were conducted in 2012. When we examine polls taken right around the time of *Hobby Lobby*, we see results similar to those from YouGov and the *Washington Post*: a nonmajoritarian split. Again, it does seem as if a majority supported the social welfare aspect (i.e., the women's health amendment requirement for contraceptive coverage).[44] Digging even deeper, a KFF poll taken immediately after *Hobby Lobby* (July 2014) reveals more nonmajoritarian evidence, as well as intensity of preferences and perceptions of the decision's impact. An overwhelming majority (85 percent) said it would not change their likelihood of voting. Nearly 80 percent of respondents did not believe that *Hobby Lobby* would have even a minor impact on health care law. In sum, public opinion polls show that there was no majority in support of or in opposition to *Hobby Lobby, Wheaton*, and *Little Sisters*.[45]

That said, Democratic lawmakers' denouncements did evoke countermajoritarian rhetoric. Representative Eddie Bernice Johnson (D-TX) claimed that "70% of Americans disagree with that heinous assertion" from *Hobby Lobby*. Meanwhile, a couple members of Congress made gender-related accountability claims. Representative Louise Slaughter (D-TX) railed against the notion that "five men on this Court decided whether women can have equal access to contraception . . . when 99% of women in this country have used some form of birth control." Senator Patty Murray (D-WA) similarly fumed, "Five men on the Supreme Court rolled back the clock on women . . . People across the country think the Supreme Court was dead wrong on this decision."[46]

Altogether, court-curbing on the three decisions was quite muted—there were only six attacks. None of them made it past introduction. They never came up for debate. They never made it close to being voted upon on the floor. In fact, perhaps the most interesting "attacks" were from conservatives. Kelly Ayotte (R-NH) introduced a bill that seemed more to uphold *Griswold v. Connecticut* (1965) in allowing women the right to purchase birth control methods (i.e., condoms, birth control pills). Sherrod Brown (D-OH), meanwhile, introduced a bill in 2018 that presaged Justices Alito and Gorsuch's concurrence in *Little Sisters*. Brown's bill required more exemptions than currently allowed by the Trump administration. In effect, this was a signal, from a Democrat no less, for the Supreme Court to take a more conservative approach to these cases.

The reaction was muted mainly because liberals had won the big policy issue: that Obamacare was constitutional. These offshoot cases were just that: offshoots. They certainly contained important constitutional and policy issues. However, it was not as if the entire

ACA was at stake. *Hobby Lobby, Wheaton,* and *Little Sisters* were not rehearings of *Sebelius.*

I suggest that conservatives' goal was relatively narrow and that their willingness to make policy concessions indicates a figurative line in the sand. Conservatives' goals were straightforward: they wanted religious objectors to be able to raise their concerns and for someone else to foot the bill for contraceptive coverage. They did not try to overturn Obamacare based on this one plank. And they were willing to comply with existing law: they did not try to exempt religious employers from providing *any* health care; they did not even try to require women to pay for contraception on their own. Practically, the litigation had no real-world effect: women still received insurance coverage for contraception, even if it did not come from their employer. If anything, conservatives' goals here seemed to violate metaconservative economic principles because they increased the likelihood of more government spending, as someone would have to pay the cost if Hobby Lobby, Wheaton, et al. did not. In this sense, conservatives acknowledged that Obamacare was a permanent fixture in American politics. But good-faith religious objections needed constitutional resolution. This was the line in the sand: Republicans could live with nationalized health care, but it had to be reconciled with free exercise.

It was almost as if Republicans acknowledged their defeat and the new politics of a post-ACA world. KFF found that Democrats were not motivated to go to the polls in the wake of *Hobby Lobby.*[47] But what if they had won the case? Would the opposite have been true: would Republicans have been more likely to vote? It is impossible to measure what did not happen, but I think disappointed Republicans would have been more likely to mobilize than disappointed Democrats.[48] Now, nonmajoritarianism works both ways: Republicans could not have built an electoral majority off a free exercise/Obamacare loss. However, because the issue was so salient to some conservatives, we could imagine the GOP using a *Hobby Lobby* loss to create a new angle on pro-life politics. For example, I believe Republican attacks (including rhetorical countermajoritarian accusations and court-curbing proposals) would have been more numerous and vociferous than the four attacks lobbed by Democratic lawmakers. Such conservative attacks would not have, say, won the White House for the GOP. But they likely would have resulted in more Republicans showing up to vote. The case was nonmajoritarian, but it was probably more salient to one side than the other. When that side won, the issue largely fizzled.

Same-Sex Marriage, Wedding Services, and Religious Liberty
Obergefell v. Hodges's protection of same-sex marriage raised free exercise issues, and Justice Kennedy's majority opinion acknowledged the likelihood of future cases and the need to protect good-faith objectors. Chief Justice Roberts's dissent, too, predicted "hard questions" arising in the wake of *Obergefell*. The first of such cases to arrive at the court was *Masterpiece Cakeshop v. Colorado Civil Rights Commission* (2018). A same-sex couple asked the bakery to make them a wedding cake. The baker declined on religious grounds, and the couple asked the commission to find the baker's response as discriminatory. The commission ruled against the baker. The court ruled that the baker had both free exercise and free expression rights and that the commission did not handle the case in a neutral manner when it showed clear hostility toward his religious beliefs. It was a relatively narrow decision that focused more on the behavior of the commission rather than the baker's free exercise. Nevertheless, the case was correctly interpreted as a conservative victory.

Similar to public opinion on the Obamacare/religious liberty cases, public opinion on same-sex wedding services was split. Table 8.6 shows various public opinion polls taken around the time of *Masterpiece*.

Democratic members of Congress did not try to claim that *Masterpiece* was countermajoritarian. The closest any lawmaker came to doing so was Speaker of the House Nancy Pelosi (D-CA) speaking on behalf of Democrats' efforts on LGBT issues: "We have fought the fight on legislation, fought the fight to present the case in the court of public opinion."[49] Moreover, they introduced only five attacks. The response is best characterized as muted.

TABLE 8.6 Public Opinion on Wedding Services

Poll[a]	Small business owners should be able to deny services	Small business owners should not be able to deny services
Penn State	52%	48%
Pew	48%	49%
PRRI	46%	50%

a. Pennsylvania State University Poll, 2017; Pew Poll 2017; Public Religion Research Institute Poll, 2018.

I do not go so far as to say that Democratic politicians were indifferent. Furthermore, LGBT advocates certainly cared. They believed this was the new frontier of civil rights: that same-sex couples not receiving their wedding cake was akin to Black patrons being denied service at a southern diner. Rather than say the issue did not matter to progressives, I contend that *conservatives'* goal was relatively narrow (at least when compared with opposition to same-sex marriage). They did not seek to ban same-sex marriage. They did not try to return the issue to the states. They wanted rearguard protection—another line in the sand: they could live with same-sex marriage, but it had to be reconciled with free exercise.

Yet, even if conservatives had lost the bakery case, they did not have much of a chance of constructing a new majority from the remnants of a hypothetical liberal *Masterpiece* decision. Whatever gains they could have made from baker-sympathetic Democrats would have likely been (more than) offset by LGBT-sympathetic Republicans. Quite likely, not many voters would have crossed party lines in the first place. The issue was certainly salient to small business owners and the New Right, but how many of them were voting Democrat and on the cusp on switching to the GOP? The issue was certainly salient to LGBT persons. But how many of them were voting Republican and ready to be won by the Democratic Party?

We might find answers to these questions soon as the Supreme Court handles more of these "hard questions." In one instance, the owner of a flower shop, Arlene's Flowers, made similar claims as the baker from Masterpiece Cakeshop: that she would not arrange flowers for a same-sex wedding. Washington state courts ruled against her. After remand from the US Supreme Court with instructions to consider the case in light of *Masterpiece*, the Washington supreme court still ruled against Arlene's Flowers, who then appealed to the US Supreme Court, twice. The case was only recently dropped after an agreed-upon settlement for the relatively paltry sum of $5000.[50]

Majorities, Nonmajoritarianism, and Judicial Nuancing in Religious Liberty Cases

Liberals won the landmark cases, and conservatives adjusted to Obamacare and same-sex marriage in the years following *Sebelius* and *Obergefell*. It was as if conservatives could live with *Sebelius* and *Obergefell*, so long as they won *Hobby Lobby* and *Masterpiece*. If anything, liberals have a majoritarian foothold on national health care and same-sex marriage. In the years following *Sebelius*, public opinion became more supportive of Obamacare—to the point where a clear majority supported the ACA. Indeed, even minor splits in the Republican Party prevented it from being unable to replace and repeal—or even just repeal—the ACA.[51] Moderate, nonlibertarian and non–Tea Party Republicans came to support—or at least tolerate—health care. They could live with *Sebelius*, as long as they had *Hobby Lobby*.

Marriage and wedding services present a similar history. In the years after *Obergefell*, support for same-sex marriage made the majoritarian turn. There were pockets of resistance (e.g., the clerk in Kentucky who refused to process same-sex marriage licenses), but these were extreme regional outliers who, in time, were forced into compliance. Libertarian, non–New Right, Republicans support—or at least tolerate—same-sex marriage. They could live with *Obergefell* as long as they had *Masterpiece*.

These cases did not meet either of the conditions necessary to cause significant electoral shifts. The issues involved did not engender cross-partisan majorities—they were partisan and nonmajoritarian. And while perhaps salient to religious or intellectual conservatives, they were not salient to a majority, or to liberals, who had won the original ACA and same-sex cases that *were* salient. Because neither condition was met, members of Congress did not have to engage in the kind of position-taking seen in other issues. This is why there are so few attacks on *Hobby Lobby* or *Masterpiece*. As with nearly all attacks, they were unlikely to change the course of policy. But unlike other case studies, such as crime and busing, they were unlikely to change the course of politics. That is, the losers of *Hobby Lobby* and *Masterpiece* had nothing to gain electorally by attacking the decisions. Thus, these cases do not match up with Supreme Court cases that caused public commotion, such as *Miranda* and *Swann*.

Instead, these cases have more in common with the follow-up cases in 1960s crime (*Warden v. Hayden* and *Terry v. Ohio*) and 1970s busing (*Milliken v. Bradley*). At the time, the original landmark decisions (again, *Mapp/Miranda* and *Swann*) had created clear winners and losers. Conservatives clamored for rearguard action against the court's rulings. They passed legislation that made *Miranda* inapplicable to the federal government. They postponed and defunded busing. Yet, these actions did not quiet all detractors, some of whom considered switching their partisan votes. Indeed, Nixon capitalized on law and order in 1968. And pro-busing Democratic members of Congress felt considerable pressure mounting in the 1974 midterm elections. The court then, in crime and busing, relieved some of the political pressure by issuing rulings that scaled back the original landmark decisions. *Warden* allowed law enforcement and prosecutors more leeway. *Terry* extended police officers' ability to stop and search suspects. *Milliken* said busing could not take place between two school districts. While liberals were surely disappointed with these follow-up cases, they had the effect of helping the Democratic coalition. Nixon might have used law and order, but the fault line was not durable over time.[52] And rather than start voting for a new Republican majority, many antibusing parents found it more profitable to retreat to a school district that evaded *Swann*.

Hobby Lobby and *Masterpiece* do differ somewhat from *Warden*, *Terry*, and *Milliken*. Mainly, the former duo did not create cross-partisan majorities that could shake the electoral calculus by transferring voters from one column to the other. Yet, had *Hobby Lobby* and *Masterpiece* been decided differently, those outcomes could have mobilized some conservatives to be more likely to show up to vote. The impact would not have been large. Nevertheless, politically, Democrats stood to lose some electoral ground if they won these religious liberty cases.[53] The court's rulings in follow-up cases met Republican's objections, but they took away a modestly winning campaign issue from Republican candidates. If anything, the court and Democrats consolidated their gains in the original cases. Just as *Mapp* and *Miranda* remained a foundational piece of constitutional law after *Terry*, so have *Obergefell* and *Sebelius* become entrenched after *Hobby Lobby* and *Masterpiece*.

The 2023 Decisions

Academic studies that analyze the current court suffer from lag. Political development continues, even as we interpret decisions, process partisan responses, and run data. For this reason, by the time we apply theory to the real world, that real world has changed since the start of the study. In what follows, I offer some cursory notes about very recent cases.

Good Governance, Continued: *Moore v. Harper*

In *Rucho v. Common Cause* (2019), Roberts had ruled that federal courts could not consider certain claims of partisan gerrymandering. That said, states could address it in their own governments. The North Carolina supreme court had struck a congressional district map drawn by the state's legislature. In *Moore v. Harper* (2023), the plaintiff argued this decision was unconstitutional due to the "independent state legislature theory," the idea that state legislatures have unchecked power to make decisions on anything related to elections. Legal experts debate the extent of the ruling, but at the very least, the Supreme Court did not adopt the theory in a 6–3 decision.[54]

Liberals have celebrated the decision because if the theory applied, they believe some Republican states would use it to gerrymander district lines and to impose voting restrictions on likely Democratic voters.[55] It is a very important ruling that ensures a more pluralistic conversation about election law among different institutions. However, it is not the type of ruling that will fire up a base or encourage partisans to switch their vote. Put simply, "independent state legislature theory" is not salient to the average voter; and there is no cross-partisan majority against the court's ruling.

Marriage Services, Continued: *303 Creative LLC v. Elenis*

303 Creative LLC v. Elenis (2023) involved graphic design of same-sex wedding websites. The plaintiff, Lorie Smith, alleged that Colorado's antidiscrimination law infringed on her free speech—that it compelled her to design websites for same-sex weddings that she opposed on religious grounds. The breakdown of votes was ideological, and the appointments of Kavanaugh and Barrett were instrumental to the outcome.[56] Justice Gorsuch wrote for the six conservatives and upheld these claims. Notably, he did so on free speech, and not free exercise, grounds.

This ruling is unlikely to shift any voters. Gorsuch's opinion did not strike down the Colorado law wholesale. In fact, he lauded these types of antidiscrimination laws. The LGBT community will understandably take offense. But as with *Masterpiece*, how many Republican-voting LGBT persons are there to switch over to the Democratic Party? Not many. And is the outcome of *303 Creative* really salient to a cross-partisan majority? Probably not.

Affirmative Action:
Students for Fair Admissions, Inc. v. Harvard College

Ruling for an ideologically split 6–2 court, Chief Justice Roberts struck down Harvard and the University of North Carolina's admission procedures.[57] In pursuing diversity, both schools relied too much on racial classifications and therefore violated the equal protection clause. Roberts said that knowing whether diversity was successful was immeasurable. For example, Harvard claimed that a more diverse group of students helped produce engaged and productive citizens, as well as future leaders. These terms were impossible for courts to assess. Moreover, admissions influenced by race required stereotyping—the belief that all students of a race think alike. Finally, race was a "negative" because college admissions are zero-sum. Some students' race propped them up, which assumedly led to some minority students taking the admission slot of others who could not claim minority status. The court said that race could come through in an applicant's file. For instance, admissions committees could consider an applicant's discussion of "how race affected the applicant's life, so long as that discussion is concretely tied to a quality of character or unique ability that the particular applicant can contribute to the university."

Unpacking public opinion on affirmative action is difficult. Fortunately, many polls ask questions specifically about college admissions. Unfortunately, even then, the wording of the question seems to impact the results.[58] A majority seems to support holistic review of applicants' files, which includes their racial background. For example, Americans for Fair Chance—an ideologically pro-affirmative action group—found that 66 percent of respondents believe that admission criteria should include students' entire backgrounds.[59] Another poll conducted by NORC found that 76 percent believe college admissions should take in account the lived experiences and whole story of a student.[60]

On the other hand, many other polls find support for banning college admission boards from considering race. Table 8.7 demonstrates that majorities (ranging from small to large) oppose use of race in college admissions. Three polls break down respondents by party. In each case, at least a quarter (and by CBS's measure, more than half) of Democrats oppose consideration of race.

Is *Students for Fair Admissions, Inc. v. Harvard College* countermajoritarian? Some might conclude that broad support for affirmative action indicates that it is countermajoritarian. At best, it would seem that the Democratic Party could mobilize a sector of its base—likely Black and Latino voters, and perhaps female Democrats. The CBS poll indicates that 18 percent of Republicans and 26 percent of independents would oppose the decision.[61] Those are significant blocs. But the same poll also found that 70 percent of *all* Americans would support the ruling.

TABLE 8.7 Public Opinion on Affirmative Action

Poll	Question	Pro-AA	Anti-AA	Other
Pew[a]	Take race and ethnicity into account in admissions decisions in order to increase diversity	33	50	Dem: 29–54 Rpb: 14–74
ABC/ Ipsos[b]	Approve of recent decision by US Supreme Court restricting the use of race as a factor in college admissions	32	52	Dem: 26 Rpb: 75 Ind: 74
CBS[c]	Should colleges be allowed to consider race in admissions	30	70	Dem: 55–44 Rpb: 82–18 Ind: 74–26
AP/ NORC[d]	Race should not be too important or at all important when colleges make decisions about admitting students	31	68	
Wa Post/ Schar School[e]	Support Supreme Court banning colleges from considering a student's race when making decisions about student admissions	36	63	

a. Pew Poll, 2022.

b. ABC/Ipsos Poll 2023.

c. CBS Poll, 2023.

d. AP/NORC Poll, 2023.

e. *Washington Post*/Schar School Poll, 2022.

CBS, and other polls, would have us believe that the ruling was in line with a majority of Americans' beliefs. If that majority exists, then it surely is cross-partisan, as indicated by the first three polls listed in table 8.7. This might be the political reality. However, it is even more likely that the American public has conflicting views on a very complex issue. This recalls views on contraceptive coverage under Obamacare and wedding services under *Obergefell*. Both issues seemingly create nonmajoritarian difficulties. Americans believe employers should provide birth control, but they also believe corporations like *Hobby Lobby* have some free exercise rights. LGBT Americans should have their cake, but evangelical bakers should be able to eat theirs, too. There might be provincial voting blocs that mobilize because of the Harvard/UNC decision. But they are likely small and were likely already aligned with the party that represented their views on affirmative action.

Student Loan Debt: *Biden v. Nebraska*

In 2022 the Biden administration announced that it would cancel up to $20,000 in student loans. A number of states challenged the move, arguing that it would affect the way they finance college students. The Biden administration argued that the HEROES Act gave the administration power to modify laws and regulations regarding student loans. The court said that meant Biden could make modest, not transformational, adjustments. Thus, Biden's cancelation of debt was overturned.

This ruling might meet the criteria for electoral pushback. For starters, *Biden v. Nebraska* appears countermajoritarian. Different polling agencies report around the same figures. For instance, Quinnipiac reports support for canceling up to $10,000 at 53 to 43 percent.[62] YouGov reports on the same question at 52 to 41 percent.[63] Fox News has the figure at 62 to 36 percent, and their question included canceling up to $20,000 or all student debt.[64] It is a slim majority, but the margin widens when we get into the details of loan forgiveness: capping monthly payments received 57 to 21 percent support; forgiving balances after ten years garnered 50 to 36 percent; and the government covering unpaid interest elicited 57 to 28 percent.[65]

The issue seems salient and that it captures a cross-partisan coalition. Politico asked how much priority Congress should give to the issue. Twenty-five percent said it should be a top priority. Breaking that group down by party identification: Thirty-five percent of Democrats, 16 percent of independents, and 15 percent of Republicans believed it should be a top priority.[66] We would expect Democrats to make up most of the pro-relief coalition; but it was not exclusively Democratic. Finally, student loan forgiveness impacted a wide swath of the electorate: fifteen percent would have had loans reduced or eliminated and 25 percent would have had the policy affect a family member.[67]

I surmise that the Democratic Party could use *Biden v. Nebraska* to expand their electoral coalition. The ruling was countermajoritarian. It has cross-partisan opposition. And it is salient. There are three possible targets for the DNC. First, they could mobilize their own base—lifelong Democrats who want to see parts of their student loans instantly extinguished. Perhaps likely Democratic voters are even more likely to vote when $10,000 is at stake. Second, they could peel away some Republicans who also want to erase thousands off their debt. Third, they could attract first-time voters. Consider college students who have not yet voted and who are in the midst of taking out these types of loans.

Yet, there is one obstacle standing in the way of the Democratic Party using the issue to win voters: the Biden administration. Soon after the court ruled, the administration announced that it would: create an "on-ramp" to repayment after the COVID pause; cut the amount borrowers have to pay each month from 10 percent to 5 percent of discretionary income; ensure that no borrower earning under 225 percent of the federal poverty level would have to make a monthly payment; forgive original balances of less than $12,000 after ten years of payment instead of after twenty years; and not charge borrowers with unpaid monthly interest.[68] If anything, these scaled-down moves are in line with another public opinion question that found that 49 percent believed Biden had exceeded his authority in canceling debt (44% believed he did not).[69] They might feel the policy outcome is both constitutionally and substantively satisfactory. In short, the Biden administration is working to fix the problem. They might be able to run retrospective campaigns in the future. That is, they can tell pro-relief voters they delivered on majoritarian sentiments. But I wonder if a better strategy would have been to use the Supreme Court as a foil—to claim that the Supreme Court had deprived the executive from acting and that there was only one solution to the *Biden v. Nebraska* problem: elect more Democrats to pass a new law.

Chapter 9

The Elephant in the Room

FOR DECADES, LIBERALS WARNED that *Roe v. Wade* stood at the precipice of reversal. Yet, despite challenge after challenge (e.g., *Webster, Casey, Box*) and one Republican appointee after another, *Roe* stood for nearly half a century.[1] Liberal suspicion that *Roe* would fall appeared like paranoia. Until 2022.

Trump Appointees

In this case, appointments mattered. A trio of Trump appointees added a new fervor to the Left's fear that *Roe* was in trouble. Justice Gorsuch's replacing Antonin Scalia might have done little to alter the bottom-line conference vote. But Justices Kavanaugh and Barrett replacing Anthony Kennedy and Ruth Bader Ginsburg, respectively, gave pro-lifers reason to believe that two votes might have switched on the court and that *Roe* could fall. Pro-choice groups agreed—and it was a major, if not the primary, reason for the Democratic Party's opposition to recent appointments, especially those of Kavanaugh and Barrett. Both had important background circumstances. Kavanaugh faced sexual assault allegations. Barrett was nominated on the eve of an election and on the heels of being told by the nominating party that such an action was undemocratic. But as Linda Greenhouse puts it, "It was always about abortion."[2]

Whatever good-faith objections Democrats might have had on these grounds, it cannot be denied that abortion hung over the nominations. Some conservatives believed the alleged sexual assault claims against Kavanaugh were a smoke screen for trying to preserve *Roe*.[3] Some liberals mixed their messaging on Republican hypocrisy and abortion.[4] And to be fair, Republicans too—from the Senate majority leader to principal pro-life advocates—all but admitted that procedure and precedent was not nearly as important as getting another conservative vote on the court, a statement that just cannot be detached from abortion.[5]

Combined with conservative Justices Thomas, Alito, and Roberts, in 2022, there now sat six justices with right-wing bona fides: conservative Segal–Cover scores, Federalist Society ties, circuit court voting records, unequivocal pro-life interest group support and pro-choice group opposition, partisan confirmation votes in the Senate, and/or presidential reassurances of conservatism. The court was stacked against *Roe*.

Dobbs v. Jackson Women's Health Organization

Pro-life hopefuls and pro-choice pessimists were correct. *Roe* fell. In *Dobbs v. Jackson Women's Health Organization* (2022), the court considered Mississippi's law prohibiting abortion after fifteen weeks. The majority opinion, written by Alito (and joined by Thomas, Gorsuch, Kavanaugh, and Barrett), overturned *Roe* and *Casey*, referring to the two cases as "egregiously wrong." Alito concluded abortion was not a right guaranteed by the Fourteenth Amendment, by the nation's history and tradition, as an essential component of ordered liberty, nor as a broader entrenched right. Stare decisis did not apply, the majority decided, because (among other items) *Roe*'s original reasoning was badly flawed, and it created major problems (e.g., circuit splits) in the judicial system. In future cases, Alito wrote, the court should use a rational basis standard to test whether challenged legislation preserves the balance between the right to choose and potential life.

A trio of conservatives wrote concurrences. Kavanaugh restated much of the majority opinion, adding that every justice over the previous century had voted to overturn some precedent. He took space to emphasize Alito's contention that *Dobbs* was not overruling other precedents (e.g., *Griswold, Loving, Obergefell*). Thomas's concurrence seems to respond to Kavanaugh's last point (or, perhaps it was vice versa). Though Thomas agreed that precedents like

Griswold, Lawrence, and *Obergefell* were not at issue in *Dobbs,* all such precedents warranted reconsideration "because any substantive due process decision is 'demonstrably erroneous.'"

Roberts did not sign on to all of the majority opinion. He voted to uphold Mississippi's restriction but did not strike down *Roe* or *Casey* wholesale. The chief justice advocated a "more measured course." He would have discarded the viability line in favor of establishing a period of time that would provide a reasonable opportunity to choose an abortion. Mississippi gave fifteen weeks, which Roberts found sufficient.

Justices Breyer, Sotomayor, and Kagan cowrote a single dissent. It hinged primarily on women's rights, saying that denying abortion took away autonomy, liberty, equality, and privacy. They criticized the majority for relying too much on the narrow intent of the Fourteenth Amendment's ratifiers, none of whom were women. They doubted the truthfulness of not challenging all privacy precedents. And they questioned Alito's stare decisis claims. All the justices understood the salience, likely interpretation of, and potential ramifications of the majority opinion.[6]

Countermajoritarian Indicators

Most of the rest of the chapter uses public opinion polls and datasets to show how a majority, including a significant percentage of Republican voters, disagree with overturning *Roe.* First, though, let us make quick observations on some of the other indicators of a countermajoritarian decision. Members of Congress have made statements on the countermajoritarian difficulty and the accountability problem. For instance, Elizabeth Warren (D-MA) stated, "Republicans stole two seats on the Supreme Court, all to force their unpopular minority agenda on the rest of Americans." Dick Durbin (D-IL) commented, "They are, in fact, judicial activists—unelected judges—who are actively undermining the rule of law."[7]

There have also been forty attacks on *Dobbs,* such as a pair of House Resolutions condemning the decision.[8] Another example:

the INFO for Reproductive Care Act (2023), introduced by Lori Trahan (D-MA), would educate health professionals about assisting patients to navigate legal issues relating to abortions. The Reproductive Freedom for All Act (2023)—introduced by Tim Kaine (D-VA) and cosponsored by Lisa Murkowski (R-AK), Krysten Simena (D-AZ; now an independent), and Susan Collins (R-ME)—would give statutory protection for *Roe* and *Casey*. Its quartet of relatively moderate sponsors hint toward the median vote (in the Senate and in the country) shading to the left. Meanwhile, on the Democrats' left wing, Alexandria Ocasio-Cortez (D-NY) has called for Gorsuch and Kavanaugh's removal from the bench.[9] There is not much cross-partisan agreement. But that is not because Republican lawmakers necessarily disagree with Democrats; it is because Republicans are largely silent after *Dobbs*.[10]

Public Opinion Polls

The data dives, here and in the next section, are deep, so where appropriate, I describe *the main takeaway message from the data in italics*. Under *Roe*, abortion became a much more partisan issue "in the government." In the 1970s the Democratic Party was split. After the Reagan victory, partisans on both sides drifted into a lockstep view on the issue. Leading up to *Dobbs*, party-line abortion votes in Congress were standard.[11] The picture "in the electorate," however, is murkier—especially within the GOP's voting ranks, where some Republicans appear mildly to extremely pro-choice.

Everything in the rest of this chapter confirms the same overarching point. *Dobbs* has created a rare opportunity for the Democratic Party: the opportunity to use an unpopular Supreme Court decision to win more votes. I start with simple public opinion polls, which give us a broad take on views on abortion. Then I unpack information from a social science dataset, which allow us to parse more complex interactions.

Numerous polls confirm that *before Dobbs the percentage of those who believed abortion should be available in all or most cases trended upward (table 9.1).*

TABLE 9.1 Public Opinion on Abortion

Poll[a]	Date	Legal in all	Legal in most	Legal in some	Illegal in all
CNN	2016	29	15	38	16
CBS	2016	29	18	39	10
Quinnipiac	2016	26	38	22	10
Gallup	2017	29	13	36	18
PRRI	2018	24	35	23	14
NBC/WSJ	2018	31	22	29	12
Pew	2018	25	34	22	15
Quinnipiac	2019	28	32	27	8
NBC/WSJ	2019	34	22	29	12
Fox	2019	31	19	34	12
Pew	2020	30	38	18	11
PRRI	2021	23	39	26	10
Quinnipiac	2021	31	31	21	11
Gallup	2021	32	13	33	19
Fox	2021	29	20	38	11

a. CNN Poll, 2016; Gallup Poll 2017, 2021; Pew Poll 2018, 2020; Quinnipiac Poll 2016, 2019, 2021; Public Religion Research Institute Poll 2018, 2021; NBC/*Wall Street Journal* Poll 2018, 2019; Fox Poll 2019, 2021; CBS Poll, 2016.

Polling organizations have asked what the trajectory of abortion should be. *They found support for Roe and/or less restrictions* (table 9.2).

TABLE 9.2 More or Less Strict Rules on Abortion

Poll[a]	Year	More strict	Less strict	Remain the same
CBS	2017	37	35	25
Gallup	2018	35	30	16
Gallup	2020	41	38	21

a. Gallup Poll, 2018, 2020; CBS Poll 2017.

More respondents believe *the Democratic Party handles abortion better than the Republican Party* (table 9.3).

TABLE 9.3 Which Party Handles Abortion Better

Poll[a]	Year	Democratic Party	Republican Party
NBC/WSJ	2014	38	23
Pew	2017	53	33
Pew	2020	50	35

a. NBC/*Wall Street Journal* Poll 2014; Pew Poll 2017, 2020.

Texas has been a fulcrum in abortion politics. There, the state legislature banned abortion after six weeks of pregnancy and instituted a unique citizen enforcement mechanism.[12] A couple of polls mentioned Texas and asked follow-up questions about it. One poll asked respondents to suppose *Roe v. Wade* was overturned and abortion was left up to the states.[13] They followed up by asking under what circumstances should abortion be allowed. The results for the nation were in line with previous polls, but the surprising finding was that of Texans' beliefs (see table 9.4). There are slight variations, but even in Texas, a majority (55 percent) of residents believe abortion should be available in all or most cases. Only 39 percent said it should be illegal in all or most cases (table 9.4). The same poll found that Americans believed *Roe* established a woman's right to an abortion by 63 to 28 percent; Texans rated at 58 to 35 percent in believing *Roe* established such a right.

TABLE 9.4 Texas's Opinion on Abortion

	Nationwide[a]	Texas
Legal in all cases	25	23
Legal in most cases	32	32
Illegal in most cases	23	29
Illegal in all cases	14	10

a. Quinnipiac Poll, 2021.

A handful of polls either explicitly asked about Texas's law or referred to states implementing similar restrictions. They all consistently found a large plurality or small majority that opposed the law. At its very least, the pro-choice group had an eleven-point margin (table 9.5).

TABLE 9.5 Opinion on Texas's Abortion Regulations

Poll[a]	Date	Strongly/somewhat disapprove	Strongly/somewhat approve
HuffPost/YouGov	Oct 2019	47	36
Quinnipiac	Sept. 2021	51	39
Economist/YouGov	Sep. 18–21, 2021	49	37
Economist/YouGov	Sept. 26–28, 2021	50	36
Economist/YouGov	Oct. 3–5, 2021	49	36
Economist/YouGov	Oct. 9–12, 2021	51	38

a. *Economist*/YouGov Poll, 2021; *Huff Post*/YouGov Poll, 2019; Quinnipiac Poll, 2021.

One poll collected data over a full year (September 2020–September 2021) on the circumstances under which abortion should be legal or illegal. With such a high N, they broke down responses by state (table 9.6).[14] A majority in three quarters of the states—representing 87 percent of the US population—responded that abortion should be legal in most or all cases. Even in the twelve pro-life-leaning states, the pro-choice responses hovered around 50 percent. Five of them (Idaho, North Dakota, Oklahoma, South Dakota, and Wyoming) registered 49 percent support; three registered 47 percent or 48 percent (Alabama, Louisiana, and Tennessee); only four (Arkansas, Kentucky, Mississippi, and West Virginia) were at 46 percent or below. All swing states (Arizona, Florida, Georgia, Iowa, Maine, Michigan, Minnesota, North Carolina, New Hampshire, Ohio, Pennsylvania, Virginia, and Wisconsin) had majorities that believed abortion should be legal in all or most cases.

While journalistic polls provide one-dimensional evidence that more Americans lean pro-choice than pro-life, social science datasets

TABLE 9.6 States' Opinions on Abortion

State	Legal	State	Legal	State	Legal	State	Legal	State	Legal
AK	57	HI	65	MI	59	NV	63	UT	52
AL	47	IA	57	MN	60	NY	65	VA	58
AR	46	ID	49	MO	52	OH	57	VT	74
AZ	58	IL	63	MS	41	OK	49	WA	66
CA	64	IN	53	MT	58	OR	68	WI	59
CO	63	KS	54	NC	56	PA	59	WV	45
CT	70	KY	44	ND	49	RI	67	WY	49
DC	79	LA	47	NE	52	SC	50		
DE	62	MA	73	NH	67	SD	49		
FL	60	MD	67	NJ	66	TN	48		
GA	54	ME	63	NM	61	TX	54		

allow for locating who, exactly, comprise the pro-choice-leaning co-alition. In what follows, I discuss two sets of comparisons: (1) views on abortion and party identification; and (2) views on abortion and political behavior (as measured by presidential vote choice). Results consistently show *a sizable cross-partisan majority disagrees with more restrictive abortion policies.*

Public Opinion Datasets and Abortion Beliefs: Primer

It is easy to feel as if too much data is exactly that: too much. To make this section as accessible as possible, I use a more conversational approach. Similar to addressing methodological choices in chapter 2, I use a question-and-answer format. Let us start by asking some baseline assumption questions.

Why should we pay attention to abortion? It is statistically significant. It might be working backward to start with regression analysis and then talk through descriptive cross-tabulations. But let us establish upfront that abortion has an impact, even when controlling for other factors. From there, let us flesh out the hypotheses that flow from that statement.

Table 9.7 shows the results of a logit model. The dependent variable is two-party presidential preference in 2020 (Biden=1; Trump=0). I account for party ID, ideology, Latino, Black, gender, age, and whether one is pro-life or pro-choice. I use CLARIFY to generate the substantive impact of significant variables. *Party ID*, of course, is the primary determinant. Holding all other variables at their means, moving two units on the seven-unit scale (e.g., from "Lean Democrat" to "Lean Republican") decreases the likelihood of voting for Biden by 44.6 percentage points. *Ideology* and *Black* are statistically and substantively significant, too. *Life/Choice* has a major effect. That it is significant at all, after controlling for other factors (especially party identification) speaks volumes. That it can affect someone's vote by 35.1 percentage points is enough evidence to warrant a deeper dive. Let's do that now.

TABLE 9.7 Logit Analysis of 2020 Presidential Vote Choice

Variable	Coeff.	Impact measurement group	Impact
Party ID	-0.97*	"Lean Democrat" to "Lean Republican"	-44.6
Ideology	-0.61*	Liberal to Conservative	-28.0
Latino	0.25		
Black	1.94*	Not Black to Black	35.3
Female	0.07		
Age	-0.001		
Life/Choice	1.49*	Pro-life to pro-choice	35.1
Constant	4.94		

*p<.001 two-tailed test. Psuedo R^2=.66

N=1131. DV=two-party vote for Biden in 2020.

What is the overall conclusion of what is to follow? *Dobbs* is unpopular, and it creates an opportunity for the Democratic Party to build its electoral coalition.

Is it inevitable that Democrats will win more votes? Unequivocally: no. Many other things can happen—other issues become more important, the economy changes, unemployment rises or falls, inflation rises or falls, wars breakout, natural disasters erupt, scandals emerge, personalities draw some voters in and discourage others from participating, etc. The Democratic Party will have to choose to align its focus, rhetoric, and strategy around abortion. It appears to be a winning issue, but the DNC might fail and/or the RNC could successfully counter (e.g., seize the agenda with another topic). *Just because the opportunity exists does not mean a party will capitalize. Still, the opportunity to campaign against a counter-majoritarian Supreme Court decision on a salient issue rarely presents itself.*

What is the data? I use the 2022 ANES. It is an N of 1585 and is nationally representative. It was conducted after *Dobbs*. The appendix has data from the 2022 GSS and 2022 CCES. I present ANES data because it has the most extensive questions on abortion and allows for what I feel is the most accurate assessment as to whether respondents are pro-life or pro-choice.

Why are there so many tables? Discussing data via prose can be lengthy. Sometimes it is easier to understand the data via visuals than through text.

When attempting to answer questions, what's the bottom line? I present tables. I explain them. But even then, it is difficult to unpack the visuals and/or words—especially when they start to blend together. It is helpful, therefore, to know what message the data conveys before moving onto the next question. I do that at the end of each answer. *I give the bottom line in italics.*

When conceptualizing all the data at once, what's the bottom line? After answering questions, I recap the overall findings and standardize the data to show the "Democratic Edge" within each grouping. For a one-stop view of all the questions asked below, and for a bottom-line calculation of how abortion benefits the Democratic Party, see table 9.18.

Why is the analysis shaded toward the GOP? My goal is not to defend or attack any policy or party. But if I argue that the GOP might be hurt by *Dobbs* (or, conversely, that the Democratic Party could take advantage), then the best line of questioning involves consideration of—or even hedging toward—the null hypothesis: that *Dobbs* has no possibility of having a significant electoral effect. I test that narrative by asking questions about data interpretations that could show that the null is true. Put differently, healthy skepticism is good research design.

Defining Our Terms
How do we know if someone is pro-life or pro-choice? The ANES asks a few questions about abortion. The most pertinent here are:

1. There has been some discussion about abortion during recent years. Which one of these opinions best agrees with your view?
   a. By law abortion should never be permitted
   b. The law should permit abortion only in case of rape, incest, or when the woman's life is in danger
   c. The law should permit abortion for reasons other than rape, incest, or danger to the woman's life, but only after the need for the abortion has been clearly established
   d. By law, a woman should always be able to obtain an abortion as a matter of personal choice
2. Regarding abortion, do you usually think of yourself as:
   a. Pro-choice
   b. Pro-life
   c. Something else
3. As you may know, the US Supreme Court overturned *Roe v. Wade*, ruling that there is no constitutional right to abortion.

Do you favor, oppose, or neither favor nor oppose the
Supreme Court's decision to overturn *Roe v. Wade*?
   a. Favor
   b. Oppose
   c. Neither favor nor oppose

Which question(s) are used? I try to create dueling categories of
pro-choice and pro-life. To do so, I started with the first question
above and placed those who believed abortion should never be legal
into the pro-life category. I placed all the respondents who believed
abortion should always be legal into the pro-choice category. I believe that question captures the poles better than any other question
and therefore was the appropriate place to start. This covered 54.4
percent of respondents. I then used the pro-choice/pro-life question, which I thought was a better worded question than the *Roe*
one (which asks if one favors the overturning of *Roe*, and not if one
favors *Roe*, which could have been confusing). This covered an additional 42.7 percent of respondents. I moved on to the *Roe* question,
but every leftover observation (2.9 percent) responded that they
neither favor nor oppose the overturning of the precedent. *In the
end, 57.5 percent were pro-choice, 39.6 percent were pro-life, and 2.9
percent were neither.*

**Would the distribution be different if we used a different ordering
of the three questions to place respondents into the pro-choice,
pro-life, and neither categories?** In a word, barely. All the responses
seem to hover around 57/39/4. Indeed, the average of all six combi-
nations is 56.9/39.4/3.7. The pro-life/pro-choice split is reliable (see
table 9.8).

**Why not just use the life/choice question if we are placing respon-
dents into pro-life and pro-choice categories?** Because that leaves
7.6 percent of respondents labeled as Something Else. I believe we
can narrow that figure.

TABLE 9.8 Sequencing of Life/Choice Questions

Sequence of sorting	Pro-choice	Pro-life	Neither
Always/Never, Life/Choice	57.5%	39.6%	2.9%
Always/Never, *Roe*	57.1%	39.5%	3.4%
Roe, Always/Never	56.3%	40.3%	3.4%
Roe, Life/Choice	56.3%	40.3%	3.4%
Life/Choice, *Roe*	57.1%	39.5%	3.4%
Life/Choice, Always/Never	56.9%	37.4%	5.7%

What about another option? Perhaps we should not place respondents into pro-life and pro-choice categories by using those very categories because it is teleological. If one wanted a very sophisticated way of placing respondents into categories, I also tried the following sequence:

1. Four-point Always=pro-choice; Four-point Nevers=pro-life
2. Abortions should be allowed in any trimester if the pregnancy is unwanted for any reason=pro-choice
3. Abortions should never be allowed in two of three categories (rape, life of the woman is at risk; serious birth defect is found)=pro-life
4. No conservative feelings about *Dobbs* (i.e., hopeful or happy); and at least two liberal feelings (i.e., angry, afraid, worried, outraged) at levels of "somewhat," "very," or "extremely"=pro-choice
5. No liberal feelings about *Dobbs*; and at least two conservative feelings at levels of "somewhat," "very," or "extremely"=pro-life.
6. Do not favor prosecuting women for abortion; and do not favor prosecuting health care professionals for abortion=pro-choice
7. Do favor prosecuting women for abortion; and do favor prosecuting health care professionals for abortion=pro-life

8. Follow *Roe v. Wade's* reversal either "a moderate amount" or "a great deal"; and oppose *Roe's* reversal=pro-choice
9. Follow *Roe v. Wade's* reversal either "a moderate amount" or "a great deal"; and favor *Roe's* reversal=pro-life

This gave the following: 57.1 percent were pro-choice; 34.5 percent were pro-life, and 8.5 percent were neither. If we want to apply the life/choice question for the 8.5 percent as a last-ditch measure to place them into a Left or Right category, then we are left with: 60 percent were pro-choice; 38.3 percent were pro-life; and 1.7 percent were neither. If anything, this method converts slightly more to the pro-choice category. The more important note, though, is: *any way I slice it, it is close to 57/39/4. I use a procedure that results in 57.5/39.6/2.9.*

Which groups deserve special focus when examining the electoral effects of abortion beliefs? I examine three types of voters. Not every person in these categories will behave in ways that perfectly correspond to their abortion preferences. However, a political party with the advantage in these categories is certainly better situated than a party saddled with a disadvantage.

1. "Probable Partisans." These are pro-choicers who believe/behave in liberal/Democratic ways and pro-lifers who believe/behave in conservative/Republican ways. They are ideologically aligned with the correct stance and party. *Dobbs* likely entrenched them deeper in their beliefs and behavior. For example, imagine a liberal Democrat who believes abortion should always be legal and who voted for Joe Biden in 2020. All else equal, that voter is probably partisan and will continue to vote Democrat after *Dobbs*.
2. "Possible Switchers." These are pro-choicers who align with and vote for the Republican Party and pro-lifers who align with and vote for the Democratic Party. Their views on abortion do not match their party and *Dobbs* could cause them to rethink their vote. Now, abortion is only one factor, and it

may not determine one's candidate preference. But abortion is such a salient issue that if we were going to see cross-partisan switching because of the issue, it would likely be among this group. They are not "switchers." They are "*possible* switchers."

3. "Capturable Independents." These are pro-choicers and pro-lifers who register as independent and/or did not vote for either the Democratic or Republican Party. Again, they might not switch just because of abortion, but if the issue were to have an effect on Independents, then we would expect pro-choice independents to be more likely to vote Democrat and pro-life independents to vote Republican. They are not "captured independents." They are "*capturable* independents."

Even if pro-choicers outnumber pro-lifers, aren't there other features that would affect whether those views translate into partisan gains or losses? Yes. Some factors might mitigate, confound, neutralize, or even reverse the effects described here. Let us examine life/choice views *within the context of party identification, vote choice, intensity of identification and beliefs, likelihood of turnout, and likelihood of changing one's vote.*

How do we know if the data presented is reliable? I ran the same data with two other datasets. The General Social Survey (GSS) is administered by the University of Chicago and the Cooperative Election Study (CES) is administered by Harvard University. The GSS had a good number of abortion-related questions. But it is a broad survey that does not focus narrowly on politics. The CES does focus on politics, but had very few abortion-related questions. There are some differences in results between the ANES and GSS or CES. Namely, the GSS and CES both contain more partisans and fewer independents. Thus, compared to the ANES, the results from the GSS and CES show the Democratic advantage as larger with probable partisans and smaller with possible switchers and capturable independents. But that is a question of scale, not direction. *Two other long-running highly regarded national polls found the same thing: Democrats have a major advantage on abortion.*

Party Identification

What is the party breakdown of the life/choice split? We can imagine a scenario in which nearly every pro-choicer is already a Democrat but the pro-life coalition is divided among Democrats, Republicans, and independents. In that scenario, the Democratic Party would have very little to gain and the GOP could seize pro-life cross-partisans and/or independents. Alternatively, maybe the GOP makes up for its ideological heterogeneity by attracting more independents, of whom most identify as pro-life. This would explain how the GOP overcomes its minoritarian position on abortion—its partisans may be divided, but nonpartisans prefer the GOP's abortion plank.

TABLE 9.9 Life/Choice by Party (N=1585)

	Democrats	Republicans	Ind/Other	Total
Pro-life	5.2%	19.1%	15.4%	39.6%
Pro-choice	26.5%	7.4%	23.6%	57.6%
Other/NA	0.4%	0.7%	1.8%	2.9%

- Probable Partisans. Many Republicans, 19.1 percent of the entire sample, code as pro-life. However, 26.5 percent of the sample are pro-choice Democrats..
- Possible Switchers. Democrats have a small advantage, as 7.4 percent are pro-choice Republicans and 5.2 percent are pro-life Democrats.
- Capturable Independents. Independents lean more toward Democratic preferences on abortion: 23.6 percent to 15.4 percent.
- *On party identification, the Democratic Party has an advantage with probable partisans, possible switchers, and capturable independents*

What about a more fine-grained partisan breakdown? Separating partisans into three boxes (Democrat, Republican, and independent) does not portray the true nature of party politics. Indeed, one driving assumption of this book is the presence of intra-party factions—that "not all Democrats/Republicans are the same." Maybe a different categorization scheme leads to a different distribution of life/choice identifiers.

Instead, a more fine-grained partisan breakdown only reinforces the narrative. The ANES uses the common seven-point party identification scheme. It asks respondents to self-place into: (1) "strong Democrat"; (2) "not very strong Democrat"; (3) "lean Democrat"; (4) "independent"; (5) "lean Republican"; (6) "not very strong Republican"; and (7) "strong Republican." Some respondents did not answer or were not sure. I placed them into the independent category.

It follows that creating a more fine-grained independent category— after we have placed "not very strong" and "lean" Democrats and Republicans—might produce a more conservative independent faction. This is quite important because the independent category represents nearly a quarter of the electorate. And it could be telling because while some voters claim to be independents, many of those who self-place into that category are actually strongly aligned with one of the two major parties.[15] Thus, after eliminating all those who think of themselves as independent but who are really just Democrats or Republicans in disguise, are we left with a bunch of pro-life independents?

TABLE 9.10 Life/Choice by Party Faction (N=1585)

Stance	Str Dem	NVS Dem	Lean Dem	Ind + NA	Lean GOP	NVS GOP	Str GOP	Total
Pro-life	2.7%	2.4%	0.8%	7.7%	6.9%	5.2%	13.9%	39.6%
Pro-choice	19.1%	7.3%	7.2%	14.3%	2.3%	3.9%	3.5%	57.6%
Other/ NA	0.2%	0.2%	0.0%	1.6%	0.3%	0.4%	0.3%	2.9%

- Probable Partisans. Democratic majorities are larger as 19.1 percent of the entire sample are pro-choice Strong Democrats and 13.9 percent are pro-life Strong Republicans.
- Possible Switchers. Republicans have more to lose. Democrats might lose 2.4 percent Not very strong pro-life Democrats and 0.8 percent Lean Democrats. But Republicans might lose

3.9 percent pro-choice Strong Republicans and 2.3 percent Lean Republicans.

- Capturable Independents. A more sifted independent group is still largely liberal on abortion. 14.3 percent of all respondents fall into the pro-choice Independent category; 7.7 percent fall into the pro-life Independent category.
- *Even with a more fine-grained measure of party identification, the Democratic Party still has an advantage with probable partisans, possible switchers, and capturable independents.*

Which party has members who demonstrate more intense preferences on abortions? There are more pro-choicers than pro-lifers. But we often see news footage of ardent antiabortion protestors, litigators, and lobbyists. Maybe more conservatives care deeply about the issue than liberals. If so, this might tell us something about the likelihood of changing views and/or participation.

ANES asks respondents how important one finds the issue of abortion. Answers include: "extremely," "very," "somewhat," "not too," and "not at all" important. I dropped those who responded "not too" or "not at all" important.[16]

TABLE 9.11 Intensity (N=1211; 76.4% of ANES sample)

	Democrats	Republicans	Ind/Other	Total
Pro-life	5.9%	18.6%	14.0%	38.4%
Pro-choice	30.9%	5.9%	23.3%	60.0%
Other/NA	0.3%	0.3%	1.1%	1.6%

- Probable Partisans. Democrats have a 12.3 percentage point advantage in probable partisans with intense preferences (30.9 percent pro-choice Democrats versus 18.6 percent pro-life Republicans).
- Possible Switchers. Neither party has a net gain with possible switchers—5.9 percent are pro-life Democrats and 5.9 percent are pro-choice Republicans.

- Capturable Independents. Independents show a significant 9.3 percentage point difference in choice (23.3 percent) versus life (14.0 percent).
- *For those with intense preferences, Democrats have a larger share of probable partisans and capturable independents.*

Political Behavior and Vote Choice

What about political behavior and how respondents vote? It is one thing to analyze abortion views through the lens of partisan "identifiers." It is another to analyze those views through the lens of how people "vote." Perhaps the distribution of voting patterns indicates a favorable landscape for the GOP. For example, perhaps every pro-choicer already votes Democrat whereas pro-lifers split between the two parties. In that case, Democrats would have no more abortion votes to gain. Meanwhile, Republicans could then use *Dobbs* to attract Democrat-voting pro-lifers. In that case, the GOP would have the advantage. Also, a considerable portion of the sample (25.2 percent) said that they did not vote for either Biden or Trump. If that portion started voting Democrat or Republican, their abortion views might influence that decision, especially after *Dobbs*. (Let's take a quick timeout to ask: **How do we measure respondents' vote?** I use presidential vote choice in 2020.)

TABLE 9.12 Candidate Support (N=1585)

	Biden supporters	Trump supporters	Other/NA	Total
Pro-life	5.9%	24.8%	8.9%	39.6%
Pro-choice	33.3%	9.3%	15.0%	57.6%
Other/NA	0.8%	0.8%	1.3%	2.9%

- Probable Partisans. Biden won a majority of pro-choice votes and Trump won a majority of pro-life votes. But Biden's edge (33.3 percent to 24.8 percent) is significantly larger.
- Possible Switchers. Trump won more pro-choicers (9.3 percent) than Biden won pro-lifers (5.9 percent). Thus, Biden has

a 3.4 percentage point advantage in trying to switch the votes of Republican voters.

- Capturable Independents. More third-party voters have liberal views on abortion than ones that have conservative views. Pro-choice third-party voters (15.0 percent) outnumber pro-life third-party voters (8.9 percent).
- *Voting patterns indicate the Democratic Party has an advantage with probable partisans, possible switchers, and capturable independents.*

How do those with intense preferences vote? Perhaps intensity of abortion preferences translates into vote choice for conservatives but not for liberals. That is, folks vote Republican when they are pro-life and believe abortion is important; but folks do not necessarily vote Democrat when they are pro-choice and find abortion important. Table 9.13 includes only respondents who find abortion "somewhat," "very," or "extremely" important.

TABLE 9.13 Intense Voters Vote Choice (N=1211; 76.4% of ANES sample)

	Biden	Trump	Other	Total
Pro-life	6.8%	23.6%	8.0%	38.4
Pro-choice	38.0%	6.9%	15.2%	60.1%
Other/NA	0.7%	0.3%	0.7%	1.3%

- Probable Partisans. 38.0 percent are intensive Biden-supporting pro-choicers; 23.6 percent are intensive Trump-supporting pro-lifers.
- Possible Switchers. In a piece of good (or neutral) news for the RNC, 6.8 percent are intense Biden-supporting pro-lifers; and 6.9 percent are intense Trump-supporting pro-choicers.
- Capturable Independents. Intense pro-choice third-party voters (15.2 percent) outnumber intense pro-life third-party voters (8.0 percent).
- *Among voters with intense views on abortion, the Democratic Party has an advantage with probable partisans and capturable independents. The margin for possible switchers is negligible.*

Most Likely Voters

I have discussed views on abortion in light of partisan identity, intensity of beliefs, and vote choice. One possibly overlooked item is the likelihood of any of these respondents actually showing up to the polls on Election Day. This section explores the beliefs and behavior of the type of citizen who makes the biggest difference in determining partisan control of Washington: likely voters.

How do we measure whether someone is a likely voter? Literature has convincingly shown that past voter turnout predicts future turnout.[17] The ANES checks governmental records for respondents in states where that is possible (about 34 percent of respondents). For the rest, they ask respondents if they voted. About 63 percent answered yes (50 percent) or no (13 percent). For the remaining 3 percent, the ANES asked them to guess whether they voted or not (about 1 percent said yes and 2 percent said no). This gave a total of 76.2 percent saying they voted. After winnowing down every observation, we have what I will refer to as "likely voters," or, *did the respondent vote or say s/he voted in the election of 2020?*

Is 76.2 percent an accurate representation of voter turnout in 2020? No. It is significantly higher than the real turnout: 62.8 percent.[18] Put simply, some people lie about whether they voted.[19] There is not much we can do about, and it could mar the analysis somewhat. On the other hand, it does remove those who: we know did not vote because government records indicate as much; those who admit they did not vote; and those who do not remember whether they voted but, when asked to guess, do not believe they voted. In other words, in wanting to answer this question, we hoped to eliminate about 35–40 percent of the sample; we eliminated about 24 percent. *It is not ideal. But two-thirds of the way toward an answer does provide some useful data.*

Do likely voters favor the GOP? It could be the case that the DNC has mobilized nearly every pro-choice voter while the RNC has not brought pro-lifers to the polls. In this case, Democrats might have a public opinion advantage with abortion, but the issue is tapped and there are no more pro-choice likely voters to be gained. In addition, Republicans could conceivably win votes by doubling down on their counter-majoritarian stance. Under these circumstances, *Dobbs* would be a winning issue for the GOP.

TABLE 9.14 Likely (N=1207; 76.2% of ANES sample) and Unlikely (N=378; 23.8% of ANES Sample) Voters

	Biden supporters		Trump supporters		Other/NA voters		Total	
	Likely	Unlikely	Likely	Unlikely	Likely	Unlikely	Likely	Unlikely
Pro-life	7.2%	1.9%	31.7%	2.9%	2.3%	29.9%	41.2%	34.7%
Pro-choice	42.8%	2.9%	11.2%	3.2%	2.7%	54.2%	56.6%	60.3%
Other/NA	1.0%	0.0%	1.1%	0.0%	0.2%	5.0%	2.2%	5.0%

- Probable Partisans. If Republicans can hold 31.7 percent likely to vote probable partisans, then Democrats can hold 42.8 percent
- Possible Switchers. If Republicans can possibly switch 7.2 percent pro-life Biden voters, then Democrats can switch 11.2 percent pro-choice Trump voters.
- Capturable Independents. If Republicans can capture 2.3 percent independents, then Democrats can capture 2.7 percent.
- *With likely voters, the Democratic Party has an advantage with probable partisans and possible switchers. The margin for capturable independents is negligible.*

What about unlikely voters—does the GOP have an untapped soon-to-be mobilized advantage? If voters who have not shown up in the past begin voting, and if they are largely pro-lifers, then we would say that there is a major source of votes just waiting to cast Republican ballots.

- Probable Partisans. Biden and Trump are tied: 2.9 percent are unlikely to vote pro-choice Biden supporters and 2.9 percent are unlikely to vote pro-life Trump supporters.

- Possible Switchers. If Republicans can switch 1.9 percent pro-life Biden-supporting nonvoters, then Democrats can switch 3.2 percent pro-choice Trump-supporting nonvoters.
- Capturable Independents. If Republicans can capture 29.9 percent pro-life third-party nonvoters, then Democrats can capture 54.2 percent pro-choice third-party nonvoters.
- *With unlikely voters, the Democratic Party has an advantage with capturable independents. The margins for probable partisans and possible switchers are negligible.*

Most Likely to Switch

Democrats might have the advantage in the entire sample on those capable of switching their votes because of abortion. But assuming a voter will switch just because of abortion ignores whether that voter is likely to switch at all—because of any issue or any candidate. Put differently, just because a voter does not agree on abortion with a party does not mean that that voter is more apt to switch. Perhaps there are other, overarching factors that must be present before one considers using abortion (or any other issue) to change one's vote.[20] In what follows, I look at a different group of voters.

Other than specific political issues, what factors would make one likely to consider switching his/her vote? How do we gather a differently stratified subset of voters with an overall tendency to consider switching their votes? I use a question from the ANES that gets at political awareness. It asks respondents how often they follow "what's going on in government and public affairs."[21] Possible answers include: "most of the time," "some of the time," "only now and then," and "hardly at all." We would assume that one who follows politics is going to be more aware about politics.[22] *For high levels of political awareness, I use those who follow government and public affairs "most of the time." For low levels, I use "only now and then" and "hardly at all."*

What is the effect of political awareness on voting behavior? The answer here is muddled because there are disagreements within the literature.[23] For instance, while one study indicates that those with high levels of political awareness are more likely to consider switching their votes, another demonstrates that citizens with low levels are more likely to switch.[24] Another says it does not matter.[25] Those with more awareness are more likely to vote "correctly" (i.e., for the party/candidate that aligns with their preferences).[26] Or maybe not.[27] Or maybe just not in presidential primaries.[28] One particularly interesting conclusion is that presidential campaigns can influence vote choice by increasing awareness through campaign strategy and spending.[29] Another area of disagreement is which party inherently benefits from lower levels of political awareness: Democrats, Republicans, or "it depends"?[30] One item seems to generate consensus: high awareness leads to a greater likelihood of turnout.[31] *Rather than choose any particular hypothesis, I present data on what I see as competing claims of which group we should focus on: those with high awareness or those with low awareness. I look at both. After, out of curiosity, I look at those with moderate awareness.*

What is the situation with those with high political awareness? As we might expect, highly aware voters strongly align their preferences (in this case, views on abortion) with vote choice. The issue, though, is that there are just more pro-choicers, and this trickles into how large of a bloc each party can consolidate and attract.

TABLE 9.15 High Awareness Vote Choice (N=773; 48.8% of ANES sample)

	Biden	Trump	Other	Total
Pro-life	4.0%	33.8%	5.4%	44.2%
Pro-choice	42.3%	6.9%	5.8%	55.0%
Other/NA	0.3%	0.9%	0.0%	1.2%

- Probable Partisans. Among those who are highly aware, there are more pro-choice Biden voters (42.3%) than pro-life Trump voters (33.8%).

- Possible Switchers. Democrats have a modest advantage (2.9 percentage points) with cross-partisans whose abortion views do not match their vote choice.
- Capturable Independents. Highly aware third-party voters are pro-choice (5.8 percent) and pro-life (5.4 percent) at about the same rate.
- *With those who are highly aware, the Democratic Party has a large advantage with probable partisans and a slight advantage with possible switchers. The margin for capturable independents is negligible.*

What is the situation with citizens with low political awareness? Whereas highly aware respondents were more likely to align with one of the two major parties, those with low awareness were more likely to support third-party candidates.

TABLE 9.16 Low Awareness Vote Choice (N=773; 22.2% of ANES sample)

	Biden	Trump	Other	Total
Pro-life	7.1%	10.8%	13.9%	31.8%
Pro-choice	16.5%	11.0%	33.0%	61.4%
Other/NA	1.7%	0.9%	4.3%	6.8%

- Probable Partisans. Among those with low awareness, Democrats have a 5.7 percentage point advantage as 16.5 percent were pro-choice Biden supporters and 10.8 percent were pro-life Trump supporters.
- Possible Switchers. Democrats have a 3.9 percentage point advantage as 11.0 percent were pro-choice Trump supporters and 7.1 percent were pro-life Biden supporters.
- Capturable Independents. About two-thirds of this group—low awareness third-party supporters—are pro-choice.
- *With those who have low awareness, the Democratic Party has a very large advantage with capturable independents. The*

Democratic Party has a relatively slighter advantage with prob-
able partisans and possible switchers.

**Out of curiosity, what about those with moderate political aware-
ness?** It is more of the same.

TABLE 9.17 Moderate Awareness Vote Choice (N=460; 29.0% of ANES sample)

	Biden	Trump	Other	Total
Pro-life	8.3%	20.4%	10.9%	39.6%
Pro-choice	29.8%	11.3%	16.5%	57.8%
Other/NA	0.9%	0.7%	1.3%	2.8%

- Probable Partisans. Moderately aware pro-choice Biden supporters (29.8 percent) outnumber moderately aware pro-life
  Trump (20.4 percent) voters by 9.4 percentage points.
- Possible Switchers. Pro-choice Trump supporters (11.3 percent) outnumber pro-life Biden voters (8.3 percent) by 3.0
  percentage points.
- Capturable Independents. Third-party voters with moderate
  awareness were more likely to be pro-choice (16.5 percent)
  than pro-life (10.9 percent).
- *With those who have moderate awareness, the Democratic
  Party has slight to modest advantages with probable partisans,
  possible switchers, and capturable independents.*

**What can we say, overall, about political awareness and abortion
preferences?** *Democratic advantages range from negligible to very
large, but the advantage is always to the Democrats.*

Recap and Two Final Thoughts
Let us recap what the data has shown:

1. We can measure it many different ways, but each time, we will
    find that more Americans are pro-choice than pro-life—by
    about fifteen to twenty points.

2. The Democratic Party has an advantage with probable partisans. There are more pro-choice Democrats than pro-life Republicans.
3. The Democratic Party has an advantage with possible switchers. There are more pro-choice Republicans than pro-life Democrats.
4. The Democratic Party has an advantage with capturable independents—both those who register as independent and/or vote third-party. There are more pro-choice capturable independents than pro-life capturable independents.
5. The Democratic Party has an advantage with those with more intense views on abortion.
6. The Democratic Party has an advantage with likely voters.
7. The Democratic Party has an advantage with unlikely—or not-yet-tapped—voters.
8. The Democratic Party has an advantage with those with high political awareness.
9. The Democratic Party has an advantage with those with low political awareness.
10. The Democratic Party has an advantage with those with moderate political awareness.

In sum, the Democratic advantage in Item number 1 is so great that it translates into any subdivision (e.g., vote choice), sub-sub-division (vote choice and likely voter), and sub-sub-sub-division (e.g., vote choice, likely voter, and political awareness).[32]

Allow me one final table. It pulls together all the other tables and summarizes many of the takeaway points discussed above. It shows the consistency of the claim that *Dobbs* was unpopular and it creates an opportunity for the Democratic Party to build its electoral coalition.

It includes a "Democratic Real Edge" column. This is the actual advantage a party (in nearly every case: Democrats) holds. For example, let us consider "Likely Voters," which comprise 76.2 percent of the electorate. 42.8 percent of that 76.2 percent of likely voters are pro-choice Biden voters. That means that 32.6 percent of the entire electorate (.428*76.2=32.6) are Democratic probable partisans. Meanwhile, 31.7 percent of that 76.2 percent of likely voters are pro-life Trump voters. That means that 24.2 percent of the entire electorate (.317*76.2=24.2) are Republican probable partisans. The "Democratic Real Edge" is +8.4 (32.6–24.2=8.4).[33] This column is helpful in that it shows how many additional points Democrats could add to their tallies were both parties to convert 100 percent of their probable partisans, possible switchers, and capturable independents.

One can reach various conclusions from the data above. I end with two. They relate to two different paths to electoral victory. First, the traditional path: convincing the median voter.[34] Despite a polarizing polity, the center still exists, and unaffiliated moderate independents still have the ability to swing elections—especially at the presidential or state (e.g., gubernatorial, Senate) levels. If abortion were a major issue in determining vote choice, Democrats would have a considerable advantage with capturable independents—especially those who have not voted in the past. Now, political scientists have made it clear that mobilizing these folks will not be easy.[35] But it is possible.[36] *Could abortion after Dobbs be that rare issue that gets people to show up to vote for the first time—and begin a pattern of more political participation?*[37] *If so, Democrats will win big.*

The second way Democrats can increase their vote margin is to appeal to their base. Abortion matters a lot to Democratic probable partisans. It is captured in the intensity measurements. And it shows across the board on probable partisans. There is a growing popular narrative and academic literature saying that the path to victory today is not through the median voter, but through mobilizing one's base.[38] Who better to mobilize than those who are already likely to vote? On this measure, Democrats have a +8.4 real edge with a group (likely to vote probable partisans from both parties) that constitutes 56.8 percent of the electorate. Set aside possible switching; consider solely getting out the Democratic vote.[39] *Might abortion after Dobbs make pro-choice Republicans less likely to vote*

TABLE 9.18 Summary and Democratic Edge

ANES 2022		Dems	GOP	Dem Edge	Dem Real Edge
Pro-choice=57.5%; Pro-life=39.6%; Other=2.9%					
Party identification (share of electorate: 100%)	Probable partisans	26.5%	19.1%	+7.4	+7.4
	Possible switchers	7.4%	5.2%	+2.2	+4.4
	Capturable independents	23.6%	15.4%	+8.2	+8.2
Intense preferences (76.4%)	Probable partisans	30.9%	18.6%	+12.3	+9.4
	Possible switchers	5.9%	5.9%	0.0	0.0
	Capturable independents	23.3%	14.0%	+9.3	+7.1
Vote choice (100%)	Probable partisans	33.3%	24.8%	+8.5	+8.5
	Possible switchers	9.3%	5.9%	+3.4	+6.8
	Capturable independents	15.0%	8.9%	+6.1	+6.1
Intense preferences + vote choice (76.4%)	Probable Partisans	38.0%	23.6%	+14.4	+11.0
	Possible switchers	6.9%	6.8%	+0.1	+0.2
	Capturable independents	15.2%	8.0%	+7.2	+5.5
Likely voters (76.2%)	Probable partisans	42.8%	31.7%	+11.1	+8.4
	Possible switchers	11.2%	7.2%	+4.0	+6.0
	Capturable independents	2.7%	2.3%	+0.4	+0.3
Unlikely voters (23.8%)	Probable partisans	2.9%	2.9%	0.0	0.0
	Possible switchers	3.2%	1.9%	+1.3	+0.6
	Capturable independents	54.2%	29.9%	+24.3	+5.8
High awareness (48.8%)	Probable partisans	42.3%	32.8%	+9.5	+4.6
	Possible switchers	6.9%	4.0%	+2.9	+2.8
	Capturable independents	5.8%	5.4%	+0.4	+0.2
Some awareness (29.0%)	Probable partisans	29.8%	20.4%	+9.4	+2.7
	Possible switchers	11.3%	8.3%	+3.0	+1.8
	Capturable independents	16.5%	10.9%	+5.6	+1.6
Low awareness (22.2%)	Probable partisans	16.5%	10.8%	+5.7	+1.3
	Possible switchers	11.0%	7.1%	+3.9	+1.8
	Capturable independents	33.0%	13.9%	+19.1	+4.2

and pro-choice Democrats more likely to vote? If so, Democrats will win big.

Conclusion

In the 1970s Pat Buchanan correctly predicted that abortion was a "political windfall" for the GOP. He said, "There is tradeoff but it leaves us with the larger share of the pie."[40] After *Dobbs*, Buchanan's logic is reversed: the windfall is the Democrats'. Today, the DNC has the larger share of the pie.

Perhaps *Dobbs* will spur some pro-life Democrats to start voting Republican. However, there just are not many Democrats who are: (1) pro-life; (2) do not already vote Republican; and (3) are ideologically centrist. Put differently, it is rare to find a weak/independent Democrat who opposed *Roe* and still voted Democrat. These rare Democrats already made the turn to the GOP. The Republican Party does not have many more cross-partisans to mine. Furthermore, Democrats have so few independents to lose on the issue of abortion. An overwhelming majority of independents who vote Democrat adhere to the party's orthodoxy on abortion.

Meanwhile, there is a significant percentage of Republicans who still vote Republican despite strong pro-choice preferences. It is unfair to say that all these partisans will change their voting behavior in light of overturning *Roe*. However, we could imagine a significant percentage of this subset rethinking their allegiance and behavior. Moreover, the GOP's views on abortion are out of line with a large percentage of independents who vote Republican. Perhaps Republicans and independents will remain in lockstep with their current voting behavior. In all likelihood, *Dobbs* will cause the GOP to lose more voters than they will gain.

Will it be enough to swing a durable majority to the Democrats? Maybe not. Maybe the Republican Party will weather the storm, control the messaging, and hit on other issues that keep their current base in place. Maybe Democrats will fail at the issue evolution aspect of party management. That is, maybe DNC leadership fails to package a national abortion campaign in a way that registers with disaffected-by-*Dobbs* centrist Americans who previously voted

Republican. Just because a winning issue exists does not mean that the party for whom it benefits will automatically capitalize.

One possible outcome is that Democrats preemptively fix the problem. Already, liberal states have become more receptive to residents of more conservative bordering states who have trouble obtaining abortions. Liberal interest groups have raised money to help transport women across state lines. State Democratic parties have initiated drives to put abortion referenda on the ballot. If abortion policy trends left—say, back to a *Roe*-like equilibrium—then pro-choice Republicans and pro-choice Republican-voting independents can continue to vote for the GOP. Put differently, if someone (the DNC, state governments, liberal activists) fixes abortion such that it is no longer a problem in a particular state or region, then voters of that state or region might disregard voting on the basis of abortion.

But what if the Democratic Party does capitalize? Let us assume that the Democratic Party runs a mildly, but not fully, effective campaign against the Supreme Court and the Republican Party that overturned *Roe v. Wade*. Let us say the Democratic Party increases margins by only a couple points nationwide. With such close elections, this would still make a difference—especially in races with larger districts (i.e., at the state level). Specifically, we might expect Democrats to be more likely to win governor's houses, US Senate seats, and electoral college votes.

Let us give this scenario more context. Let us say that Democrats net 10 percent of all probable partisans, possible switchers, and capturable independents. This would increase their overall vote share by 2.14 percentage points.[41] In some contexts, that is the margin of victory for the Republican Party. For example, if Democrats had had an across-the-board 2.14 point bump, Hillary Clinton would have won Michigan, Pennsylvania, Wisconsin, and Florida. Put differently, Clinton would have won the election.[42]

Even under this 10 percent scenario, the GOP would still have hope. They could win state legislatures and the House of Representatives (especially if boundary lines were drawn in a way that maximized their electoral chances). The electoral college might give them more of a chance, too, than they would have if the president selected by a national popular vote. Furthermore, equal representation in the Senate might make it possible for Republicans to take a majority in the upper chamber. At the very least, with only a mildly effective Democratic counterstrike, Republicans would likely be able to mount a filibuster defense in the Senate. And conservatives certainly have a majority on the Supreme Court for the foreseeable future, especially after turning Kennedy and Ginsburg's seats into Kavanaugh and Barrett.

But what if the Democrats fully capitalize? What if we witness, say, a five-point swing nationwide? How many more seats in the House could Democrats win?[43] Could they win a filibuster-proof majority in the Senate? Probably not.[44] But what if they added, say, two more seats and if every Democrats' seat became just a little safer? Would that allow the DNC to turn the screws—or not even have to rely—on moderates like Joe Manchin (D-WV)?

In presidential contests, every state would shade bluer. Purple states—Arizona, Georgia, Pennsylvania, Michigan, Wisconsin— would become blue-leaning. Recent red-leaning states—Ohio, Florida—might be more in play for Democratic presidential candidates. If the unlikely Republican doomsday scenario happened— if Texas became a purple swing state—the margin of error for the Republican Party in presidential contests would be razor-thin.[45]

More concerning for the theme of this book, why wouldn't Democrats attack the Supreme Court? They might not pack the court in the way that FDR sought. But attacks do not have to pass to succeed. Like the New Deal Court, as well as the Warren Court during the communism cases, a reeling Roberts Court might think twice before upsetting a hypothetical dominant Democratic coalition the way they did in *Dobbs*.

This is not to say that Democrats should thank the court's conservatives for overturning *Roe*. However, recent developments mirror previous eras. The conservative Supreme Court of the late twentieth and early twenty-first centuries has, for the most part, exemplified what regime politics scholars tell us: like earlier courts, they have mostly avoided countermajoritarian decisions on issues that are highly salient to the electorate. But the court *is* countermajoritarian sometimes. Indeed, the last time the court issued a decision that helped rearrange political coalitions was in 1973, with *Roe v. Wade*. Are we again on the cusp of abortion pushback?

Appendix

Democratic Factions

To give an overall sense of the intracoalitional factions in the Democratic Party, I created a way to separate all Democrats in the 1960s and 1970s into one of three mutually exclusive categories: southern, liberal, and northern conservative. I used the second dimension Common Space scores, which look at the social liberalism/conservatism of a member of Congress. I also used the religious affiliation of the lawmaker and the percentage of Catholics and evangelicals in their home state.[1] The figure on the next page shows how each Democrat was placed into one of the three categories.

Counting Attacks

Court-curbing can be an *institutional* attack on the Supreme Court. Here, Congress seeks to change the structure or rules of the court. For instance, FDR's court-packing plan sought to encourage *Lochner*-era conservatives to retire from the court and/or to tack on additional justices to overcome their votes. Although the outcome would be to seat justices who would legitimize New Deal policies, the court-packing plan sought to alter the court itself. Alternatively, there are *issue-based* attacks, such as passing new laws that seemingly contradict a court decision or trying to amend the Constitution to overturn a decision.[2]

I differ from previous scholars' counts of attacks against the court in that I more generously include proposed constitutional amendments. The amendment gauntlet is daunting, and surely members of Congress know that their proposals stand little chance of garnering two-thirds majorities in both chambers, let alone three-fourths of the state legislatures to ratify. Yet, the mere introduction of these

FIGURE 1. Democratic Faction Flow Chart

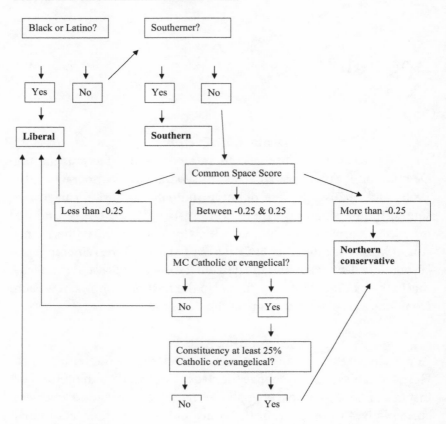

amendments says something important. This is the key: though not all bills and resolutions that are introduced face equal odds of passing, they are all equal in that they signal something larger—about the court, policy, and/or coalitional politics. For instance, from 1989 to 2013, Senator Orrin Hatch (R-UT) repeatedly proposed to amend the Constitution to ban flag burning. He must have known that each proposal would fail; yet he continually introduced resolution after resolution. Why? Electoral considerations are the most likely and most parsimonious explanation.[3] But even then, what does it say that a Republican senator from Utah can electorally benefit from taking positions on flag burning for nearly a quarter of a century? This type of attack counts—in politics and in the database.

I extend a previously existing database, which looked at attacks from 1955 to 1984. I use the same method and take the count through 2023. I used the index of the *Congressional Record* to conduct a sweep of attacks. For every year, I looked at proposals in the sections in the index titled "Courts," "Supreme Court," and "Constitution." Within "Constitution," there was a subheading that listed all proposed amendments to the Constitution made during a particular session of Congress. I confirmed court-curbing measures by looking up the content of relevant amendments. In addition, when amendments pointed to a certain issue that took root immediately following a Supreme Court decision (e.g., abortion after *Roe v. Wade* in 1973), I also turned to that issue in the index to look at proposals. Often, proposals listed there overlapped with the amendments in the "Constitution" heading. For each proposal, I turned to its text to determine if it was a court-curbing effort.

Admittedly, some measures were likely not captured. Short of reading every single legislative proposal and contextualizing its text, debate, and sponsor within the date of its introduction, there is no way of gathering a bulletproof database of attacks. I could have prioritized reliability. For instance, had I only looked under the "amendments" subheading of the "Constitution" section, then anyone could replicate the database. However, this left out a substantial number of attacks. Instead, I prioritized accuracy and volume, on the assumption that gathering all the attacks I could find and providing them in one place was a more worthwhile contribution than providing a system for how others could go about finding a more limited number of attacks. In the future, if others find an issue that members of Congress seemed to have attacked on, they can add to the database and expand upon it. In this way, the database here could be thought of as a continuation of previous work toward a comprehensive catalog of court-curbing measures. It might not be 100 percent complete. But it is the most complete count we currently have.

From 1955 to 2023, members of Congress launched 3649 attacks against the Supreme Court. For each attack, the database identifies the following: year, congressional session, bill number, member of Congress, whether the proposal was a constitutional amendment, home state of the attacking member, party identification of the

attacking member, and the issue involved. House members introduced 82 percent of attacks; Senators introduced 18 percent. Almost
two-thirds (65 percent) were proposed constitutional amendments.

Table A1 shows the ten most attacked issues. Examples of institutional attacks include election of justices, elimination of judicial
review, judicial ethics bills, etc. Other issue-based court-curbing
that totaled at least ten proposals include: segregation, Second
Amendment, Obamacare, crime, same-sex marriage, pledge of allegiance, line-item veto, electoral college, death penalty, eminent do-
main, federalism, communism, homeschooling, and war on terror.

TABLE A1 Overview of Attacks Database

Issue	N	Issue	N
Prayer	808	Apportionment/ redistricting	244
Abortion	538	Flag burning	134
Institutional	503	Pro-choice	89
Campaign finance	424	Voter ID	78
Busing	247	Free exercise	64

Salience

I use Clark, Lax, and Rice's database for Supreme Court case salience. It uses mentions of Supreme Court cases on the front pages of the *New York Times*, *Los Angeles Times*, and *Washington Post*.
One issue with newspaper coverage is that salience can be measured
retrospectively—that salience is determined after the fact rather than
being measured as a true product of its time. Clark, Lax, and Rice
include a measure of newspaper mentions before the court even
decides a case. They find that it roughly matches any retrospective
measure of salience and that the two are highly correlated. That is,
a case mentioned on the front page of a newspaper the day after it
is handed down is likely to be a case mentioned on the front page
of the newspaper years after it comes out. Similarly, they find that
contemporaneous newspaper coverage is correlated with experts'
opinions on which cases prove important over time. In sum, "there

is a common underlying trait that attracts the attention of both the media and the experts; we believe that this is salience."[4]

Table A2 highlights cases discussed in preceding chapters. For communism and crime, I select the highest ranking pair of cases. Cases in communists' rights, crime, busing, and abortion rank in the top 1 percent of Clark, Lax, and Rice's database. Oddly, *Roe v. Wade* appears relatively nonsalient. But *Doe v. Bolton*, a sister case to *Roe* which came out the same day, rates as very salient. Thus, the take-away is that the court's foray into abortion in 1973 was salient.

School prayer could be interpreted as salient. *Engel v. Vitale* is in the top 8 percent of Supreme Court cases reported on by newspapers. That said, *Engel's* raw score of salience is much more middle-of-the-pack. The difference in raw score between *Milliken* (284th in rank) and *Engel* (545th) is the same as that between *Engel* and the 995th ranked case. Moreover, if we were to add up the salience scores of cases on the issues above, we'd see that newspapers reported on all the other issues far more than school prayer and Bible readings. For example, *Doe v. Bolton* + *Roe v. Wade*=3.46; *Engel* + *Schempp*=1.34. At least on raw numbers, abortion appears about two-and-a-half more times salient than school prayer. This fits well with my narrative.

TABLE A2 Salience in Mature New Deal Era

Issue • Cases	My claim	CLR's database	Overall rank of 7181 (raw score [-1.35–3.5])
Communists' rights	Salient	Salient	
• *Cole v. Young*			13 (2.70)
• *Service v. Dulles*			19 (2.58)
Prayer	Not salient	Not salient (at	
• *Engel v. Vitale*		least compared to	545 (1.11)
• *Abington v. Schempp*		others)	2069 (0.23)
Crime	Salient	Salient	
• *Miranda v. AZ*			5 (3.24)
• *Escobedo v. IL*			206 (1.60)
Busing	Salient	Salient	
• *Swann v. Charlotte*			49 (2.26)
• *Milliken v. Bradley*			284 (1.43)
Abortion	Salient	Salient	
• *Doe v. Bolton*			51 (2.25)
• *Roe v. Wade*			442 (1.21)

Unfortunately, Clark, Lax, and Rice's database does not capture the more recent cases discussed in chapters 8 and 9. It would be tempting to just speculate. But we might be able to match recent cases with those from before 2008 to see if the latter measured as salience. Table A3 presents those matches.

TABLE A3 Salience in Modern Era

Issue/case that I discuss	Pre-2009 proxy case	Proxy's rank of 7181 (raw score [-1.35–3.5])
Citizens United (2010)	*McConnell v. FEC* (2003)	137 (1.77)
Redistricting (2015–19)	*Vieth v. Jubelirer* (2004)	768 (.092)
Voter ID/*Shelby* (2013)	*Crawford v. Marion* (2008)	468 (1.18)
Obergefell (2015)	*Lawrence v. Texas* (2004)	79 (2.05)
Free exercise: *Hobby Lobby* (2014) and *Masterpiece* (2018)	*Locke v. Davey* (2004)	239 (1.52)
Dobbs (2022)	*Gonzales v. Carhart* (2007)	63 (2.13)

Some might squabble, but overall these classifications work. *Lawrence* is not the same as *Obergefell*. But they both are about LGBT rights. *Locke v. Davey* is not a perfect proxy for *Hobby Lobby* and *Masterpiece*. Some might think *Lawrence* captures *Masterpiece* better—that it is an LGBT rights case and not a free exercise case. Some might even think it is a free speech case. Some might see *Hobby Lobby* as a women's rights case, in which case *United States v. Virginia* (1995) would be the appropriate proxy. It scored 1.07. *National Federation of Independent Businesses v. Sebelius* is missing. I could not find a match for upholding Obamacare. Perhaps some of the early New Deal cases would have sufficed, but the database does not go that far back. I am comfortable, though, saying *Sebelius* was salient.

GSS & CES

Below are tabulations from the GSS and CES. Neither had as wide a range of questions on abortion as the ANES. Neither asked about intensity of abortion views. GSS did not have a good awareness question. CES had very few questions on abortion, and I had to use ideology as a proxy. For both, I had to use a "born again/evangelical" proxy as a last-ditch way to code life/choice. It is not perfect, but it also was the final labeling mechanism in the sequence. Those who were not born again after that mechanism were labeled "other." Thus, it is possible that I overreport pro-lifers.

I used the following sequence to assign pro-life and – choice views for GSS:

1. Women should be able to obtain an abortion for any reason =pro-choice
2. Self-reported strongly or slightly pro-life=pro-life
3. Self-reported strongly or slightly pro-choice=pro-choice
4. Abortion should not be legal after 4.5 months=pro-life
5. Abortion should be legal after 4.5 months=pro-choice
6. Abortion should not be available in cases where the health of the woman is in jeopardy=pro-life
7. Abortion should not be available in cases of rape=pro-life
8. Abortion should be available in at least four of the following five instances: defect in fetus, health of the woman, married woman does not want more children, low income woman cannot afford more children, and cases of rape=pro-choice
9. Born-again=pro-life

TABLE A4 GSS Reliability, Summary, and Democratic Edge

GSS		Dems	GOP	Dem Edge	Real Edge
Pro-choice=54.9%; Pro-life=37.2%; Other=7.9%					
Party identification (100%)	Probable partisans	32.2%	21.0%	+11.2	+11.2
	Possible switchers	8.8%	7.0%	+1.8	+3.6
	Capturable independents	14.0%	9.2%	+4.8	+4.8
Vote choice (100%)	Probable partisans	35.4%	21.0%	+14.4	+14.4
	Possible switchers	10.2%	9.1%	+1.1	+2.2
	Capturable independents	9.3%	7.1%	+2.2	+2.2
Likely voters (69.8%)	Probable partisans	44.5%	23.6%	+20.9	+14.6
	Possible switchers	10.2%	9.5%	+0.7	+1.0
	Capturable independents	3.3%	2.8%	+0.5	+0.3
Unlikely voters (30.2%)	Probable partisans	14.3%	14.9%	-0.6	-0.2
	Possible switchers	10.4%	8.1%	+2.3	+1.4
	Capturable independents	23.2%	16.9%	+6.3	+1.9

I used the following sequence to assign pro-life and – choice views for CES:

1. Abortions should be illegal in all circumstances=pro-life
2. Women should always be able to obtain an abortion as a matter of choice=pro-choice
3. Prohibit all abortions after the twentieth week of pregnancy =pro-life
4. Very conservative, conservative, somewhat conservative= pro-life
5. Very liberal, liberal, somewhat liberal=pro-choice
6. Born-again=pro-life

TABLE A5 CES Reliability, Summary, and Democratic Edge

CES (2022)		Dems	GOP	Dem Edge	Real Edge
Pro-choice=65.6%; Pro-life=31.1%; Other=3.4%					
Party identification (100%)	Probable partisans	42.3%	21.0%	+21.3	+21.3
	Possible switchers	11.7%	5.6%	+6.2	+12.4
	Capturable independents	11.5%	4.5%	+7.1	+7.1
Vote choice (100%)	Probable partisans	41.3%	20.7%	+20.6	+20.6
	Possible switchers	11.1%	5.2%	+5.8	+11.6
	Capturable independents	13.2%	5.1%	+8.1	+8.1
Likely voters (72.9%)	Probable partisans	48.1%	24.9%	+23.2	+16.9
	Possible switchers	11.6%	5.4%	+6.2	+9.0
	Capturable independents	5.0%	2.1%	+2.9	+2.1
Unlikely voters (27.1%)	Probable partisans	22.8%	9.4%	+13.4	+3.6
	Possible switchers	9.6%	4.7%	+4.9	+2.6
	Capturable independents	35.4%	13.3%	+22.1	+6.0
High awareness (47.9%)	Probable partisans	49.4%	26.7%	+22.7	+10.9
	Possible switchers	9.6%	4.1%	+5.5	+5.2
	Capturable independents	5.1%	2.4%	+2.7	+1.3

TABLE A5 *(continued)*

CES (2022)		Dems	GOP	Dem Edge	Real Edge
Some awareness (26.9%)	Probable partisans	40.7%	18.9%	+21.8	+5.9
	Possible switchers	12.5%	6.8%	+5.7	+3.0
	Capturable independents	12.5%	5.1%	+7.4	+2.0
Low awareness (22.1%)	Probable partisans	27.6%	12.0%	+15.6	+3.4
	Possible switchers	13.0%	5.7%	+7.3	+3.2
	Capturable independents	27.8%	9.5%	+18.3	+4.0

Notes

Preface

1. Dan DiSalvo and Eric Schickler pursue a similar scope of analysis in their respective foundational monographs on party factions and racial politics. DiSalvo writes, "I do not attempt to offer a parsimonious theory of political change, since such a theory is likely to remain elusive . . . My aim is rather to offer a set of mid-range theories . . . there is virtue in today's specialized academy to taking a step back to look for broader patterns of political development" (*Engines of Change: Party Factions in American Politics: 1868–2010*, xv). Schickler writes, "Systematically tracing the interplay of multiple historical processes over time can yield insight into the sources of political development even when clean causal identification is simply not possible" (*Racial Realignment: The Transformation of American Liberalism, 1932–1965*, 278).

Introduction

1. Caro writes that Johnson thought it was a bad bill. He also notes that Johnson knew he would be hailed a savior by the liberal wing of the party. Robert A. Caro, *Master of the Senate: The Years of Lyndon Johnson*.

2. Stephen M. Engel, *American Politicians Confront the Court: Opposition Politics and Changing Responses to Judicial Power*, 299; C. Herman Pritchett, *Congress versus the Supreme Court, 1957–1960*, 35.

3. Walter Murphy, *Congress and the Court*, 210. In a rare moment of confusion, Johnson had no plan forward. A colleague had to advise, "Lyndon, you'd better adjourn this place. They're going to pass this g****** bill" (Caro, *Master of the Senate*, 1031).

4. Agreeing to adjourn was, itself, difficult. Anti-court leaders insisted on a roll call, at which point, LBJ visibly wrote down the name of every senator who did not vote to adjourn. After eighteen names were taken, everyone else felt sufficiently bullied to adjourn. Caro, *Master of the Senate*, 1031.

5. Pairing allows absent two absent senators with opposite votes to take positions without voting. The votes are not tabulated when calculating results of the roll call. Sometimes, a present senator will graciously not vote (but announce his/her preference) to pair with an absent senator who votes the opposite way. In reality, Johnson might not have added a tally in his own column, but he prevented court-curbing advocates from adding one to theirs by insincerely pairing it. "How Our Laws Are Made," accessed October 13, 2023, https://www.congress.gov/help/learn-about-the-legislative-process/how-our-laws-are-made.

6. Murphy describes how Eisenhower—whom no one would call a friend to communists—supported judicial independence. When asked by the press about congressional bills that sought to curb the court on communism, the president waffled and

refused to put institutional support behind the legislation. Eisenhower likely would have vetoed the bill had it passed. In fact, even before the Senate's vote, policy entrepreneurs in the Justice Department, including the attorney general, began strategizing about the ways in which to lobby President Eisenhower to veto the bill. Murphy, *Congress and the Court*. See also William G. Ross, "Attacks on the Warren Court by State Officials: A Case Study of Why Court-Curbing Movements Fail"; Robert J. Steamer, "Statesmanship or Craftsmanship: Current Conflict over the Supreme Court."

7. Caro, *Master of the Senate*.

8. Murphy, *Congress and the Court*, 217.

9. LBJ had lobbied Bennett as extra insurance but did not feel he had fully persuaded the Utah Senator to vote "nay." Johnson had counted Bennett as voting for court-curbing. In the end, his was the extra vote that stopped the bill.

10. *Congressional Record* 1957, 18928. Hereafter, I will use *CR* for *Congressional Record*.

11. Some commentators believe that the quartet of decisions are compatible and that the 1959 cases did not overrule the earlier ones. Pritchett, *Congress versus the Supreme Court*; Robert J. Steamer, *The Supreme Court in Crisis: A History of Conflict*. The consensus, though, is that the court "felt the heat" and "effectively reversed its earlier decisions." Many others make this claim and it is discussed in a later chapter. Arthur J. Sabin, *In Calmer Times: The Supreme Court and Red Monday*, 196; Gerald N. Rosenberg, "Judicial Independence and the Reality of Political Power," 391; Lucas A. Powe Jr., *The Warren Court and American Politics*.

12. Roger K. Newman, "The Warren Court and American Politics: An Impressionistic Appreciation," 677. The quote comes from the diary of Drew Pearson, a prominent liberal journalist who covered the Warren Commission. The quote seems off. It should probably read either "*Sweezy* was exactly the same thing as *Uphaus*," or, "*Watkins* was exactly the same thing as *Barenblatt*." Regardless, the tone indicates both Warren's frustration and his belief that the court had reversed itself.

13. In chapter 2, I will explain the factions of the Democratic Party and how I sorted them. For now, let us assume there were southern, liberal, and northern conservative Democrats.

14. *CR* 1957, 15955. Earl Warren, *The Memoirs of Chief Justice Earl Warren*, 6. Republican senators had shepherded the 1958 court-curbing bill against Democrats' parliamentary maneuvers. And President Dwight Eisenhower was no friend to communists' rights. Indeed, when Warren asked Eisenhower what he would do with the communists, the president responded, "I would kill the SOBs."

15. Michael J. Klarman, *From Jim Crow to Civil Rights: The Supreme Court and the Struggle for Racial Equity*; Murphy, *Congress and the Court*; Steamer, "Statesmanship or Craftsmanship"; Paul A. Freund, "The Supreme Court under Attack"; Arno Van Alstyne, "Self-Government and the Supreme Court: The Constitution in Crisis"; Pritchett, *Congress versus the Supreme Court*; Ross, "Attacks on the Warren Court."

16. *CR* 1955, 7123.

17. Jeff Woods, *Black Struggle, Red Scare: Segregation and Anti-Communism in the South, 1948–1968*, 57.

18. Republicans might have struggled to pass such measures after their historic 1958 midterm defeats. To be sure, that election mattered. Still, introducing bills is an action that can be taken regardless of majority or minority status. Sabin, *In Calmer Times*;

Barry Friedman, "The Birth of an Academic Obsession: The History of the Counter-majoritarian Difficulty, Part Five"; Woods, *Black Struggle, Red Scare*. Others note that the intersection of race and GOP politics started in 1964: Joseph Crespino, "Goldwater in Dixie: Race, Region, and the Rise of the Right"; Doug McAdam and Karina Kloos, *Deeply Divided: Racial Politics and Social Movements in Postwar America*; Thomas Byrne Edsall and Mary D. Edsall, *Chain Reaction: The Impact of Race, Rights, and Taxes on American Politics*.

19. Stuart S. Nagel, "Court Curbing Periods in American History"; Rosenberg, "Judicial Independence"; Tom S. Clark, *The Limits of Judicial Independence*; Engel, *American Politicians Confront the Court*; H. Chris Tecklenburg, *Congressional Constraint and Judicial Responses: Examining Judiciary Committee Court Curbing and Court Structuring Bills*. There are a couple exceptions: Laura P. Moyer and Ellen M. Key, "Political Opportunism, Position Taking, and Court-Curbing Legislation," which looks at attacks against the lower federal courts, and Michael A. Catalano, "Ex Ante and Ex Post Control over Courts in the US States: Court Curbing and Political Party Influence," which looks at state court attacks before a court even acts.

20. To clarify the grammar: "pushback" is a noun and a single word (e.g., the pushback following *Roe*); "push back" is a verb and two words (e.g., conservatives would push back following *Roe*.)

21. As noted in the preface, the work here is not conclusive. In generating hypotheses, I use guarded, rather than definitive, language. And I recognize that other factors played a role.

Chapter 1. The Countermajoritarian Difficulty and Regime Politics

1. William G. Ross, *A Muted Fury: Populists, Progressives, and Labor Unions Confront the Courts, 1890–1937*.

2. James Bradley Thayer, *The Origin and Scope of the American Doctrine of Constitutional Law*, 135.

3. Thayer, *Origin and Scope*, 18; Thayer, "John Marshall," 86. See also Mark Tushnet, "Alternative Forms of Judicial Review"; Mark A. Graber, "Judicial Supremacy Revisited: Independent Constitutional Authority in American Constitutional Law and Practice"; and Evan H. Caminker, "Thayerian Deference to Congress and the Supreme Court Supermajority Rule: Lessons from the Past."

4. Other notable jurisprudential minimalists took classes from Professor Thayer, including Roscoe Pound and Learned Hand. See Andrew Porwancher et al., *The Prophet of Harvard Law: James Bradley Thayer and His Legal Legacy*.

5. *Louisville Gas Company v. Coleman* (1928). This is different from Holmes's reliance on the "reasonable man," now "reasonable person," standard. Applying to common law, negligence, and tort, Holmes believed that litigants had a baseline responsibility to act in a reasonable manner. For instance, in *Baltimore & Ohio Railroad Company v. Goodman* (1927), Nathan Goodman had been killed in his truck when he had failed to look for an oncoming train at a railroad crossing. The court ruled, with Holmes writing, that Goodman's failure to see the train had caused the accident. That is not how a reasonable person acts.

6. *Lochner v. New York* (1905). See Howard Gillman, *The Constitution Besieged: The Rise and Demise of Lochner Era Police Powers Jurisprudence*; Owen M. Fiss, *Troubled Beginnings of the Modern State, 1888–1910*.

7. *Lochner v. New York* (1905).

8. *New State Ice Co. v. Liebmann* (1932). For the differences among Thayer, Holmes, and Brandeis, see Vicki C. Jackson, "Thayer, Holmes, Brandeis: Conceptions of Judicial Review, Factfinding, and Proportionality."

9. Jay Hook, "A Brief Life of James Bradley Thayer," 8.

10. Nigel Anthony Sellars, "'Cold, Hard Facts': Justice Brandeis and the Oklahoma Ice Case," 266.

11. David Luban, "Justice Holmes and the Metaphysics of Judicial Restraint," 451. Frankfurter did not always treat his self-appointed mentee and ostensible friend Harlan II with charity. Charles Nesson, "The Harlan-Frankfurter Connection: An Aspect of Justice Harlan's Judicial Education"; Brad Snyder, *Democratic Justice: Felix Frankfurter, the Supreme Court, and the Making of the Liberal Establishment.*

12. *West Virginia State Board of Education v. Barnette* (1943).

13. The memo read, "The legislative history of the [Fourteenth]Amendment is, in a word, inconclusive." Ron Collins, "Foreword—Looking Back while Looking Forward," *SCOTUSblog*, August 13, 2012, https://www.scotusblog.com/2012/08/online-a lexander-bickel-symposium-foreword-looking-back-while-moving-forward/.

14. Sanford Levinson, "Online Alexander Bickel Symposium: Alexander Bickel Has Left the Building," *SCOTUSblog*, August 20, 2012, https://www.scotusblog.com/2012/08 /online-alexander-bickel-symposium-alexander-bickel-has-left-the-building/.

15. Richard Epstein, "Online Alexander Bickel Symposium: An Affectionate, but Contrarian, Remembrance," *SCOTUSblog*, August 17, 2012, https://www.scotusblog.com /2012/08/online-alexander-bickel-symposium-an-affectionate-but-contrarian-remembrance/.

16. Alexander M. Bickel, *The Least Dangerous Branch: The Supreme Court at the Bar of Politics*, 16–17. Bickel admitted that the design of the Senate can mean the upper chamber might occasionally act counter to the majority. But he generally assumed that legislative acts represented majority preferences.

17. The countermajoritarian difficulty and accountability problem are related, but still separate critiques. On one hand, we can imagine an institution that could produce countermajoritarian policy while still being held accountable to the people. For instance, the House of Representatives could pass an unpopular bill; but the members of Congress would still be directly accountable. On the other hand, we can imagine an institution that is majoritarian but unaccountable. For instance, if the Federal Reserve made popular fiscal policy, the outcome would be majoritarian, but the institution's members are still not directly accountable. Dave Bridge, "The Supreme Court, Factions, and the Counter-Majoritarian Difficulty"; Bridge, "Holding the Accountability Problem Accountable: Response Mechanisms to Counter-Majoritarian Supreme Court Decisions."

18. Alexander M. Bickel, "The Supreme Court 1960 Term. Foreword: The Passive Virtues."

19. Steve Vladeck, "Online Alexander Bickel Symposium: The Passive Virtues as a Means, Not Ends," *SCOTUSblog*, August 21, 2012, https://www.scotusblog.com/2012/08 /online-alexander-bickel-symposium-the-passive-virtues-as-means-not-ends.

20. Barry Friedman describes it more explicitly: "There was a tension in Alex Bickel: a commitment to a hands-off Court deferential to democracy, set against the promise of an activist one . . . principles were great, but they had to bend to the force of real-world

realities" ("Online Alexander Bickel Symposium: Learning about the Supreme Court," *SCOTUSblog*, August 20, 2012, https://www.scotusblog.com/2012/08/online-alexander -bickel-symposium-learning-about-the-supreme-court/). Adam White offers a simi-lar perspective: "The Court should look to the long arc of national experience to de-duce the principles that could be enforced against present majorities in the Supreme Court's work of judicial review." Adam White, "Online Alexander Bickel Symposium: Bickel's Principled Prudence," *SCOTUSblog*, August 15, 2012, https://www.scotusblog .com/2012/08/online-alexander-bickel-symposium/.

21. Bickel was especially fond of: Learned Hand, *The Bill of Rights*; Herbert Wechsler, "Toward Neutral Principles of Constitutional Law." See also Barry Friedman, "Neutral Principles: A Retrospective."

22. Bickel himself never articulated it this way. As Louis Seidman writes, "Should the Court, on such occasions, abandon its devotion to legal principle? . . . One thing is cer-tain: If Bickel thought that it should, he would never have told us so. For if, indeed, the Court's politics must remain secret when they infect its substantive decision making, it would hardly do for the Court's defenders to spill the beans" ("Online Alexander Bick-el Symposium: Too Principled to Stand on Principle?" *SCOTUSblog*, August 14, 2012, https://www.scotusblog.com/2012/08/online-bickel-symposium-too-principled-to -stand-on-principle/); see also Gerald Gunther's cutting critique which interprets Bickel as "100% insistence on principle, 20% of the time" ("The Subtle Vices of the 'Passive Virtues': A Comment on Principle and Expediency in Judicial Review," 3).

23. Kenneth D. Ward and Cecilia R. Castillo, eds., *The Judiciary and American De-mocracy: Alexander Bickel, the Countermajoritarian Difficulty, and Contemporary Con-stitutional Theory*; Friedman, "Learning about the Supreme Court"; Adam J. White, "The Lost Greatness of Alexander Bickel," *Commentary Magazine*, March 2012.

24. To be fair, the left has lobbed these critiques, too. For instance, Akhil Amar co-authored an editorial with Steven Calabresi on instituting term limits: "Term Limits for the High Court," *Washington Post*, August 9, 2002. Often, these calls occur after an un-favorable ruling. For instance, Jamelle Bouie, "The Case for Supreme Court Term Limits Just Got a Lot Better," *New York Times*, November 22, 2022. For analysis on this issue, see Keith E. Whittington, "The New Originalism"; Barry Friedman, "The Cycles of Consti-tutional Theory"; Jack M. Balkin, "Why Liberals and Conservatives Flipped on Judicial Restraint: Judicial Review in the Cycles of Constitutional Time"; Jack Balkin, *The Cycles of Constitutional Time*. Still, the argument is associated more with conservatives. This has taken different forms. For example: Randy Barnett puts institutional procedure be-fore substantive outcome in "Health Care Ruling: A Strange Constitutional Win," *Wash-ington Examiner*, June 28, 2012. Others have proposed other ideas, including Ted Cruz, "Constitutional Remedies to a Lawless Supreme Court," *National Review*, June 26, 2015.

25. James F. Simon, *What Kind of Nation: Thomas Jefferson, John Marshall, and the Epic Struggle to Create a United States*; G. Edward White and Gerald Gunther, *The Mar-shall Court and Cultural Change, 1815–1831*; R. Kent Newmyer, *John Marshall and the Heroic Age of the Supreme Court*.

26. Barry Friedman, *The Will of the People: How Public Opinion Has Influenced the Supreme Court and Shaped the Meaning of the Constitution*.

27. Keith Whittington, *Constitutional Construction: Divided Powers and Constitution-al Meaning*.

28. Barry Friedman, "The History of the Countermajoritarian Difficulty, Part One: The Road to Judicial Supremacy," 362, 363; Mark A. Graber, "Federalist or Friends of Adams: The Marshall Court and Party Politics"; Graber, "The Passive-Aggressive Virtues: *Cohens v. Virginia* and the Problematic Establishment of Judicial Power"; Graber, "Establishing Judicial Review? *Schooner Peggy* and the Early Marshall Court."

29. The dean of the Dickinson Law School at Penn State commented, "These nine men can quash the legislation of the representatives of 90 millions of people." Barry Friedman, "The History of the Countermajoritarian Difficulty, Part Three: The Lesson of *Lochner*," 1443; Friedman, "Popular Dissatisfaction with the Administration of Justice: A Retrospect (and a Look Ahead)."

30. Howard Gillman, "The Collapse of Constitutional Originalism and the Rise of the Notion of the 'Living Constitution' in the Course of American State-Building"; Barry Friedman, "The History of the Countermajoritarian Difficulty, Part Four: Law's Politics."

31. Soon after *The Nine Old Men* was published, FDR received many letters from people complaining about "nine old men" on the court. Drew Pearson and Robert S. Allen, *The Nine Old Men*.

32. Friedman, "Part Four," 1000.

33. Laura Kalman, *FDR's Gambit: The Court Packing Fight and the Rise of Legal Liberalism*.

34. Laura Kalman, "The Constitution, the Supreme Court, and the New Deal"; William E. Leuchtenburg, "Comment on Laura Kalman's Article"; Barry Cushman, *Rethinking the New Deal Court: The Structure of a Constitutional Revolution*.

35. Erwin Chemerinsky, "It's Alexander Bickel's Fault," *SCOTUSblog*, August 16, 2012, https://www.scotusblog.com/2012/08/online-alexander-bickel-symposium-its-alexander-bickels-fault/.

36. John Hart Ely, *Democracy and Distrust*, 71.

37. Cass R. Sunstein, *One Case at a Time: Judicial Minimalism on the Supreme Court*; Sunstein, "Problems with Minimalism"; Sunstein, "The Minimalist Constitution." Mark Tushnet has referred to Sunstein as the "jurisprudential heir" to Bickel. Tushnet, "Law and Prudence in the Law of Justiciability: The Transformation and Disappearance of the Political Question Doctrine."

38. Anthony T. Kronman, "Alexander Bickel's Philosophy of Prudence"; Edward A. Purcell Jr., "Alexander M. Bickel and the Post-Realist Constitution."

39. Nicholas Buccola, "In Defense of Judicial Prudence: American Constitutional Theory, Virtue, and Judicial Review in Hard Cases"; Brad Snyder, "The Former Clerks Who Nearly Killed Judicial Restraint."

40. David Wolitz, "Alexander Bickel and the Demise of Legal Process Jurisprudence"; Tushnet, "Law and Prudence."

41. Roger Pilon, "Online Alexander Bickel Symposium: Bickel and Bork beyond the Academy," *SCOTUSblog*, August 16, 2012, https://www.scotusblog.com/2012/08/online-alexander-bickel-symposium-bickel-and-bork-beyond-the-academy. Incidentally, when Yale created the Alexander Bickel Chair of Law, Bork was the first professor to fill the seat. See also Laura Kalman, *Yale Law School and the Sixties: Revolt and Reverberations*.

42. Robert H. Bork, *The Tempting of America: The Political Seduction of the Law*, 264.

43. Michael Avery and Danielle McLaughlin, *The Federalist Society: How Conservatives Took the Law back from Liberals*; Amanda Hollis-Brusky, *Ideas with Consequences: The Federalist Society and the Conservative Counterrevolution*.

44. Antonin Scalia, *A Matter of Interpretation*; Scalia, "The Rule of Law as a Law of Rules."

45. Barack Obama, "The President's Press Conference," April 2, 2012; Donald Trump, "Statement on the Sanctuary Cities Ruling," April 25, 2017.

46. Robert Dahl, *How Democratic Is the American Constitution?*; Sanford Levinson, *Our Undemocratic Constitution*.

47. Maureen Dowd, "Men in Black," *New York Times*, April 3, 2012; Glenn Beck, "Frightening Obama," October 27, 2008, quoted in Bridge, "Holding the Accountability Problem Accountable," 18.

48. Keith E. Whittington, "'Interpose Your Friendly Hand': Political Supports for the Exercise of Judicial Review by the United States Supreme Court." The following provide overviews of the paradigm: Mark A. Graber, "The Problematic Establishment of Judicial Review"; Graber, "Regime Politics and the Countermajoritarian Problem," *Balkanization* (blog), June 6, 2008, http://balkin.blogspot.com/2008/06/regime-politics -and-countermajoritarian.html; Graber, "The Countermajoritarian Difficulty: From Courts to Congress to Constitutional Order"; Cornell W. Clayton, "The Supply and Demand Sides of Judicial Policy-Making"; Cornell W. Clayton and David May, "The New Institutionalism and Supreme Court Decision-Making toward a Political Regimes Approach"; Keith E. Whittington, "Once More unto the Breach: Post-Behavioralist Approaches to Judicial Politics"; Whittington, *Political Foundations of Judicial Supremacy: The Presidency, the Supreme Court, and Constitutional Leadership in U.S. History*; Howard Gillman, "Regime Politics, Jurisprudential Regimes, and Unenumerated Rights"; Jeb Barnes, "Bringing the Courts Back In: Interbranch Perspectives on the Role of Courts in American Politics and Policy Making"; Thomas M. Keck, "Party Politics or Judicial Independence: The Regime Politics Literature Hits the Law Schools"; Keck, "Party, Policy, or Duty: Why Does the Supreme Court Invalidate Statutes?"; George I. Lovell and Scott E. Lemieux, "Assessing Juristocracy: Are Judges Rulers or Agents?"; Scott E. Lemieux and David J. Watkins, "Beyond the 'Countermajoritarian Difficulty': Lessons from Contemporary Democratic Theory"; Corinna Barrett Lain, "Upside-Down Judicial Review"; Kevin J. McMahon, "Will the Court Still 'Seldom Stray Very Far'? Regime Politics in a Polarized America."

49. Bridge, "Supreme Court, Factions."

50. Rosenberg asks fair questions about the regime. I try to answer his questions here briefly in [brackets]. More detailed answers are in the text in this section, the next chapter (which deals with political parties), and throughout the book, where I try to identify the different players of a regime and their intercurrent interactions. Rosenberg writes: "What is such a beast? [complex and multi-faceted coalitions] How does the Court know when a ruling regime has come into existence or has disintegrated? [existence via electoral and policy changes; disintegration with shifts to secondary preferences] Does its political strength matter [yes], and if so, how can the Court determine it [I provide ways to measure majoritarianism]? To whom does the Court look to identify its interests? [according to regime politics scholars, the "presidential wing"] What if its

members disagree, as they undoubtedly will, over important issues? [this is my book: under certain conditions, there will be pushback]." Rosenberg closes it out by admitting, "There are no simple or easy answers to these questions." He is right. I try to answer these issues, but a concept as amorphous as "the regime" is admittedly tough to nail down. Gerald N. Rosenberg, "The Wonder of It All," 684.

51. Walter Dean Burnham, *Critical Elections and the Mainsprings of American Politics*; Curt Nichols and Adam S. Myers, "Exploiting the Opportunity for Reconstructive Leadership: Presidential Responses to Enervated Presidential Regimes"; Curt Nichols, "The Presidency and the Political Order: In Context"; Cohen et al., *The Party Decides: Presidential Nominations before and after Reform*.

52. V. O. Key, *Politics, Parties, and Pressure Groups*.

53. Coalitional leadership is not confined to this list. Some Supreme Court justices, such as Abe Fortas, have been central to the passage and execution of coalitional policies. Lobby groups, such as the NRA or teachers' union, have strong pulls within their respective coalitions. Internal party leaders, such as Mark Hanna, Karl Rove, and Rahm Emanuel, can also play a central role.

54. Robert Dahl, "Decision-Making in a Democracy: The Supreme Court as a National Policy-Maker." To wit, Google Scholar notes that it has 2991 citations, with 200 citations in 2022 alone. Notably, the first two listings are Ely's *Democracy and Distrust* and Bickel's *The Least Dangerous Branch*. The next three listings are some of the most influential works in all of law and courts: Marc Galanter's "Why the 'Haves' Come Out Ahead: Speculations on the Limits of Legal Change," Gerald Rosenberg's *The Hollow Hope: Can Courts Bring about Social Change?*, and Jeffrey A. Segal and Harold J. Spaeth's *The Supreme Court and the Attitudinal Model Revisited*.

55. Gerald Rosenberg, "The Road Taken: Robert A. Dahl's Decision-Making in a Democracy: The Supreme Court as a National Policy-Maker," 615.

56. Dahl, "Decision-Making in a Democracy," 293.

57. Dahl, "Decision-Making in a Democracy," 293; Keith E. Whittington, "Legislative Sanctions and the Strategic Environment of Judicial Review."

58. Jonathan D. Casper, "The Supreme Court and National Policy Making."

59. Michael W. McCann, "Reform Litigation on Trial."

60. Dahl, "Decision-Making in a Democracy," 293–94.

61. Howard Gillman, "Robert G. McCloskey, Historical Institutionalism, and the Arts of Judicial Governance," 338.

62. Robert G. McCloskey, *The American Supreme Court*, xv.

63. McCloskey, *American Supreme Court*, 230.

64. McCloskey, *American Supreme Court*, 26; Graber, "Passive-Aggressive Virtues"; Graber, "Establishing Judicial Review?"; Graber, "Federalist or Friends of Adams."

65. Robert G. McCloskey, *The Modern Supreme Court*, 307–8.

66. McCloskey, *American Supreme Court*, 230.

67. McCloskey, *American Supreme Court*, 230–31.

68. Martin Shapiro, *Law and Politics in the Supreme Court: New Approaches to Political Jurisprudence*. For an overview of Shapiro's contributions, see Howard Gillman, "Martin Shapiro and the Movement from 'Old' Institutionalist Studies to 'New' Institutionalist Studies in Public Law."

69. Herbert M. Kritzer, "Martin Shapiro: Anticipating the New Institutionalism," 390.

70. Martin Shapiro, "Public Law and Judicial Politics," 366.

71. Graber, "Nonmajoritarian Difficulty."

72. Don E. Fehrenbacher, *The Dred Scott Case: Its Significance in American Law and Politics*.

73. For example: Jefferson Davis, D-MS, *Congressional Globe* 1851, 154: "We are entitled to a decision of the Supreme Court"; Lewis Cass, D-MI, *Congressional Globe* 1851, 531: "Let the Supreme Court determine the question"; Stephen Douglas, D-IL, *Congressional Globe* 1855, 1258: "I am willing to leave that to the Supreme Court." James Buchanan, "1857 Inaugural Address": "It is a judicial question, which legitimately belongs to the Supreme Court."

74. Graber, *Dred Scott*.

75. Klarman, "Rethinking the History of American Freedom." These include: *Gideon v. Wainwright* (requiring states to provide legal counsel to defendants in felony cases); *Pierce v. Society of Sisters* (allowing children to attend private schools); *Harper v. Virginia Board of Elections* (banning poll taxes); *Coker v. Georgia* (forbidding the death penalty in cases of rape); and *Moore v. City of East Cleveland* (allowing blood relatives the right to live in a single household).

76. Connecticut, Rhode Island, Massachusetts, and New York.

77. Perhaps telling of the majoritarian nature of these decisions, *dissenters* in both cases used the exact same phrase to describe the laws at issue. Potter Stewart called Connecticut's anti-contraceptive law "uncommonly silly." Clarence Thomas used the same phrase for Texas's law.

78. Howard Gillman, "Courts and the Politics of Partisan Coalitions."

79. Mark A. Graber, "Constructing Judicial Review," 446.

80. Thomas M. Keck, *Judicial Politics in Polarized Times*; McMahon, "Will the Court Still 'Seldom Stray Very Far'?"; Howard Gillman, "Party Coalitions and Supreme Court Politics: Additional Lessons from Whittington's *Repugnant Laws*."

Chapter 2. Theory

1. An early form of this structure can be found in Dave Bridge, "Supreme Court, Factions, and the Counter-Majoritarian Difficulty."

2. E. E. Schattschneider, *Party Government*; Seymour Martin Lipset and Stein Rokkan, *Party Systems and Voter Alignments: Cross-National Perspectives*; James Sundquist, *Dynamics of the Party System*.

3. David Karol, *Party Position Change in American Politics: Coalition Management*; DiSalvo, *Engines of Change*; Gary Miller and Norman Schofield, "The Transformation of the Republican and Democratic Party Coalitions in the U.S."

4. Schattschneider, *Party Government*; see also Gary Miller and Norman Schofield, "Activists and Partisan Realignment in the United States"; Norman Schofield and Gary Miller, "Elections and Activist Coalitions in the United States."

5. Kevin J. McMahon, *Reconsidering Roosevelt on Race: How the Presidency Paved the Road to Brown*; Graber, "Constructing Judicial Review"; Graber, "Countermajoritarian Difficulty"; Howard Gillman, "Party Politics and Constitutional Change: The Political Origins of Liberal Judicial Activism"; Whittington, *Political Foundations of Judicial Supremacy*; Keck, "Party, Policy, or Duty"; Balkin, "Why Liberals and Conservatives Flipped"; Balkin, *Cycles of Constitutional Time*; Curt Nichols, "The 'Second Wave' of

Political Time Scholarship. And Beyond!". Bradley Hays gives a very helpful description of the "presidential wing," saying that it might be better conceived of as the "dominant" or "elite" wing. (He notes that regime scholars use these terms interchangeably.) In any case, the presidency matters, obviously, to the selection of justices. The expansion of executive power—especially after the New Deal—has made other institutions dependent on presidential leadership. Power grabs, congressional deferrals, symbolic heads of party, de facto and de jure veto power, Kernell's "going public," Tulis's "rhetorical presidency"—these are all reasons why regime politics falls back on the term "presidential wing." See Bradley D. Hays, "Party with the Court: Political Parties and the National Judiciary in the Creation, Maintenance, and Transformation of Political Orders." See also Samuel Kernell, *Going Public: New Strategies of Presidential Leadership*; Jeffrey K. Tulis, *The Rhetorical Presidency*; Sarah Burns, *The Politics of War Powers: The Theory and History of Presidential Unilateralism*; Clement Fatovic and Benjamin A. Kleinerman, eds., *Extra-Legal Power and Legitimacy: Perspectives on Prerogative*.

6. Daniel Cook and Andrew J. Polsky, "Political Time Reconsidered: Unbuilding and Rebuilding the State under the Reagan Administration."

7. Cook and Polsky, "Political Time Reconsidered"; Karol, *Party Position Change in American Politics*; Andrew J. Polsky, "Partisan Regimes in American Politics."

8. Nichols and Myers, "Exploiting the Opportunity"; Nichols, "Presidency and the Political Order"; Stephen Skowronek, *Presidential Leadership in Political Time: Reprise and Reappraisal*.

9. Friedman uses a similar term, "dialogic" to describe the relationship between the Supreme Court and public opinion. Friedman, *Will of the People*; Barry Friedman, "Dialogue and Judicial Review"; Jenna Bednar, "The Dialogic Theory of Judicial Review: A New Social Science Research Agenda"; Rosenberg, "Wonder of It All"; Gerald N. Rosenberg, "Romancing the Court."

10. Nichols and Myers, "Exploiting the Opportunity."

11. Graber, "Constructing Judicial Review," 446.

12. McMahon, *Reconsidering Roosevelt*; Graber, "Constructing Judicial Review"; Graber, "Countermajoritarian Difficulty"; Gillman, "Party Politics and Constitutional Change"; Whittington, *Political Foundations of Judicial Supremacy*; Keck, "Party, Policy, or Duty"; Balkin, "Why Liberals and Conservatives Flipped"; Balkin, *Cycles of Constitutional Time*; Nichols, "'Second Wave' of Political Time Scholarship"; Hays, "Party with the Court."

13. An early form of this structure can be found in Dave Bridge, "Supreme Court, Factions."

14. Key, *Politics, Parties, and Pressure Groups*.

15. Friedman, "History of the Countermajoritarian Difficulty, Part One," 349.

16. For a full discussion, see Murphy, *Congress and the Court*; Pritchett, *Congress versus the Supreme Court*; Ross, "Attacks on the Warren Court." The following comes from Bridge, "Supreme Court, Factions," 436: "*Pennsylvania v. Nelson* (1956) ruled against Pennsylvania's anti-sedition law; *Konigsberg v. State Bar* (1957) and *Schware v. Board of Examiners* (1957) held that state bars could not deny applications because of Communist Party affiliation; *Cole v. Young* (1956) reversed the dismissal of a federal employee based on 'sympathetic association' with a communist organization; *Slochower v. Board of Education* (1956) reversed the dismissal of a professor who refused to answer questions regarding communist affiliations; *Service v. Dulles* (1957) reversed the discharge of a

foreign service officer suspected of being a communist; *Jencks v. United States* (1957) forced government prosecutors to cooperate in the sharing of evidence in criminal cases; *Yates v. United States* (1957) made it more difficult for the government to prosecute Communist organization and advocacy; *Sweezy v. New Hampshire* (1957) narrowed the definition of 'subversive persons' to exclude activity remotely and unconsciously connected to subversion; and *Watkins v. United States* (1957) declared the House Committee on Un-American Activities to have reached beyond the scope of congressional power."

17. Murphy, *Congress and the Court*, 111.

18. Gordon Silverstein and John Hanley, "The Supreme Court and Public Opinion in Times of War and Crisis."

19. National Opinion Research Center, "Poll: Communism, Conformity, and Civil Liberties," 1954.

20. This is one possible solution to the problem: examine polls before the court decided an issue. This would give us insight into what the public believes before the court brings more attention to an issue. When possible, I turn to these polls. Even so, the fact that a case is pending before the court—or even just making its way through lower state or federal courts—still makes it difficult to measure public opinion completely independent from judicial intervention.

21. William Jenner, R-IN, *CR* 1957, 12806; see also Harold Collier, R-IL, *CR* 1957, 15974; Wint Smith, R-KS, *CR* 1957, 16981.

22. *CR* 1957, 9887; see also John Williams, D-MS, *CR* 1957, 4339; Strom Thurmond, D-SC, *CR* 1957, 10333.

23. Curt Nichols, Dave Bridge, and Adam Carrington, "Court-Curbing via Attempt to Amend the Constitution: An Update of Congressional Attacks on the Supreme Court from 1955–1984."

24. Applying this expectation to communists' rights decisions, we find a small handful of attacks against the court on that very topic. The previous chapter mentioned the bill that LBJ thwarted. In addition, Strom Thurmond (D-SC) and William Colmer (D-MS) sponsored separate bills that would have allowed states to pass laws further restricting communist rights.

25. David R. Mayhew, *Congress: The Electoral Connection*.

26. H. W. Brands, *Reagan: The Life*.

27. For instance, in a 1960 letter he wrote to Richard Nixon about John F. Kennedy, Reagan commented, "Under the tousled boyish haircut is still old Karl Marx." *Time*, "The Crist Switch: Top 10 Political Defections."

28. Some examples: Edward G. Carmines and James A. Stimson, *Issue Evolution: Race and the Transformation of American Politics*; Greg D. Adams, "Abortion: Evidence of an Issue Evolution"; Kara Lindaman and Donald P. Haider-Markel, "Issue Evolution, Political Parties, and the Culture Wars"; Edward G. Carmines and Michael W. Wagner, "Political Issues and Party Alignments: Assessing the Issue Evolution Perspective"; Byron E. Shafer and William J. M. Claggett, *The Two Majorities: The Issue Context of Modern American Politics*; Geoffrey Layman, *The Great Divide: Religious and Cultural Conflict in American Party Politics*; Christina Wolbrecht, *The Politics of Women's Rights: Parties, Positions, and Change*.

29. Adams, "Abortion," 720.

30. Adams, "Abortion," 720.

31. *CR* 1957, 15955.

32. Keck, *Judicial Politics*, 4.

33. Jeb Barnes, *Overruled? Legislative Overrides, Pluralism, and Contemporary Court-Congress Relations*; J. Mitchell Pickerill, *Constitutional Deliberation in Congress: The Impact of Judicial Review in a Separated System.*

34. This could be in a single election or over the course of time. I refrain from using the term "realignment," following Elizabeth Sanders, to "not to be encumbered with its baggage." When a party uses the same issue to win elections over and over (e.g., the post-*Roe* GOP with abortion), that seems durable. When one group goes from durably voting for one party to durably voting for another (e.g., the solid south going from blue to red), that seems like "realigning." That said, I am not going to extensively debate the merits and drawbacks of realignment theory, and I relegate it to this note. Does the American electorate realign every thirty years? Maybe not. But even realignment's fiercest critic, David Mayhew, would agree with the answers to the following questions. *Can a political party opposed to unpopular Supreme Court decisions advertise their positions in such a way to attract new voters to that party?* Yes. Mayhew notes "much contingency in politics and history. Wars, depressions, disasters, assassinations, fads, fancies, emergent circumstances, and leadership idiosyncrasies." Surely countermajoritarian Supreme Court rulings count. *Can it work for more than one election cycle?* Yes. Mayhew says we should aim for "clear, exhaustively stated, replicable, and if possible simple, decision rules" that allow for "periodization [to] emerge from the data rather than be imposed on it." That is my goal: to use the observable expectations to drive the data collection and interpretation; and to see what trends emerge and what hypotheses can be drawn and studied further. At the very least, Edward Carmines and Michael Wagner's synthesis of the issue evolution literature describes the compelling effect that parties can have when attracting cross-partisans on certain issues. My argument is that, under certain conditions, a court ruling can create that opportunity. See Elizabeth Sanders, "In Defense of Realignment and Regimes: Why We Need Periodization," 538; Carmines and Wagner, "Political Issues and Party Alignments"; Burnham, *Critical Elections*; Key, *Politics, Parties, and Pressure Groups*; David R. Mayhew, *Electoral Realignments: A Critique of an American Genre*; Stephen Skowronek, *The Politics Presidents Make: Leadership from John Adams to George Bush*; Karen Orren and Stephen Skowronek, "Beyond the Iconography of Order: Notes for a 'New Institutionalism'"; Andrew J. Polsky, "No Tool Is Perfect: Periodization in the Study of American Political Development"; David R. Mayhew, "Suggested Guidelines for Periodization," 532–34.

35. Daniel Schlozman, *When Movements Anchor Parties: Electoral Alignments in American History*; Christopher Baylor, *First to the Party: The Group Origins of Political Transformation.*

36. Murphy, *Congress and the Court*, 111.

37. Robert M. Lichtman, *The Supreme Court and McCarthy-Era Repression: One Hundred Decisions*; Engel, *American Politicians Confront the Courts.*

38. Murphy, *Congress and the Court*, 119.

39. Newman, "Warren Court and American Politics."

40. We know in hindsight that Eisenhower's appointees shifted the court to the left. Some of this had to do with choosing Earl Warren as chief justice. Richard M. Fried, *Nightmare in Red: The McCarthy Era in Perspective*; Powe, *Warren Court*. But even

contemporary scholars of the time believed that Brennan was a clear liberal. Murphy, *Congress and the Court*; Pritchett, *Congress versus the Court*.

41. *Slochower v. Board of Higher Education of New York City*, *Pennsylvania v. Nelson*, and *Cole v. Young*.

42. *Sweezy v. New Hampshire*, *Jencks v. US*, *Service v. Dulles*, *Watkins v. US*, *Schware v. Board of Bar Examiners of New Mexico*, and *Konigsberg v. State Bar of California*. He joined a week too late to participate in *Yates v. US*, but he presided over *Jencks v. US* on only his second day on the job.

43. *Uphaus v. Wyman* (which scaled back, or reversed, *Sweezy v. New Hampshire*) and *Barenblatt v. US* (which scaled back, or reversed, *Watkins v. US*).

44. Whittaker, thus, participated in only one of the 1956–57 cases. He voted with the unanimous liberal majority in *Service v. Dulles*.

45. Only one case, *Slochower v. Board of Higher Education of New York City*, was a 5–4 decision. Even then, Reed and Burton (as well as Minton) dissented. Replacing them with another dissenter would not have changed the majority opinion.

46. Steamer, *Supreme Court in Crisis*. Pritchett, somewhat half-heartedly and without any citations as to who made the suggestion, writes, "It was suggested by some that the decisions of June 8, 1959 [*Uphaus* and *Barenblatt*], were not in fact reversals of the actual holdings of the earlier cases, but only amounted to a clarification and explanation of the rather general language used there." Pritchett, *Congress versus the Court*, 13. Friedman similarly acknowledges that possibility without really endorsing it: "There are legal arguments that the decisions before and after the congressional proceedings can be reconciled with one another." Yet, Friedman also convincingly explains why, "It is very difficult to reconcile the Court's legislative investigation decisions *Watkins* and *Barenblatt*." Friedman, *Will of the People*, 255, 514.

47. Friedman, *Will of the People*.

48. Sabin, *In Calmer Times*; Rosenberg, "Judicial Independence"; Powe, *Warren Court*; Lucas A. Powe Jr., *The Supreme Court and the American Elite, 1789–2008*; Geoffrey R. Stone, *Perilous Times: Free Speech in Wartime*; Pritchett, *Congress versus the Court*; Murphy, *Congress and the Court*; Fried, *Nightmare in Red*; Mark V. Tushnet, ed., *The Warren Court in Historical and Political Perspective*; C. Peter Magrath, "'Nine Deliberative Bodies': A Profile of the Warren Court," *Commentary Magazine*, November 1961; Van Alstyne, "Self-Government and the Supreme Court."

49. Sabin, *In Calmer Times*; Friedman, "Birth of an Academic Obsession"; Woods, *Black Struggle, Red Scare*.

50. See also Dave Bridge, "Supreme Court, Factions"; Bridge, "Holding the Accountability Problem Accountable"; Bridge, "Catholics in the 'Mature' New Deal Era: How the Republican Party Used Supreme Court Attacks to Pursue Catholic Voters"; Bridge, "Supreme Court Attacks as a Mechanism for Coalition Building: How the Republican Party Used Court-Curbing Proposals to Pursue Southern Voters"; Dave Bridge and Curt Nichols, "Congressional Attacks on the Supreme Court: A Mechanism to Maintain, Build, and Consolidate."

51. To wit, 92.3 percent of the 3,315 Democratic members of Congress from 1961–79 had Common Space economic scores in the negative (i.e., on the liberal end). Of the outliers, around 90 percent came from the South. All of this confirms what previous scholars have argued—that economic issues had united the disparate factions of the

1930s–50s. This was partly ideological. For example, leading liberals united mostly white labor unions with returning Black soldiers under claims of personal economic freedom. And it was partly practical, as various factions approved increased federal spending on "alphabet soup" proposals because the bills promoted their faction's particular cause: liberals supported the Social Security Act; blue-collar Catholics liked the National Industrial Recovery Act; southerners endorsed the Tennessee Valley Authority; and so on. By the 1960s the economic bills that split the Democratic Party had more to do with race (e.g., Great Society, appropriations to fight crime) than fiscal policy (see chapter 5). Put differently, the very small economic differences in the Democratic Party from 1961–79 (i.e., the 7.7 percent split that mostly comes from the South) seemed to load on region and race. See John Gerring, *Party Ideologies in America: 1828–1996*; Schickler, *Racial Realignment*; DiSalvo, *Engines of Change*; David R. Mayhew, *Placing Parties in American Politics: Organization, Electoral Settings, and Government Activity in the Twentieth Century*; Steve Fraser and Gary Gerstle, *The Rise and Fall of the New Deal Order, 1930–1980*; Roger Biles, *The South and the New Deal*; Joseph Lowndes, Julie Novkov, and Dorian T. Warren, eds., *Race and American Political Development*; Earl Black and Merle Black, *The Rise of Southern Republicans*.

52. In 1952 liberals converted the platform from a "populist" ideology to a "universalist" ideology. That year, the liberal delegation also held an effective veto on the presidential nomination. After the 1958 congressional elections, non-southern Democrats nearly doubled the number of southern Democrats in both chambers of Congress. Gerring, *Party Ideologies*; Walter Johnson, *How We Drafted Adlai Stevenson*; Bruce Miroff, *The Liberals' Moment: The McGovern Insurgency and the Identity Crisis of the Democratic Party*; Schickler, *Racial Realignment*; Robert Mason and Iwan Morgan, eds., *Seeking a New Majority: The Republican Party and American Politics, 1960–1980*; John Allswang, *The New Deal and American Politics: A Study in Political Change*; David Plotke, *Building a Democratic Political Order: Reshaping Liberalism in the 1930s and 1940s*; Robert M. Collins, *More: The Politics of Economic Growth in Postwar America*; James L. Sundquist, *Politics and Policy: The Eisenhower, Kennedy, and Johnson Years*; Karen Orren, "Union Politics and Postwar Liberalism in the United States, 1946–1979"; Taylor Dark, *The Unions and the Democrats: An Enduring Alliance*; Mary L. Dudziak, *Cold War Civil Rights: Race and the Image of American Democracy.*

53. DiSalvo notes that they tried to centralize power to move the party to the left. Their goals were to "complete" the New Deal and broaden Black civil rights. Their methods were party caucus and congressional leadership control, "from which they could command their southern Democratic adversaries" (*Engines of Change*, 103). See also Daniel DiSalvo, "Party Factions in Congress," 38; Michael Foley, *The New Senate: Liberal Influence on a Conservative Institution, 1959–1972*; James L. Sundquist, *The Decline and Resurgence of Congress*; Julian E. Zelizer, *On Capitol Hill: The Struggle to Reform Congress and Its Consequences, 1948–2000*; Emily Caitlin Baer-Bositis, "Organizing for Reform: The Democratic Study Group and the Role of Party Factions in Driving Institutional Change in the House of Representatives."

54. A slim majority supported *Brown* in 1954. Matthew E. K. Hall, *The Nature of Supreme Court Power*, 128; Klarman, *From Jim Crow to Civil Rights*, 450. Polls from 1955 and 1957 show that a national majority (56 percent) favored *Brown*. Ross, "Attacks on the Warren Court," 606.

55. The following notes' citations are not even approximately comprehensive. They are highlights and representations of a much larger literature.

56. Robert J. Cottrol, Raymond T. Diamond, and Leland B. Ware, *Brown v. Board of Education: Caste, Culture, and the Constitution*; Richard Kluger, *Simple Justice: The History of Brown v. Board of Education and Black America's Struggle for Equality*; Mark V. Tushnet, *Brown v. Board of Education: The Battle for Integration*; Wechsler, "Toward Neutral Principles of Constitutional Law"; Hand, *Bill of Rights*; Austin Sarat, ed., *Race, Law and Culture: Reflections on Brown v. Board of Education*; Michael W. McConnell, "Originalism and the Desegregation Decisions"; Michael J. Klarman, "*Brown*, Originalism, and Constitutional Theory: A Response to Professor McConnell"; Jack Balkin, ed., *What Brown v. Board Should Have Said*.

57. For example: *Virginia Law Review*, "Symposium: 50 Years of *Brown v. Board of Education*"; *Cornell Law Review*, "Symposium: Revisiting *Brown v. Board of Education*: 50 Years of Legal and Social Debate"; *Stetson Law Review*, "Symposium: Commemorating the 50th Anniversary of *Brown*"; *Washburn Law Journal*, "*Brown v. Board of Education* Revisited: Fiftieth Anniversary Symposium"; *New York Law School Law Review*, "*Brown* Is Dead? Long Live *Brown!*"; *Harvard Law Review*, "Symposium: *Brown* at Fifty."

58. Peter F. Lau, ed., *From the Grassroots to the Supreme Court: Brown v. Board of Education and American Democracy*; Mark Tushnet, "Implementing, Transforming, and Abandoning *Brown*." This seems to have been true, too, in the North. See Brian Purnell, Jeanne Theoharis, and Komozi Woodard, eds., *The Strange Careers of the Jim Crow North: Segregation and Struggle outside of the South*; Harvard Sitkoff, *The Struggle for Black Equality*.

59. Rosenberg, *Hollow Hope*; Michael J. Klarman, "*Windsor* and *Brown*: Marriage Equality and Racial Equality," 152. But see McCann, "Reform Litigation on Trial"; Mark V. Tushnet, "The Significance of *Brown v. Board of Education*"; Tushnet, "Some Legacies of *Brown v. Board of Education*."

60. Klarman, *From Jim Crow to Civil Rights*.

61. In terms of policy, just a small handful of examples: Derrick Bell, *Silent Covenants: Brown v. Board of Education and the Unfulfilled Hopes for Racial Reform*; Doug McAdam, *Political Process and the Development of Black Insurgency, 1930–1970*; Richard M. Valelly, *The Two Reconstructions: The Struggle for Black Enfranchisement*; Michelle Alexander and Cornel West, *The New Jim Crow: Mass Incarceration in the Age of Colorblindness*; Richard Rothstein, *The Color of Law: A Forgotten History of How Our Government Segregated America*; Brian J. Glenn and Steven M. Teles, eds., *Conservatism and American Political Development*; Anders Walker, *The Burning House: Jim Crow and the Making of Modern America*; Walker, *The Ghost of Jim Crow: How Southern Moderates Used Brown v. Board to Stall Civil Rights*. In terms of politics, examples include, among others: Schickler, *Racial Realignment*; Timothy N. Thurber, *Republicans and Race: The GOP's Frayed Relationship with African Americans, 1945–1974*; Carmines and Stimson, *Issue Evolution*; Crespino, "Goldwater in Dixie"; Byron E. Shafer and Richard Johnston, *The End of Southern Exceptionalism: Class, Race, and Partisan Change in the Postwar South*; Joseph E. Lowndes, *From the New Deal to the New Right: Race and the Origins of Modern Conservatism*.

62. The final chapter looks at splits in the modern GOP. The GOP was not homogenous in the 1960s–70s, either. What few southern Republicans served were quite

conservative. There was a wing that was quite progressive on civil rights, as well as a southwestern contingent (including Barry Goldwater) that defined itself as anti–Great Society and anti–Civil Rights Act of 1964. McAdam and Kloos, *Deeply Divided*; Edsall and Edsall, *Chain Reaction*; Nicole C. Rae, *The Decline and Fall of the Liberal Republicans*; Andrew E. Busch, *Reagan's Victory: The Presidential Election of 1980 and the Rise of the Right*; DiSalvo, *Engines of Change*; Donald T. Critchlow, *The Conservative Ascendancy: How the GOP Right Made Political History*; Matthew D. Lassiter, *The Silent Majority: Suburban Politics in the Sunbelt South*; Lowndes, *From the New Deal to the New Right*; Daniel Galvin, *Presidential Party Building: Dwight D. Eisenhower to George W. Bush*.

63. This stands in contrast to significant breaks in the contemporary Democratic ranks, some of which are clearly based on economics. For instance, the "Blue Dog" faction still sees itself as more concerned with smaller deficits and excess spending. Meanwhile, some members of Congress today even go so as to call themselves "socialists." It is not that there are not racial/social factions in the DNC; it is that they exist alongside economic fault lines.

64. Patrick J. Buchanan, *Nixon's White House Wars*, 142. He devotes an entire chapter of a book to the issue. It is striking. Buchanan labeled four issues as key: social conservatism (e.g., morality, sexuality), anticommunism, parochial aid, and right to life.

65. Indeed, the chapter on *Roe* shows how evangelicals became a major part of the GOP coalition. Even then, it took evangelical willingness to merge their pro-life goals with those that Catholics had already long been leading.

66. Roy Morey, "Memorandum to Ken Cole and Ed Harper: The Catholic Vote and 1972." September 16, 1971.

67. Pat Buchanan, "Memorandum to John Ehrlichman, H. R. Haldeman, and Charles Colson," September 23, 1971.

68. Michael Novak, *The Rise of the Unmeltable Ethnics: The New Political Force of the Seventies*, 56.

69. Buchanan, *Nixon's White House Wars*, 149.

70. This includes South Carolina, Mississippi, Florida, Alabama, Georgia, Louisiana, Texas, Virginia, Arkansas, North Carolina, and Tennessee. In 2014, fivethirtyeight.com investigated the regions boundaries by asking respondents "Which states do you consider part of the south?" The results are largely in line with those on the eve of secession. West Virginia, Oklahoma, and Missouri did not make the cut. Texas, Arkansas, and Virginia did, although, at a smaller rate than, say, Georgia. The only state that might be different between the 1860s and 2010s is Kentucky. Was the Bluegrass State a southern state in the 1960s and 1970s? Perhaps, but either way, it would not change the overall analysis. Walt Hickey, "Which States Are in the South?" *FiveThirtyEight*, April 30, 2014, https://fivethirtyeight.com/features/which-states-are-in-the-south/.

71. Tom S. Clark, *The Limits of Judicial Independence*; Nichols, Bridge, and Carrington, "Court-Curbing."

72. Clark, *Limits of Judicial Independence*. The difference is my counting constitutional amendments more extensively. Nevertheless, Clark's database should be commended. I found only one missing legislative bill attack (.002 percent of the population) in the time period listed here. In other words, Clark's work is remarkably reliable.

73. This does not count Nixon's failed nominations of Clement Haynsworth and G. Harrold Carswell, nor LBJ's withdrawn nominations of Abe Fortas (to chief justice) and Homer Thornberry. One might conclude that the GOP acquired an extra nomination

by delaying the confirmation of Earl Warren's replacement until Nixon took office and named Warren Burger the new chief.

74. David Alistair Yalof, *Pursuit of Justices: Presidential Politics and the Selection of Supreme Court Nominees*; Henry J. Abraham, *Justices, Presidents, and Senators: A History of the U.S. Supreme Court Appointments from Washington to Bush II*. For example: Truman prioritized "cronyism"; Nixon prioritized southerners; Reagan prioritized conservative ideologues; and Obama and Biden prioritized diversity.

75. For example, some speculate Eisenhower put Earl Warren on the bench as payback for Warren dutifully stepping aside in the 1952 GOP convention and then campaigning for Eisenhower. Later, on the eve of the 1956 election, Eisenhower wanted a nominee who had impeccable qualifications and would not meet any Senate resistance. He also preferred a Catholic who supported *Brown*. He ended up with William Brennan. Harry Blackmun was appointed only after the failed nominations of Clement Haynsworth and G. Harrold Carswell. After that episode, Lewis Powell was appointed because Nixon wanted "a qualified southerner" [Burger told the president, "I recognize that geographical factors cannot be ignored"] and "to be sure that my nominees would be confirmed." Even then, Powell turned Nixon down three times before relenting. William Rehnquist very well might have made it to the court because the ABA declared Mildred Lillie (who would have been the first female justice, and whom Pat Nixon ardently lobbied for) unqualified. Meanwhile, the other candidate, Senator Howard Baker (R-TN), had flown to Tennessee to discuss a possible appointment with his wife. Nixon impatiently wanted to announce the next day and could not get a hold of Baker. Nixon said, "Maybe we leave him [Baker] off the list . . . I still think that the Rehnquist thing is a damn good possibility, you know." Gerald Ford, also, wanted to avoid a fight at all costs. He appointed John Paul Stevens because so little was known of him—other than he was a "lawyer's lawyer." Ed Cray, *Chief Justice: A Biography of Earl Warren*; Yalof, *Pursuit of Justices*; Abraham, *Justices, Presidents, and Senators*; Schickler, *Racial Realignment*; Byron J. Moraski and Charles R. Shipan, "The Politics of Supreme Court Nominations: A Theory of Institutional Constraints and Choices"; Pritchett, *Congress versus the Supreme Court*; Murphy, *Congress and the Court*; Richard Nixon, *The Memoirs of Richard Nixon*, 422; John Ehrlichman, *Witness to Power: The Nixon Years*; Buchanan, *Nixon's White House Wars*, 110; Bob Woodward and Scott Armstrong, *The Brethren: Inside the Supreme Court*, 160, 400.

76. For instance, Gerald Ford appointee, John Paul Stevens, served for thirty-five years—it took six presidents (Carter, Reagan, H. W. Bush, Clinton, George W. Bush, and Obama) before that seat opened up.

77. For instance, when insisting on unanimity in *Brown*, Chief Justice Earl Warren did much to all but compel Stanley Reed to join the majority. Powe, *Warren Court*.

78. Alternatively, some justices vote exactly how their appointer prefers on specific—perhaps even litmus test—issues. But on other issues, justices diverge from their appointer. For instance, Brennan and Warren delivered on Eisenhower's desire to see desegregation through; they disappointed Eisenhower on communist rights cases. Michael A. Kahn, "Shattering the Myth about President Eisenhower's Supreme Court Appointments." (Others might disagree on Eisenhower's commitment to desegregation. See James F. Simon, *Eisenhower vs. Warren: The Battle for Civil Rights and Civil Liberties*.) Nixon's appointees, meanwhile, were all tough on crime: Burger, Blackmun, Powell, and Rehnquist "got their seats on the bench because of their supposed or known lack of sympathy for the rights of the criminally accused." Leonard W. Levy, *Against the Law:*

Notes for Chapter 3

The Nixon Court and Criminal Justice, 422; Friedman, *Will of the People*.

79. Clark, *Justice Brennan*, 75.

80. Lee Epstein and Jeffrey A. Segal, *Advice and Consent: The Politics of Judicial Appointments*, 119.

81. Teddy Roosevelt said he could "carve out of a banana a judge with more backbone" than Oliver Wendell Holmes. Jeffrey A. Segal, Richard J. Timpone, and Robert M. Howard, "Buyer Beware? Presidential Success through Supreme Court Appointments," 559. Truman referred to Tom Clark as "my biggest mistake . . . that damn fool . . . [who] hasn't made one right decision I can think of . . . It's just that he's such a dumb son of a b****." Merle Miller, *Plain Speaking: An Oral Biography of Harry S. Truman*, 225–26; Bridge and Nichols, "Congressional Attacks on the Supreme Court," 104.

82. Lee Epstein et al., "Ideological Drift among Supreme Court Justices: Who, When, and How Important"; Lee Epstein et al., "Do Political Preferences Change? A Longitudinal Study of US Supreme Court Justices"; Lee Epstein and Eric A. Posner, "Supreme Court Justices' Loyalty to the President."

83. Segal-Cover scores are derived from newspaper editorials at the time of an appointment. They quantify the opinions of editorials, which theorize on the nominee's ideology. The scores range from – 1.00 (extremely conservative) to 1.00 (extremely liberal). None of Eisenhower's five appointees rated conservative: Warren (.50); Harlan (.75); Brennan (1.00); Whittaker (.00); and Stewart (.50). Nixon and Ford had more success in placing thought-to-be conservatives on the bench: Burger (-.77); Blackmun (-.77); Powell (-.67); Rehnquist (-.71); and Stevens (-.50). Now, Segal-Cover scores are not perfect proxies (e.g., John Paul Stevens did not turn out to be as conservative as originally predicted by the newspapers). But because they derive from contemporary sources, they do indicate what people at the time thought of the justices at the time of their nomination—and they knew, to some extent, that some of these nominees had liberal tendencies.

84. Episodes that saw jurisprudential waffling include: from *Sweezy* and *Watkins* to *Uphaus* and *Barenblatt*; from *Mapp*, *Miranda*, et al. to *Terry v. Ohio* and *Warden v. Hayden*; and from *Swann* to *Milliken*.

Chapter 3. Prayer

1. Bruce J. Dierenfield, *The Battle over School Prayer: How* Engel v. Vitale *Changed America*, 72.

2. Justice Byron White did not participate and Justice Felix Frankfurter was indisposed.

3. Thomas M. Mengler, "Public Relations in the Supreme Court: Justice Tom Clark's Opinion in the School Prayer Case"; Corinna Barrett Lain, "God, Civic Virtue, and the American Way: Reconstructing Engel."

4. Ted Dracos, *UnGodly: The Passions, Torments, and Murder of Atheist Madalyn Murray O'Hair*.

5. Dierenfield, *School Prayer*.

6. Lain would disagree. She writes that *Engel* was not countermajoritarian. Based on the criteria in the previous chapter, though, evidence strongly suggests *Engel* had a lot of opposition. This is not to take away from Lain—her article is certainly worthwhile, both for its bold argument and the rich historical detail. Lain, "God, Civic Virtue."

7. Gallup Poll, 1963, 1964; Harris Poll, 1966.

8. American National Election Studies Survey (hereafter "ANES"), 1964, 1966, 1968.

9. General Social Survey (hereafter "GSS"), 1974, 1975, 1976, 1977, 1978.

10. ANES, 1964; GSS, 1974; GSS, 1977.

11. *CR* 1962, 6378, 12624, 13455. See also *CR* 1962, Joseph Waggoner, D-LA, 11777; Robert Sikes, D-FL, 11775; Thomas O'Brien, D-IL, 12226; William Hull, D-MO, 12624; William McCulloch, R-OH; 11755; CR 1963, Bob Wilson, R-CA, 21171..

12. *CR* 1962, 11675, 11841, 11843.

13. The remark was made by George Andrews (D-AL). *Congressional Quarterly Almanac 1962*, "Supreme Court Prayer Decision."

14. Don Fuqua, D-FL, *CR* 1963, 11215.

15. *CR* 1962, 12120. See also *CR* 1962, Thomas Abernethy, D-MS, 11718; L. Mendel Rivers D-SC, 11718; Joseph Waggoner D-LA, 11777; CR 1963, Don Fuqua D-FL, 11215.

16. Billy B. Hathorn, "The Changing Politics of Race: Congressman Albert William Watson and the SC Republican Party, 1965–1970."

17. He later lost a gubernatorial race in Georgia to a more strident Democratic segregationist. *New York Times*, "Howard H. Callaway, Strategist Who Helped GOP Rise in South, Dies at 86," March 21, 2014.

18. Of course, that could also refer to desegregation. Thomas M. Keck, *The Most Activist Supreme Court in History: The Road to Modern Judicial Conservatism*, 97.

19. This is an imperfect measure of Catholic-related interests, but without representative-level data, it is hard to zero in on where, exactly, Catholics reside and are represented. Those five states, though, seem uncontroversial.

20. For instance, Thomas Johnson (D-MD) said, "It is noteworthy that this same organization in the guise of champion of civil liberties has defended communists in several instances." *CR* 1962, 13598, 11779.

21. *America*, editorial, "Black Monday Decision," July 7, 1962, 456: "It is not only an unpopular decision with the vast majority of the American people. It is quite literally, a stupid decision, a doctrinaire decision, an unrealistic decision, a decision that spits in the face of our history, our tradition, and our heritage as a religious people . . . enslaving limitations of secularistic dogma." Roscoe Balch, *America*, "Religious Liberty in New York," November 3, 1962, 983: "Courts might go on to establish an America which is secularist at every point." *Commonweal*, editorial, "The Court on Prayer," July 1962, 387: "nightmarish implications into this ruling: that the cause of Communism has been served, that the Court has proclaimed secularism . . . there is nothing in the actual decision to support any of these conclusions." William B. Ball, *Commonweal*, "The Forbidden Prayer," July 1962, 420: "the effort further to press for the elimination of all orthodoxies, save secularism, from every remaining aspect of religion in American public life."

22. Robert S. Alley, *School Prayer*, 124.

23. James Zeigler, *Red Scare Racism and Cold War Black Radicalism*.

24. *CR* 1962, 11782.

25. *CR* 1963, 11931.

26. Sabin, *In Calmer Times*; Woods, *Red Scare*. Some would say Eisenhower slyly courted southern votes. No one would claim Ike espoused George Wallace–type rhetoric. Jeffrey R. Young, "Eisenhower's Federal Judges and Civil Rights Policy: A Republican 'Southern Strategy' for the 1950s"; Simon, *Eisenhower vs. Warren*; William I. Hitchcock, *The Age of Eisenhower: America and the World in the 1950s*. But see the following for an argument that Ike was at the forefront of civil rights: David A. Nichols, *A Matter of Justice: Eisenhower and the Beginning of the Civil Rights Revolution*.

27. *CR* 1962, 12300. See also *CR* 1962, 11780; *CR* 1963, A5394.

28. *CR* 1962, 116, 11719.

29. *New York Times*, "Frank J. Becker, 82, Is Dead; Represented L.I. in Congress," September 6, 1981, 36.

30. Dierenfield, *School Prayer*, 176.

31. Dierenfield, *School Prayer*, 179.

32. Patrick Buchanan, "Dividing the Democrats: Memorandum to the Attorney General H. R. Haldeman."

33. Buchanan, "Dividing the Democrats."

34. Patrick Buchanan, "Assault Book"; Buchanan, "Dividing the Democrats."

35. *America*, editorial: "On Praying in Schools," 1962, 715. See also: *America* editor Francis Canavan, "Implications of the School Prayer and Bible Reading Decisions: The Welfare State"; Catholic intellectual Philip Scharper, "Catholics and Public Schools," *Commonweal* 79, no. 18 (1964): 533–38.

36. John C. Jeffries Jr. and James E. Ryan, "A Political History of the Establishment Clause," 323.

37. Dierenfield, *School Prayer*, 161.

38. Republican Party Platform, 1968.

39. Buchanan, *Nixon's White House Wars*, 143.

40. Lawrence McAndrews, "Unanswered Prayers: Church, State, and School in the Nixon Era," 86–87.

41. Republican Party Platform, 1964.

42. Daniel K. Williams, *God's Own Party: The Making of the Christian Right*, 75.

43. In 2011 Mitt Romney said there should be more prayer in schools. See Rachel Streitfeld, "Romney: More Prayer in Schools," CNN, December 16, 2011. In 2016 Ted Cruz tried to win the GOP nomination by appealing to evangelicals with the need for school prayer. See Robert Draper, "Ted Cruz's Evangelical Gamble," *New York Times*, January 26, 2016. In 2020 Donald Trump promised "big action" on school prayer. See Franco Ordóñez, "Trump Defends School Prayer. Critics Say He's Got It All Wrong," NPR, January 16, 2016.

44. William M. Beaney and Edward N. Beiser, "Prayer and Politics: The Impact of *Engel* and *Schempp* on the Political Process"; Ellis Katz, "Patterns of Compliance with the *Schempp* Decision"; Kenneth M. Dolbeare and Phillip E. Hammond, *The School Prayer Decisions from Court Policy to Local Practice*.

45. Dolbeare and Hammond, *School Prayer Decisions*.

46. Dierenfield, *School Prayer*, 148.

47. Robert H. Birkby, "The Supreme Court and the Bible Belt: Tennessee Reaction to the *Schempp* Decision," 148.

48. Beaney and Beiser, "Prayer and Politics," 489.

49. Katz, "Patterns of Compliance," 404. Again, it should be stressed that these attitudes were not confined to the south. For instance, Katz quotes an anonymous state superintendent of public education from a western state: "I wonder if it is not a treasonable act intended to undermine the morals of the country and make it ripe for Godless communism to take over."

50. Birkby, "Supreme Court and the Bible Belt," 315. One superintendent claimed, "99% of the people in the United States feel as I do about the Supreme Court's decision— that it was an outrage and that Congress should have it amended." For good measure,

he added, "The remaining 1% do not belong in the free world." Another board member added, "If Bible reading is offensive to a very small minority, then this minority may do homework or look out the window."

51. Birkby, "Supreme Court and the Bible Belt," 317.

52. Beaney and Beiser, "Prayer and Politics," 487.

53. H. Frank Way Jr., "Survey Research of Judicial Decisions: The Prayer and Bible Reading Cases." These figures are, in all likelihood, deflated as survey respondents might have been reticent to admit they were in defiance of a Supreme Court ruling. At the very least, though, more than a third of those surveyed defied *Engel* and just under a quarter defied *Schempp*.

54. Donald E. Reich, "Schoolhouse Religion and the Supreme Court: A Report on Attitudes of Teachers and Principals and on School Practices in Wisconsin and Ohio."

55. Way, "Survey Research."

56. Way, "Survey Research."

57. It read, "We thank you for the flowers so sweet; We thank you for the food we eat; We thank you for the birds that sing; We thank you for everything."

58. Dolbeare and Hammond, *School Prayer Decisions*, 42.

59. Alley, *School Prayer*, 115. The inscription remains above the speaker's desk today.

60. *New York Times*, "Rep. Becker Renews Drive on Prayer Bill," June 16, 1964.

61. Bruce J. Dierenfield, "'Somebody Is Tampering with America's Soul': Congress and the School Prayer Debate."

62. Donald Boles, *The Bible, Religion, and the Public Schools*.

63. Beaney and Beiser, "Prayer and Politics"; Lain, "God, Civic Virtue."

64. *CR* 1964, 24043.

65. Alley, *School Prayer*. Antiprayer journalist Robert Alley was the last person to testify before Bayh's committee. As he walked out of the hearing with Bayh, the two chatted and Bayh admitted that he was committed to defeating the Dirksen Amendment.

66. Alley, *School Prayer*, 163.

67. Dierenfield, *School Prayer*, 179.

68. Dierenfield, *School Prayer*.

69. Joan DelFattore, *The Fourth R: Conflicts over Religion in America's Public Schools*, 137.

70. Dierenfield, *School Prayer*, 183.

71. DelFattore, *Fourth R*, 138.

72. Alley, *School Prayer*, 187.

73. Powe, *Warren Court*; Dierenfield, *School Prayer*; Daryl J. Levinson, "Parchment and Politics: The Positive Puzzle of Constitutional Government"; Michael J. Klarman, "Rethinking the History of American Freedom"; Tara Leigh Grove, "A (Modest) Separation of Powers Success Story"; Rodney K. Smith, *Public Prayer and the Constitution*.

74. Gallup Poll, 2014.

75. Mengler, "Public Relations," 340. This practice was not entirely new. In the segregation cases, the court purposely listed *Brown v. Board* as the styled case. Justice Clark later revealed it was a conscious choice, too, "We consolidated them and made *Brown* the first so that the whole question would not smack of being a purely southern one."

76. Lain, "God, Civic Virtue." 535.

77. John B. Ryan and Caitlin Milazzo, "The South, the Suburbs, and the Vatican Too: Partisanship in Context."

Chapter 4. Crime

1. The petty thug was let off the hook because of the oversight. Ronald Steiner, Rebecca Bauer, and Rohit Talwar, "The Rise and Fall of the Miranda Warnings in Popular Culture."

2. In fact, the court occasionally ruled in favor of law enforcement. See *Hoffa v. United States*, *Lewis v. United States* (1966), *Ker v. California* (1967), *McCray v. Illinois* (1967), *Terry v. Ohio* (1967), and *Warden v. Hayden* (1967). At the end of this chapter, I discuss this shift.

3. A quick word on *Gideon v. Wainwright* (1963), the historic case that provided indigent criminal defendants with legal counsel. I exclude *Gideon* from the list of cases the spurred mass opposition because, quite simply, it was a very popular decision—perhaps the best-received (at the time) of any Warren Court ruling. There are two obvious reasons as to why. The decision was unanimous, which prohibited losers from pointing to a dissent that legitimized their legal point of view. Also, *Gideon* only applied to five "local outlier" states (Alabama, Florida, Mississippi, North Carolina, and South Carolina); all other states already provided counsel for indigent defendants. In sum, it was a popular and narrow ruling. Politicians would later debate *when* counsel *needed* to be present. But nearly everyone agreed that poor defendants had a right to a lawyer at trial. This stands in contrast to the other headliner criminal cases of the 1960s. Klarman, "Rethinking the Civil Rights and Civil Liberties Revolutions"; Sara Mayeux, "What *Gideon* Did."

4. Justice Potter Stewart claimed counsel was warranted in *Massiah* but not *Escobedo* because of the federal versus state implications. Moreover, Stewart believed right-to-counsel only took effect after indictment. Justice John Marshall Harlan II echoed some of White's concerns: "I think the rule announced today is most ill-conceived and that it seriously and unjustifiably fetters perfectly legitimate methods of criminal law enforcement."

5. Justice Harlan's concurrence said there should be a reasonableness standard for determining whether someone should expect privacy in a setting. This—not Stewart's articulation—became the test used in later cases. There were other, relatively unimportant, opinions. Justice White claimed the president or attorney general had the right to wiretap for national security issues. Douglas responded to this saying it would be beyond the executive's powers. Justice Black, meanwhile, wrote an opinion saying the text of the Fourth Amendment applied to tangible "things."

6. "The Court added what the press would call 'a surprising postscript': if the officers had simply obtained a warrant first, their actions would have been constitutionally permissible. In one short paragraph, the Court erased years of unease with the notion of subjecting electronic eavesdropping to Fourth Amendment scrutiny by reassuring all concerned that the practice could nevertheless survive it—and that was major news." Corinna Barrett Lain, "Countermajoritarian Hero or Zero? Rethinking the Warren Court's Role in the Criminal Procedure Revolution," 1436.

7. ANES, 1964.

8. Hall, *Nature of Supreme Court Power*.

9. Gallup Poll, 1966, 1968, 1969, 1972, 1973; Harris Poll, 1966, 1968, 1969; Life Poll, 1969. To be fair, Lain argues that the questions inaccurately represented the court's jurisprudence. This is a good point, and to be clear, I am not arguing that Lain is wrong. I would add that sometimes the *perception* of the court is more important than the reality. Had everyday Americans understood the complexities of criminal and constitutional

law, would a majority of them have agreed with *Miranda* in the mid-1960s? Maybe. But given what average Americans did (or did not) understand, did a majority of them agree with *Miranda*? Probably not. Lain, "Countermajoritarian Hero or Zero," 1422.

10. ANES, 1970.

11. GSS, 1972.

12. Thaddeus Dulski, D-NY, *CR* 1966, A5841; Stuart Symington, D-MO, *CR* 1970, 10991.

13. Sam Ervin, D-NC, *CR* 1966, 21040; John McClellan, D-AR, *CR* 1968, 17601; Strom Thurmond, D-SC, *CR* 1968, 28776.

14. I am not setting aside race altogether. That is untenable. My only claim is that southerners were more likely to rhetorically disparage the court as a representative institution. Now, that could very well be because of race and leftover hostility from *Brown*. So perhaps it is impossible to set aside race for a moment. Again, I do address the issue in this chapter.

15. Herman Talmadge, D-GA, *CR* 1968, 14004; James Allen, D-AL, *CR* 1971, 30983.

16. *CR* 1968, 28776.

17. *CR* 1966, 14975.

18. *CR* 1968, 9241, 5052, 22725, 16021.

19. Hugh Scott, R-PA, *CR* 1968, 15148; Louis Wyman, R-NH, *CR* 1968, 8888; Glenn Cunningham, R-NE, *CR* 1967, 17270; *CR* 1967, 21188.

20. In part, this was because in the immediate aftermath, some detectives found ways around *Miranda*. I discuss this in the grassroots pushback section.

21. Robert Byrd, D-WV, *CR* 1966, 13513; James Corman, D-CA, *CR* 1966, A3981; Herman Talmadge, D-GA, *CR* 1966, 13861.

22. Charles Bennett, D-FL, *CR* 1967, 2110; Peter Rodino, D-NJ, *CR* 1967, 21089; Sam Ervin, D-NC, *CR* 1968, 25435.

23. We might have expected a sectional rift, with southerners claiming that the Warren Court's criminal procedure revolution was really just an extension of its racial jurisprudence. *Mapp*, *Escobedo*, and *Miranda* all involved nonwhite suspects who were eventually freed because of due process violations. And to be sure, criminal justice in any southern state likely fluctuated with the race of the defendant. The southern police, too, played a part in reinforcing Jim Crow. For the most part, though, southern rhetoric on crime excluded denunciations of Black defendants. Maybe they did not have to link criminal procedure to race because it was always lurking in the background. Yale Kamisar, "Can (Did) Congress 'Overrule' *Miranda*?" See Ian Haney-López, *Dog Whistle Politics: How Coded Racial Appeals Have Reinvented Racism and Wrecked the Middle Class*; Alexander and West, *New Jim Crow*; Elizabeth Hinton, *From the War on Poverty to the War on Crime: The Making of Mass Incarceration in America*; Kevin Drakulich et al., "Race and Policing in the 2016 Presidential Election: Black Lives Matter, The Police, and Dog Whistle Politics."

24. While liberals used terms such as "slums," "ghettos," and "Negroes," non-liberals spoke of "chaos," "subversion," and "anarchy." For example, John McClellan (D-AR), who would lead the opposition against liberal measures in the Senate, warned, "The thrust of the *Miranda* ruling, if it is not changed, will sweep us into the throes of anarchy." John McClellan, D-AR, *CR* 1968, 11206; Watkins Abbitt, D-VA, *CR* 1967, 22131; John McCormack, D-MA, *CR* 1968, 16750; John Rooney, D-NY, *CR* 1968, 16804; Roy Taylor, D-NC, *CR* 1968, 16279;

25. If this was the case, then it is even more likely that Democratic Party leaders must have seen the nonracial fault line created by the Warren Court's criminal procedure decisions.

26. If political leaders linked anticommunism to segregation in the 1950s, maybe they linked anticommunism to racism in the 1960s. And while Reagan coined terms such as "welfare queen" and "strapping young bucks buying T-bone steaks," maybe he was not the first to invoke the unspoken connection between federal spending and racist preferences.

27. Lain, "Countermajoritarian Hero or Zero"; Allen J. Matusow, *The Unraveling of America: A History of Liberalism in the 1960s*; Mark Tushnet, "The Warren Court as History: An Interpretation."

28. Lain, "Countermajoritarian Hero or Zero," 1413.

29. 1968 Report from the National Advisory Commission on Civil Disorders.

30. LBJ advisor Harry McPherson privately admitted, "We talk about the multitude of good programs going into the cities, and yet there are riots, which suggests that the programs are no good, or the Negroes are past saving." Harry McPherson, *A Political Education: A Washington Memoir*, 360.

31. *CR* 1967, 21103.

32. ANES, 1970, 1972.

33. GSS, 1972.

34. Frank Horton, R-NY, *CR* 1963, 14734; Bob Dole, R-KS, *CR* 1966, 15949; Samuel Devine, R-OH, *CR* 1967, 6093.

35. *CR* 1967, 13089.

36. Glenn Cunningham, R-NE, *CR 1967*, 17270.

37. Some scholars doubt Nixon's claim. López, *Dog Whistle Politics*; Vesla M. Weaver, "Frontlash: Race and Development of Punitive Crime Policy"; Mark Peffley, "The Racial Component of 'Race-Neutral' Crime Policy Attitudes"; Brian P. Tilley, "'I Am the Law and Order Candidate': A Content Analysis of Donald Trump's Race-Baiting Dog Whistles in the 2016 Presidential Campaign."

38. Michael W. Flamm, *Law and Order: Street Crime, Civil Unrest, and the Crisis of Liberalism in the 1960s*, 175. Nixon's 1968 acceptance speech has similar rhetoric: "And to those who say that law and order is the code word for racism, there and here is a reply: Our goal is justice for every American." I recognize that both now and in 1968, many would find these statements unconvincing. My argument is not that race was absent; my argument is that other ideologies (anticommunism, anticrime, antispending) were present. And once again, I fully recognize that these other issues might funnel through the racial dimension. They are not mutually exclusive.

39. John Ehrlichman, *Witness to Power: The Nixon Years*.

40. Rick Perlstein, "Exclusive: Lee Atwater's Infamous 1981 Interview on the Southern Strategy," *Nation*, November 13, 2012. Furthermore, *Time* quoted a George Wallace supporter, "Y'all know about law and order. It's spelled n******." "Nixon's Hard-Won Chance to Lead," *Time*, November 15, 1968.

41. Robert Denney, R-NE, *CR* 1967, 21207.

42. *CR* 1967, 21187.

43. At the risk of sounding like a broken record, I again acknowledge that these statements might have been racially motivated. William Bates, R-MA, *CR* 1968, 16251; Jimmy Quillen, R-TN, *CR* 1968, 16276.

44. Flamm, *Law and Order*, 33.

45. Richard Nixon, "What Has Happened to America?" *Reader's Digest*, October 1967.

46. The GOP version of the bill could have been motivated, at least in part, by race. See Weaver, "Frontlash." But it started as a liberal measure.

47. *CR* 1967, 21083.

48. William Ryan, D-NY, *CR* 1967, 21103; Herbert Tenzer, D-NY, *CR* 1967, 21103; Jacob Gilbert, D-NY, *CR* 1967, 21193.

49. William Cahill, R-NJ, *CR* 1967, 21093; Gerald Ford, R-MI, *CR* 1967, 21200; John McCulloch, R-OH, *CR* 1967, 20188.

50. Leslie Arends, R-IL, *CR* 1967, 21199.

51. Clark MacGregor, R-MN, *CR* 1967, 21094.

52. J. Edward Hutchinson, R-MI, *CR* 1967, 21188.

53. Nixon, *Memoirs*.

54. Powe, *Warren Court*, 410.

55. *Congressional Quarterly Almanac*, 1968, "Congress Passes Extensive Anticrime Legislation."

56. Stephen E. Ambrose, *Nixon: The Triumph of a Politician, 1962–1972*.

57. Paul L. Murphy, *The Constitution in Crisis Times, 1918–1969*, 381.

58. Powe, *Warren Court*, 391.

59. Barry Goldwater, "1964 Acceptance Speech."

60. Ambrose, *Nixon*.

61. Richard Nixon, "Order & Justice under the Law," September 29, 1968.

62. Ambrose, *Nixon*, 202.

63. Ambrose, *Nixon*, 144.

64. "The McGovern Record" (from *Hearings before the Select Committee on the Presidential Activities of the United States Senate: Watergate and Related Activities*).

65. Patrick Buchanan and Ken Khachigian, "Memorandum to John Mitchell: Attack Organization & Strategy," March 14, 1972.

66. Patrick Buchanan, "Memorandum to HR Haldeman, John Ehrlichman, and Charles Colson," September 13, 1972.

67. Republican Party Platform, 1968, 1972.

68. Republican Party Platform, 1968, 1972, 1976, 1980.

69. Conservatives worried about the restrictions on wiretapping, too. See "Editorial: Wiretapping a Potent Weapon," *Tribune-Democrat*, February 27, 1967; "Editorial: Wiretapping Has a Place," *Ashville Times*, March 11, 1967; "Statement of William Cahn, District Attorney of Nassau County, State of New York," in *Controlling Crime through More Effective Law Enforcement: Hearings before the Subcommittee on Criminal Laws and Procedures*, 545; "Statement of Michael Dillon, District Attorney, Erie County, Buffalo, NY," in *Hearings before the Subcommittee*, 864.

70. "Statement of Arlen Specter," in *Hearings before the Subcommittee*, 199.

71. See *Washington Evening Star*, February 21, 1967; Aurora (IL) *Beacon News*, January 30, 1967; *Chicago Daily News*, January 31, 1967; *Arkansas Democrat*, February 1, 1967; *New York World Journal Tribune*, February 22, 1967.

72. *CR* 1966, A5841.

73. *CR* 1967, 4242.

74. "Laurence T. Wren," in *Hearings before the Subcommittee*, 526.

75. Cyril D. Robinson, "Police and Prosecutor Practices and Attitudes Relating to Interrogation as Revealed by Pre and Post-*Miranda* Questionnaires: A Construct of Policy Capacity to Comply"; Richard H. Seeburger and R. Stanton Wettick Jr., "Miranda in Pittsburgh—A Statistical Study"; Michael Wald, "Interrogations in New Haven: The Impact of *Miranda*"; Richard Medalie, Leonard Zeitz, and Paul Alexander, "Custodial Police Interrogation in Our Nation's Capital: The Attempt to Implement *Miranda*."

76. Otis Stephens Jr., Robert L. Flanders, and J. Lewis Cannon, "Law Enforcement and the Supreme Court: Police Perceptions of the *Miranda* Requirements," 407.

77. Wald, "Interrogations in New Haven," 1545.

78. Lawrence S. Leiken, "Police Interrogation in Colorado: The Implementation of *Miranda*."

79. Wald, "Interrogations in New Haven."

80. Leiken, "Police Interrogation in Colorado," 25.

81. David W. Neubauer, *Criminal Justice in Middle America*.

82. López, *Dog Whistle Politics*; Alexander and West, *New Jim Crow*; Hinton, *War on Crime*; Drakulich et al., "Race and Policing in the 2016 Presidential Election."

83. Powe, *Warren Court*, 394; Richard A. Leo, "The Impact of *Miranda* Revisited," 665.

84. Martin H. Belsky, "Whither *Miranda*."

85. Stephen L. Wasby, *Continuity and Change: From the Warren Court to the Burger Court*; Edsall and Edsall, *Chain Reaction*; Morton J. Horowitz, "The Warren Court and the Pursuit of Justice."

86. William J. Stuntz, *The Collapse of American Criminal Justice*; Welsh S. White, "Defending Miranda: A Reply to Professor Caplan"; Yale Kamisar, "Remembering the 'Old World' of Criminal Procedure: A Reply to Professor Grano"; Yale Kamisar, "Miranda Does Not Look So Awesome Now," *Legal Times*, June 10, 1996; Jerold H. Israel, "Criminal Procedure, the Burger Court, and the Legacy of the Warren Court"; Liva Baker, *Miranda, Crime, Law, and Politics*; George C. Thomas and Richard A. Leo, *Confessions of Guilt: From Torture to Miranda and Beyond*; George C. Thomas III and Richard A. Leo, "The Effects of *Miranda v. Arizona*: 'Embedded' in Our National Culture?"

87. Perlstein, "Exclusive"; Ehrlichman, *Witness to Power*.

88. Robert Mason, *Richard Nixon and the Quest for a New Majority*; Kevin McMahon, *Nixon's Court*; Buchanan, *Nixon's White House Wars*. To be fair, unrest with LBJ's Vietnam policy, the counterculture movement, and civil rights also were important.

89. Nixon, *Memoirs*, 316.

90. Leo, "Impact of Miranda Revisited."

91. Powe, *Warren Court*, 405.

92. Segal-Cover scores would have us believe all three made the court more liberal: Goldberg (0.50) replaced Frankfurter (0.33); Marshall (1.00) replaced Clark (0.50); and Fortas (1.00) replaced Goldberg (0.50). Jeffrey A. Segal and Albert D. Cover, "Ideological Values and the Votes of U.S. Supreme Court Justices."

93. To be fair, Clark wrote *Mapp*, though.

94. As mentioned earlier, if anything, *Katz* clarified rules for law enforcement—even if Congress scaled it back soon thereafter.

95. Indeed, the headline after *Katz* in the *New York Times* was, "High Court Eases Curbs on Bugging; Adds Safeguard," December 19, 1967. The subheading was, "Insists

Police Must Obtain Warrant to Act—Doesn't Forbid Eavesdropping." Lain, "Counter-majoritarian Hero or Zero?" 1436. Compare this to the headline on the day after *Miranda*: Fred P. Graham, "High Court Puts New Curb on Powers of the Police to Interrogate Suspects," *New York Times*, June 14, 1966.

96. William J. Stuntz, "Local Policing after the Terror," 2152.

97. Lain, "Countermajoritarian Hero or Zero?"

98. Powe, *Warren Court*, 407; see also Tracy Maclin, "*Terry v. Ohio*'s Fourth Amendment Legacy: Black Men and Police Discretion."

99. Watergate, without question, played a role, too.

Chapter 5. Busing

1. Dean J. Kotlowski, *Nixon's Civil Rights: Politics, Principle, and Policy*.

2. As mentioned earlier in this book, the literature on *Brown*'s decade of ineffectiveness is extensive. The paradigmatic studies are Rosenberg, *Hollow Hope*; Klarman, *From Jim Crow to Civil Rights*.

3. *Briggs v. Elliot*, 1952.

4. Bernard Schwartz, *Swann's Way: The School Busing Case and the Supreme Court*.

5. Gallup 1971a, 1971b; ANES 1972, 1974, 1976; GSS 1972, 1974, 1975, 1976.

6. ANES, 1972. See also: ANES, 1974, 1976; Gallup, 1971; GSS, 1972, 1974, 1975, 1976. Later in the chapter, I explain why Catholics disliked busing.

7. This included: California in 1972 at 63–37 percent; Florida in 1972 at 74–26 percent; Colorado in 1974 at 69–31 percent; Washington in 1978 at 66–44 percent; Massachusetts in 1978 at 70–30 percent; and California (again) in 1979 at 69–31 percent. "Race and Ethnicity on the Ballot," Ballotpedia, accessed October 24, 2023, https://ballotpedia.org/Race_and_ethnicity_on_the_ballot.

8. David Gambrell, D-GA, *CR* 1971, 38959; Edith Green, D-OR, *CR* 1974, 3515; Wilmer Mizell, R-NC, *CR* 1974, 18072.

9. D. Sunshine Hillygus and Todd G. Shields, *The Persuadable Voter: Wedge Issues in Presidential Campaigns*, 131.

10. "Testimony of Patrick Buchanan," *Hearings before the Select Committee on the Presidential Campaign Activities of the United States Senate: Watergate and Related Activities*, 3903. Now, perhaps it was more rhetoric than substance—in fact, Nixon's own attorney general told the press, "Watch what we do, not what we say," hinting that the administration would surreptitiously pursue civil rights. McMahon, *Nixon's Court*, 65; Laura Kalman, *The Long Reach of the Sixties: LBJ, Nixon, and the Making of the Sixties*, 248; Kotlowski, *Nixon's Civil Rights*.

11. *CR* 1973, 8349. See also: *CR* 1971, 47768; *CR* 1973, 37053.

12. *CR* 1977, 20938. See also: *CR* 1972, 630; *CR* 1974, 24482.

13. *CR* 1975, 26287. See also: *CR* 1971, 11012, 32122; *CR* 1975, 28900.

14. Joseph Waggoner, D-LA, *CR* 1971, 11093; Tom Bevill, D-AL, *CR* 1971, 31873; Bill Nichols, D-AL, *CR* 1971, 32120.

15. John Stennis, D-MS, *CR* 1971, 39715; William Colmer, D-MS, *CR* 1972, 28830.

16. Robert Casey, D-TX, *CR* 1971, 13340; Jack Brinkley, D-GA, *CR* 1971, 18449; James Allen, D-AL, *CR* 1971, 30982.

17. *CR* 1971, 11014.

18. *CR* 1971, 11152; see also Joseph Waggoner, D-LA, *CR* 1971, 11094.

19. *CR* 1970, 2892.

20. Representative Herbert Burke (R-FL) later commented, "There are numerous bills before the House Judiciary Committee on this question, but they are going nowhere because of an obvious reluctance on the part of the entrenched liberals." *CR* 1975, 42354.

21. Jon Meachem, "A Man Out of Time," *Newsweek*, December 22, 2002.

22. Edward M. Kennedy Institute for the United States Senate, "Chester Trent Lott Oral History."

23. Meachem, "Man Out of Time"; "The Making of Senator Smootie," *Newsweek*, January 26, 1997.

24. "Lott Oral History."

25. Roger Chapman, *Culture Wars: An Encyclopedia of Ideas, Viewpoints, and Voices*, 327.

26. Jesse Helms, *Here's Where I Stand: A Memoir*, 63.

27. "Excerpts—The GOP Tapes: Frank Rouse," July 6, 1997.

28. Bridge, "Supreme Court, Factions."

29. I did a Lexis-Nexis keyword search of US District Court and Circuit Court cases from 1970–1980 containing the word "busing." I checked each case to make sure it dealt with school busing proper, as some of the cases involved the busing of prisoners, the right of citizens to protest school board busing policies, and so on. I found that at least nineteen (56 percent) northern Democratic attacks came within a year of a lower federal court busing ruling in the attacker's state. I believe this figure is an underestimation because it does not account for ongoing legal battles resolved outside of the one-year time frame. For example, federal courts constantly ruled on busing in California in the 1970s. However, my limited search did not uncover any decided cases in 1978 or 1979, and thus Rep. Jerry Patterson's (D-CA) (who represented Los Angeles) 1979 attack on busing does not count toward the 56 percent, despite the fact that litigation in Los Angeles was ongoing in 1979.

30. An earlier version of this argument can be found in Bridge, "Catholics in the 'Mature' New Deal Era."

31. Mary T. Hanna, *Catholics and American Politics*.

32. David J. O'Brien, *American Catholics and Social Reform: The New Deal Years*; Mark M. Gray, Paul M. Perl, and Mary E. Bendyna, "Camelot Only Comes but Once? John F. Kerry and the Catholic Vote"; Gregory A. Smith, "One Church, Many Messages: The Politics of the U.S. Catholic Clergy." Catholics do not have a political philosophy that neatly maps onto partisan splits. This was true in the 1970s and still holds today. It is precisely this reason that allows critical masses of the faction to waffle between the two parties.

33. John T. McGreevy, *Parish Boundaries: The Catholic Encounter with Race in the Twentieth Century Urban North*.

34. Michael Novak, *Unmeltable Ethnics: Politics and Culture in American Life*.

35. Pope Pius XI, *Quadragesimo Anno: Encyclical Letter on Reconstructing the Social Order*.

36. Ronald P. Formisano, *Boston against Busing: Race, Class, and Ethnicity in the 1960s and 1970s*.

37. ANES, 1960, 1970.

38. Andrew M. Greeley, *The American Catholic: A Social Portrait*; Lawrence J. McAndrews, *What They Wished For: American Catholics and American Presidents, 1960–2004*.

As a group, their collective opinion on race in the early 1970s is virtually indistinguishable from the rest of the nation, and certainly better than those in the south. In 1972 the ANES asked respondents to rate their feelings toward Blacks on a "thermometer" from 0 (negative) to 100 (positive). The national average was 63.7; the Catholic average was 64.0. The northern suburban Catholic average was 70.0. In comparison, the average in the south was 58.2. See ANES, 1972.

39. Hanna, *Catholics and American Politics*, 116, 140.

40. For example, Thomas Downey (R-NY) said, "Before I discuss my views on busing in detail, let me state exactly what this position is not. It is not a retreat from the noble mandate of *Brown against Board of Education*. De jure segregation-racial separation ordained and enforced by law was and is a disgrace to America. Nor is my position in any sense a withdrawal from a commitment to an integrated society, or the just goals of equal opportunity for all. We have come too far, made too much substantive progress, and most importantly have seen too clearly the wrongs of our past to ever renege on these national commitments." *CR* 1976, 5250. See also *CR* 1973, 28796; *CR* 1976, 1770.

41. Jonathan Kelly, "The Politics of School Busing."

42. Southern Democrats brought up the point, such as Rep. Bill Nichols (D-AL) who quoted a George Wallace speech, "This federal intervention in our schools is Communist motivated." *CR* 1971, 32120. And some non-Catholic northerners likely harbored similar suspicions, such as those in Kansas City who attempted to peg the appointed busing consultant as leader in a Communist-front organization. See Peter William Moran, "Difficult from the Start: Implementing the *Brown* Decision in Kansas City, Missouri Public Schools."

43. Todd Scribner, *A Partisan Church: American Catholicism and the Rise of Neoconservative Catholics.*

44. "Letter to Judge Garrity from Jamaica Plain Resident," *Garrity Papers.*

45. Gadsden, *Between North and South.*

46. Teasingly, Helms chimed in, "The Senator from North Carolina welcomes the Senator from Delaware to the ranks of the enlightened," *CR* 1975, 29103.

47. *CR* 1977, 21256.

48. *CR* 1977, 118.

49. *CR* 1975, 30659.

50. Bill Brock, R-TN, *CR* 1972, 30241; Lawrence Hogan, R-MD, *CR* 1974, 3525; Marvin Esch, R-MI, *CR* 1974, 32627; William Cramer, R-FL, *CR* 1970, 630; Gene Snyder, R-KY, *CR* 1974, 4794; Marjorie Holt, R-MD, *CR* 1975, 29823; Howard Baker, R-TN, *CR* 1975, 34814.

51. Mike McKevitt, R-CO, *CR* 1971, 11581; Bill Brock, R-TN, *CR* 1971, 18874.

52. *CR* 1971, 12523.

53. John Hall Buchanan, R-AL, *CR* 1970, 3159; Bill Brock, R-TN, *CR* 1971, 18874; Charles Bennett, R-FL, *CR* 1971, 29380; Marvin Esch, R-MI, *CR* 1971, 38090; Jack McDonald, R-MI, *CR* 1971, 39676.

54. They used the exact phrase "neighborhood school," in the following: Richard Nixon, "Statement about Assistance to Local Communities for School Desegregation Plans," February 16, 1970; Richard Nixon, "Remarks in Asheville, NC," October 20, 1970; Richard Nixon, "The President's News Conference," April 29, 1971; Richard Nixon, "Address to the Nation on Equal Educational Opportunities and School Busing," March 16, 1972; Richard Nixon, "Radio Address about American Education," March 23, 1974; Gerald

Ford, "Statement on the Education Amendments of 1974," August 21, 1974; Gerald Ford, "Remarks in Dallas at the Biennial Convention of the National Federation of Republican Women," September 13, 1975.

55. John Schmitz, R-CA, *CR* 1972, 20941.

56. *CR* 1970, 9286.

57. *CR* 1972, 8134.

58. Richard Nixon, "Statement on Signing the Education Amendments of 1972."

59. Allen objected to the reading of the bill on two separate occasions, which kept the measure on the floor and forced it to be scheduled for debate. Apparently, Senate Majority Leader Mike Mansfield (D-MT) was caught off guard.

60. The LSC provides civil legal aid to those who cannot afford it. The bill was sponsored by John Dellenbeck (R-OR), John Erlenborn (R-IL), Marvin Esch (R-MI), Edwin Eshelman (R-PA), Orval Hansen (R-ID), Carl Perkins (D-KY), William Steiger (R-WI), and David Towell (R-NV).

61. Gerald Ford, "Statement on School Busing," May 29, 1976.

62. The diary is more of an appointment book. In some places, Haldeman uses fragments instead of full sentences.

63. H. R. Haldeman, *The Haldeman Diaries: Inside the Nixon White House*, 128.

64. Again, Nixon's civil rights policy was complicated. He seemed privately committed to doing something, even if he publicly appeared as an obstructionist. Kalman, *Long Reach of the Sixties*; Kotlowski, *Nixon's Civil Rights*.

65. Presumably, this meant that Democrats would seize the initiative and guide the legislative debate in a way that did not leave their party in disarray.

66. Lawrence J. McAndrews, "The Politics of Principle: Richard Nixon and School Desegregation," 190.

67. Richard Nixon, "Statement about the Busing of Schoolchildren," August 3, 1971; Nixon, "Remarks and a Question-and-Answer Session with Guests Following a Dinner at Secretary Connally's Ranch in Floresville, TX," April 30, 1972; Richard Nixon, "The President's News Conference," October 5, 1972.

68. Kevin Phillips, "School Busing and Public Opinion," *Bryan Times*, March 4, 1972.

69. McAndrews, "Politics of Principle," 194.

70. Richard Nixon, "The President's News Conference," April 29, 1971.

71. McAndrews, "Politics of Principle ," 196.

72. Ehrlichman, *Witness to Power*, 232. On the whole, Nixon tried for moderate domestic policy—to "go gung-ho for blue collar Catholics but *not* hard right reactionary." Kotlowski, *Nixon's Civil Rights*, 22.

73. Haldeman, *Diaries*, 276.

74. Quoted in Kotlowski, *Nixon's Civil Rights*, 34.

75. McMahon, *Nixon's Court*, 275.

76. Nixon Tapes, January 2, 1973.

77. Quoted in Kotlowski, *Nixon's Civil Rights*, 40.

78. Haldeman, *Diaries*, 351.

79. "Testimony of Donald H. Segretti," *Watergate Hearings*, 3982. These actions might have been at Nixon's request. On the Nixon tapes, the president suggests to "have some civil rights people praise him [Muskie] for his defense of busing . . . I don't know if you've got any people to do that or not but I think that would be very clever," *Nixon Tapes*, September 22, 1971.

80. Patrick Buchanan, "Memorandum to the President: The Muskie Watch."

81. Patrick Buchanan, "Memorandum to the Attorney General H. R. Haldeman: Dividing the Democrats," October 5, 1971.

82. Hillygus and Shields, *Persuadable Voter*, 131.

83. Almost immediately after *Swann*, Owen Fiss predicted its implications would reach into the North. Owen M. Fiss, "The Charlotte-Mecklenburg Case—Its Significance for Northern School Desegregation."

84. George R. Metcalf, *From Little Rock to Boston: The History of School Desegregation*; Jeanne F. Theoharis, "'We Saved the City': Black Struggles for Educational Equality in Boston, 1960–1976."

85. Louis P. Masur, *The Soiling of Old Glory: The Story of a Photograph That Shocked America*; Laura Kalman, *Right Star Rising: A New Politics, 1974–1980*.

86. Celia Wren, "Stars and Strife," *Smithsonian Magazine* (April 2006).

87. Jon Hillson, *The Battle of Boston: Busing and the Struggle for School Desegregation*, 15–18.

88. Joyce A. Baugh, *The Detroit School Busing Case: Milliken v. Bradley and the Controversy over Desegregation*, 118.

89. Carrie Sharlow, "Michigan Lawyers in History: Stephen J. Roth."

90. Dimond, *Beyond Busing*.

91. Metcalf, *Little Rock to Boston*.

92. "Michigan Women Hike 620 Miles to Urge Congress to Bar Busing," *New York Times*, April 28, 1972.

93. Metcalf, *Little Rock to Boston*, 162.

94. To clarify, Celler's opposition did not stem so much from the merits of the antibusing movement—he had been instrumental in protecting northern de facto segregation from the 1964 Civil Rights Act. It likely stemmed from denying the GOP a winning issue. See Matthew F. Delmont, *Why Busing Failed: Race, Media, and the National Resistance to School Desegregation*.

95. Congress does not record or report the exact number of signatures. According to journalistic reports, which relied on interviews with Lent, it seems that the congressman had gathered about 145 signatures before Celler scheduled debate. Delmont, *Why Busing Failed*.

96. *CQ Almanac*, "Busing Constitutional Amendment," 1972.

97. *CQ Almanac*, "President's Two Anti-Busing Measures Shelved," 1972.

98. *Milliken v. Bradley* (1974).

99. Nixon told his attorney general, "I want you to have a specific talk with whatever man we consider and I have to have an absolute commitment from him on busing and integration . . . Tell him that we totally respect his right to do otherwise, but if he believes otherwise, I will not appoint him to the Court." Quoted in Myron Orfield, *"Milliken, Meredith*, and Metropolitan Segregation," 385.

100. Orfield, *"Milliken."*

101. William H. Rehnquist, "A Random Thought on the Segregation Cases."

102. Rehnquist himself claimed he was not a segregationist. See Brad Snyder, "What Would Justice Holmes Do (WWJGD)? Rehnquist's *Plessy* Memo, Majoritarianism, and *Parents Involved*." Some claim Rehnquist was truthful. See Mark Tushnet, *A Court Divided: The Rehnquist Court and the Future of Constitutional Law*; Mark Tushnet and Katyz Lezin, "What Really Happened in *Brown v. Board of Education*"; Dennis J. Hutchinson,

"Unanimity and Desegregation: Decisionmaking in the Supreme Court, 1948–1958."
Others claim the memo represents Rehnquist's feelings at the time: Kluger, *Simple Justice*; John A. Jenkins, *The Partisan: The Life of William Rehnquist*; John W. Dean, *The Rehnquist Choice: The Untold Story of the Appointment that Redefined the Supreme Court*.

103. McMahon, *Nixon's Court*; Sue Davis, "Justice Rehnquist's Equal Protection Clause: An Interim Analysis."

104. Jeffries takes it further: at least in the immediate aftermath, Powell disagreed with *Brown*. To be fair, Jeffries also notes that Powell took steps to help integration more than others might have. And he swore in the first Black governor of Virginia, proclaiming, "It's a great day for Virginia!" John C. Jeffries Jr., *Justice Louis F. Powell*. Also, see: Mark Tushnet, "Justice Lewis F. Powell and the Jurisprudence of Centralism."

105. Anders Walker argues that Powell's opposition to MLK had more to do with anti-communism than race relations. Anders Walker, "A Lawyer Looks at Civil Disobedience: How Lewis F. Powell, Jr. Reframed the Civil Rights Revolution."

106. Adreanne Stephenson, "Two Sides of the Same Coin: Justice Powell and Justice Marshall's Perspectives on Education and the Law," 36.

107. Earl M. Maltz, "The Triumph of the Southern Man: *Dowell, Shelby County*, and the Jurisprudence of Lewis F. Powell, Jr."

108. This is a generous interpretation, since Powell's predecessor, Hugo Black, was mostly antibusing. As Earl Warren had done with the Kentuckian Stanley Reed on *Brown*, Warren Burger had to lobby the Alabaman Black to secure unanimity on *Swann*. Black's various defenses included: children should go to the school nearest to them, the justice knew a Black man who opposed busing, busing would trigger massive violence, and Congress's taxing power prohibited the court from requiring districts to purchase buses. It is impossible to say how Black would have voted in *Milliken*. But it is clear that Black was no Brennan or Marshall, and that it is possible he *could* have voted with the conservative majority against interdistrict busing. Woodward and Armstrong, *Brethren*, 98.

109. Richard Nixon Tapes, April 21, 1971.

110. One of Brennan's clerks believed that "Nixon . . . had given Burger his marching orders." Woodward and Armstrong, *Brethren*, 156.

111. Fred. P. Graham, "Burger Cautions Lower Tribunals on Busing Orders," *New York Times*, September 10, 1971.

112. J. Harvie Wilkinson, *From Brown to Bakke: The Supreme Court and School Integration: 1945–1978*; Orfield, "*Milliken.*"

113. Burger—like all the justices—wanted unanimity on *Swann*. He used Hugo Black's conservatism to try to extract concessions from the liberal majority. "Black was willing to budge . . . the others would have to compromise." Other justices thought this was a ploy that exposed Burger's true preferences, as well as his ability, as chief justice, to control the opinion. Woodward and Armstrong, *Brethren*, 107.

114. Wilkinson, *From Brown to Bakke*.

115. Nathaniel R. Jones, "An Anti-Black Strategy and the Supreme Court," 203.

116. Haynesworth had upheld Virginia's desegregation resistance efforts, such as closing schools and freedom of choice plans. Carswell once declared support for white supremacy. Orfield, "*Milliken,*" 381.

117. Segal and Cover, "Ideological Values."

118. Linda Greenhouse, *Becoming Justice Blackmun*; Tinsley Yarbrough, *Harry A. Blackmun: The Outsider Justice*; Harold Hongju Koh, "Justice Blackmun and the 'World Out There'"; Owen Fiss writes that Blackmun "began his career . . . readily lending his support to the other Nixon appointees." Owen Fiss, "The Law of Narrow Tailoring," 880.

119. Baugh, *Milliken*; Erwin Chemerinsky, "The Segregation and Resegregation of American Public Education: The Court's Role"; James R. Freeswick, "*Milliken v. Bradley*."

120. Fiss, "Law of Narrow Tailoring," 889. Orfield calls Stewart's threshold for conscious segregationist preferences "cryptic." He points out that housing discrimination was a main cause of school segregation, but that residential patterns were "unknown and unknowable." Orfield, "*Milliken*," 412.

121. Owen M. Fiss, "School Desegregation: The Uncertain Path of the Law," 31.

122. One contemporary law professor theorized that *Milliken* would be used to determine the conditions under which interdistrict busing *would* be allowed. Steven E. Asher, "Interdistrict Remedies for Segregated Schools."

123. Woodward and Armstrong, *Brethren*.

124. "All of the Justices who formed the majority in *Milliken* are sensitive about public reactions." Fiss, "School Desegregation," 31; "It is important to recognize that *Milliken* was not decided in a political vacuum. On the contrary, *Milliken* came during a period of intense antibusing political activity, which began shortly after the Court's decision in *Swann* . . . the public consistently expressed strong opposition to mandatory busing in polls, and state and national politicians worked hard to limit it . . . the Supreme Court was influenced by the dominant and widespread political opposition to busing." James E. Ryan and Michael Heise, "The Political Economy of School Choice," 2052, 2056; "Political forces are mobilizing around race relations and racial equality, and you see that start to have an influence in changing the trajectory of what the Supreme Court had been doing up until that point on desegregation. Importantly, President Nixon takes office in 1969, and he has explicit opposition to busing," 5–4 Pod: "*Milliken v. Bradley*," podcast, accessed October 24, 2023, https://www.fivefourpod.com/episodes/miliken-v-bradley/.

125. James E. Ryan, "*Brown*, School Choice, and the Suburban Veto"; Richard Nixon, "Address to the Nation on Equal Educational Opportunities and School Busing."

126. Rosenberg, *Hollow Hope*.

Chapter 6. Abortion

1. Issues of justiciability were raised. For instance, could a woman sue for the right to an abortion if she were not, in fact, pregnant? Because these issues did not present a serious obstacle at any court, I focus on the substantive issues.

2. Mary Ziegler, *Beyond Abortion: Roe v. Wade and the Battle for Privacy*.

3. Margaret G. Farrell, "Revisiting *Roe v. Wade*: Substance and Process in the Abortion Debate."

4. The background on *Doe* is as follows: Georgia had a less restrictive antiabortion law than Texas. Texas allowed abortion only to save the mother's life. Georgia allowed for that, as well as for serious injury, birth defects, and cases of rape. The district court ruling in *Doe v. Bolton* was similar to the district court ruling in *Roe v. Wade*: it struck down the statute under privacy but did not provide injunctive relief.

5. Accordingly, then, he assigned the opinion. Burger was notorious for behaving in this manner. This rankled Douglas, who believed Burger had manipulated his powers as

chief justice. Still, Burger had told Douglas, in clear terms, that the case should be rear-gued. Woodward and Armstrong, *Brethren*; Linda Greenhouse, "How Not to Be Chief Justice: The Apprenticeship of William H. Rehnquist"; Kaitlyn L. Sill, Joseph Daniel Ura, and Stacia L. Haynie, "Strategic Passing and Opinion Assignment on the Burger Court"; Forrest Maltzman, James F. Spriggs, and Paul J. Wahlbeck, *Crafting Law on the Supreme Court: The Collegial Game.*

6. N. E. H. Hull and Peter Charles Hoffer, *Roe v. Wade: The Abortion Rights Controversy in American History.* Another analysis has a different line-up of judicial votes: White upholding restrictions; Burger upholding restrictions but without a clear vote; Douglas, Brennan, and Marshall granting a broad constitutional right to an abortion; Stewart and Blackmun striking laws on the basis of professional discretion of the doctor. Woodward and Armstrong, *Brethren.*

7. Linda Greenhouse and Reva B. Siegel, *Before Roe v. Wade: Voices That Shaped the Abortion Debate before the Supreme Court's Ruling,* 251.

8. Harris Poll, 1972.

9. Gallup Poll, 1973.

10. Gallup Poll, 1972.

11. Gallup Poll, 1975.

12. Gallup Poll, 1973, 1975.

13. Judith Blake, "The Supreme Court's Abortion Decisions and Public Opinion in the United States." A number of polls find that from 1970 to 1975, somewhere between 50 percent and 76 percent disapproved. Blake examines the specifics of the polls and concludes that the correct figure probably stood somewhere around 60 percent.

14. Graber, "Nonmajoritarian Difficulty."

15. Graber, "Nonmajoritarian Difficulty"; Lemieux and Lovell, "Legislative Defaults."

16. *CR* 1975, 6101. In Arizona's Third District, 37 percent preferred an amendment to prohibit abortion in all but extreme circumstances (hereafter, "prohibit") and 28 percent wanted states to decide the issue (hereafter, "states' rights"). In Arkansas's Third, 24 percent would prohibit and 34 percent wanted states' rights. In California's Twenty-Fifth, 63 percent disagreed that the proper solution to the abortion controversy was a *Roe*-like solution. In Illinois's Eleventh, 43 percent would prohibit (44 percent would not). In Illinois's Seventeenth, 59 percent wanted states' rights. In Indiana's Fifth, 44 percent would prohibit and 23 percent wanted states' rights. In Kentucky's Fourth, 51.3 percent opposed *Roe*. In Mississippi's Fifth, 48.1 percent opposed *Roe* (40.4 percent approved). In Missouri's Sixth, 42 percent opposed *Roe's* allowance for first-trimester abortions (46 percent approved). In New Jersey's First, 47 percent wanted states' rights (42 percent would do nothing and 11 percent were undecided). In Ohio's Seventeenth, 36 percent would prohibit with exceptions for the mother's health, 7 percent would outlaw all abortions, and 8 percent wanted states' rights. In South Dakota's Second, 55 percent opposed *Roe*. In Wisconsin's Eighth district, 52 percent would prohibit and 5 percent would outlaw all abortions.

17. *CR* 1973, 23999. See also: Richard Ichord, D-MO, *CR* 1973, 30144; Harold Froe-lich, R-WI, *CR* 1973, 33452; Lawrence Hogan, R-MD, *CR* 1973, 16581.

18. *CR* 1977, 19713.

19. Carmines and Stimson, *Issue Evolution*; Adams, "Abortion."

20. National Conference of Catholic Bishops, "Human Life in Our Day," November 15, 1968.

21. Greenhouse and Siegel, *Before Roe v. Wade*, 258.

22. National Right to Life homepage, accessed October 24, 2023, Nrlc.org.

23. National Conference of Catholic Bishops, "Resolution on the Pro-Life Constitutional Amendment," November 13, 1973.

24. George J. Marlin, *The American Catholic Voter: 200 Years of Political Impact*, 258.

25. Eva R. Rubin, *Abortion, Politics, and the Courts: Roe v. Wade and Its Aftermath*, 90.

26. *New York Times*, Statements by 2 Cardinals, January 23, 1973; Rev. Msgr. James T. McHugh, Statement, 34; Rubin, *Abortion, Politics, and the Courts*, 90.

27. Patrick T. Conley and Robert J. McKenna, "The Supreme Court on Abortion: A Dissenting Opinion"; William H. Marshner, "Urges Excommunication of Brennan," *Wanderer*, February 8, 1973; Marshner, "Some Catholic-Political Considerations," *Triumph*, April 1973; "Editorial: Abortion and the Church," *America* 128, no. 5 (1973): 10–11; "Editorial: The Abortion Decision," *Commonweal* 97, no. 19 (1973): 435–436.

28. Pro-life responses include "abortion should never be permitted" and "abortion should only be permitted when the life of the woman was in danger." Prochoice responses include "abortion should be permitted if, due to personal reasons, the woman would have difficulty in caring for the child" and "abortion should never be forbidden, since one should not require a woman to have a child she doesn't want." GSS figures are similar, but not as nuanced. Until 1977, the GSS did not ask a broad abortion question. In 1977 it asked whether the respondent believed if, a woman wanted an abortion for any reason, should she able to get one. Of Catholic respondents, 68 percent said "no." Once again, Strong Democrats were more likely to respond "no" (74 percent) than Strong Republicans (64 percent).

29. William Whitehurst, R-VA, *CR* 1973, 7569; Mark Hatfield, R-OR, *CR* 1973, 17558; Earl Landgrebe, R-IN, *CR* 1973, 34988; George O'Brien, R-IL, *CR* 1973, 10650; Robert Hanrahan, R-IL, *CR* 1973, 24008; Robin Beard, R-TN, *CR* 1973, 37113; Philip Crane, R-IL, *CR* 1975, 11982.

30. *CR* 1973, 23997, 23996, 24004.

31. On the other hand, Nixon condoned abortion for rape victims (as well as for pregnancies resulting from interracial couples). See Nixon Tapes, January 23, 1973.

32. Buchanan, "The Muskie Watch."

33. *CQ Almanac 1977*, "Abortion Agreement Ends Funding Deadlock."

34. Representatives George Mahon (D-TX) and Jim Wright (D-TX) tried to convince the House to adopt the Senate's relatively liberal position on the Hyde Amendment. Later, Mahon and then Ernest Hollings (D-SC) tried to include language on reporting rape or incest: it would need not be prompt; it could be reported to the police, a public health agency, rape crisis center, family planning center, or counseling service; and it could be done by the victim, doctor, attorney, or other third party. The House rejected this proposal 183–205 (Republicans voting 31–98; southern Democrats voting 41–38).

35. *CQ Almanac 1977*, "Abortion Agreement."

36. "The group is now named Reproductive Freedom for All."

37. *CQ Almanac 1977*, "Abortion Agreement."

38. The Ford administration also sought to take pro-life stances, but the purposiveness and consistency of Ford's attempts were not as vigorous as Nixon's. For instance, Ford wavered on rescinding Nixon's military abortions policy, even as his political advisers explained to him the Catholic losses he would suffer. Caspar Weinberger, "Memorandum for the President," June 24, 1975. Nevertheless, by Election Day 1976, Ford

advisers understood the cache of prolife politics. Mason, *Richard Nixon and the Quest*, 230.

39. Patrick Buchanan, "Memorandum to the Attorney General: Democratic and Republican Contenders," July 2, 1971.

40. Buchanan, *Nixon's White House*, 150.

41. Henry Cashen, "Memoradum to John Ehrlichman," December 7, 1971; Henry Cashen, "Memorandum to Charles Colson," May 15, 1971; Henry Cashen, "Memorandum to H. R. Haldeman," May 17, 1971.

42. Buchanan, "Muskie Watch."

43. Phillips, "How Nixon Will Win," *New York Times*, August 6, 1972.

44. Louis Cassels, "Swing to Right Seen among Catholics, Jews," August 5, 1972. Quoted in Greenhouse and Siegel, *Before Roe v. Wade*, 212.

45. Phillips, "How Nixon Will Win"; Cashen, "Memorandum to Ehrlichman"; Buchanan, "Muskie Watch"; Buchanan, "Memorandum to the President," September 6, 1973; Buchanan, "Memorandum to Harlow," September 18, 1973; Buchanan, "Dividing the Democrats."

46. Blake, "Supreme Court's Abortion Decisions," 61.

47. Rosenberg, *Hollow Hope*; but see Hall, *Nature of Supreme Court Power*.

48. Gerald Rosenberg, "The Surprising Resilience of State Opposition to Abortion: The Supreme Court, Federalism, and the Role of Intense Minorities in the US Politics System."

49. M. David Bryant Jr., "State Legislation on Abortion after *Roe v. Wade*: Selected Constitutional Issues"; Rosenberg, *Hollow Hope*.

50. Stanley K. Henshaw, Jacqueline Darroch Forrest, and Ellen Blaine, "Abortion Services in the United States, 1981 and 1982," 122.

51. Reva B. Siegel, "The Right's Reasons: Constitutional Conflict and the Spread of Woman-Protective Antiabortion Abortion Argument"; Robert Post and Reva Siegel, "*Roe* Rage: Democratic Constitutionalism and Backlash"; Michael J. Klarman, "Courts, Social Change, and Political Backlash"; Mary Ziegler, "Beyond Backlash: Legal History, Polarization, and *Roe v. Wade*"; Caitlin E. Borgmann, "Roe v. Wade's 40th Anniversary: A Moment of Truth for the Anti-Abortion Rights Movement?"; Neal Devins, "Rethinking Judicial Minimalism: Abortion Politics, Party Polarization, and the Consequences of Returning the Constitution to Elected Government; Rubin, *Abortion, Politics, and the Courts*.

52. Caitlin E. Borgmann, "Abortion, the Undue Burden Standard, and the Evisceration of Women's Privacy."

53. Alan Abramowitz, "It's Abortion, Stupid: Policy Voting in the 1992 Presidential Election"; Mitchell Killian and Clyde Wilcox, "Do Abortion Attitudes Lead to Party Switching?"; Mary Ziegler, "The Framing of a Right to Choose: *Roe v. Wade* and the Changing Debate on Abortion Law; Michael Hout, "Abortion Politics in the United States, 1972–1994: From Single Issue to Ideology"; Ted G. Jelen and Clyde Wilcox, "Causes and Consequences of Public Attitudes toward Abortion: A Review and Research Agenda"; Laurence H. Tribe, *Abortion: The Clash of Absolutes*; Cynthia Gorney, *Articles of Faith: A Frontline History of the Abortion Wars*.

54. Neil A. O'Brian, "Before Reagan: The Development of Abortion's Partisan Divide"; Daniel K. Williams, *Defenders of the Unborn: The Pro-Life Movement before Roe v. Wade*; Samantha Luks and Michael Salamone, "Abortion"; Michael Hout, Stuart Perrett, and

Sarah K. Cowan, "Stasis and Sorting of Americans' Abortion Opinions: Political Polarization Added to Religious and Other Differences"; John H. Evans, "Polarization in Abortion Attitudes in US Religious Traditions, 1972–1998"; Ziegler, "Beyond Backlash"; Jerome L. Himmelstein, *To the Right: The Transformation of American Conservatism*; Michele McKeegan, *Abortion Politics: Mutiny in the Ranks of the Right*.

55. Mary Ziegler, *After Roe: The Lost History of the Abortion Debate*; Barry Friedman, *The Will of the People*.

56. Williams, *Defenders of the Unborn*.

57. Williams, *Defenders of the Unborn*, 193.

58. Timothy A. Byrnes, *Catholic Bishops in American Politics*.

59. Rubin, *Abortion*.

60. Betty Ford commented that *Roe* was "the best thing in the world." Laura Kalman, "On 'Roe' at Forty"; Donald T. Critchlow, *Intended Consequences: Birth Control, Abortion, and the Federal Government in Modern America*.

61. Byron W. Daynes and Raymond Tatalovich, "Presidential Politics and Abortion, 1972–1988."

62. David Karol and Chloe N. Thurston, "From Personal to Partisan: Abortion, Party, and Religion Among California State Legislators"; Lou Cannon, *Governor Reagan: His Rise to Power*; Daniel K. Williams, "Reagan's Religious Right: The Unlikely Alliance between Southern Evangelicals and a California Conservative."

63. Ziegler, "Beyond Backlash"; Tribe, *Abortion*. One scholar believes Reagan would have lost to Carter and that losing the 1976 primary to Ford enabled the Reagan Revolution. See Donald T. Critchlow, "The Rise of Conservative Republicanism: A History of Fits and Starts."

64. Carter said, "I think abortion is wrong. I don't think the government ought to do anything to encourage abortion, but I don't favor a constitutional amendment on the subject. But short of a constitutional amendment, and within the confines of a Supreme Court ruling, I will do everything I can to minimize the need for abortions with better sex education, family planning, and with better adoptive procedures. I personally don't believe that the federal government ought to finance abortions, but I draw the line and don't support a constitutional amendment. I honor the right of people to seek a constitutional amendment on abortion, but I don't actively work for its passage." Carter-Ford Debate, October 22, 1976.

65. Byrnes, *Catholic Bishops in American Politics*.

66. Robert N. Karrer, "The National Right to Life Committee: Its Founding, Its History, and the Emergence of the Pro-Life Movement Prior to *Roe v. Wade*."

67. Mary Ziegler, *Dollars for Life: The Anti-Abortion Movement and the Fall of the Republican Establishment*.

68. These costs were not only monetary. For example, the Americans United for Life—probably the second largest national pro-life group behind the Catholic Church's National Right to Life Committee—suffered internal splits on exceptions to abortion bans. Ziegler details the infighting within the pro-life movement and the rift between pragmatic incrementalists who sought abortion restrictions and ideological absolutists who sought to ban abortion wholesale. Ziegler, *After Roe*.

69. Williams, *Defenders of the Unborn*; Byrnes, *Catholic Bishops in American Politics*.

70. Greenhouse and Siegel, *Before Roe v. Wade*, 112–13.

71. Williams, *Defenders of the Unborn*.

72. Greenhouse and Siegel, *Before Roe v. Wade*.

73. Ziegler, "Beyond Backlash"; Kalman, "On '*Roe*' at Forty"; Hall, *Nature of Supreme Court Power*.

74. Rubin, *Abortion*; Ziegler, *After Roe*.

75. Greenhouse and Siegel, *Before Roe v. Wade*, 227.

76. Greenhouse and Siegel, *Before Roe v. Wade*, 82.

77. Greenhouse and Siegel, *Before Roe v. Wade*, 196, 257, 268, 280, 310.

78. Ziegler, *After Roe*; Kalman, "On '*Roe*' at Forty"; Robert Self, *All in the Family: The Realignment of American Democracy since the 1960s*; Friedman, *Will of the People*.

79. Greenhouse and Siegel, *Before Roe v. Wade*, 79.

80. Ziegler, *After Roe*.

81. Rubin, *Abortion*.

82. Ziegler, *After Roe*.

83. Daniel K. Williams, "Voting for God and the GOP: The Role of Evangelical Religion in the Emergence of the Republican South"; Charles S. Bullock et al., *The South and the Transformation of U.S. Politics*; Black and Black, *Rise of Southern Republicans*; Mason, *Richard Nixon and the Quest*.

84. There is much written about the rise of the New Right. Direct activists have recorded their experiences: Richard A. Viguerie, *The New Right: We're Ready to Lead*; Kevin P. Phillips, *Post-Conservative America: People, Politics, and Ideology in a Time of Crisis*. There are more journalistic or popular accounts: Thomas Frank, *What's the Matter with Kansas? How Conservatives Won the Heart of America*; Colin Woodard, *American Nations: A History of the Eleven Rival Regional Cultures of North America*. Scholars, I believe, best capture the complexity. That includes monographs: Kalman, *Right Star Rising*; Lowndes, *From the New Deal to the New Right*. And it includes edited volumes: Mason and Morgan, *Seeking a New Majority*; Bruce J. Schulman and Julian E. Zelizer, eds., *Rightward Bound: Making America Conservative in the 1970s*.

85. Kalman, *Right Star Rising*.

86. Michael J. McVicar, "The Religious Right in America."

87. Williams, *God's Own Party*.

88. Ziegler, "Beyond Backlash."

89. Siegel, "Right's Reasons."

90. Sara Diamond, *Not by Politics Alone: The Enduring Influence of the Christian Right*; Friedman, *Will of the People*.

91. Greenhouse and Siegel, *Before Roe v. Wade*, 297; Siegel, "Right's Reasons."

92. William C. Martin, *With God on Our Side: The Rise of the Religious Right in America*, 196.

93. Reva Siegel, "Sex Equality Arguments for Reproductive Rights: Their Critical Basis and Evolving Constitutional Expression"; Ziegler, "Beyond Backlash," 1011.

94. Phyllis Schlafly, "A Short History of the ERA."

95. Concerned Women for America Legislative Action Committee, "About Us," accessed October 24, 2023, https://concernedwomen.org/about-us/.

96. "Wives, submit to your own husbands, as it is fitting in the Lord . . .And whatever you do, do it heartily, as to the Lord and not to men"; Beverly LaHaye, *The Spirit-Controlled Woman*, 129.

97. Williams, "Reagan's Religious Right," 138. The United States needed a national "redemption" against "godless" communism and the "evil empire."

98. Williams, *God's Own Party*.

99. Concerned Women for America Legislative Action Committee, "About Us,"

100. McKeegan, *Abortion Politics*, 20.

101. Mason and Morgan, *Seeking a New Majority*, 2; *Federalist no. 1*; David R. Mayhew, "Wars and American Politics"; Mayhew, "Events as Causes." In 1980 this included: racial resentment, reaction to the counterculture movement, the Vietnam War, the Iranian hostage crisis, inflation, high gas prices, dissatisfaction with the Carter administration, and Reagan's personal charisma.

102. Paul Weyrich, "Comments," 25.

103. Some of these have obvious or subversive racial undertones.

104. The following sources do not discuss every possible connective thread between all issues, but they do discuss some of the ideological linkages: Kalman, "On '*Roe*' at Forty"; Lisa McGirr, *Suburban Warriors: The Origins of the New American Right*; Glenn and Teles, *Conservatism and American Political Development*; Self, *All in the Family*; Friedman, *Will of the People*; Glenn Feldman, ed., *Painting Dixie Red: When, Where, Why, and How the South Became Republican*; Ziegler, "Beyond Backlash"; Siegel, "Right's Reasons"; Siegel, "Sex Equality"; Mason and Morgan, *Seeking a New Majority*; Greenhouse and Siegel, *Before Roe v. Wade*; Busch, *Reagan's Victory*; Himmelstein, *To the Right*; Sidney Blumenthal, *The Rise of the Counter-Establishment: The Conservative Ascent to Political Power*; Viguerie, *New Right*; George H. Nash, *The Conservative Intellectual Movement in American since 1945*; Mary C. Brennan, *Turning Right in the Sixties: The Conservative Capture of the GOP*; Critchlow, *Conservative Ascendancy*; William C. Berman, *America's Right Turn: From Nixon to Bush*; Kim Philips-Fein, *Invisible Hands: The Making of the Conservative Movement from the New Deal to Ronald Reagan*; Lassiter, *Silent Majority*; Williams, *God's Own Party*; Martin, *With God on Our Side*; Kalman, *Right Star Rising*; Lowndes, *From the New Deal to the New Right*; Schulman and Zelizer, *Rightward Bound*.

105. Greenhouse and Siegel, *Before Roe v. Wade*, 297; Crespino, "Goldwater in Dixie."

106. Keck, *Most Activist Supreme Court in History*; also, Jerold Waltman, *Principled Judicial Restraint: A Case against Activism*; Michael Klarman, "*Windsor* and *Brown*: Marriage Equality and Racial Equality."

107. Greenhouse and Siegel, *Before Roe v. Wade*, 290.

108. Buchanan, "Assault Book."

109. Phillips, "How Nixon Will Win."

110. Devins, "Rethinking Judicial Minimalism," 30.

111. Kalman, *Right Star Rising*. Ford said, "I believe also that there is some merit to an amendment that Senator Everett Dirksen proposed very frequently, an amendment that would change the Court decision as far as voluntary prayer in public schools. It seems to me that there should be an opportunity, as long as it's voluntary, as long as there is no compulsion whatsoever, that an individual ought to have that right."

112. To be fair, political advisers in the Nixon administration (e.g., Buchanan, Phillips) understood how to build a conservative majority. But after Watergate, it seems like the party's leadership focused more on distancing itself from scandal (and from Nixon's advisers) rather than putting forward a positive constitutional vision that could translate into electoral majorities.

113. Ronald Reagan, *The Greatest Speeches of Ronald Reagan*.

114. Naturally, it was more complicated than this, with nuance and personalities playing a role. See Kalman, *Right Star Rising*.

115. Clayton and Pickerill, "Politics of Criminal Justice"; Clayton, "The Bush Presidency and the New Right Constitutional Regime"; Pickerill and Clayton, "Rehnquist Court."

116. "Presidential Debate in Baltimore," September 21, 1980. Reagan had said, "I have found a great hunger in America for a spiritual revival. For a belief that law must be based on a higher law. For a return to traditions and values that we once had. Our government, in its most sacred documents—the Constitution and the Declaration of Independence and all—speak of man being created, of a Creator. That we're a nation under God."

117. Ziegler, "Beyond Backlash," 1010–11; see also Siegel, "Right's Reasons." Note that Reagan did not have to deliver on his overall vision or policy promises. Indeed, while rhetorically he galvanized religious conservatives, he did not do much to overturn *Roe*. His appointment of Sandra Day O'Connor, for example, was not met enthusiastically. Prudence Flowers, "A Prolife Disaster: The Reagan Administration and the Nomination of Sandra Day O'Connor."

118. Focus on the Family was founded in 1977.

119. Thomas M. Keck and Kevin J. McMahon, "Why *Roe* Still Stands: Abortion Law, the Supreme Court, and the Republican Regime."

120. Mary Ziegler, *Reproduction and the Constitution in the United States*; Melissa Murray, Katherine Shaw, and Reva B. Siegel, eds., *Reproductive Rights and Justice Stories*; Mark A. Graber, *Rethinking Abortion: Equal Choice, the Constitution, and Reproductive Politics*.

121. Greenhouse and Siegel, *Before Roe v. Wade*, 294.

Chapter 7. Lessons

1. Bickel, *Least Dangerous Branch*.

2. John W. Kingdon, *Agendas, Alternatives, and Public Policies*; Adam D. Sheingate, "Political Entrepreneurship, Institutional Change, and American Political Development."

3. David A. Crockett, *The Opposition Presidency*; Crockett, *Running against the Grain: How Opposition Presidents Win the White House*; Andrew J. Polsky, "Shifting Currents: Dwight Eisenhower and the Dynamic of Presidential Opportunity Structure."

4. Karen Orren and Stephen Skowronek, *The Search for American Political Development*; Nichols and Myers, "Exploiting the Opportunity."

5. Kalman, "Constitution, the Supreme Court, and the New Deal"; McMahon, *Reconsidering Roosevelt*; Kalman, *FDR's Gambit*.

6. Pritchett, *Congress versus the Supreme Court*; Murphy, *Congress and the Court*; McMahon, *Nixon's Court*; Kalman, *Long Reach of the Sixties*; Kalman, *Right Star Rising*.

7. Fraser and Gerstle, *Rise and Fall of the New Deal Order*.

8. McMahon, *Reconsidering Roosevelt*; Graber, "Constructing Judicial Review"; Graber, "Countermajoritarian Difficulty"; Gillman, "Party Politics and Constitutional Change"; Whittington, *Political Foundations of Judicial Supremacy*.

9. Cook and Polsky, "Political Time Reconsidered"; Nichols, "Presidency and Political Order"; Graber, "Nonmajoritarian Difficulty."

10. McMahon, *Reconsidering Roosevelt*.

11. DiSalvo, *Engines of Change*; Schickler, *Racial Realignment*.

12. Gillman, "Party Politics and Constitutional Change."

13. Bickel, *Least Dangerous Branch*.

14. Nagel, "Court Curbing"; Rosenberg, "Judicial Independence."

15. Dahl, "Decision-Making in a Democracy."

16. Jordan T. Cash, "The Isolated Presidency: John Tyler and Unilateral Presidential Power"; Benjamin A. Kleinerman, *The Discretionary President: The Promise and Peril of Executive Power*; Rottinghaus, "Assessing the Unilateral Presidency."

17. Dudziak, *Cold War Civil Rights*.

18. Kamisar, "Can (Did) Congress 'Overrule' Miranda?"

19. Kernell, *Going Public*.

20. William B. Gould, "Right to Travel and National Security."

21. John F. Kennedy, "The President's News Conference," June 27, 1962.

22. Richard Nixon, "Statement about Policy on Abortions at Military Base Hospitals in the United States," April 3, 1971.

23. Greenhouse and Siegel, *Before Roe v. Wade*, 297.

24. Orren and Skowronek, *Search*; Pickerill, *Constitutional Deliberation*; Barnes, *Overruled*.

25. Mayhew, *Electoral Connection*.

26. Carmines and Stimson, "Issue Evolution"; Adams, "Abortion."

27. Laura Kalman, *Abe Fortas: A Biography*.

28. Howard Gillman, "Review: What's Law Got to Do with It? Judicial Behavioralists Test the 'Legal Model' of Judicial Decision Making."

29. Kalman, *FDR's Gambit*. It was closer to passing than commonly acknowledged.

30. Barack Obama, "The President's Press Conference," April 2, 2012; Donald Trump, "Statement on the Sanctuary Cities Ruling," April 25, 2017.

31. See notes to chapters 1 and 2 detailing regime politics literature.

32. Terri Peretti, *In Defense of a Political Court*; Lemieux and Watkins, "Beyond the 'Countermajoritarian' Difficulty"; Jeb Barnes, "Congressional Compromise on Election Reform: A Look Forward and Backward"; Laura Kalman, *The Strange Career of Legal Liberalism*.

33. Chemerinsky is particularly critical. He examines infamous historical cases (e.g., *Buck v. Bell*, *Dred Scott*, *Lochner*), as well as recent controversial ones (e.g., *Bush v. Gore*, *Citizens United*, *Shelby*). See Erwin Chemerinsky, *The Case against the Supreme Court*. See also Barry Friedman, "Letter to Supreme Court" (Erwin Chemerinsky Is Mad. Why You Should Care)"; Friedman, "Dialogue and Judicial Review"; Girardeau A. Spann, *Race against the Court: The Supreme Court and Minorities in Contemporary America*; Powe, *Supreme Court and the American Elite*; Matthew E. K. Hall, "Rethinking Regime Politics"; Thomas R. Marshall, *American Public Opinion and the Modern Supreme Court, 1930–2020*; Gerald N. Rosenberg, "The Broken-Hearted Lover: Erwin Chemerinsky's Romantic Longings for a Mythical Court"; Rosenberg, "Wonder of It All"; Adam Cohen, *Supreme Inequality: The Supreme Court's Fifty-Year Battle for a More Unjust America*; Michael J. Klarman, *The Framers' Coup: The Making of the United States*.

34. Gordon Silverstein, *Law's Allure: How Law Shapes, Constrains, Saves, and Kills Politics*; Jeb Barnes and Thomas F. Burke, *How Policy Shapes Politics: Rights, Courts, Litigation and the Struggle over Injury Compensation*; Hall, *Nature of Supreme Court Power*.

35. Corinna Barrett Lain, "Three Supreme Court 'Failures' and a Story of Supreme Court Success."

Chapter 8. Contemporary Issues

1. Another option exists here: for a countermajoritarian opinion to mobilize an otherwise latent opposition party. I discuss this later in the chapter when addressing Obamacare and religious liberty.

2. Philip Moniz and Chistopher Wlezien, "Issue Salience and Political Decisions."

3. Colton Heffington, Brandon Beomseob Park, and Laron K. Williams, "The 'Most Important Problem' Dataset (MIPD): A New Dataset on American Issue Importance"; Will Jennings and Christopher Wlezien, "Preferences, Problems, and Representation"; Christopher Wlezien, "On the Salience of Political Issues: The Problem with 'Most Important Problem.'"

4. David R. Mayhew, *Divided We Govern: Party Control, Lawmaking, and Investigations, 1946–2002*. Hall uses a similar technique in *Nature of Supreme Court Power*.

5. Tom S. Clark, Jeffrey R. Lax, and Douglas Rice, "Measuring the Political Salience of Supreme Court Cases." This article updates and improves upon Lee Epstein and Jeffrey A. Segal, "Measuring Issue Salience."

6. Harold J. Spaeth et al., 2022 Supreme Court Database, Version 2022 Release 1, http://Supremecourtdatabase.org.

7. One difference between recent and historical cases deserves mention: rising levels of partisanship. Put simply, because modern congressional Democrats and Republicans vote the party line more often, they are typically less willing to reach across the aisle and form an anti-court cross-partisan majority. Nevertheless, court rulings still deserve examination via their impact on national politics. And even in an era of hyperpartisanship, at least one issue looms as a possible landmine for the judiciary and national party politics.

8. *New York Times* Poll, 2015.

9. Gallup Poll, 2010.

10. Pew Poll, 2012.

11. Pew Poll, 2012; Fox Poll, 2012; Gallup Poll, 2016.

12. University of Delaware's Center for Political Communication Poll, 2012.

13. Pew Poll, 2018.

14. Tiger Li and Nadja Linke, "Poll Shows Strong Bipartisan Opposition to Partisan Gerrymandering," *Common Cause*, September 17, 2017.

15. Dan Eggen, "Poll: Large Majority Opposes Supreme Court's Decision on Campaign Financing," *Washington Post*, February 17, 2010.

16. *CR* 2012, S102; *CR* 2010, S354; *CR* 2013, 6103; *CR* 2016, E1378.

17. The odd Republican-introduced bills are a combination of seemingly nonpartisan measures (e.g., separating internet contribution disclosures from direct check disclosures), conservative-oriented good-governance proposals (e.g., a candidate cannot spend more than s/he has in the war chest), or more ideologically motivated bills (e.g., eliminating direct contribution limits altogether).

18. Russell Falcon et al., "Beto O'Rourke, Others Testify against Elections Overhaul Bills at Texas Capitol," *KXAN*, July 11, 2021; Sean Morales-Doyle, "We're Suing Texas over Its New Voter Suppression Law," Brennan Center for Justice, September 7, 2021.

19. Daniel Béland, Philip Rocco, and Alex Waddan, "Policy Feedback and the Politics of the Affordable Care Act."

20. Gallup Poll, "Health Care System," 2000–2022.

21. Kaiser Family Foundation Poll, "KFF Health Tracking Poll: The Public's Views on the ACA," 2010–22.

22. Gallup Poll, 2013.

23. Tom Graves, R-GA, CR 2012, 10521; Louie Gohmert, R-TX, CR 2012, 10764.

24. Senator Mark Pryor (D-AR) sought to include qualifying churches' health plans for meeting the mandate. Senator Sherrod Brown (D-OH) wanted to allow religious exemptions for individuals from health coverage responsibility. Brown still sought to require everyone to have coverage for "routine dental, vision and hearing services, midwifery services, vaccinations, necessary medical services provided to children, services required by law or by a third party, and such other services as the Secretary of Health and Human Services may provide."

25. S.J. Res 16, 2013.

26. Josh Blackman, *Unprecedented: The Constitutional Challenge to Obamacare*.

27. Béland, Rocco, and Waddan, "Affordable Care Act."

28. Gallup Poll, "Health Care System"; Kaiser Family Foundation Poll, "Health Tracking."

29. Kaiser Family Foundation Poll, "Health Tracking."

30. Jordan T. Cash and Dave Bridge, "Donald Trump and Institutional Change Strategies."

31. Neither of the parties had shown they had been injured by the other and that their claims could be redressed by the requested relief.

32. I do not have data to back up the statement that Obamacare was salient. I am comfortable, though, making that statement.

33. Granted, it could have mobilized inactive Republicans, though the election of 2012 returns indicate it was not too durable.

34. *CR* 2015, H2493; Louie Gohmert (R-TX), *CR* 2015, H4646; Keith Rothfus (R-PA), *CR* 2015, H4764.

35. Pew Poll, 2015.

36. Michael J. Klarman, *From the Closet to the Altar: Courts, Backlash, and the Struggle for Same-Sex Marriage*.

37. Klarman, "Rethinking the Civil Rights and Civil Liberties Revolutions"; Powe, *Warren Court*.

38. "Same-Sex Marriage, State by State," Pew Research Center, June 26, 2015.

39. Objectors pointed out that the Trump regulation went into effect without a public comment period. The court rejected this claim.

40. Justices Roberts, Thomas, and Kavanaugh believed the administration did not *have to* issue these guidelines. Justices Alito and Gorsuch disagreed, writing a concurrence that would have taken the decision further by mandating that the exemptions be available.

41. In a separate case, *Zubik v. Burwell* (2016), the court heard arguments regarding religious freedom and the contraceptive mandate. The court unanimously vacated a lower court decision and remanded. Justice Kennedy's decision made quite clear that the remand was not a decision on the merits. Neither side won nor lost *Zubik*.

42. *Washington Post* poll, 2014.

43. Public Religion Research Institute poll, 2012.

44. Kaiser Family Foundation poll, 2014. This poll conducted immediately before the court released *Hobby Lobby*, found that 58 percent supported, and 32 percent opposed,

the ACA's requirement that private insurers cover the full cost of birth control. However, when we dig deeper into the religious exemption issue, we find a more mixed story. In that same poll, the KFF found that 53 percent believed for-profit companies should be required to cover birth control, even if it violated their owners' personal religious beliefs; 41 percent believed they should not have to cover it. Even if it appears there is a majority opposed to *Hobby Lobby*, the 58–32 versus 53–41 split is noticeable. It shows that a significant number of women's health amendment supporters were willing to grant religious institutions an exemption.

45. Kaiser Family Foundation Poll, 2014.

46. *CR* 2014, H2373, E1186, S4535.

47. Kaiser Family Foundation Poll, 2014.

48. Michael Klarman might agree: "A court decision is more likely to generate backlash when opponents of the ruling are more intensely committed on the underlying issue than supporters are." I believe liberals were more committed to the primary cases (*Sebelius* and *Obergefell*), but also that conservatives were more committed on the religious liberty follow-ups (*Hobby Lobby* and *Masterpiece*). Klarman, "*Windsor* and *Brown*," 149.

49. *CR* 2019, H3943.

50. Why would the same-sex couple take such a low figure? I suspect that they looked at the composition of the court. Four justices (Gorsuch, Alito, Thomas, and Roberts) voted in favor of Masterpiece Cakeshop. Justice Kagan had concurred. And there is good reason to think Justices Kavanaugh and Barrett would have more conservative stances than their predecessors (Justices Kennedy and Ginsburg, respectively). Perhaps settling was the best way to avoid the kind of precedent that would lock-in religious liberty over LGBT rights.

51. It took only a single Republican, Senator John McCain (R-AZ), to stop the movement to repeal health care. Granted, other than McCain, the GOP was quite united, so one interpretation could be that Republicans were only one vote away from repealing the ACA. But the Obamacare as majoritarian story is further magnified when we consider electoral institutions (e.g., Senate, Electoral College) that advantaged the GOP. In addition, Keith Whittington has shown how partisan actors can purposely ensure a negative outcome (i.e., the measure fails) even when they supposedly want a positive one. For instance, Reconstruction Republicans engineered a removal vote to save Andrew Johnson by a single vote. Perhaps the GOP would have done the same had a more conservative senator sat in McCain's place. Perhaps they would have found a different Republican to take the fall. After all, McCain had a reputation and was on his way out of politics—he was the perfect Republican to ensure the party did not pass countermajoritarian policy while also allowing Republicans to look like they were trying to do everything possible to repeal Obamacare. See Whittington, *Constitutional Construction*.

52. Or, at least, it was not durable enough to overcome the Watergate scandal.

53. Some Democrats might still have traded the mild electoral loss for judicial victories.

54. Alito, Gorsuch, and Thomas dissented. Amy Howe, "Supreme Court Rules against North Carolina Republicans over Election Law Theory," SCOTUSblog, June 27, 2023; Nina Totenberg, "Supreme Court Rejects Independent State Legislature Theory, but Leaves Door Ajar," NPR, June 27, 2023.

55. In all likelihood, some Democratic states would gerrymander lines, too.

56. Appointments played a role here. Essentially, we can swap Kennedy and Ginsburg in *Masterpiece* with Kavanaugh and Barrett in *303 Creative*. The next chapter details the Trump appointments more fully.

57. Justice Jackson did not sit on the Harvard case because she had been involved with Harvard admissions. She dissented, along with Justices Kagan and Sotomayor, in the North Carolina case.

58. Amelia Thomson-DeVeaux and Zoha Qamar, "The Supreme Court Could Overturn Another Major Precedent. This Time, Americans Might Agree," FiveThirtyEight, October 28, 2023; Monica Potts, "Most Americans Wanted the Supreme Court to End Affirmative Action—Kind Of," *FiveThirtyEight*, June 29, 2023, https://fivethirtyeight .com/features/american-opinion-affirmative-action/.

59. "National Poll Shows Strong Public Support for Affirmative Action, Diversity of College and University Campuses," Harvard University, Graduate School of Education, https://www.gse.harvard.edu/news/01/05/national-poll-shows-strong-public-support -affirmative-action-diversity-college-and.

60. NORC Affirmative Action Survey, 2022.

61. The 2022 GSS asks respondents if they favor a preference in hiring Blacks. Only 10 percent of Republicans and 28 percent of independents responded favorably.

62. Quinnipiac Poll, 2022.

63. *Economist*/YouGov Poll, 2022.

64. Fox Poll, 2022.

65. *Economist*/YouGov Poll, 2022.

66. Morning Consult-Politico Poll, 2022.

67. William A. Galston, "Do Americans Support President Biden's Student Loan Plan?" Brookings Institution, September 6, 2022, https://www.brookings.edu/articles/do-amer icans-support-president-bidens-student-loan-plan/.

68. "FACT SHEET: President Biden Announces New Actions to Provide Debt Relief and Support for Student Loan Borrowers," White House, June 30, 2023.

69. Fox Poll, 2023.

Chapter 9. The Elephant in the Room

1. Keck and McMahon, "Why *Roe* Still Stands."

2. Linda Greenhouse, *Justice on the Brink*, 185.

3. Matt Lewis, "Kavanaugh Fight Leads 'Never Trumper' Erick Erickson back to Trump," *Daily Beast*, September 27, 2018.

4. Jennifer Weiss-Wolf, "Amy Coney Barrett's 'Much-Touted Cloak of Decency,'" *Ms.*, October 12, 2020.

5. Amber Phillips, "'Oh, We'd Fill It': How McConnell Is Doing a 180 on Supreme Court Vacancies in an Election Year," *Washington Post*, May 29, 2019; Michael Barbaro, "A Historical Opening for Anti-Abortion Activists," *Daily*, September 23, 2020.

6. Alito noted "public approval of the Court weighs heavily in favor of retaining *Roe*." Thomas called abortion "a policy goal." Kavanaugh wrote, "To be sure, many Americans will disagree with the Court's decisions." Roberts quoted Felix Frankfurter: "Observe the wise limitations of our function." And the dissent said, "*Roe* and *Casey* continue to reflect, not diverge from, broad trends in American society."

7. *CR* 2022, S2395, S3235. Christine Smith (D-MN): "Americans don't want to over-turn *Roe*, and anti-choice Republicans know this," *CR* 2022, S2303; Maria Cantwell (D-WA): "70% of Americans believe that we should not overturn *Roe v. Wade*"; Tim Kaine (D-VA): "overturning *Roe* and *Casey* goes directly against the will of the people." *CR* 2022, S3806.

8. Both were introduced by Adriano Espaillat (D-NY).

9. Adam Carrington, "The Squad's Wild, Illogical Attacks on the Supreme Court," *Washington Examiner*, July 6, 2023.

10. Oriana González, "Republicans Abortion Silence Backfires in Midterms," *Axios*, November 10, 2022, https://www.axios.com/2022/11/10/republicans-abortion-midterms-results-silence; Josh Dawsey et al., "Abortion Divides 2024 Candidates and Confounds Many within the GOP," *Washington Post*, April 20, 2023; Isabella Murray, "Most Leading Republicans Remain Quiet on Abortion Pill Ruling as Democrats Blast Decision," *ABC News*, April 11, 2023.

11. For instance, in 2018, the House passed an iteration of the Hyde Amendment 238–183. No Republican voted against it; only three Democrats voted in favor. Daniel Lipinski (D-IL) voted against Obamacare, refused to endorse Obama in 2012, voted against decriminalization of marijuana, and personally opposes same-sex marriage. He lost his primary bid in 2020. Collin Peterson (D-MN) had a record of party-bucking conservative votes and was long considered the most conservative Democrat in Congress. He voted: against the impeachment of Donald Trump, against DC statehood, against decriminalization of marijuana, and against Obamacare. His bipartisan garage band was named the Second Amendments. In 2020 Peterson lost his reelection bid to a Republican. Henry Cuellar (D-TX) was appointed secretary of state of Texas under Republican governor Rick Perry, voted against decriminalization of marijuana, and voted with Trump 75 percent of the time. Clare Malone, "A Q&A with the House Democrat Who's Voted with Trump 75% of the Time," FiveThirtyEight, February 10, 2017.

12. Sarah McCammon, "What the Texas Abortion Ban Does—and What It Means for Other States." *NPR*, September 1, 2021.

13. Quinnipiac Poll, 2021.

14. YouGov Poll, 2021.

15. Both academics and journalists tell this story. See: Bruce E. Keith et al., *The Myth of the Independent Voter*; David B. Magleby, Candice J. Nelson, and Mark C. Westlye, "The Myth of the Independent Voter Revisited"; John Richard Petrocik, "Measuring Party Support: Leaners Are Not Independents"; Shankar Vedantam, "Are Independents Just Partisans in Disguise?" *Hidden Brain*, NPR, August 22, 2012; Geoffrey Skelley, "Few Americans Who Identify As Independent Are Actually Independent. That's Really Bad for Politics," FiveThirtyEight, April 15, 2021; "Political Independents: Who They Are, What They Think," Pew Research Center, March 14, 2019, https://www.pewresearch.org/politics/2019/03/14/political-independents-who-they-are-what-they-think/.

16. I ran figures when dropping Somewhat Important responders. They were similar as those reported above. Splitting partisanship with the more fine-grained, seven-point identification also yielded similar results.

17. Alan S. Gerber, Donald P. Green, and Ron Shachar, "Voting May Be Habit-Forming: Evidence from a Randomized Field Experiment"; Markus Prior, "You've Either Got It or You Don't? The Stability of Political Interest over the Life Cycle."

18. Drew Desilver, "Turnout in US Has Soared in Recent Elections but by Some Measures Still Trails That of Many Other Countries," Pew Research Center, November 1, 2022. https://www.pewresearch.org/short-reads/2022/11/01/turnout-in-u-s-has-soared-in-recent-elections-but-by-some-measures-still-trails-that-of-many-other-countries/.

19. W. T. Harbaugh, "If People Vote Because They Like to, Then Why Do So Many of Them Lie?"; Matthew K. Berent, Jon A. Krosnick, and Arthur Lupia, "Measuring Voter Registration and Turnout in Surveys: Do Official Government Records Yield More Accurate Assessments?"

20. I stay away from examining other political issues. Instead, I look for overarching factors that would cause someone to be more likely to switch their vote. Still, as I mention throughout the book, shifts in the electorate are almost never due to one cause. *Dobbs* is just one factor. There are certainly others, including but not limited to: tax policy, federal spending, business regulation, inflation, foreign policy, LGBT issues, critical race in schools, religious freedom, the charisma of any individual candidate, natural disasters, emerging violence across the world, domestic terrorism, and so forth.

21. ANES 2022 codebook, 3.

22. I also looked at a variable that looks at respondents' interest in the news. Naturally, it was very highly correlated (82.1 percent) with how closely one follows politics.

23. The following is a terrific literature review on the topic: Lauri Rapeli, "Does Sophistication Affect Electoral Outcomes?"

24. Cindy D. Kam, "Who Toes the Party Line? Cues, Values, and Individual Differences"; Larry M. Bartels, "Uninformed Votes: Information Effects in Presidential Elections."

25. Arthur Lupia, "Shortcuts versus Encyclopedias: Information and Voting behavior in California Insurance Reform Elections."

26. Michael X. Delli Carpini and Scott Keeter, *What Americans Know about Politics and Why It Matters.*

27. Matthew A. Baum and Angela S. Jamison, "The Oprah Effect: How Soft News Helps Inattentive Citizens Vote Consistently"; Sean Richey, "The Social Basis of Voting Correctly."

28. Richard R. Lau, "Correct Voting in the 2008 US Presidential Nominating Elections."

29. Matthew L. Bergbower, Scott D. McClurg, and Thomas Holbrook, "Presidential Campaign Spending and Correct Voting from 2000 to 2008."

30. Bartels, "Uninformed Votes"; Jay K. Dow, "Political Knowledge and Electoral Choice in the 1992–2004 United States Presidential Elections: Are More and Less Informed Citizens Distinguishable?"; Anthony Fowler and Michele Margolis, "The Political Consequences of Uninformed Voters"; Scott L. Althaus, "Information Effects in Collective Preferences."

31. Dow, "Political Knowledge"; David Dreyer Lassen, "The Effect of Information on Voter Turnout: Evidence from a Natural Experiment"; Markus Prior, "News vs. Entertainment: How Increasing Media Choice Widens Gaps in Political Knowledge and Turnout"; Scott L. Althaus, "Who's Voted in When the People Tune Out? Information Effects in Congressional Elections."

32. I ran these numbers. They tell the same story: Democrats have an advantage on abortion.

33. One more note: the possible switcher column is multiplied by two. This is because switching someone's vote not only adds one to a party's column; it also takes one away from the opposition party. The net effect is two votes.

34. Anthony Downs, *An Economic Theory of Democracy*.

35. Pedro C. Magalhães, John H. Aldrich, and Rachel K. Gibson, "New Forms of Mobilization, New People Mobilized? Evidence from the Comparative Study of Electoral Systems."

36. Simeon Nichter, "Vote Buying or Turnout Buying? Machine Politics and the Secret Ballot"; Lisa García Bedolla and Melissa R. Michelson, *Mobilizing Inclusion: Transforming the Electorate through Get-Out-the-Vote Campaigns*; Daniel E. Bergan et al., "Grassroots Mobilization and Voter Turnout in 2004."

37. See Edward G. Carmines and Eric R. Schmidt, "Critical Elections, Partisan Realignment, and Long-Term Electoral Change in American Politics"; Burnham, *Critical Elections*. Realignment theory's biggest critic, David Mayhew, would disagree with Burnham on the singular causes and lasting effects of critical elections. But Mayhew would agree that in any single election, external forces (e.g., countermajoritarian rulings) can have electoral impacts. See Mayhew, "Events as Causes" and Mayhew, "Electoral Realignments."

38. Daniel W. Drezner, "The End of the Median Voter Theorem in Presidential Politics?" *Washington Post*, May 29, 2015; David Wasserman, "House Democrats' Keys to Victory: Suburbs, Money, and Fired-Up Women College Grads," *NBC News*, November 8, 2018; Bradley Jones, "House Republicans Who Lost Re-Election Bids Were More Moderate Than Those Who Won," Pew Research Center, December 7, 2018, https://www.pewresearch.org/short-reads/2018/12/07/house-republicans-who-lost-re-election-bids-were-more-moderate-than-those-who-won/; Geoffrey Skelley, "Just How Many Swing Voters Are There?" FiveThirtyEight, September 19, 2019; Galvin, "Party Domination and Base Mobilization"; Corwin D. Smidt, "Polarization and the Decline of the American Floating Voter"; William G. Mayer, ed., *The Swing Voter in American Politics*; Gary C. Jacobson, "The Triumph of Polarized Partisanship in 2016: Donald Trump's Improbable Victory"; Jacobson, "Extreme Referendum: Donald Trump and the 2018 Midterm Elections"; Carlos Algara et al., "Nail in the Coffin or Lifeline? Evaluating the Electoral Impact of COVID-19 on President Trump in the 2020 Election."

39. Though this is still important. See Seth J. Hill, Daniel J. Hopkins, and Gregory A. Huber, "Not by Turnout Alone: Measuring the Sources of Electoral Change, 2012 to 2016."

40. Buchanan, "Memo to Harlow"; Buchanan, "Dividing the Democrats."

41. Let us use vote choice from 2020. Democrats have a +8.5 Real Edge in probable partisans, a +6.8 Real Edge with possible switchers, and a +6.1 Real Edge with capturable independents. The cumulative total is +21.4, and 10% of that figure is 2.14 added points.

42. This might be an apples to oranges comparison because I am using 2020 returns to retroactively assess 2016 results. The takeaway is that a 2.14 point bump is considerable in some contexts—especially the race for the White House. That said, in the presidential election of 2016: the margin was so close; abortion is so explosive; and the Democrats have such an advantage on the issue. Put those items together, and I speculate that Hillary Clinton would have won the presidency had *Roe* been overturned in 2015 or 2016. But it is exactly that: speculation.

43. In 2022, with five more points, Democrats would have turned nineteen seats. They would have gone from a nine-seat minority to a thirty-seat majority.

44. In 2022 the answer is "no." They would have won two additional seats and instead of a 50–50 split into a 52–48 majority. (Note: Independents Kyrsten Sinema and Bernie Sanders caucus with the 48 Democrats.)

45. I do not see Texas swinging. If Texas ever became a blue-leaning state, the general election would effectively be over before it started. The real race, then, would be the Democratic primary.

Appendix

1. Dave Bridge, "Living on a Prayer: Descriptive Representation of Catholics and Evangelicals, 1962–1980." We do not have district-level data.

2. Engel, *American Politicians Confront the Courts*.

3. Mayhew, *Congress*.

4. Clark, Lax, and Rice, "Measuring the Political Salience," 53.

Bibliography

Primary Sources
Public Opinion Polls and Datasets
ABC/Ipsos
ABC/*Washington Post*
American National Election Survey
Americans for Fair Chance
AP/NORC
CBS
Cooperative Congressional Election Study
CNN
Economist/YouGov
Fox
Gallup
General Social Science Survey
Harris
HuffPost/YouGov
Kaiser Family Foundation
Life
Morning Consult/*Politico*
National Opinion Research Center
NBC/*Wall Street Journal*
New York Times
Pennsylvania State University
Pew
Public Religion Religious Institute
Quinnipiac
Washington Post
Washington Post/Schar School
YouGov

Primary Documents Holdings
Americanpresidency.org
Congressional Globe

Congressional Record

Controlling Crime through More Effective Law Enforcement: Hearings before the Subcommittee on Criminal Laws and Procedures

Gerald Ford Papers

Hearings before the Select Committee on the Presidential Campaign Activities of the United States Senate: Watergate and Related Activities

Richard Nixon Papers

Richard Nixon Tapes

Southern Oral History Program

Wendel Arthur Garrity Papers on the Boston School Desegregation Case, 1972–1997

White House

Newspapers, Periodicals, and Other Media Sources

ABC News

America

Ashville Times

Axios

Balkinization

Bryan Times

CNN

Commentary Magazine

Common Cause

Commonweal

CQ Almanac

Daily

Daily Beast

FiveThirtyEight

KXAN

Legal Times

Ms.

Nation

National Review

New York Times

Newsweek

NPR

Reader's Digest

SCOTUSblog

Time

Tribune-Democrat

Triumph

Wanderer

Washington Examiner
Washington Post

Websites
Ballotpedia.org
Brennancenter.org
Brookings.edu
Concernedwomen.org
Eagleforum.org
Emkinstitute.org
Nrlc.org
Pewresearchcenter.org
Sfpl.org
Usccb.org

Secondary Sources

Abraham, Henry Julian. *Justices, Presidents, and Senators: A History of the U.S. Supreme Court Appointments from Washington to Bush II*. Lanham, MD: Rowman & Littlefield, 2008.

Abramowitz, Alan I. "It's Abortion, Stupid: Policy Voting in the 1992 Presidential Election." *Journal of Politics* 57, no. 1 (1995): 176–86.

Adams, Greg D. "Abortion: Evidence of an Issue Evolution." *American Journal of Political Science* 41, no. 3 (July 1997): 718–37.

Alexander, Michelle, and Cornel West. *The New Jim Crow: Mass Incarceration in the Age of Colorblindness*. New York: New Press, 2012.

Algara, Carlos, Sharif Amlani, Samuel Collitt, Issac Hale, and Sara Kazemian. "Nail in the Coffin or Lifeline? Evaluating the Electoral Impact of COVID-19 on President Trump in the 2020 Election." *Political Behavior*. 2022. Online.

Alley, Robert S. *School Prayer*. Buffalo, NY: Prometheus Books, 1994.

Allswang, John. *The New Deal and American Politics: A Study in Political Change*. New York: Wiley, 1978.

Althaus, Scott L. "Information Effects in Collective Preferences." *American Political Science Review* 92, no. 3 (1998): 545–58.

———. "Who's Voted in When the People Tune Out? Information Effects in Congressional Elections." In *Communication in U.S. Elections: New Agendas*, edited by Roderick P. Hart and Daron Shaw, 33–54. Lanham, MD: Rowman & Littlefield, 2001.

Ambrose, Stephen E. *Nixon: The Triumph of a Politician, 1962–1972*. New York: Simon & Schuster, 2014.

Asher, Steven E. "Interdistrict Remedies for Segregated Schools." *Columbia Law Review* 79, no. 6 (1979): 1168–90.

Avery, Michael, and Danielle McLaughlin. *The Federalist Society: How Conservatives Took the Law Back from Liberals*. Nashville, TN: Vanderbilt University Press, 2013.

Baer-Bositis, Emily Caitlin. "Organizing for Reform: The Democratic Study Group and the Role of Party Factions in Driving Institutional Change in the House of Representatives." PhD diss., University of Minnesota, 2017.

Baker, Liva. *Miranda: Crime, Law, and Politics*. New York: Atheneum, 1983.

Balkin, Jack M. *The Cycles of Constitutional Time*. Oxford: Oxford University Press, 2020.

———. "Why Liberals and Conservatives Flipped on Judicial Restraint: Judicial Review in the Cycles of Constitutional Time." *Texas Law Review* 98, no. 215 (2019): 215–68.

Balkin, Jack, ed. *What Brown v. Board Should Have Said*. New York: NYU Press, 2002.

Barnes, Jeb. "Bringing the Courts Back In: Interbranch Perspectives on the Role of Courts in American Politics and Policy Making." *Annual Review of Political Science* 10 (2007): 25–43.

———. "Congressional Compromise on Election Reform: A Look Forward and Backward." In *After 2000: The Politics of Election Reform*, edited by Ann N. Crigler, Marion R. Just, and Edward J. McCaffery, 117–32. New York: Oxford University Press, 2003.

———. *Overruled? Legislative Overrides, Pluralism, and Contemporary Court-Congress Relations*. Stanford, CA: Stanford University Press, 2004.

Barnes, Jeb, and Thomas F. Burke. *How Policy Shapes Politics: Rights, Courts, Litigation, and the Struggle over Injury Compensation*. New York: Oxford University Press, 2015.

Bartels, Larry M. "Uninformed Votes: Information Effects in Presidential Elections." *American Journal of Political Science* 40, no. 1 (February 1996): 194–230.

Baugh, Joyce A. *The Detroit School Busing Case: Milliken v. Bradley and the Controversy over Desegregation*. Lawrence: University of Kansas Press, 2011.

Baum, Howell S. *Brown in Baltimore: School Desegregation and the Limits of Liberalism*. Ithaca, NY: Cornell University Press, 2010.

Baum, Matthew A., and Angela S. Jamison. "The Oprah Effect: How Soft News Helps Inattentive Citizens Vote Consistently." *Journal of Politics* 68, no. 4 (2006): 946–59.

Baylor, Christopher. *First to the Party: The Group Origins of Political Transformation*. Philadelphia: University of Pennsylvania Press, 2017.

Beaney, William M., and Edward N. Beiser. "Prayer and Politics: The Impact of Engel and Schempp on the Political Process." *Journal of Public Law* 13 (1964): 475–503.

Bednar, Jenna. "The Dialogic Theory of Judicial Review: A New Social Science Research Agenda." *George Washington Law Review* 78, no. 6 (September 2010): 1178–90.

Béland, Daniel, Philip Rocco, and Alex Waddan. "Policy Feedback and the Politics of the Affordable Care Act." *Policy Studies Journal* 47, no. 2 (October 2018): 395–422.

Bell, Derrick. *Silent Covenants: Brown v. Board of Education and the Unfulfilled Hopes for Racial Reform*. Oxford: Oxford University Press, 2004.

Bell, Lauren C. "Monitoring or Meddling: Congressional Oversight of the Judicial Branch." *Wayne Law Review* 64, no. 1 (Spring 2018): 23–62.

Bell, Lauren C., and Kevin M. Scott. "Policy Statements or Symbolic Politics: Explaining Congressional Court-Limiting Attempts." *Judicature* 89, no. 4 (2006): 196–201.

Belsky, Martin H. "Whither Miranda." *Texas Law Review* 62 (1984): 1341–62.

Berent, Matthew K., Jon A. Krosnick, and Arthur Lupia. "Measuring Voter Registration and Turnout in Surveys: Do Official Government Records Yield More Accurate Assessments?" *Public Opinion Quarterly* 80, no. 3 (2016): 597–621.

Bergan, Daniel E., Alan S. Gerber, Donald P. Green, and Costas Panagopoulos. "Grassroots Mobilization and Voter Turnout in 2004." *Public Opinion Quarterly* 69, no. 5 (January 2005): 760–77.

Bergbower, Matthew L., Scott D. McClurg, and Thomas Holbrook. "Presidential Campaign Spending and Correct Voting from 2000 to 2008." *Social Science Quarterly* 96, no. 5 (November 2015): 1196–213.

Berman, William C. *America's Right Turn: From Nixon to Bush*. Baltimore: Johns Hopkins University Press, 1994.

Bickel, Alexander M. *The Least Dangerous Branch: The Supreme Court at the Bar of Politics*. New York: Bobs-Merrill, 1962.

———. "The Supreme Court 1960 Term—Foreword: The Passive Virtues." *Harvard Law Review* 75, no. 40 (November 1961): 40–244.

Biles, Roger. *The South and the New Deal*. Lexington: University Press of Kentucky, 1994.

Birkby, Robert H. "The Supreme Court and the Bible Belt: Tennessee Reaction to the Schempp Decision." *Midwest Journal of Political Science* 10, no. 3 (August 1966): 304–19.

Black, Earl, and Merle Black. *The Rise of Southern Republicans*. Cambridge, MA: Belknap Press, 2002.

Blackman, Josh. *Unprecedented: The Constitutional Challenge to Obamacare*. New York: PublicAffairs, 2013.

Blackstone, Bethany. "An Analysis of Policy-Based Congressional Responses to the U.S. Supreme Court's Constitutional Decisions." *Law and Society Review* 47, no. 1 (2013): 199–228.

Blake, Judith. "The Supreme Court's Abortion Decisions and Public Opinion in the United States." *Population and Development Review* 3, no. 1/2 (1977): 45–62.

Blumenthal, Sidney. *The Rise of the Counter-Establishment: The Conservative Ascent to Political Power.* New York: Union Square Press, 2008.

Boles, Donald. *The Bible, Religion, and the Public Schools.* Ames: Iowa State University Press, 1963.

Borgmann, Caitlin E. "Abortion, the Undue Burden Standard, and the Evisceration of Women's Privacy." *William and Mary Journal of Women and the Law* 16, no. 2 (February 2010): 291–325.

———. "*Roe v. Wade*'s 40th Anniversary: A Moment of Truth for the Anti-Abortion-Rights Movement." *Stanford Law and Policy Review* 24, no. 1 (2013): 245–70.

Bork, Robert H. *The Tempting of America: The Political Seduction of the Law.* New York:

Brands, H. W. *Reagan: The Life.* New York: Doubleday, 2015.

Brennan, Mary C. *Turning Right in the Sixties: The Conservative Capture of the GOP.* Chapel Hill: University of North Carolina Press, 1995.

Bridge, Dave. "Catholics in the 'Mature' New Deal Era: How the Republican Party Used Supreme Court Attacks to Pursue Catholic Voters." *US Catholic Historian* 34, no. 4 (2016): 79–106.

———. "Holding the Accountability Problem Accountable: Response Mechanisms to Counter-Majoritarian Supreme Court Decisions." *American Review of Politics* 35, no. 1 (2015): 18–43.

———. "Living on a Prayer: Descriptive Representation of Catholics and Evangelicals, 1962–1980." *Journal of Church and State* 59, no. 2 (2017): 163–84.

———. "Supreme Court Attacks as a Mechanism for Coalition Building: How the Republican Party Used Court-Curbing Proposals to Pursue Southern Voters." *Journal of Political Science* 44, no. 1 (2016): 61–88.

———. "The Supreme Court, Factions, and the Counter-Majoritarian Difficulty." *Polity* 47, no. 4 (2015): 420–60.

Bridge, Dave, and Curt Nichols. "Congressional Attacks on the Supreme Court: A Mechanism to Maintain, Build, and Consolidate." *Law and Social Inquiry* 41, no. 1 (2016): 100–25.

Bryant, M. David, Jr. "State Legislation on Abortion after *Roe v. Wade*: Selected Constitutional Issues." *American Journal of Law and Medicine* 2, no. 1 (Summer 1976): 101–32.

Buccola, Nicholas. "In Defense of Judicial Prudence: American Constitutional Theory, Virtue, and Judicial Review in Hard Cases." *Journal Jurisprudence* 49 (2013): 49–72.

Buchanan, Patrick. *Nixon's White House Wars.* New York: Crown Forum, 2017.

Bullock, Charles S., Susan A. MacManus, Jeremy D. Mayer, and Mark J. Rozell. *The South and the Transformation of U.S. Politics.* Oxford: Oxford University Press, 2019.

Burnham, Walter Dean. *Critical Elections and the Mainstream of American Politics.* New York: W. W. Norton, 1970.

Burns, Sarah. *The Politics of War Powers: The Theory and History of Presidential Unilateralism.* Lawrence: University Press of Kansas, 2019.

Busch, Andrew E. *Reagan's Victory: The Presidential Election of 1980 and the Rise of the Right.* Lawrence: University Press of Kansas, 2005.

Byrnes, Timothy A. *Catholic Bishops in American Politics.* Princeton: Princeton University Press, 2016.

Caminker, Evan H. "Thayerian Deference to Congress and Supreme Court Supermajority Rule: Lessons from the Past." *Indiana Law Journal* 78, no. 1 (2003): 73–122.

Canavan, Francis. "Implications of the School Prayer and Bible Reading Decisions: The Welfare State." *Journal of Public Law* 13 (1964): 439–46.

Cannon, Lou. *Governor Reagan: His Rise to Power.* New York: PublicAffairs, 2003.

Carmines, Edward G., and Eric R. Schmidt. "Critical Elections, Partisan Realignment, and Long-Term Electoral Change in American Politics." In *Oxford Bibliographies Online*, edited by L. Sandy Maisel. New York: Oxford University Press, 2018.

Carmines, Edward G., and James A. Stimson. *Issue Evolution: Race and the Transformation of American Politics.* Princeton: Princeton University Press, 1989.

Carmines, Edward G., and Michael W. Wagner. "Political Issues and Party Alignments: Assessing the Issue Evolution Perspective." *Annual Review of Political Science* 9, no. 1 (June 2006): 67–81.

Caro, Robert A. *Master of the Senate: The Years of Lyndon Johnson.* New York: Vintage Books, 2002.

Cash, Jordan T. "The Isolated Presidency: John Tyler and Unilateral Presidential Power." *American Political Thought* 7, no. 1 (Winter 2018): 26–56.

Cash, Jordan T., and Dave Bridge. "Donald Trump and Institutional Change Strategies." *Laws* 7, no. 3 (2018): 1–21.

Casper, Jonathan D. "The Supreme Court and National Policy Making." *American Political Science Review* 70, no. 1 (1976): 50–63.

Catalano, Michael A. "Ex Ante and Ex Post Control over Courts in the US States: Court Curbing and Political Party Influence." *Justice System Journal* 43, no. 4 (October 2022): 503–23.

Chapman, Roger. *Culture Wars: An Encyclopedia of Issues, Viewpoints, and Voices.* Armonk, NY: M. E. Sharpe, 2010.

Chemerinsky, Erwin. *The Case against the Supreme Court*. New York: Penguin Random House, 2014.

———. "The Segregation and Resegregation of American Public Education: The Court's Role." *North Carolina Law Review* 81, no. 4 (May 2003): 1597–622.

Chutkow, Dawn M. "Jurisdiction Stripping: Litigation, Ideology, and Congressional Control of the Courts." *Journal of Politics* 70, no. 4 (October 2008): 1053–64.

Clark, Hunter R. *Justice Brennan: The Great Conciliator*. New York: Birch Lane, 1995.

Clark, Tom S. *The Limits of Judicial Independence*. New York: Cambridge University Press, 2011.

Clark, Tom S., Jeffrey R. Lax, and Douglas Rice. "Measuring the Political Salience of Supreme Court Cases." *Journal of Law and Courts* 3, no. 1 (2015): 37–65.

Clayton, Cornell W. "The Bush Presidency and the New Right Constitutional Regime." *Law and Courts* 15, no. 1 (2005): 6–14.

———. "The Supply and Demand Sides of Judicial Policy-Making." *Law and Contemporary Problems* 65 (Summer 2002): 69–86.

Clayton, Cornell W., and David D. May. "The New Institutionalism and Supreme Cout Decision-Making: Toward a Political Regimes Approach." *Polity* 32, no. 2 (1999): 233–52.

Clayton, Cornell W., and J. Mitchell Pickerill. "The Politics of Criminal Justice: How the New Right Regime Shaped the Rehnquist Court's Criminal Justice Jurisprudence." *Georgetown Law Journal* 94, no. 5 (June 2006): 1385–426.

———. "The Rehnquist Court and the Political Dynamics of Federalism." *Perspectives on Politics* 2, no. 2 (June 2004): 233–48.

Cohen, Adam. *Supreme Inequality: The Supreme Court's Fifty-Year Battle for a More Unjust America*. New York: Penguin Press, 2020.

Cohen, Marty, David Karol, Hans Noel, and John Zaller. *The Party Decides: Presidential Nominations before and after Reform*. Chicago: University of Chicago Press, 2008.

Collins, Robert M. *More: The Politics of Economic Growth in Postwar America*. New York: Oxford University Press, 2000.

Conley, Patrick T., and Robert J. McKenna. "The Supreme Court on Abortion: A Dissenting Opinion." *Catholic Lawyer* 19, no. 1 (Winter 1973): 19–28.

Cook, Daniel, and Andrew J. Polsky. "Political Time Reconsidered: Unbuilding and Rebuilding the State under the Reagan Administration." *American Politics Research* 33, no. 4 (July 2005): 577–605.

Cottrol, Robert J., Raymond T. Diamond, and Leland Ware. *Brown v. Board of Education: Caste, Culture, and the Constitution*. Landmark Law Cases & American Society. Lawrence: University Press of Kansas, 2003.

Cray, Ed. *Chief Justice: A Biography of Earl Warren.* New York: Simon & Schuster, 2008.

Crespino, Joseph. "Goldwater in Dixie: Race, Region, and the Rise of the Right." In *Barry Goldwater and the Remaking of the American Political Landscape*, edited by Elizabeth Tandy Shermer, 144–69. Tucson: University of Arizona Press, 2013.

Critchlow, Donald T. *The Conservative Ascendancy: How the GOP Right Made Political History.* Cambridge, MA: Harvard University Press, 2007.

———. *Intended Consequences: Birth Control, Abortion, and the Federal Government in Modern America.* Oxford: Oxford University Press, 1999.

———. "The Rise of Conservative Republicanism: A History of Fits and Starts." In Mason and Morgan, *Seeking a New Majority*, 13–31.

Crockett, David A. *The Opposition Presidency: Leadership and the Constraints of History.* College Station: Texas A&M University Press, 2002.

———. *Running against the Grain: How Opposition Presidents Win the White House.* College Station: Texas A&M University Press, 2008.

Cushman, Barry. *Rethinking the New Deal Court: The Structure of a Constitutional Revolution.* New York: Oxford University Press, 1998.

Dahl, Robert A. "Decision-Making in a Democracy: The Supreme Court as a National Policy-Maker." *Journal of Public Law* 6 (Fall 1957): 279–95.

———. *How Democratic Is the American Constitution?* New Haven: Yale University Press, 2003.

Dark, Taylor. *The Unions and the Democrats: An Enduring Alliance.* Ithaca, NY: Cornell University Press, 1999.

Davis, Sue. "Justice Rehnquist's Equal Protection Clause: An Interim Analysis." *Nebraska Law Review* 63, no. 2 (1984): 288–313.

Daynes, Byron W., and Raymond Tatalovich. "Presidential Politics and Abortion, 1972–1988." *Presidential Studies Quarterly* 22, no. 3 (Summer 1992): 545–61.

Dean, John W. *The Rehnquist Choice: The Untold Story of the Appointment That Redefined the Supreme Court.* New York: Free Press, 2002.

DelFattore, Joan. *The Fourth R: Conflicts over Religion in America's Public Schools.* New Haven: Yale University Press, 2004.

Delli Carpini, Michael X., and Scott Keeter. *What Americans Know about Politics and Why It Matters.* New Haven: Yale University Press, 1996.

Delmont, Matthew F. *Why Busing Failed: Race, Media, and the National Resistance to School Desegregation.* Berkeley: University of California Press, 2016.

Devins, Neal. "Rethinking Judicial Minimalism: Abortion Politics, Party Polarization, and the Consequences of Returning the Constitution to Elected Government." *Vanderbilt Law Review* 69, no. 4 (2016): 935–90.

Diamond, Sara. *Not by Politics Alone: The Enduring Influence of the Christian Right*. New York: Guilford Press, 1998.

Dierenfield, Bruce J. *The Battle over School Prayer: How Engel v. Vitale Changed America*. Lawrence: University Press of Kansas, 2007.

———. "'Somebody Is Tampering with America's Soul': Congress and the School Prayer Debate." *Congress and the Presidency* 24, no. 2 (1997): 167–204.

Dimond, Paul R. *Beyond Busing: Reflections on Urban Segregation, the Courts, and Equal Opportunity*. Ann Arbor: University of Michigan Press, 2009.

DiSalvo, Daniel. *Engines of Change: Party Factions in American Politics: 1868–2010*. Oxford: Oxford University Press, 2012.

———. "Party Factions in Congress." *Congress and the Presidency* 36, no. 1 (March 2009): 27–57.

Dolbeare, Kenneth M., and Phillip E. Hammond. *The School Prayer Decisions from Court Policy to Local Practice*. Chicago: University of Chicago Press, 1971.

Dow, Jay K. "Political Knowledge and Electoral Choice in the 1992–2004 United States Presidential Elections: Are More and Less Informed Citizens Distinguishable?" *Journal of Elections, Public Opinion and Parties* 21, no. 3 (2011): 381–405.

Downs, Anthony. *An Economic Theory of Democracy*. New York: Harper Press, 1957.

Dracos, Ted. *UnGodly: The Passions, Torments, and Murder of Atheist Madalyn Murray O'Hair*. New York: Free Press, 2003.

Drakulich, Kevin, Kevin H. Wozniak, John Hagan, and Devon Johnson. "Race and Policing in the 2016 Presidential Election: Black Lives Matter, the Police, and Dog Whistle Politics." *Criminology* 58, no. 2 (2020): 370–402.

Dudziak, Mary L. *Cold War Civil Rights: Race and the Image of American Democracy*. Princeton: Princeton University Press, 2011.

Edsall, Thomas Byrne, and Mary D. Edsall. *Chain Reaction: The Impact of Race, Rights, and Taxes on American Politics; with a New Afterword*. New York: Norton, 1992.

Ehrlichman, John. *Witness to Power: The Nixon Years*. New York: Simon & Schuster, 1982.

Ely, John Hart. *Democracy and Distrust*. Cambridge, MA: Harvard University Press, 1981.

Engel, Stephen M. *American Politicians Confront the Courts: Opposition Politics and Changing Responses to Judicial Power*. New York: Cambridge University Press, 2011.

Epstein, Lee, Valerie Hoekstra, Jeffrey A. Segal, and Harold J. Spaeth. "Do Political Preferences Change? A Longitudinal Study of U.S. Supreme Court Justices." *Journal of Politics* 60, no. 3 (August 1998): 801–18.

Epstein, Lee, Andrew D. Martin, Kevin M. Quinn, and Jeffrey A. Segal. "Ideological Drift among Supreme Court Justices: Who, When, and How Important?" *Northwestern Law Review* 101, no. 4 (2007): 1483–1542.

Epstein, Lee, and Eric Posner. "Supreme Court Justices' Loyalty to the President." *Journal of Legal Studies* 45, no. 2 (June 2016): 401–36.

Epstein, Lee, and Jeffrey A. Segal. *Advice and Consent: The Politics of Judicial Appointments.* Oxford: Oxford University Press, 2007.

———. "Measuring Issue Salience." *American Journal of Political Science* 44, no. 1 (2000): 66–83.

Eskridge, William N., Jr. "Overriding Supreme Court Statutory Interpretation Decisions." *Yale Law Journal* 101, no. 2 (November 1991): 331–53.

Evans, John H. "Polarization in Abortion Attitudes in US Religious Traditions, 1972–1998." *Sociological Forum* 17, no. 3 (2002): 397–422.

Farrell, Margaret G. "Revisiting *Roe v. Wade*: Substance and Process in the Abortion Debate." *Indiana Law Journal* 68, no. 2 (1993): 269–362.

Fatovic, Clement, and Benjamin A. Kleinerman, eds. *Extra-Legal Power and Legitimacy: Perspectives on Prerogative.* New York: Oxford University Press, 2013.

Fehrenbacher, Don E. *The Dred Scott Case: Its Significance in American Law and Politics.* New York: Oxford University Press, 1978.

Feldman, Glenn, ed. *Painting Dixie Red: When, Where, Why, and How the South Became Republican.* Gainesville: University Press of Florida, 2011.

Fiss, Owen M. "The Charlotte-Mecklenburg Case—Its Significance for Northern School Desegregation." *University of Chicago Law Review* 38, no. 4 (1971): 697–706.

———. "The Law of Narrow Tailoring." *University of Pennsylvania Journal of Constitutional Law* 23, no. 5 (2021): 879–906.

———. "School Desegregation: The Uncertain Path of the Law." *Philosophy and Public Affairs* 4, no. 1 (Autumn 1974): 3–39.

———. *Troubled Beginnings of the Modern State, 1888–1910.* History of the Supreme Court of the United States. Vol. 8. New York: Macmillan, 1993.

Flamm, Michael W. *Law and Order: Street Crime, Civil Unrest, and the Crisis of Liberalism in the 1960s.* New York: Columbia University Press, 2005.

Flowers, Prudence. "'A Prolife Disaster': The Reagan Administration and the Nomination of Sandra Day O'Connor." *Journal of Contemporary History* 53, no. 2 (2018): 391–414.

Foley, Michael. *The New Senate: Liberal Influence on a Conservative Institution, 1959–1972.* New Haven: Yale University Press, 1980.

Formisano, Ronald P. *Boston against Busing: Race, Class, and Ethnicity in the 1960s and 1970s.* Chapel Hill: University of North Carolina Press, 1991.

Fowler, Anthony, and Michele Margolis. "The Political Consequences of Uninformed Voters." *Electoral Studies* 34, no. 1 (2014): 100–10.

Frank, Thomas. *What's the Matter with Kansas? How Conservatives Won the Heart of America*. New York: Henry Holt, 2005.

Fraser, Steve, and Gary Gerstle. *The Rise and Fall of the New Deal Order, 1930–1980*. Princeton: Princeton University Press, 1989.

Freeswick, James R. "*Milliken v. Bradley*." *Hofstra Law Review* 3, no. 2 (1975): 487–515.

Freund, Paul A. "The Supreme Court under Attack." *University of Pittsburgh Law Review* 25, no. 1 (October 1963): 1–8.

Fried, Richard M. *Nightmare in Red: The McCarthy Era in Perspective*. New York: Oxford University Press, 1991.

Friedman, Barry. "The Birth of an Academic Obsession: The History of the Countermajoritarian Difficulty, Part Five." *Yale Law Journal* 112 (November 2002): 153–259.

——. "The Cycles of Constitutional Theory." *Law and Contemporary Problems* 67, no. 3 (Summer 2004): 149–74.

——. "Dialogue and Judicial Review." *Michigan Law Review* 91, no. 4 (1993): 577–682.

——. "The History of the Countermajoritarian Difficulty, Part Four: Law's Politics." *University of Pennsylvania Law Review* 148, no. 4 (April 2000): 971–1064.

——. "The History of the Countermajoritarian Difficulty, Part One: The Road to Judicial Supremacy." *New York University Law Review* 73, no. 2 (May 1998): 333–433.

——. "The History of the Countermajoritarian Difficulty, Part Three: The Lesson of Lochner." *New York University Law Review* 76, no. 5 (November 2001): 1383–455.

——. "Letter to the Supreme Court (Erwin Chemerinsky Is Mad. Why You Should Care)." *Vanderbilt Law Review* 69, no. 4 (May 2016): 995–1018.

——. "Neutral Principles: A Retrospective." *Vanderbilt Law Review* 50, no. 2 (March 1997): 503–36.

——. "Popular Dissatisfaction with the Administration of Justice: A Retrospective (and a Look Ahead)." *Indiana Law Journal* 82, no. 5 (2007): 1193–1214.

——. *The Will of the People: How Public Opinion Has Influenced the Supreme Court and Shaped the Meaning of the Constitution*. New York: Farrar, Straus, and Giroux, 2009.

Frymer, Paul. "Acting When Elected Officials Won't: Federal Courts and Civil Rights Enforcement in U.S. Labor Unions, 1935–85." *American Political Science Review* 97, no. 3 (2003): 483–99.

Gadsden, Brett. *Between North and South: Delaware, Desegregation, and the Myth of American Sectionalism*. Philadelphia: University of Pennsylvania Press, 2013.

Galanter, Marc. "Why the 'Haves' Come Out Ahead: Speculations on the Limits of Legal Change." *Law and Society Review* 9, no. 1 (1974): 95–160.

Galvin, Daniel J. "Party Domination and Base Mobilization: Donald Trump and Republican Party Building in a Polarized Era." *Forum* 18, no. 2 (2020): 135–68.

———. *Presidential Party Building: Dwight D. Eisenhower to George W. Bush.* Princeton: Princeton University Press, 2009.

García Bedolla, Lisa, and Melissa R. Michelson. *Mobilizing Inclusion: Transforming the Electorate through Get-Out-the-Vote Campaigns.* New Haven: Yale University Press, 2012.

Gerber, Alan S., Donald P. Green, and Ron Shachar. "Voting May Be Habit-Forming: Evidence from a Randomized Field Experiment." *American Journal of Political Science* 47, no. 3 (2003): 540–50.

Gerring, John. *Party Ideologies in America: 1828–1996.* New York: Cambridge University Press, 1998.

Gillman, Howard. "The Collapse of Constitutional Originalism and the Rise of the Notion of the 'Living Constitution' in the Course of American State-Building." *Studies in American Political Development* 11, no. 2 (1997): 191–247.

———. *The Constitution Besieged: The Rise and Demise of Lochner Era Police Powers Jurisprudence.* Durham, NC: Duke University Press, 1993.

———. "Courts and the Politics of Partisan Coalitions." In *The Oxford Handbook of Law and Politics*, edited by Gregory A. Caldeira, R. Daniel Keleman, and Keith E. Whittington, 644–82. Oxford: Oxford University Press, 2008.

———. "How Political Parties Can Use the Courts to Advance Their Agendas: Federal Courts in the United States, 1875–1891." *American Political Science Review* 96, no. 3 (September 2002): 511–24.

———. "Martin Shapiro and the Movement from 'Old' Institutionalist Studies to 'New' Institutionalist Studies in Public Law." *Annual Review of Political Science* 7 (2004): 363–82.

———. "Party Coalitions and Supreme Court Politics: Additional Lessons from Whittington's Repugnant Laws." *Georgetown Journal of Law and Public Policy* 19, no. 2 (2021): 405–23.

———. "Party Politics and Constitutional Change: The Political Origins of Liberal Judicial Activism." In *The Supreme Court and American Political Development*, edited by Ken Kersch and Ronald Kahn, 138–62. Lawrence: University Press of Kansas, 2006.

———. "Regime Politics, Jurisprudential Regimes, and Unenumerated Rights." *University of Pennsylvania Journal of Constitutional Law* 9, no. 1 (2006): 107–19.

———. "Review: What's Law Got to Do with It? Judicial Behavioralists Test the 'Legal Model' of Judicial Decision Making." *Law and Social Inquiry* 26, no. 2 (Spring 2001): 465–504.

———. "Robert G. McCloskey, Historical Institutionalism, and the Arts of Judicial Governance." In Maveety, *Pioneers of Judicial Behavior*, 336–60.

Glenn, Brian J., and Steven M. Teles, eds. *Conservatism and American Political Development*. New York: Oxford University Press, 2009.

Gorney, Cynthia. *Articles of Faith: A Frontline History of the Abortion Wars*. New York: Simon & Schuster, 2000.

Gould, William B. "Right to Travel and National Security." *Washington University Law Review* 4 (1961): 334–66.

Graber, Mark A. "Constructing Judicial Review." *Annual Review of Political Science* 8 (2005): 425–51.

———. "The Countermajoritarian Difficulty: From Courts to Congress to Constitutional Order." *Annual Review of Law and Social Science* 4, no. 1 (2008): 361–84.

———. *Dred Scott and the Problem of Constitutional Evil*. New York: Cambridge University Press, 2006.

———. "Establishing Judicial Review? Schooner Peggy and the Early Marshall Court." *Political Research Quarterly* 51, no. 1 (March 1998): 221–39.

———. "Federalist or Friends of Adams: The Marshall Court and Party Politics." *Studies in American Political Development* 12 (October 1998): 229–66.

———. "Judicial Supremacy Revisited: Independent Constitutional Authority in American Constitutional Law and Practice." *William and Mary Law Review* 58, no. 5 (2016–17): 1549–607.

———. "The Nonmajoritarian Difficulty: Legislative Deference to the Judiciary." *Studies in American Political Development* 7 (Spring 1993): 35–73.

———. "The Passive-Aggressive Virtues: *Cohens v. Virginia* and the Problematic Establishment of Judicial Power." *Constitutional Commentary* 12, no. 2 (Spring 1995): 67–92.

———. "The Problematic Establishment of Judicial Review." In *The Supreme Court and American Politics: New Institutionalist Interpretations*, edited by Howard Gillman and Cornell Clayton, 28–42. Lawrence: University Press of Kansas, 1999.

———. *Rethinking Abortion: Equal Choice, the Constitution, and Reproductive Politics*.

Gray, Mark M., Paul M. Perl, and Mary E. Bendyna. "Camelot Only Comes but Once? John F. Kerry and the Catholic Vote." *Presidential Studies Quarterly* 36, no. 2 (2006): 203–22.

Greeley, Andrew M. *The American Catholic: A Social Portrait*. New York: Basic Books, 1977.

Greenhouse, Linda. *Becoming Justice Blackmun: Harry Blackmun's Supreme Court Journey*. New York: Times Books, 2005.

——— . "How Not to Be Chief Justice: The Apprenticeship of William H. Rehnquist." *University of Pennsylvania Law Review* 154, no. 6 (June 2006): 1365–72.

——— . *Justice on the Brink.* New York: Random House, 2022.

Greenhouse, Linda, and Reva B. Siegel. *Before Roe v. Wade: Voices That Shaped the Abortion Debate before the Supreme Court's Ruling.* New Haven: Yale Law Library, 2012.

Grove, Tara Leigh. "A (Modest) Separation of Powers Success Story." *Notre Dame Law Review* 87, no. 4 (2012): 1647–72.

Gunther, Gerald. "The Subtle Vices of the 'Passive Virtues': A Comment on Principle and Expediency in Judicial Review." *Columbia Law Review* 64, no. 1 (January 1964): 1–25.

Haldeman, H. R. *The Haldeman Diaries: Inside the Nixon White House.* New York: G. P. Putnam's Sons, 2017.

Hall, Matthew E. K. *The Nature of Supreme Court Power.* New York: Cambridge University Press, 2013.

——— . "Rethinking Regime Politics." *Law and Social Inquiry* 37, no. 4 (2012): 878–907.

Hand, Learned. *The Bill of Rights.* Cambridge, MA: Harvard University Press, 1958.

Haney-López, Ian. *Dog Whistle Politics: How Coded Racial Appeals Have Reinvented Racism and Wrecked the Middle Class.* New York: Oxford University Press, 2015.

Hanna, Mary T. *Catholics and American Politics.* Cambridge, MA: Harvard University Press, 1979.

Harbaugh, W. T. "If People Vote because They Like to, Then Why Do So Many of Them Lie?" *Public Choice* 89, no. 2 (October 1996): 63–76.

Hathorn, Billy B. "The Changing Politics of Race: Congressman Albert William Watson and the S.C. Party, 1965–1970." *South Carolina Historical Magazine* 89, no. 4 (October 1988): 227–41.

Hays, Bradley D. "Party with the Court: Political Parties and the National Judiciary in the Creation, Maintenance, and Transformation of Political Orders." PhD diss., University of Maryland, College Park, 2005.

Heffington, Colton, Brandon Beomseob Park, and Laron K. Williams. "The 'Most Important Problem' Dataset (MIPD): A New Dataset on American Issue Importance." *Conflict Management and Peace Science* 36, no. 3 (May 2019): 312–35.

Helms, Jesse. *Here's Where I Stand: A Memoir.* New York: Random House, 2005.

Henshaw, Stanley K., Jacqueline Darroch Forrest, and Ellen Blaine. "Abortion Services in the United States, 1981 and 1982." *Family Planning Perspectives* 16, no. 3 (March–April 1984): 119–27.

Hill, Seth J., Daniel J. Hopkins, and Gregory A. Huber. "Not by Turnout Alone: Measuring the Sources of Electoral Change, 2012 to 2016." *Science Advances* 7, no. 17 (April 2021): 1–10.

Hillson, Jon. *The Battle of Boston: Busing and the Struggle for School Desegregation.* New York: Pathfinder Press, 1997.

Hillygus, D. Sunshine, and Todd G. Shields. *The Persuadable Voter: Wedge Issues in Presidential Campaigns.* Princeton: Princeton University Press, 2008.

Himmelstein, Jerome L. *To the Right: The Transformation of American Conservatism.* Berkeley: University of California Press, 1992.

Hinton, Elizabeth. *From the War on Poverty to the War on Crime: The Making of Mass Incarceration in America.* Cambridge, MA: Harvard University Press, 2016.

Hitchcock, William I. *The Age of Eisenhower: America and the World in the 1950s.* New York: Simon & Schuster, 2018.

Hollis-Brusky, Amanda. *Ideas with Consequences: The Federalist Society and the Conservative Counterrevolution.* New York: Oxford University Press, 2015.

Hook, Jay. "A Brief Life of James Bradley Thayer." *Northwestern University Law Review* 88, no. 1 (Fall 1993): 1–8.

Horn, Teena F., Alan Huffman, and John Griffin Jones. *Lines Were Drawn: Remembering Court-Ordered Integration at a Mississippi High School.* Oxford, MS: University of Mississippi Press, 2016.

Horowitz, Morton J. "The Warren Court and the Pursuit of Justice." *Washington and Lee Law Review* 50, no. 1 (1993): 5–13.

Hout, Michael. "Abortion Politics in the United States, 1972–1994: From Single Issue to Ideology." *Gender Issues* 17, no. 2 (1999): 3–34.

Hout, Michael, Stuart Perrett, and Sarah K. Cowan. "Stasis and Sorting of Americans' Abortion Opinions: Political Polarization Added to Religious and Other Differences." *Socius* 8 (January 2022): 1–11.

Hull, N. E. H., and Peter Charles Hoffer. *Roe v. Wade: The Abortion Rights Controversy in American History.* Lawrence: University Press of Kansas, 2021.

Hutchinson, Dennis J. "Unanimity and Desegregation: Decisionmaking in the Supreme Court, 1948–1958." *Georgetown Law Journal* 68, no. 1 (October 1979): 1–96.

Israel, Jerold H. "Criminal Procedure, the Burger Court, and the Legacy of the Warren Court." *Michigan Law Review* 75, no. 7 (June 1977): 1320–425.

Jackson, Vicki C. "Thayer, Holmes, Brandeis: Conceptions of Judicial Review, Factfinding, and Proportionality." *Harvard Law Review* 130, no. 9 (2017): 2348–96.

Jacobson, Gary C. "Extreme Referendum: Donald Trump and the 2018 Midterm Elections." *Political Science Quarterly* 134, no. 1 (2019): 9–38.

———. "The Triumph of Polarized Partisanship in 2016: Donald Trump's Improbable Victory." *Political Science Quarterly* 132, no. 1 (2017): 9–41.

Jeffries, John C., Jr. *Justice Louis F. Powell, Jr.* New York: Scribner, 1994.

Jeffries, John C., Jr., and James E. Ryan. "A Political History of the Establishment Clause." *Michigan Law Review* 100, no. 2 (November 2001): 279–370.

Jelen, Ted G., and Clyde Wilcox. "Causes and Consequences of Public Attitudes toward Abortion: A Review and Research Agenda." *Political Research Quarterly* 56, no. 4 (2003): 489–500.

Jenkins, John A. *The Partisan: The Life of William Rehnquist.* New York: Public Affairs, 2012.

Jennings, Will, and Christopher Wlezien. "Preferences, Problems and Representation." *Political Science Research and Methods* 3, no. 3 (2015): 659–81.

Johnson, Walter. *How We Drafted Adlai Stevenson.* New York: Knopf, 1955.

Jones, Nathaniel R. "An Anti-Black Strategy and the Supreme Court." *Journal of Law and Education* 4, no. 1 (January 1975): 203–8.

Kahn, Michael A. "Shattering the Myth about President Eisenhower's Supreme Court Appointments." *Presidential Studies Quarterly* 22, no. 1 (1992): 47–56.

Kalman, Laura. *Abe Fortas: A Biography.* New Haven: Yale University Press, 1992.

———. "The Constitution, the Supreme Court, and the New Deal." *American Historical Review* 100, no. 4 (October 2005): 1052–80.

———. *FDR's Gambit: The Court Packing Fight and the Rise of Legal Liberalism.* Oxford: Oxford University Press, 2002.

———. "On 'Roe' at Forty." *Reviews in American History* 41, no. 4 (2013): 756–66.

———. *The Long Reach of the Sixties: LBJ, Nixon, and the Making of the Contemporary Supreme Court.* New York: Oxford University Press, 2017.

———. *Right Star Rising: A New Politics, 1974–1980.* New York: W.W. Norton, 2010.

———. *The Strange Career of Legal Liberalism.* New Haven: Yale University Press, 1996.

———. *Yale Law School and the Sixties: Revolt and Reverberations.* Chapel Hill: University of North Carolina Press, 2005.

Kam, Cindy D. "Who Toes the Party Line? Cues, Values, and Individual Differences." *Political Behavior* 27, no. 2 (June 2005): 163–82.

Kamisar, Yale. "Can (Did) Congress 'Overrule' *Miranda?*" *Cornell Law Review* 85, no. 4 (2000): 936–50.

———. "Remembering the 'Old World' of Criminal Procedure: A Reply to Professor Grano." *University of Michigan Journal of Law Reform* 23, no. 4 (1990): 537–89.

Karol, David. *Party Position Change in American Politics: Coalition Management.* New York: Cambridge University Press, 2009.

Karol, David, and Chloe N. Thurston. "From Personal to Partisan: Abortion, Party, and Religion among California State Legislators." *Studies in American Political Development* 34, no. 1 (April 2020): 91–109.

Karrer, Robert N. "The National Right to Life Committee: Its Founding, Its History, and the Emergence of the Pro-Life Movement Prior to *Roe v. Wade.*" *Catholic Historical Review* 97, no. 3 (July 2011): 527–77.

Katz, Ellis. "Patterns of Compliance with the *Schempp* Decision." *Journal of Public Law* 14 (1965): 396–408.

Keck, Thomas M. *Judicial Politics in Polarized Times.* Chicago: University of Chicago Press, 2014.

———. *The Most Activist Supreme Court in History: The Road to Modern Judicial Conservatism.* Chicago: University of Chicago Press, 2004.

———. "Party, Policy, or Duty: Why Does the Supreme Court Invalidate Statutes?" *American Political Science Review* 101, no. 2 (May 2007): 321–38.

———. "Party Politics or Judicial Independence: The Regime Politics Literature Hits the Law Schools." *Law and Social Inquiry* 32, no. 2 (Spring 2007): 511–44.

———. "The Relationship between Courts and Legislatures." In *Oxford Handbook of U.S. Judicial Behavior*, edited by Lee Epstein and Stefanie A. Lindquist, 381–98. Oxford: Oxford University Press, 2017.

Keck, Thomas M., and Kevin J. McMahon. "Why *Roe* Still Stands: Abortion Law, the Supreme Court, and the Republican Regime." *Studies in Law, Politics, and Society* 70 (2016): 33–83.

Keith, Bruce E., David B. Magleby, Candice J. Nelson, Elizabeth A. Orr, Mark C. Westlye, and Raymond E. Wolfinger. *The Myth of the Independent Voter.* Berkeley: University of California Press, 1992.

Kelley, Jonathan. "The Politics of School Busing." *Public Opinion Quarterly* 38, no. 1 (Spring 1971): 23–39.

Kernell, Samuel. *Going Public: New Strategies of Presidential Leadership.* Washington, DC: CQ Press, 1986.

Key, V. O. *Politics, Parties, and Pressure Groups.* New York: Thomas Y. Cromwell, 1942.

Killian, Mitchell, and Clyde Wilcox. "Do Abortion Attitudes Lead to Party Switching?" *Political Research Quarterly* 61, no. 4 (2008): 561–73.

Kingdon, John W. *Agendas, Alternatives, and Public Policies*

Kirp, David L. "Race, Schooling, and Interest Politics: The Oakland Story." *School Review* 87, no. 4 (August 1979): 355–97.

Klarman, Michael J. "Brown, Originalism, and Constitutional Theory: A Response to Professor McConnell." *Virginia Law Review* 81, no. 7 (October 1995): 1881–1936.

———. "Courts, Social Change, and Political Backlash." Hart Lecture at Georgetown Law Center, March 31, 2011. Available at http://scholarship.law.georgetown.edu/cgilviewcontent.cgi?article= 1001&context-hartlecture.

———. *The Framers' Coup: The Making of the United States Constitution.* New York: Oxford University Press, 2016.

———. *From the Closet to the Altar: Courts, Backlash, and the Struggle for Same-Sex Marriage.* New York: Oxford University Press, 2014.

———. *From Jim Crow to Civil Rights: The Supreme Court and the Struggle for Racial Equality.* Oxford: Oxford University Press, 2006.

———. "Rethinking the Civil Rights and Civil Liberties Revolutions." *Virginia Law Review* 82, no. 1 (February 1996): 1–67.

———. "Rethinking the History of American Freedom." *William and Mary Law Review* 42, no. 1 (October 2000): 265–88.

———. "*Windsor* and *Brown*: Marriage Equality and Racial Equality." *Harvard Law Review* 127, no. 1 (November 2013): 127–160.

Kleinerman, Benjamin A. *The Discretionary President: The Promise and Peril of Executive Power.* Lawrence: University Press of Kansas, 2009.

Kluger, Richard. *Simple Justice: The History of Brown v. Board of Education and Black America's Struggle for Equality.* New York: Vintage Books, 2004.

K'Meyer, Tracy E. *From Brown to Meredith: The Long Struggle for School Desegregation in Louisville Kentucky, 1954–2007.* Chapel Hill: University of North Carolina Press, 2013, 67.

Koh, Harold Hongju. "Justice Blackmun and the 'World Out There.'" *Yale Law Journal* 104, no. 1 (October 1994): 23–31.

Kotlowski, Dean J. *Nixon's Civil Rights: Politics, Principle, and Policy.* Cambridge, MA: Harvard University Press, 2001.

Kritzer, Herbert M. "Martin Shapiro: Anticipating the New Institutionalism." In *Pioneers of Judicial Behavior,* 387–417.

Kronman, Anthony T. "Alexander Bickel's Philosophy of Prudence." *Yale Law Journal* 95, no. 7 (June 1985): 1567–616.

LaHaye, Beverly. *The Spirit Controlled Woman.* Eugene, OR: Harvest House, 1976.

Lain, Corinna Barrett. "Countermajoritarian Hero or Zero? Rethinking the Warren Court's Role in the Criminal Procedure Revolution." *University of Pennsylvania Law Review* 152, no. 4 (2004): 1361–452.

———. "God, Civic Virtue, and the American Way: Reconstructing *Engel.*" *Stanford Law Review* 67, no. 3 (2015): 479–555.

———. "Three Supreme Court 'Failures' and a Story of Supreme Court Success." *Vanderbilt Law Review* 69, no. 4 (2016): 1019–74.

———. "Upside-Down Judicial Review." *Georgetown Law Journal* 101, no. 1 (2012): 113–83.

Lassen, David Dreyer. "The Effect of Information on Voter Turnout: Evidence from a Natural Experiment." *American Journal of Political Science* 49, no. 1 (January 2005): 103–18.

Lassiter, Matthew D. *The Silent Majority: Suburban Politics in the Sunbelt South.* Princeton: Princeton University Press, 2007.

Lau, Peter F., ed. *From the Grassroots to the Supreme Court: Brown v. Board of Education and American Democracy*. Constitutional Conflicts. Durham, NC: Duke University Press, 2004.

Lau, Richard R. "Correct Voting in the 2008 U.S. Presidential Nominating Elections." *Political Behavior* 35, no. 2 (2013): 331–55.

Layman, Geoffrey. *The Great Divide: Religious and Cultural Conflict in American Party Politics*. New York: Columbia University Press, 2001.

Leiken, Lawrence S. "Police Interrogation in Colorado: The Implementation of Miranda." *Denver Law Journal* 47, no. 1 (1970): 1–53.

Lemieux, Scott E., and George Lovell. "Legislative Defaults: Interbranch Power Sharing and Abortion Politics." *Polity* 42, no. 2 (2010): 210–43.

Lemieux, Scott E., and David J. Watkins. "Beyond the 'Countermajoritarian Difficulty': Lessons from Contemporary Democratic Theory." *Polity* 41, no. 1 (2009): 30–62.

Leo, Richard A. "The Impact of Miranda Revisited." *Journal of Criminal Law and Criminology* 86, no. 3 (Spring 1996): 621–92.

Leuchtenburg, William E. "Comment on Laura Kalman's Article." *American Historical Review* 100, no. 4 (October 2005): 1081–93.

Levinson, Daryl J. "Parchment and Politics: The Positive Puzzle of Constitutional Government." *Harvard Law Review* 124, no. 3 (January 2011): 659–746.

Levinson, Sanford. *Our Undemocratic Constitution*. Oxford: Oxford University Press, 2008.

Levy, Leonard W. *Against the Law: The Nixon Court and Criminal Justice*. New York: Harper & Row, 1976.

Lichtman, Robert M. *The Supreme Court and McCarthy-Era Repression: One Hundred Decisions*. Champaign: University of Illinois Press, 2012.

Lindaman, Kara, and Donald P. Haider-Markel. "Issue Evolution, Political Parties, and the Culture Wars." *Political Research Quarterly* 55, no. 1 (March 2002): 91–110.

Littlejohn, Jeffrey L., and Charles H. Ford. *Elusive Equality: Desegregation and Resegregation in Norfolk's Public Schools*. Charlottesville: University of Virginia Press, 2012.

Lovell, George. *Legislative Deferrals: Statutory Ambiguity, Judicial Power, and American Democracy*. Cambridge, UK: Cambridge University Press, 2003.

Lovell, George I., and Scott E. Lemieux. "Assessing Juristocracy: Are Judges Rulers or Agents?" *Maryland Law Review* 65, no. 1 (2006): 100–14.

Lowndes, Joseph E. *From the New Deal to the New Right: Race and the Origins of Modern Conservatism*. New Haven: Yale University Press, 2009.

Lowndes, Joseph E., Julie Novkov, and Dorian T. Warren. *Race and American Political Development*. New York: Routledge, 2008.

Luban, David. "Justice Holmes and the Metaphysics of Judicial Restraint." *Duke Law Journal* 43, no. 3 (December 1994): 449–523.

Luks, Samantha, and Salamone Michael. 2008. "Abortion." In *Public Opinion and Constitutional Controversy*, edited by Nathaniel Persily, Jack Citrin, and Patrick J. Egan, 80–107. Oxford, UK: Oxford University Press, 2008.

Lupia, Arthur. "Shortcuts versus Encyclopedias: Information and Voting Behavior in California Insurance Reform Elections." *American Political Science Review* 88, no. 1 (1994): 63–76.

Maclin, Tracy. "*Terry v. Ohio's* Fourth Amendment Legacy: Black Men and Police Discretion." *St. John's Law Review* 72, no. 3–4 (1998): 1271–317.

Magalhães, Pedro C., John H. Aldrich, and Rachel K. Gibson. "New Forms of Mobilization, New People Mobilized? Evidence from the Comparative Study of Electoral Systems." *Party Politics* 26, no. 5 (2020): 605–18.

Magleby, David B., Candice J. Nelson, and Mark C. Westlye. "The Myth of the Independent Voter Revisited." In *Facing the Challenge of Democracy: Explorations in the Analysis of Public Opinion and Political Participation*, edited by Paul M. Sniderman and Benjamin Highton, 238–66. Princeton: Princeton University Press, 2011.

Maltz, Earl M. "The Triumph of the Southern Man: *Dowell, Shelby County*, and the Jurisprudence of Lewis F. Powell, Jr." *Duke Journal of Constitutional Law and Public Policy* 14, no. 1 (June 2019): 169–232.

Maltzman, Forrest, James F. Spriggs, and Paul J. Wahlbeck. *Crafting Law on the Supreme Court: The Collegial Game*. New York: Cambridge University Press, 2000.

Marlin, George J. *The American Catholic Voter: 200 Years of Political Impact*. South Bend, IN: St. Augustine's Press, 2004.

Marshall, Thomas R. *American Public Opinion and the Modern Supreme Court, 1930–2020: A Representative Institution*. Lanham, MD: Lexington Books, 2022.

Martin, William. *With God on Our Side: The Rise of the Religious Right in America*. New York: Broadway Books, 2005.

Mason, Robert. *Richard Nixon and the Quest for a New Majority*. Chapel Hill: University of North Carolina Press, 2004.

Mason, Robert, and Iwan Morgan, eds. *Seeking a New Majority: The Republican Party and American Politics, 1960–1980*. Nashville, TN: Vanderbilt University Press, 2013.

Masur, Louis P. *The Soiling of Old Glory: The Story of a Photograph That Shocked America*. New York: Bloomsbury Press, 2008.

Matusow, Allen J. *The Unraveling of America: A History of Liberalism in the 1960s*. New York: Harper & Row, 1984.

Maveety, Nancy, ed. *The Pioneers of Judicial Behavior*. Ann Arbor: University of Michigan Press, 2003.

Mayer, William G., ed. *The Swing Voter in American Politics*. Washington, DC: Brookings Institution Press, 2008.

Mayeux, Sara. "What *Gideon* Did." *Columbia Law Review* 116, no. 1 (2016): 15–104.

Mayhew, David. *Congress: The Electoral Connection*. New Haven: Yale University Press, 1974.

———. *Divided We Govern: Party Control, Lawmaking, and Investigations, 1946–2002*. 2nd ed. New Haven: Yale University Press, 2005.

———. "Electoral Realignments." *Annual Review of Political Science* 3, no. 1 (June 2000): 449–74.

———. *Electoral Realignments: A Critique of an American Genre*. New Haven: Yale University Press, 2004.

———. "Events as Causes." In *Political Contingency: Studying the Unexpected, the Accidental, and the Unforeseen*, edited by Ian Shapiro and Sonu Bedi, 95–119. New York: New York University Press, 2007.

———. *Placing Parties in American Politics: Organization, Electoral Settings, and Government Activity in the Twentieth Century*. Princeton: Princeton University Press, 1986.

———. "Suggested Guidelines for Periodization." *Polity* 37, no. 4 (October 2005): 531–35.

———. "Wars and American Politics." *Perspectives on Politics* 3, no. 3 (September 2005): 473–93.

McAdam, Doug. *Political Process and the Development of Black Insurgency, 1930–1970*. Chicago: University of Chicago Press, 1999.

McAdam, Doug, and Karina Kloos. *Deeply Divided: Racial Politics and Social Movements in Postwar America*. Oxford: Oxford University Press, 2014.

McAndrews, Lawrence J. "The Politics of Principle: Richard Nixon and School Desegregation." *Journal of Negro History* 83, no. 3 (Summer 1998): 187–200.

———. "Unanswered Prayers: Church, State, and School in the Nixon Era." *U.S. Catholic Historian* 13, no. 4 (1995): 86–87.

———. *What They Wished For: American Catholics and American Presidents, 1960–2004*. Athens: University of Georgia Press, 2014.

McCann, Michael W. "Reform Litigation on Trial." *Law and Social Inquiry* 1, no. 4 (Fall 1992): 715–43.

McCloskey, Robert G. *The American Supreme Court*. Chicago: University of Chicago Press, 2000.

———. *The Modern Supreme Court*. Cambridge, MA: Harvard University Press, 1972.

McConnell, Michael W. "Originalism and the Desegregation Decisions." *Virginia Law Review* 81, no. 4 (May 1995): 947–1140.

McGirr, Lisa. *Suburban Warriors: The Origins of the New American Right*. Princeton: Princeton University Press, 2015.

McGreevy, John T. *Parish Boundaries: The Catholic Encounter with Race in the Twentieth-Century Urban North*. Chicago: University of Chicago Press, 1996.

McHugh, Rev. Msgr. James T. "Statement." *Catholic Lawyer* 19, no. 1 (Winter 1973): 33–34.

McKeegan, Michele. *Abortion Politics: Mutiny in the Ranks of the Right.* New York: Free Press, 1992.

McMahon, Kevin J. *Nixon's Court.* Chicago: University of Chicago Press, 2011.

———. *Reconsidering Roosevelt on Race: How the Presidency Paved the Road to Brown.* Chicago: University of Chicago Press, 2004.

———. "Will the Court Still 'Seldom Stray Very Far'? Regime Politics in a Polarized America." *Chicago-Kent Law Review* 93, no. 2 (2018): 343–71.

McPherson, Harry. *A Political Education: A Washington Memoir.* Austin: University of Texas Press, 1995.

McVicar, Michael J. "The Religious Right in America." In *The Oxford Encyclopedia of Religion in America*, edited by John Corrigan. New York: Oxford University Press, 2018.

Medalie, Richard, Leonard Zeitz, and Paul Alexander. "Custodial Police Interrogation in Our Nation's Capital: The Attempt to Implement *Miranda.*" *Michigan Law Review* 66, no. 7 (1968): 1347–422.

Metcalf, George R. *From Little Rock to Boston: The History of School Desegregation.* Westport, CT: Greenwood Press, 1983.

Miller, Gary, and Norman Schofield. "Activists and Partisan Realignment in the United States." *American Political Science Review* 97, no. 2 (May 2003): 245–60.

———. "The Transformation of the Republican and Democratic Party Coalitions in the U.S." *Perspectives on Politics* 6, no. 3 (September 2008): 433–50.

Miller, Merle. *Plain Speaking: An Oral Biography of Harry S. Truman.* New York: Putnam Books, 1974.

Miroff, Bruce. *The Liberals' Moment: The McGovern Insurgency and the Identity Crisis of the Democratic Party.* Lawrence: University Press of Kansas, 2007.

Moniz, Philip, and Christopher Wlezien. "Issue Salience and Political Decisions." In *Oxford Research Encyclopedia of Politics.* New York: Oxford University Press, 2020.

Moran, Peter William. "Difficult from the Start: Implementing the Brown Decision in Kansas City, Missouri Public Schools." *Equity and Excellence in Education* 37, no. 2 (2004): 278–88.

Moraski, Bryon J., and Charles R. Shipan. "The Politics of Supreme Court Nominations: A Theory of Institutional Constraints and Choices." *American Journal of Political Science* 43, no. 4 (1999): 1069–95.

Moyer, Laura P., and Ellen M. Key. "Political Opportunism, Position Taking, and Court-Curbing Legislation." *Justice System Journal* 39, no. 2 (April 2018): 155–70.

Murphy, Paul L. *The Constitution in Crisis Times, 1918–1969.* New York: Harper and Row, 1972.

Murphy, Walter F. *Congress and the Court*. Chicago: University of Chicago Press, 1962.

Murray, Melissa, Katherine Shaw, and Reva B. Siegel, eds. *Reproductive Rights and Justice Stories*. St. Paul, MN: Foundation Press, 2019.

Nagel, Stuart S. "Court Curbing Periods in American History." *Vanderbilt Law Review* 18 (1965): 925–44.

Nash, George H. *The Conservative Intellectual Movement in America since 1945*. New York: Basic Books, 1976.

Nesson, Charles. "The Harlan-Frankfurter Connection: An Aspect of Justice Harlan's Judicial Education." *New York Law School Law Review* 36, no. 1 (January1991): 179–97.

Neubauer, David W. *Criminal Justice in Middle America*. Morristown, NJ: General Learning Press, 1974.

Newman, Roger K. "The Warren Court and American Politics: An Impressionistic Appreciation." *Constitutional Commentary* 18 (2001): 661–98.

Newmyer, R. Kent. *John Marshall and the Heroic Age of the Supreme Court*. Baton Rouge: Louisiana State University Press, 2007.

Nichols, Curt. "The Presidency and the Political Order: In Context." *Polity* 43, no. 4 (October 2011): 513–32.

———. "The 'Second Wave' of Political Time Scholarship. And, Beyond!" *USAbroad—Journal of American History and Politics* 5, no. 1 (2022): 29–42.

Nichols, Curt, Dave Bridge, and Adam Carrington. "Court-Curbing via Attempt to Amend the Constitution: An Update of Congressional Attacks on the Supreme Court from 1955–1984." *Justice Systems Journal* 35, no. 4 (2014): 1–13.

Nichols, Curt, and Adam S. Myers, "Exploiting the Opportunity for Reconstructive Leadership: Presidential Responses to Enervated Presidential Regimes." *American Politics Research* 38, no 5. (September 2010): 806–41.

Nichols, David A. *A Matter of Justice: Eisenhower and the Beginning of the Civil Rights Revolution*. New York: Simon & Schuster, 2007.

Nichter, Simeon. "Vote Buying or Turnout Buying? Machine Politics and the Secret Ballot." *American Political Science Review* 102, no. 1 (2008): 19–31.

Nixon, Richard. *The Memoirs of Richard Nixon*. New York: Rosset & Dunlap, 1978.

Novak, Michael. *The Rise of the Unmeltable Ethnics: The New Political Force of the Seventies*. New York: Macmillan, 1972.

———. *Unmeltable Ethnics: Politics and Culture in American Life*. New Brunswick, NJ: Transaction, 1995.

O'Brian, Neil A. "Before Reagan: The Development of Abortion's Partisan Divide." *Perspectives on Politics* 18, no. 4 (2020): 1031–47.

O'Brien, David J. *American Catholics and Social Reform: The New Deal Years*. New York: Oxford University Press, 1968.

Orfield, Myron. "*Milliken, Meredith,* and Metropolitan Segregation." *UCLA Law Review* 62, no. 2 (2015): 364–462.

Orren, Karen. "Union Politics and Postwar Liberalism in the United States, 1946–1979." *Studies in American Political Development* 1, no. 1 (Spring 1986): 215–252.

Orren, Karen, and Stephen Skowronek. "Beyond the Iconography of Order: Notes for a 'New Institutionalism." In *The Dynamics of American Politics: Approaches and Interpretations,* edited by Lawrence C. Dodd and Calvin Jillson, 311–330. Boulder, CO: Westview Press, 1994.

———. *The Search for American Political Development.* New York: Cambridge University Press, 2004.

Pearson, Drew, and Robert S. Allen. *The Nine Old Men.* Garden City, NY: Doubleday, Doran, 1937.

Peffley, Mark, and Jon Hurwitz. "The Racial Component of 'Race-Neutral' Crime Policy Attitudes." *Political Psychology* 23 (March 2002): 1–31.

Peretti, Terri. *In Defense of a Political Court.* Princeton: Princeton University Press, 1999.

———. *Partisan Supremacy: How the G.O.P Enlisted Courts to Rig America's Elections Rules.* Lawrence: University Press of Kansas, 2020.

Petrocik, John Richard. "Measuring Party Support: Leaners Are Not Independents." *Electoral Studies* 28, no. 4 (December 2009): 562–72.

Phillips, Kevin. *Post-Conservative America: People, Politics, and Ideology in a Time of Crisis.* New York: Vintage Books, 1983.

Philips-Fein, Kim. *Invisible Hands: The Making of the Conservative Movement from the New Deal to Ronald Reagan.* New York: W. W. Norton, 2009.

Pickerill, J. Mitchell. *Constitutional Deliberation in Congress: The Impact of Judicial Review in a Separated System.* Durham, NC: Duke University Press, 2004.

Pius XI, Pope. *Quadragesimo Anno = Encyclical Letter on Reconstructing the Social Order.* Washington, DC: National Catholic Welfare Conference, 1942.

Plotke, David. *Building a Democratic Political Order: Reshaping Liberalism in the 1930s and 1940s.* New York: Cambridge University Press, 1996.

Polsky, Andrew J. "No Tool Is Perfect: Periodization in the Study of American Political Development." *Polity* 37, no. 4 (October 2005): 523–30.

———. "Partisan Regimes in American Politics." *Polity* 44, no. 1 (January 2012): 51–80.

———. "Shifting Currents: Dwight Eisenhower and the Dynamic of Presidential Opportunity Structure." *Presidential Studies Quarterly* 45, no. 1 (2015): 91–109.

Porwancher, Andrew, Jake Mazeitis, Taylor Jipp, and Austin Coffey. *The Prophet of Harvard Law: James Bradley Thayer and His Legal Legacy.* Lawrence: University Press of Kansas, 2002.

Post, Robert, and Reva Siegel. "*Roe* Rage: Democratic Constitutionalism and Backlash." *Harvard Civil Rights-Civil Liberties Law Review* 42 (2007): 373–433.

Powe, Lucas A., Jr. *The Supreme Court and the American Elite, 1789–2008.* Lawrence: University Press of Kansas, 2008.

———. *The Warren Court and American Politics.* Cambridge, MA: Belknap Press of Harvard University Press, 2000.

Pratt, Robert. A. *The Color of Their Skin, Education and Race in Richmond, Virginia.* Charlottesville: University Press of Virginia, 1992.

Pride, Richard A., and J. David Woodard. *The Burden of Busing: The Politics of Desegregation in Nashville, Tennessee.* Knoxville: University of Tennessee Press, 1985.

Prior, Markus. "News vs. Entertainment: How Increasing Media Choice Widens Gaps in Political Knowledge and Turnout." *American Journal of Political Science* 49, no. 3 (July 2005): 577–92.

———. "You've Either Got It or You Don't? The Stability of Political Interest over the Life Cycle." *Journal of Politics* 72, no. 3 (2010): 747–66.

Pritchett, C. Herman. *Congress versus the Supreme Court.* Minneapolis: University of Minnesota Press, 1960.

Purcell, Edward A. Jr. "Alexander M. Bickel and the Post-Realist Constitution." *Harvard Civil Rights-Civil Liberties Law Review* 11, no. 3 (1976): 521–64.

Purnell, Brian, Jeanne Theoharis, and Komozi Woodard, eds. *The Strange Careers of the Jim Crow North: Segregation and Struggle outside of the South.* New York: NYU Press, 2019.

Rae, Nicole C. *The Decline and Fall of the Liberal Republicans.* New York: Oxford University Press, 1989.

Rapeli, Lauri. "Does Sophistication Affect Electoral Outcomes?" *Government and Opposition* 53, no. 2 (April 2018): 181–204.

Rehnquist, William. "A Random Thought on the Segregation Cases." Memo from law Clerk William H. Rehnquist to Justice Robert H. Jackson, December 12, 1952.

Reich, Donald E. "Schoolhouse Religion and the Supreme Court: A Report on Attitudes of Teachers and Principals and on School Practices in Wisconsin and Ohio." *Journal of Legal Education* 23, no. 1 (1970): 123–43.

Richey, Sean. "The Social Basis of Voting Correctly." *Political Communication* 25, no. 4 (2008): 366–76.

Robinson, Cyril D. "Police and Prosecutor Practices and Attitudes Relating to Interrogation as Revealed by Pre – and Post-*Miranda* Questionnaires: A Construct of Police Capacity to Comply." *Duke Law Journal* (1968): 425–524.

Rosenberg, Gerald N. "The Broken-Hearted Lover: Erwin Chemerinsky's Romantic Longings for a Mythical Court." *Vanderbilt Law Review* 69, no. 4 (2019): 1075–113.

———. *The Hollow Hope: Can Courts Bring about Social Change?* Chicago: University of Chicago Press, 1991.

———. "The Importance of Being Political: How to Understand the US Supreme Court's Approach to Affirmative Action in Education." *National Law School Journal* 16, no. 1 (2022): 66–98.

———. "Judicial Independence and the Reality of Political Power." *Review of Politics* 54 (Summer 1992): 391.

———. "The Road Taken: Robert A. Dahl's Decision-Making in a Democracy: The Supreme Court as a National Policy-Maker." *Emory Law Journal* 50, no. 2 (2001): 613–30.

———. "Romancing the Court." *Boston University Law Review* 89, no. 2 (April 2009): 563–79.

———. "The Surprising Resilience of State Opposition to Abortion: The Supreme Court, Federalism, and the Role of Intense Minorities in the U.S. Politics System." *Saint Louis University Public Law Review* 34, no. 2 (2015): 241–58.

———. "The Triumph of Politics: The Republican Party's Takeover of the US Supreme Court." *National Law School Journal* 16, no. 1 (2022): 99–106.

———. "The Wonder of It All." *Tulsa Law Review* 45, no. 4 (Summer 2010): 679–89.

Ross, William G. "Attacks on the Warren Court by State Officials: A Case Study of Why Court-Curbing Movements Fail." *Buffalo Law Review* 50, no. 2 (April 2002): 483–612.

———. *A Muted Fury: Populists, Progressives, and Labor Unions Confront the Courts, 1890–1937.* Princeton: Princeton University Press, 1994.

Rothstein, Richard. *The Color of Law: A Forgotten History of How Our Government Segregated America.* New York: Liveright, 2018.

Rottinghaus, Brandon. "Assessing the Unilateral Presidency: Constraints and Contingencies." *Congress and the Presidency* 42, no. 3 (2015): 287–92.

Rubin, Eva R. *Abortion, Politics, and the Courts: Roe v. Wade and Its Aftermath.* Westport, CT: Greenwood Press, 1987.

Ryan, James E. "'*Brown*,' School Choice, and the Suburban Veto." *Virginia Law Review* 90, no. 6 (2004): 1635–47.

Ryan, James E., and Michael Heise. "The Political Economy of School Choice." *Yale Law Journal* 111, no. 1 (October 2001): 2043–136.

Ryan, John B., and Caitlin Milazzo. "The South, the Suburbs, and the Vatican Too: Partisanship in Context." *Political Behavior* 37, no. 2 (June 2015): 441–63.

Sabin, Arthur J. *In Calmer Times: The Supreme Court and Red Monday.* Philadelphia: University of Pennsylvania Press, 1999.

Sanders, Elizabeth. "In Defense of Realignment and Regimes: Why We Need Periodization." *Polity* 37, no. 4 (October 2005): 536–40.

Sarat, Austin, ed. *Race, Law and Culture: Reflections on Brown v. Board of Education*. Oxford: Oxford University Press, 1997.

Scalia, Antonin. *A Matter of Interpretation*. Princeton: Princeton University Press, 1998.

——. "The Rule of Law as a Law of Rules." *University of Chicago Law Review* 54, no. 4 (Fall 1989): 1175–88.

Schlafly, Phyllis. "A Short History of the E.R.A.," *Phyllis Schlafly Report*, September 1986.

Schattschneider, E. E. *Party Government*. New York: Holt, Rinehart, and Winston, 1942.

Schickler, Eric. *Racial Realignment: The Transformation of American Liberalism, 1932–1965*. Princeton: Princeton University Press, 2016.

Schlozman, Daniel. *When Movements Anchor Parties: Electoral Alignments in American History*. Princeton: Princeton University Press, 2015.

Schofield, Norman, and Gary Miller. "Elections and Activist Coalitions in the United States." *American Journal of Political Science* 51, no. 3 (July 2007): 518–31.

Schulman, Bruce J., and Julian E. Zelizer, ed. *Rightward Bound: Making America Conservative in the 1970s*. Cambridge, MA: Harvard University Press, 2008.

Schwartz, Bernard. *Swann's Way: The School Busing Case and the Supreme Court*. Oxford: Oxford University Press, 1986.

Scribner, Todd. *A Partisan Church: American Catholicism and the Rise of Neoconservative Catholics*. Washington, DC: Catholic University Press, 2015.

Seeburger, Richard H., and R. Stanton Wettick Jr. "*Miranda* in Pittsburgh—A Statistical Study." *University of Pittsburgh Law Review* 29, no. 1 (1967): 1–26.

Segal, Jeffrey A., and Albert D. Cover. "Ideological Values and the Votes of U.S. Supreme Court Justices." *American Political Science Review* 83, no. 2 (June 1989): 557–565.

Segal, Jeffrey A., and Harold J. Spaeth. *The Supreme Court and the Attitudinal Model Revisited*. Cambridge, UK: Cambridge University Press, 2002.

Segal, Jeffrey A., Richard J. Timpone, and Robert M. Howard. "Buyer Beware? Presidential Success through Supreme Court Appointments." *Political Research Quarterly* 53, no. 3 (2000): 557–73.

Self, Robert O. *All in the Family: The Realignment of American Democracy since the 1960s*. New York: Hill and Wang, 2012.

Sellars, Nigel Anthony. "Cold Hard Facts: Justice Brandeis and the Oklahoma Ice Case." *Historian* 63, no. 2 (Winter 2001): 249–67.

Seymour, Martin Lipset, and Stein Rokkan. *Party Systems and Voter Alignments: Cross-National Perspectives*. Toronto, ON: Free Press, 1967.

Shafer, Byron E., and William J. M. Claggett. *The Two Majorities: The Issue Context of Modern American Politics*. Baltimore: Johns Hopkins University Press, 1995.

Shafer, Byron E., and Richard Johnston. *The End of Southern Exceptionalism: Class, Race, and Partisan Change in the Postwar South*. Cambridge, MA: Harvard University Press, 2009.

Shapiro, Martin. *Law and Politics in the Supreme Court: New Approaches to Political Jurisprudence*. New York: Free Press of Glencoe, 1964.

———. "Public Law and Judicial Politics." In *Political Science: The State of the Disciple II*, edited by Ada W. Finifter, 365–81. Washington, DC: American Political Science Association, 1993.

Sharlow, Carrie. "Michigan Lawyers in History: Stephen J. Roth." *Michigan Bar Journal* (October 2012): 44–45.

Sheingate, Adam D. "Political Entrepreneurship, Institutional Change, and American Political Development." *Studies in American Political Development* 17, no. 2 (2003): 185–203.

Siegel, Reva B. "The Right's Reasons: Constitutional Conflict and the Spread of Woman-Protective Anti-Abortion Argument." *Duke Law Journal* 57, no. 6 (2008): 1641–92.

———. "Sex Equality Arguments for Reproductive Rights: Their Critical Basis and Evolving Constitutional Expression." *Emory Law Journal* 56, no. 4 (2007): 815–42.

Sill, Kaitlyn L., Joseph Daniel Ura, and Stacia L. Haynie. "Strategic Passing and Opinion Assignment on the Burger Court." *Justice System Journal* 31, no. 2 (2010): 164–79.

Silverstein, Gordon. *Law's Allure: How Law Shapes, Constrains, Saves, and Kills Politics*. New York: Cambridge University Press, 2009.

Silverstein, Gordon, and John Hanley. "The Supreme Court and Public Opinion in Times of War and Crisis." *Hastings Law Journal* 61, no.6 (2010): 1453–501.

Simon, James F. *Eisenhower vs. Warren: The Battle for Civil Rights and Liberties*. New York: Liveright, 2018.

———. *What Kind of Nation: Thomas Jefferson, John Marshall, and the Epic Struggle to Create a United States*. New York: Simon & Schuster, 2006.

Sitkoff, Harvard. *The Struggle for Black Equality*. 25th anniversary ed. New York: Hill and Wang, 2008.

Skowronek, Stephen. *The Politics Presidents Make: Leadership from John Adams to George Bush*. Cambridge, MA: Harvard University Press, 1997.

———. *Presidential Leadership in Political Time: Reprise and Reappraisal*. Lawrence: University Press of Kansas, 2011.

Smidt, Corwin. "Polarization and the Decline of the American Floating Voter." *American Journal of Political Science* 61, no. 2 (2015): 365–81.

Smith, Gregory A. "One Church, Many Messages: The Politics of the U.S. Catholic Clergy." In *Catholics and Politics: The Dynamic Tension Between Faith and Power*, edited by Kristin E. Heyer, Mark J. Rozell, and Michael A. Genovese, 43–60. Washington, DC: Georgetown University Press, 2008.

Smith, Rodney K. *Public Prayer and the Constitution*. Wilmington, NC: Scholarly Resources, 1987.

Snyder, Brad. *Democratic Justice: Felix Frankfurter, the Supreme Court, and the Making of the Liberal Establishment*. New York: W. W. Norton, 2022.

——— . "The Former Clerks Who Nearly Killed Judicial Restraint." *Notre Dame Law Review* 89, no. 5 (2014): 2129–54.

——— . "What Would Justice Holmes Do (WWJHD)? Rehnquist's *Plessy* Memo, Majoritarianism, and *Parents Involved*." *Ohio State Law Journal* 69, no. 5 (2008): 873–910.

Spann, Girardeau A. *Race against the Court: The Supreme Court and Minorities in Contemporary America*. New York: NYU Press, 1994.

Steamer, Robert J. "Statesmanship or Craftsmanship: Current Conflict over the Supreme Court." *Western Political Quarterly* 11, no. 2 (1958): 265–77.

——— . *The Supreme Court in Crisis: A History of Conflict*. Amherst, MA: University of Massachusetts Press, 1971.

Steiner, Ronald, Rebecca Bauer, and Rohit Talwar. "The Rise and Fall of the *Miranda* Warnings in Popular Culture." *Cleveland State Law Review* 59, no. 2 (2011): 219–36.

Stephens Jr., Otis, Robert L. Flanders, and J. Lewis Cannon. "Law Enforcement and the Supreme Court: Police Perceptions of the *Miranda* Requirements." *Tennessee Law Review* 39, no. 3 (1972): 407–31.

Stephenson, Adreanne. "Two Sides of the Same Coin: Justice Powell and Justice Marshall's Perspectives on Education and the Law." *Notre Dame Journal of Law, Ethics & Public Policy Online* (2014): 27–60.

Stone, Geoffrey R. *Perilous Times: Free Speech in Wartime*. New York: W. W. Norton, 2004.

Stuntz, William J. *The Collapse of American Criminal Justice*. Cambridge, MA: Belknap Press of Harvard University Press, 2011.

——— . "Local Policing after the Terror." *Yale Law Journal* 111, no. 8 (June 2002): 2137–94.

Sundquist, James L. *The Decline and Resurgence of Congress*. Washington, DC: Brookings Institution, 1981.

——— . *Dynamics of the Party System*. Washington, DC: Brookings Institution, 1983.

——— . *Politics and Policy: The Eisenhower, Kennedy, and Johnson Years*. Washington, DC: Brookings Institution, 1968.

Sunstein, Cass R. "The Minimalist Constitution." In *The Constitution in 2020*, edited by Jack M. Balkin and Reva B. Siegel, 37–44. New York: Oxford University Press, 2009.

———. *One Case at a Time: Judicial Minimalism on the Supreme Court.* Cambridge, MA: Harvard University Press, 2001.

———. "Problems with Minimalism." *Stanford Law Review* 58, no. 6 (April 2006): 1899–918.

Tecklenburg, H. Chris. *Congressional Constraint and Judicial Responses: Examining Judiciary Committee Court Curbing and Court Structuring Bills.* New York: Palgrave Pivot, 2020.

Thayer, James Bradley. "John Marshall." In *James Bradley Thayer, Oliver Wendell Holmes, and Felix Frankfurter on John Marshall,* edited by James Bradley Thayer, Oliver Wendell Holmes, and Felix Frankfurter, 1–86. Chicago: University of Chicago Press, 1966.

———. *The Origin and Scope of the American Doctrine of Constitutional Law.* Boston, MA: Little, Brown, 1893.

Theoharis, Jeanne F. "'We Saved the City': Black Struggles for Educational Equality in Boston, 1960–1976." *Radical History Review* 81 (Fall 2001): 61–93.

Thomas, George C., and Richard A. Leo. *Confessions of Guilt: From Torture to Miranda and Beyond.* Oxford: Oxford University Press, 2012.

———. "The Effects of *Miranda v. Arizona*: 'Embedded' in Our National Culture?" *Crime and Justice* 29 (2002): 203–71.

Thomas, Kenneth. "Limiting Court Jurisdiction over Federal Constitutional Issues: 'Court-Stripping.'" *Congressional Research Service,* January 2005. Library of Congress: Washington, DC.

Tilley, Brian. "'I Am the Law and Order Candidate': A Content Analysis of Donald Trump's Race-Baiting Dog Whistles in the 2016 Presidential Campaign." *Psychology* 11, no. 12 (2020): 1941–74.

Thurber, Timothy N. *Republicans and Race: The GOP's Frayed Relationship with African Americans, 1945–1974.* Lawrence: University Press of Kansas, 2013.

Tribe, Laurence H. *Abortion: The Clash of Absolutes.* New York: Norton, 1992.

Tulis, Jeffrey. *The Rhetorical Presidency.* Princeton: Princeton University Press, 2017.

Tushnet, Mark. "Alternative Forms of Judicial Review." *Michigan Law Review* 101, no. 8 (2003): 2781–802.

———. *Brown v. Board of Education: The Battle for Integration.* Historic Supreme Court Cases. New York: Franklin Watts, 1995.

———. *A Court Divided: The Rehnquist Court and the Future of Constitutional Law.* New York: W. W. Norton, 2005.

———. "Implementing, Transforming, and Abandoning *Brown.*" In *Brown at 50: The Unfinished Legacy: A Collection of Essays,* edited by Deborah Rhode and Charles Ogletree, Chicago: American Bar Association, 2004.

———. "Justice Lewis F. Powell and the Jurisprudence of Centralism." *Michigan Law Review* 93, no. 6 (1995): 1854–84.

———. "Law and Prudence in the Law of Justiciability: The Transformation and Disappearance of the Political Question Doctrine." *North Carolina Law Review* 80, no. 4 (May 2002): 1203–35.

———. "The Significance of *Brown v. Board of Education.*" *Virginia Law Review* 80, no. 1 (February 1994): 173–84.

———. "Some Legacies of '*Brown v. Board of Education.*'" *Virginia Law Review* 90, no. 6 (October 2004): 1693–720.

———. "The Warren Court as History: An Interpretation." In Tushnet, *Warren Court in Historical and Political Perspective*, 1–36.

Tushnet, Mark, ed. *Warren Court in Historical and Political Perspective*. Charlottesville: University of Virginia Press, 1993.

Tushnet, Mark, and Katya Lezin. "What Really Happened in *Brown v. Board of Education.*" *Columbia Law Review* 91, no. 8 (December 1991): 1867–930.

Valelly, Richard M. *The Two Reconstructions: The Struggle for Black Enfranchisement. American Politics and Political Economy*. Chicago: University of Chicago Press, 2004.

Van Alstyne, Arvo. "Self-Government and the Supreme Court: The Constitution in Crisis." *Law in Transition* 22, no. 1 (Spring 1962): 1–18.

Viguerie, Richard A. *The New Right: We're Ready to Lead*. Falls Church, VA: Viguerie, 1981.

Wald, Michael. "Interrogations in New Haven: The Impact of *Miranda.*" *Yale Law Journal* 76, no. 8 (1967): 1520–648.

Walker, Anders. *The Burning House: Jim Crow and the Making of Modern America*. New Haven: Yale University Press, 2018.

———. *The Ghost of Jim Crow: How Southern Moderates Used Brown v Board of Education to Stall the Civil Rights Movement*. New York: Oxford University Press, 2009.

———. "A Lawyer Looks at Civil Disobedience: Why Lewis F. Powell Jr. Divorced Diversity from Affirmative Action." *University of Colorado Law Review* 86, no. 4 (2015): 1230–72.

Ward, Kenneth D., and Cecilia R. Castillo, eds. *The Judiciary and American Democracy: Alexander Bickel, the Countermajoritarian Difficulty, and Contemporary Constitutional Theory*. Albany: State University Press of New York, 2005.

Warren, Earl. *The Memoirs of Chief Justice Earl Warren*. New York: Doubleday, 1977.

Wasby, Stephen L. *Continuity and Change: From the Warren Court to the Burger Court*. Pacific Palisades, CA: Goodyear, 1976.

Watras, Joseph. *Politics, Race, and Schools: Racial Integration, 1954–1994*. New York: Garland Publishing, 1997.

Way, H. Frank, Jr. "Survey Research of Judicial Decisions: The Prayer and Bible Reading Cases." *Western Political Quarterly* 21, no. 2 (June 1968): 189–205.

Weaver, Vesla M. "Frontlash: Race and the Development of Punitive Crime Policy." *Studies in American Political Development* 21, no. 2 (2007): 230–65.

Wechsler, Herbert. "Toward Neutral Principles of Constitutional Law." *Harvard Law Review* 73, no. 1 (November 1959): 1–35.

Weyrich, Paul. "Comments." In *No Longer Exiles: The Religious New Right in American Politics*, edited by Michael Cromartie. Washington, DC: Ethics and Public Policy Center, 1993.

White, G. Edward, and Gerald Gunther. *The Marshall Court and Cultural Change, 1815–1835*. New York: Oxford University Press, 1991.

White, Welsh S. "Defending *Miranda*: A Reply to Professor Caplan." *Vanderbilt Law Review* 39, no. 1 (January 1986): 1–22.

Whittington, Keith E. *Constitutional Construction: Divided Powers and Constitutional Meaning*. Cambridge, MA: Harvard University Press, 1999.

———. "'Interpose Your Friendly Hand': Political Supports for the Exercise of Judicial Review by the United States Supreme Court." *American Political Science Review* 99, no. 4 (November 2005): 1–14.

———. "Legislative Sanctions and the Strategic Environment of Judicial Review." *I-CON: The International Journal of Constitutional Law* 1, no. 3 (2003): 446–74.

———. "The New Originalism." *Georgetown Journal of Law and Public Policy* 2, no. 2 (2004): 500–613.

———. "Once More unto the Breach: Post-Behavioralist Approaches to Judicial Politics." *Law and Social Inquiry* 25, no. 2 (April 2000): 601–34.

———. *Political Foundations of Judicial Supremacy: The Presidency, the Supreme Court, and Constitutional, Leadership in U.S. History*. Princeton: Princeton University Press, 2007.

Wilkinson, *From Brown to Bakke: The Supreme Court and School Integration: 1945–1978*. New York: Oxford Academic, 1979.

Williams, Daniel K. *Defenders of the Unborn: The Pro-Life Movement before Roe v. Wade*. New York: Oxford University Press, 2016.

———. *God's Own Party: The Making of the Christian Right*. New York: Oxford University Press, 2010.

———. "Reagan's Religious Right: The Unlikely Alliance between Southern Evangelicals and a California Conservative." In *Ronald Reagan and the 1980s: Perceptions, Policies, Legacies*, edited by Cheryl Hudson and Gareth Davies, 135–49. New York: Palgrave MacMillan, 2008.

———. "Voting for God and the GOP: The Role of Evangelical Religion in the Emergence of the Republican South." In *Painting Dixie Red: When, Where, Why, and How the South Became Republican*, edited by Glenn Feldman, 21–37. Gainesville: University Press of Florida, 2011.

Wlezien, Christopher. "On the Salience of Political Issues: The Problem with 'Most Important Problem.'" *Electoral Studies* 24, no. 4 (December 2005): 555–79.

Wolbrecht, Christina. *The Politics of Women's Rights: Parties, Positions, and Change*. Princeton: Princeton University Press, 2000.

Wolitz, David. "Alexander Bickel and the Demise of Legal Process Jurisprudence." *Cornell Journal of Law and Public Policy* 29, no. 1 (2019): 153–209.

Woodard, Colin. *American Nations: A History of the Eleven Rival Regional Cultures of North America*. New York: Penguin Books, 2012.

Woods, Jeff. *Black Struggle, Red Scare: Segregation and Anti-Communism in the South, 1948–1968*. Baton Rouge: Louisiana State Press, 2004.

Woodward, Bob, and Scott Armstrong. *The Brethren: Inside the Supreme Court*. New York: Simon & Schuster, 2005.

Wren, Celia. "Stars and Strife." *Smithsonian Magazine*, April 2006. https://www.smithsonianmag.com/history/stars-and-strife-113668570/.

Yalof, David Alistair. *Pursuit of Justices: Presidential Politics and the Selection of Supreme Court Nominees*. Chicago: University of Chicago Press, 1999.

Yarbrough, Tinsley E. *Harry A. Blackmun: The Outsider Justice*. New York: Oxford University Press, 2008.

Young, Jeffrey R. "Eisenhower's Federal Judges and Civil Rights Policy: A Republican 'Southern Strategy' for the 1950s." *Georgia Historical Quarterly* 78, no. 3 (1994): 536–65.

Zelizer, Julian E. *On Capitol Hill: The Struggle to Reform Congress and Its Consequences, 1948–2000*. New York: Cambridge University Press, 2004.

Ziegler, Mary. *Abortion in America: A Legal History from Roe to the Present*. New York: Cambridge University Press, 2020.

———. *After Roe: The Lost History of the Abortion Debate*. Cambridge, MA: Harvard University Press, 2015.

———. *Beyond Abortion: Roe v. Wade and the Battle for Privacy*. Cambridge, MA: Harvard University Press, 2018.

———. "Beyond Backlash: Legal History, Polarization, and *Roe v. Wade*." *Washington and Lee Law Review* 71 (2014): 969–1021.

———. *Dollars for Life: The Anti-Abortion Movement and the Fall of the Republican Establishment*. New Haven: Yale University Press, 2022.

———. "The Framing of a Right to Choose: *Roe v. Wade* and the Changing Debate on Abortion Law." *Law and History Review* 27, no. 2 (2009): 281–330.

———. *Reproduction and the Constitution in the United States*. New York: Routledge, 2022.

Zeigler, James. *Red Scare Racism and Cold War Radicalism*. Oxford: University Press of Mississippi, 2015.

Index

Inouye, Daniel, 58

Jackson, Robert, 17, 137
Jaynes, Richard, 165
Jean-Louis, Andre Yvon, 134
Jenner, William, 39
Jim Crow, 102, 142
Johnson, Eddie Bernice, 218
Johnson, Lyndon B., 3–5, 86, 89, 90, 182, 188
Johnston, Paul F., 66
Jones, Nathaniel R., 139

Kagan, Elena, 216, 233
Kaine, Tim, 234
Kalman, Laura, 280nn33–34, 280n41, 301n10, 304n64, 305n85, 311n60, 312n73, 312n78, 312nn84–85, 313n104, 313n111, 313n114, 314nn5–6, 315n27, 315n29, 315n32
Kansas-Nebraska Act, 28
Kaptur, Marcy, 205
Kastenmeier, Robert, 75
Katz v. United States, 82–83, 90, 107, 184, 190
Kavanaugh, Brett, 18, 211, 225, 231, 232, 234, 262
Keck, Thomas, 173, 281n48, 283n5, 283n80, 284n12, 286n32, 293n18, 313n106, 314n119, 319n1
Kennedy, Anthony, 212, 220, 231, 262
Kennedy, John F., 118, 141, 189
Kennedy, Robert, 106
Kent v. Dulles, 189
Kerr, Robert, 3–5
Key, V. O., 20, 35
Keyes v. School District of Denver, 143
Khachigian, Ken, 92
King, Martin Luther Jr., 106, 138, 141
Klarman, Michael, 28, 276n15, 283n75, 288n64, 289n56, 289nn59–60, 295n73, 296n3, 301n2, 310n51, 313n106, 315n33, 317nn36–37, 318n48
Knights of Columbus, 78, 157
Krol, John, 152

Ku Klux Klan, 132, 134–35

LaHaye, Beverly, 170–71
Lain, Corinna Barrett, 281n48, 292n3, 292n6, 295n63, 295n76, 296n6, 296n9, 298nn27–28, 301n95, 301n97, 315n35
Lamone v. Benisek, 203
Lawrence v. Texas, 28–29, 233
Leahy, Patrick, 205
legislative deference, 27
Lemieux, Scott E., 208n15, 281n48, 315n32
Lent, Norman, 128, 136
LGBT rights, 31, 214, 220–21, 225, 228
connected to desegregation, 221
See also same-sex marriage
Liebmann, Ernest and Paul, 13
Little Sisters of the Poor Saints Peter and Paul Home v. Pennsylvania, 216–19
Lochner v. New York, 12, 17
Lott, Trent, 118
Lovell, George, 281n48, 308n15
Loving v. Virginia, 197, 232
Lowndes, Joseph E., 288n51, 289n61, 290n62, 312n84, 313n104

Manchin, Joe, 262
Mapp, Dollree, 80
Mapp v. Ohio, 80, 83, 87, 101, 107, 192–93, 223–24
Marbury v. Madison, 16
Marshall, John, 16
Marshall, Thurgood, 51, 104, 106, 107, 137, 146, 193
Massiah v. United States, 80
Masterpiece Cakeshop v. Colorado Civil Rights Commission, 220–25, 270
McCloskey, Robert, 20, 23–25
McClure, James, 87
McCray v. Illinois, 104
McCulloch v. Maryland, 22
McGovern, George, 92, 108, 118, 131, 155, 157, 162, 173
McHugh, James T., 152
McMahon, Kevin J., 281n48, 283n5